Speaking the Truth in Love

Speaking the Truth in Love
Christian Public Rhetoric

DANIEL R. BERGER

Wipf & Stock
PUBLISHERS
Eugene, Oregon

SPEAKING THE TRUTH IN LOVE
Christian Public Rhetoric

ISBN 10: 1-55635-118-6
ISBN 13: 978-1-55635-118-1

Manufactured in the U.S.A.

To my parents
Bill and Ruth Berger
Glenn and Edna Sonsteng
And my grandparents
Don and Faith Turner
Rudy and Mary Berger

Supporters, who assisted me throughout my life.
Practitioners, who showed me how to speak.
Scholars, who taught me to love learning.
Professors, who trained me in research.
Guides, who led me to God in faith.
Companions, who stood beside me.
Family, who provided belonging.
Elders, who gave me direction.
Leaders, who believed in me
Parents, who gave me life.
For giving of yourselves.
Thank you

Contents

Acknowledgements

THANK YOU Glenda, my wife, my partner, my lover, my companion, my co-laborer, my best friend. I appreciate you and thank you for the countless sacrifices you have made to enable me to research and write this book. Thank you for choosing to live with a boy who refuses to grow up.

A special thanks goes to my editor, colleague, and friend Alan Rose. For the innumerable suggestions you made to help with the clarity and quality of the content and the myriad grammatical and punctuation errors you corrected, I cannot give adequate appreciation, only thank you.

Thank you too to my Dean Robin Dummer and Provost Stanley Clark for freeing up my time and encouraging me in writing this text.

Thank you also to Jennifer Rupert, my TA, who did a significant amount of research for this text.

I also want to thank Jim Tedrick of Wipf and Stock Publishers for his encouragement and work in getting this project to press.

Most important, I want to thank my Father for revealing his love and message, my Lord and Savior, Jesus Christ for his sacrifice, and the Holy Spirit for his voice in speaking the truth.

Many others gave of their time, advice, and encouragement in the development of this manuscript over the past three years. Thank you to my students who read rough drafts of this text and made innumerable suggestions as to the content, clarity, and style of the book.

To God be the glory. Amen

Foreword

WRITING AND speaking in the Name of the Lord, representing his content to others is not an easy task. A liberal arts approach to Christian rhetoric will attempt to bring threads from numerous fields into a comprehensive understanding of the tapestry of communication. Setting up the warp and woof of the cloth with theological, ethical, and philosophical discussions will provide a strong beginning. Adding to that will a short representative history of the development of rhetorical thought demonstrating a rich heritage. The next part of our tapestry is to provide the theoretical design adding some ways to see patterns in written and oral rhetoric. Finally we will address the practice of being a Christian communicator.

The Apostle Peter says:

> "If anyone speaks, he should do it as one speaking the very words of God." I Peter 4:11 NIV

The Apostle Paul says:

> "Let your speech always be with grace, seasoned with salt, that you may know how you ought to answer each one." Colossians 4:6 NKJV

These are a simple beginning to the way God looks at our words. My prayer is that you will weave your own rhetorical tapestry, coming to communicate truth spoken in love (Ephesians 4:15).

PART I

Entering the Dialogue

A LIBERAL ARTS approach to persuasive rhetoric begins by looking through a philosophical telescope. Taking in a broad view of the constellations of rhetoric: Defining the field, developing the content of truth, using a medium of language, and expressing in an attitude of love that leads to spiritual maturity. Key issues for writing, reading, and speaking may uncover unanswerable questions and directions for thought. Writing this section, I assume the reader has a grasp of philosophical ideas along with some of the vocabulary of the field and can envision the landscape of philosophical thought. In the third chapter, I assume a belief in the Bible as true, that God is real and Jesus is God incarnate who gave himself for people.

Beginning with the most difficult subject, philosophy, we will address the questions: What is rhetoric? What is truth? What is meaning? What is language? And, how do I know? Because an increasing number of the audience will accept deconstructive perspectives of truth we will attempt to deal in some depth in the area where that philosophy touches Christian rhetoric. If you have ever had someone say to you, "Well, that's your truth." Or "I could not believe that kind of God." Then you will want to read this difficult chapter.

Next to philosophy is the constellation of ethics. What is right and wrong? What is good and bad? What is the meaning of life? What is aesthetically beautiful? We will consider some of the ways to look at these questions in order to understand virtuous public rhetoric. Clear decision making will lead to convincing rhetoric. I will propose an ethical synthesis from a Christian virtue perspective.

The third constellation we will study through our telescope is that of theology. What does God say about our language, our words, and how we say what we say. He is the God who is speaking (Hebrews 12:25) and his rhetoric is powerfully effectual (Isaiah 55). One of the primary ways of understanding God is that he speaks to us through his Word (Hebrews 1:1-2; John 1:1). Theology is not simply a separate chapter but spiritual issues will be integrated into theory and practice of influential argumentation throughout the book.

1

These three: Philosophy, ethics, and theology are the conceptual basis upon which we can understand the spiritual discipline of public rhetoric. Through this rigorous examination of rhetoric, a map of the ideas will begin to emerge from which we can intentionally create, communicate, and critique our own finite words.

Chapter 1

Philosophy: The Direction and Ideals of Rhetorical Persuasion

Speaking the truth in love
Ephesians 4:15

The Impact of Rhetorical Persuasion

THE USE of words has often changed the course of history. Inspiring persuasive speeches and writings move the thoughts and attitudes of audiences to the point of change where deeply rooted beliefs, values, and attitudes transform into new ways of thinking and acting. In many ways the pen is mightier than the sword because, through persuasion, people willingly modify themselves while the sword only has the power of coercion through violence. The ancient prophet Isaiah claimed that rhetoric could uproot thorn bushes and briars while fertilizing pine and myrtle trees in the lives of listeners (55:13). This use of metaphor suggests the impact of persuasive words on people moving us to eliminate evil from our lives and grow what is good. Persuasive public communication moves and inspires people to become better people. Theologically this is called sanctification—the process of becoming more holy.

Consider some of the ways words frame the paradigms of others resulting in changed thinking patterns, perceptions, values, assumptions and actions. The fiery words of Patrick Henry fanned the flames of fledging patriotism before the Virginia Convention on March 23, 1775:

Our brethren are already in the field! Why stand we here idle? What
is it that gentlemen wish? What would they have? Is life so dear, or
peace so sweet, as to be purchased at the price of chains and slavery?
Forbid it Almighty God! I know not what course others may take;
but as for me, give me liberty, or give me death!

The resulting commitment to the revolution brought about a vote that
helped bring about independence from England for the United States. The
American revolution would not have happened without rhetoric.

In another era the calm demeanor of Winston Churchill called his
country to action on May 31, 1940:

I have nothing to offer but blood, toil, tears and sweat. We have
before us an ordeal of the most grievous kind. We have before us
many, many months of struggle and suffering.

You ask, What is our policy? I say it is to wage war by land, sea, and
air. War with all our might and with all the strength God has given
us, and to wage war against a monstrous tyranny never surpassed
in the dark and lamentable catalogue of human crime. That is our
policy.

*You ask, What is our aim? I can answer in one word. It is victory.
Victory at all costs. Victory in spite of all terrors. Victory, how ever
long and hard the road may be, for without victory there can be no
survival.*

This speech began the process of reorganizing the English government
while catapulting the people of England into a massive winning effort during World War II.

Martin Luther King Jr. elicited a social awareness into the seared
consciousness of a nation through his words on the steps of the Lincoln
Memorial on August 28, 1963:

*In a sense we've come to our nation's capital to cash a check. When the ar-
chitects of our Republic wrote the magnificent words of the Constitution
and the Declaration of Independence, they were signing a promissory
note to which every American was to fall heir. This was a promise that
all men—yes, black men as well as white men—would be guaranteed
the unalienable rights of life, liberty and the pursuit of happiness.*

It is obvious today that America has defaulted on this promissory note insofar as her citizens of color are concerned. Instead of honoring this sacred obligation, America has given the Negro people a bad check, a check marked "insufficient funds."

But we refuse to believe that the bank of justice is bankrupt. We refuse to believe that there are insufficient funds in the great vaults of opportunity of this nation.

So we've come to cash this check—a check that will give us upon demand the riches of freedom and the security of justice.

With these words conveying the dream of equality, the civil rights revolution gained full force, winning many people of different ethnic origins to join together to change an unjust situation. The dream took root in the nation and began a mighty march toward reality in these simple words.

These brief reminders of the power of words to create peace or to move to war, to heal or to hurt, to create love or frustration. No revolution, no political campaign, no social issue, not even intimate interpersonal relationships happen without the use of influential human symbolic interaction—persuasive rhetoric.

Relational Persuasion

One of the most overlooked aspects of persuasive communication is the relational dimension. If my wife were to tell me the tie I choose to wear with my shirt doesn't match, I would listen far more carefully than if a salesperson, who was trying to sell me another tie, said the same thing. I know my wife would have my best interests at heart while the salesperson's advice would probably be motivated to a degree by profit. I take compliments from students who are in my courses far less seriously than the same statements from a colleague, friend, or an alumnus because the power balance is different in the relationship.

In many cases persuasion is primarily relational. Even the fake relational communication of a telemarketer's script will tell you that people are hungry for the personal emotional touch of interpersonal dimension within persuasive communication. At the other end of the spectrum, Billy Graham usually spends time in his introduction establishing relational ties with the audience before launching into his persuasive, evangelistic sermons. Paul in his letters usually began by reestablishing his relational connection to the readers. *Persuasive communication based on a foundation of a positive relationship is more affective.*

More than *ethos*, the audience's perception of the speaker's character, relational dimensions of rhetoric help define the meaning of words and non-verbal behavior based on mutual history, intimacy, and empathy. Picking up a new book by your favorite author is not a hard decision while deciding on whether to pay hard-earned cash and spend a significant amount of time reading a book by someone you have never heard of is a more difficult decision-because of the relationship. Reading an editorial in a newspaper by someone you respect from past articles places you in a mindset in which you are more likely to believe what is said than if you have never heard of the author-because of the relationship. Listening to a radio talk show from someone you recognize as an authority is easier than sorting out messages from those who call in to the host-because of the relationship. A speech by a trusted pastor or elected official will be far more influential in your thinking than one by someone you strongly disagree with-because of the relationship. Likewise a speech by the President of our country will have a greater impact than the same speech by the president of a country you have a hard time placing on the map-because of the relationship.

Philosophy of Rhetoric

Over thousands of years of debate and through hundreds of volumes of text, the conceptual basis of rhetoric has been tossed from paradigm to paradigm. Usually, when talking about persuasive rhetoric, philosophy is simply overlooked. On the rare occasions when philosophy is taken into account, more often than not general philosophical schools of thinking take precedence over rhetorical reflection. From the complexity of scientific models to the simplicity of conversation, some scholars allow rhetorical methodology to lead the way in a discussion of persuasion. From calling all communication rhetoric to limiting the scope to only persuasive speeches, some allow definitions to control the scope of rhetoric. Others choose to allow elements outside of the discipline such as a political agenda, a religious belief, or a sociological group to provide the path for rhetorical studies. Language, psychology, gender, semiotics or other disciplines may take precedence in studying persuasion. This first chapter is an attempt to ground persuasive rhetoric in a philosophy rooted in its classical beginnings coupled with spiritual realities, and then to provide direction and content with a perspective of the discipline. Rhetorical philosophy points out the significance and value of persuasive speech furnishing an impetus to current theory along with significance and impact.

A philosophy differs from theory in that philosophy involves wisdom, direction, values, and ethics-not simply descriptive or effectual knowledge. Approaching rhetoric from a philosophical perspective means the nature, causes, logic, assumptions, principles, and values of persuasive public rhetoric will be given precedence over channels, technique, and delivery. It also gives direction, scope, and process in a manner that begins with foundational questions and moves toward answers in dialogue. The result of a philosophy is an ideal (what ought to happen) rather than pragmatics (way to make it happen) or technique (how to make it happen) or knowledge (what happens). Hopefully your understanding will be deepened through a philosophy-based learning process in a manner that gives wisdom for both critique and use. A philosophy is founded on a worldview, in this text that is an evangelical Christian perspective informed by secular rhetoric.

Other approaches to rhetoric include: 1. the amount of influence (did the customer buy the product?), 2. lasting impact (can a student pass a standardized test?), 3. favorable impression (does the audience honor/ vote for the writer or speaker?), 4. establishment of a power base (did the rhetor win the argument/account), 5. amount of change (did the auditor change?). You can often recognize the differences of approach in the speeches, articles, and books themselves.

As we travel back through the dusty annals of time, we will find that the Greek philosophers Plato and Aristotle along with the Roman rhetors Cicero and Quintilian will lead in directing the philosophy of this text. Cicero based his ideas on the solid foundation of Aristotle, Plato, and Isocrates attempting to train *citizen orators*. He believed students of rhetoric should first learn high moral character, understanding of truth, and then eloquence. Quintilian followed Cicero fighting the *grammarians* (Sophists) who were usurping the ground of rhetoric. According to Quintilian, literature and grammar should lay the foundations of speaking and writing correctly and then rhetoric should take over the training of the character and speech so that a properly trained individual would be "a good man speaking well." A person who is involved in rhetoric, whether as a writer, speaker, or audience, can be called a rhetor. Individuals in the audience, whether as a reader or listener, can be called an auditor.

Development, organization, and exercise of virtue and virtuous ideas expressed influentially sets the direction and scope of rhetorical persuasion and argumentation. This philosophy focuses on good character and positive empowering (virtue). Persuasive communication is formed of logical thinking about the good (virtuous ideas that are true). The content is expressed (whether orally, written, and with intentional nonverbals) in a persuasive manner (influentially). The communication should form into a comprehensive whole called *rhetorical persuasion*.

Classical thought is process oriented rather than product focused. Aristotle's canons of rhetoric include—1. the invention of the message, 2. organizing the message into form, 3. articulating the message in a style, 4. dedicating the message to the mind, and 5. delivery of the message to an audience—are active processes enabling and shaping knowledge through the use of language for the good of individuals and communities. The end of philosophical rhetoric is good people speaking well—great speeches, conversations, stories, and writings result from the rhetors themselves. This means delivery technique along with speeches or writings are secondary to truth, people, and virtue. Changing people and culture for the better is the result or end of good rhetoric not publication of an article or payment for a speech.

The philosophy proposed here is also spiritual, for people are spiritual beings. Socrates defined the essence of humanity as being the soul. The body is a "prison" for the spiritual aspect of people. The relationship with God and each other dominates the persuasive aspects of communication. Without the spiritual dimension, communication would be coercive or informative but not persuasive. The still small voice of the Holy Spirit speaking to the spirit can be exceptionally persuasive, yet never manipulative. The Christian rhetor speaks with words developed from and enveloped in the Spirit.

Definition of Rhetorical Persuasion

Persuasive public communication taught from a rhetorical perspective encompasses a number of divergent strands. One of the primary methods of inquiry used since the time of Socrates is to provide a complete definition. Many have tried and failed to universalize persuasive rhetoric. We will attempt to cover some of the significant issues and develop a working definition instead of a categorical definition. As an art of oratory, persuasive rhetoric involves eloquent style and delivery of well-articulated argument. As a communication science, persuasive rhetoric involves principles of developing, organizing, and presenting sound argument. As literary composition, rhetorical argument formulates the process and product of written communication. As an intellectual faculty, rhetoric addresses epistemological questions in the formation and transmission of knowledge through argument. As logical process, rhetoric includes development and arrangement of reasonable argument. As a human activity, persuasive rhetoric engages an audience within a situation and environment. Virtually every act that uses human symbols in an attempt to engage or influence another's character, thought, behavior, or emotion is under the sphere of rhetoric.

Yet *rhetoric* remains a dirty term to many. Journalists shun the thought of writing articles branded *rhetoric* by their editors. To them, the appellation *rhetoric* means the article has no substance or significance. Politicians are fond of insulting opponents by calling their speeches or arguments *mere rhetoric* or President Bush's phrase *only rhetoric*. To them, calling an adversary's words rhetoric signifies empty promises and thoughts with no follow-through or commitment. Professionals insulting and cheapening each other through identifying another's communication as rhetoric is a mudslinging activity in our society. Although widely used in this manner, the degradation of rhetoric to the level of unethical human actions demonstrates a misrepresentation of a honorable field of study and a worthwhile endeavor.

Different thinkers throughout time have placed the emphasis of the study of rhetoric in unique "places." In defining rhetoric, Plato focused on the knack or art of influencing others based on opinion, not fact. Later he reconciled his thought to the activity of rhetoric by defining it as expressing secondary truth through the character of passionate love. On the other hand, Aristotle understood persuasion to be the foundation of rhetoric focusing on the discovery or invention of argument. Cicero aligned rhetoric on the life-changing content of speech for the development of citizen orators. The Apostle Paul encapsulates rhetoric as primary truth spoken in self-giving love. The notion that "Rhetoric is a good man speaking well," Quintilian's standpoint, has been debated for centuries. Francis Bacon considered rhetoric to be applying reason to the imagination to move the will of the audience. Immanuel Kant viewed rhetoric as bringing about conviction in an audience that motivates them to change. I. A. Richards (1936) notes, bad writers are more common than good ones and they play a larger part in bandying notions about in the world. Therefore, "Rhetoric . . . should be a study of misunderstanding and its remedies" (p. 3). Perelman classified persuasive rhetoric as the convincing power of human symbolic interaction in the mind of the audience. Burke identified rhetoric as a process of creating community through language. Today, Ross believes that attitude formation and change is the primary aspect of rhetoric. Trapp's notion of rhetoric is synonymous with communication. The list could go on and on, with no resolution, no universal definition, no unconditional agreement on the specific meaning of the term, or the full extent of the concept, we call persuasive rhetoric.

All of these strands of definitions point out that the art and science of rhetoric deals with *the use of symbols to convey meaning between people.* The English word *rhetoric* etymologically comes through the French word, *rhetorique,* from the Greek concept of *rhema* or "word." The Greek verb *eiro* means "I say," and *rhetor* refered to a speaker or a teacher of oratory. In ancient Greece the study of the use of words in speaking, that eventually included writing, was called *rhetorike techne.*

The writer or speaker and audience (people), the speech artifact (words and nonverbals of communication), the aesthetic process (beauty), and the influential results (impact) are all involved in the rhetorical event. Any discussion of rhetorical persuasion should include these ideas. As an understanding of rhetorical persuasion develops, these concepts will be emphasized in numerous ways. Recognizing the imperfection of any definition, we will focus this study on the invention and implementation of human symbolic interaction intentionally attempting to engage, influence, or impact an audience's character, thought, behavior, or emotion.

Persuasive rhetoric is the best influential public communication-focusing on truth and virtue. This book encompasses advanced public speaking and writing from a distinctly Christian perspective in the tradition of the Apostle Paul and Augustine.

Along with the philosophy, the development and exercise of virtue and virtuous ideas expressed influentially (or a good person speaking well), we must examine the content, direction and scope of rhetorical persuasion and argumentation.

Philosophy of Language

Historical-comparative-temporal methodology dominated linguistics and the philosophy of language until the early 1900s. The history, development, and interrelationships of modern languages provided significant knowledge about the broad categories of language classification and interrelationships.

Structural Linguistics: Saussure

Saussure (1966) changed that focus by trying to understand how language works as an independent system. He divided language into two general components: *langue* (the grammatical structure and rules of an ideal) and *parole* (language as it is spoken). Words are the essential building blocks of language. From these words people construct sentences and thoughts—we invent ideas. But language is more than cognition; it calls forth appropriate emotions to the appropriate intensity. Language creates the impetus to action as well. *Langue,* for Saussure, is the structured signs that have no independent meaning, but must function as a part of *parole.* Through words we are called to take up arms against a common enemy, and through words we again lay down those weapons. Meaning is not inherent in the signs themselves but as a socio-cultural by-product embodied in *langue.*

Words are arbitrary socially constructed vehicles through which we experience meaning. Socio-cultural influences shape language, and language in turn forms and creates society. Thoughts become ordered, and sounds articulated in a combination of structure we call language. These sound-images have a number of related aspects for study: phonology (sound patterns), phonetics (production and perception of sound), syntax (arrangement of sentence structure), morphology (individual words), semantics (meaning of words), and pragmatics (how language is used).

Language is comprised of a speaker communicating signs to a listener. For Saussure, written language is a representation of spoken language making the pen secondary to the voice. The linguistic value of a word (signifier) structurally stands for a concept or thing (signified). The communicative value is derived from the unification of the signifier and the signified within the meaning. The signs call forth meaning within the people because of the collective meaning derived through *langue.*

Structural linguistics enables rhetors to understand the style, form, and grammatical organization of messages. The signifier (sounds, written letters, or nonverbal cues) calls forth a culturally determined signified (the associated concept or image in the brain) making language a transaction of meaning between individuals within a community. Besides these elements the message and collective meaning are stressed so that we can comprehend the kinds of meaning within public communication.

Psycholinguistics: Chomsky

Observing the multitude of languages both living and dead are too similar for coincidence, and that none of us learn the rules of grammar before we learn to speak, Chomsky (1965) postulated children are born with an innate universal grammar in their thinking processes enabling them to learn any particular language. Assuming the underlying psychological processes of thinking provide a deep structure for the surface structure of language use, psycholinguists primarily concentrate on language acquisition and performance.

Chomsky is interested in learning the surface structure of how language is used but only in relationship to the deep structure or universal grammar that underlies all thinking within any language. Viewed as a speech chain, language links the brain of an individual with that of another through auditory transactions that call forth the deep structures of both the speaker and the listener. Communication begins as the brain puts a message into linguistic form and interprets it as articulation commands emerging as an acoustic signal (oral speech). The listener receives the acoustically digitized message through the ear, then physiologically transmits the message through the sensory nerves to the brain which interprets the message as comprehension or misunderstanding. With a great deal of "unpacking," Noam Chomsky attempts to describe the process by which the brain puts the message into linguistic form (generative grammar) along with the intentional psychological and acoustic levels (performance) as well as the reception and interpretation (lexical access and syntactic processing). As with Saussure, written language plays second fiddle to spoken rhetoric.

Psycholinguistic principles assist rhetoricians through a model of language processing—how we form ideas and messages, then how they are transmitted, and finally how they are interpreted. Chomsky also tied these processes to the physical makeup of the brain. Perception and comprehension of meaning are essential to public rhetoric. But psycholinguistic theory also gives us some understanding of the creative genius behind aesthetically pleasing unique constructions of language, through innovative use of the brain. We have the capacity to understand communications and increase our capability to produce better language constructions through thinking.

Functional Linguistics: Givon

How people use language forms the basis of understanding linguistic phenomena. Natural discourse is the primary artifact for studying language; competence is the most important variable in language variation (as opposed to Chomsky's focus on performance or Saussure's focus on structure). Givon (1979) demonstrates that the structural properties of syntax emanate from the use of language in discourse. In the thinking of Saussure, *parole* (use) takes precedence over *langue* (ideal structure) instead of the structural approach where *langue* determines *parole*. He goes on to challenge Chomsky's psychological, performance, and acquisitional arguments in that syntax cannot be explained or understood without discourse. Functional linguistic theory attempts to account for a speaker's ability to combine phonemes into morphemes, morphemes into words, words into sentences, and sentences into discourses. Within this process Givon is interested in the grammatical properties that involve questions of style, appropriateness, cohesiveness, rhetorical force, along with arrangement and logic of content.

Language use is dynamic and complex, and in order to explain the myriad changes of meaning through communication, discourse pragmatics—how language actually functions in discourse—is therefore primary to understanding rhetoric. The function and context of an individual utterance within a discourse will be essential in determining its meaning. Communicative competence in producing grammatical sentences that are intelligible to other speakers of the language demonstrate the linguistic ability of the rhetor.

Grice (1975) discusses four maxims to understand discourse: 1) Quantity—to say neither more nor less than appropriate in the situation. 2) Relevance—say only what is relevant to the situation, people, and topic. 3) Manner—be brief and clear. 4) Quality—truthful using logic or evidence to support information. Native speakers will naturally understand these maxims and adapt their communication accordingly.

Varying degrees of clarity, beauty, and intensity are a result of the skill of the communicators in the use of language. In rhetorical persuasion we call these elements the competency of style. Also vital for the rhetor are the concepts of function and context in that language is meaningful only as it happens in actual discourse. Functional linguistics also gives the speaker the primary responsibility for the communication.

Deconstructive Linguistic Philosophy: Derrida

Ever have someone come up to you and ask, "How does that grab you?" Or perhaps after a speech you will hear a comment dismissing everything you carefully articulated by saying "that's your truth." Someone else will think that all religions are equally valid and equally arbitrary making spiritual persuasion exceptionally difficult. Philosophy of language makes a difference in how people listen to public communication.

Wading through this section may seem like trying to ford a deep river at a category 5 rapid. No footing can be gripped as you attempt to navigate through a torrent of water catapulting you into whitewater and whirlpools, or dashing your brain against philosophical boulders. Public communication is in the vortex of a philosophical fight that is vital for communication as we know it while communicators are losing the traction of truth. The popular form of deconstructive philosophy is already leading people to think in terms of "your truth," and "my truth" in a way that facts, historical events, and states of being become impossible to talk about or use persuasively because the audience can believe that a public speaker can present information that contradicts their belief system, yet remain unaffected and unmoved. Persuasive public address is in danger of becoming the whim of emotional experience rather than reasoned discourse. So, at the very start of this book, I ask you to struggle through the philosophical implications of postmodern deconstructive philosophy of language for public communication.

Backing up through time, let's get a running start into the postmodern mindset. In the spirit of Cicero, the enabling and empowering transfer of meaning that alters the participants' character, so that they become better individuals, will receive the bulk of attention in rhetorical persuasion. This focus does not deny the negative nature of some communication, nor that misunderstanding is common. Modernism in philosophy is an Enlightenment synthesis of logical reason and empirical methodology with science as primary and experience as reality. Postmodernism brought about a distrust of concepts such as truth and fact with an emphasis on relativity, world-view, and perspectives of the individual. For people who fall into this kind of thinking, perception becomes more important than reality (image is everything), choice more significant than truth, thus leaving what is *right* (good ethical truth) impossible to know, if it exists at all. Image becomes a transitory truth through human perception, this is an outright rejection of modernism. Nihilistic subjectivism is at the heart of this kind of thinking—nothing exists, and if it did, you cannot know it, so all that is left is belief and power. Objective and absolute truth with ethics, the heart of a classical rhetorical perspective, are denied from the start.

Postmodern philosophy follows Husserl's phenomenology examining meanings by pure impersonal consciousness. However, Heidigger's (1962) focus of language as "being-in-the-world" or *dasein* changes further the definition of language and words from semi-objective observations of reality to relationships of meaning within people. This postmodern emphasis leads to either deconstructivism or constructivism. Knowledge is no longer about identifiable referents (objects like a rock, or concepts such as freedom) but instead language creates networks of "relations" where "belonging" replaces conventional concepts of meaning. The result of Heidigger's philosophy is a fusion of language and the speaker in a "presencing" where meaning is beyond simple human speech. Words take on an "unknowable" element and impact. In this relationship, language is the "master," the human is the "servant." "Thus, the entire framework for understanding reason and knowledge and thus education, professional work, political life, and thinking itself has collapsed in contemporary philosophy" (Crosswhite, 1996). Experience takes precedence over knowledge and truth, right and wrong. A rhetorical perspective of language steps back from this kind of thinking into a classical understanding of meaning and language that speaks of facts, objectivity, subjectivity and truth through denotative and connotative meaning that can be competently shared in language.

Constructive postmodern reasoning questions certainty and universal truth, rejects authority, distrusts perceptions, and asserts relativity of knowledge. Articulation of positive aspects does not reflect the "real world" while at the same time questioning the individual's ability to understand reality allowing construction of knowledge through experience and revision, as seen in Hauerwas and Willimon. A positive vision of communication arises in that perceptions can be verbalized and those "essences" transferred to others' perceptions. This process places a strong emphasis on world-view, values, flexibility of thinking, and the ability to put experience into descriptive words. All this is done as an influence on the emerging consciousness of the world and world-view of others. Persuasion thus takes a major role in the process of constructing a new world order as well as influencing individuals. Communication becomes experience centered rather than meaning centered in this postmodern thought. As people persuade each other, we create meaning.

Deconstructivists like Derrida (1976), Irigaray, Hartman, and Foucault exaggerate the emphasis of Heidigger into a radical skepticism of language and meaning. Deconstruction attempts to "unbuild" communication and identity with a negative hermeneutic focused on a consciousness of being, rather than a positive rhetorical hermeneutic focused on understanding the original intent of the communicators (Moore & Bruder, 1996). Recognizing the inadequacies of metaphysical systems that attempt to categorize ideals such as "truth," "reality," "objectivity," "reason," "emotion," "being," and "presence," deconstructivist thinkers propose differences disguising mutual dependence and sameness through an infinite number of meanings (rather than picture or reflect reality). This can be a strength when it enables us to think critically about the ways we are influenced by worldviews that are embedded in our language. However, when this is carried too far doubt becomes primary (de Mann, 1983) and seemingly, absolute.

Derrida (1981) uses the metaphor of a cloth to describe language. The threads of a language are the phonemes (sound units) and graphemes (written marks). These are interwoven to create a cloth or system of language. The resulting textile is the text that can only be used to contrast and transform other texts of meaning. Nothing is either present or absent but only differences and traces of traces of meaning. Therefore, no final meaning can exist. I believe Derrida's metaphorical analogy breaks down where his theory does—shirts, pants, and coats do exist even if they are part of a larger system of textiles. Individual phonemes may have arbitrary conditional meaning, but in the context of a discourse, we have much more than "traces of traces" or "differences," in rhetoric we have a text that calls forth meaning within in and of itself. The vividness and clarity of meaning elicited through a text is directly proportional to the congruence of the message and the competence of the author. The truth of a text is dependent on correspondence to reality and not the perceptions of the rhetors. The competence of M.L. King, Jr.'s *I have a dream* speech still draws out meaning decades after the "cloth" was "unmade" not simply in contrast (Derrida) but in construction (Aristotle) of shared meaning.

Deconstructive, postmodern philosophy is effectively eliminating universal principles and absolutes with deductive logic as well as existential experience and observations in inductive logic because perceptions are flawed and finite. Taking the Heraclitean idea that "You can't step into the same river twice" and applying it to language "You can't understand the same statement in the same way twice" Derrida explains an individual cannot understand the same words in the same way a second time (Moore & Bruder, 1996). The communicator is therefore forced to constantly "defer" the meaning through "overwriting" (Derrida, 1981). Understanding, truth, and shared meaning are thus impossible to attain and all persuasion would be self-convincing in the present situation. For instance, you could never communicate verbally or nonverbally the passionate love you feel for your spouse, because of the infinite variety of meanings possible for the word *love*. No amount of explanation, no poetry, no nonverbal actions, nothing could ever communicate the intensity and passion of the emotion even if your partner were experiencing a similar emotion at the same time. Transferring meaning through communication is therefore impossible to achieve, regulating rhetoric to the realm of relational impacts rather than meaning.

For deconstructivist thinkers, objectivity and presence are impossible making all meaning subjective, or to use de Mann's term, "absent." Experience becomes everything--other's intentions, meanings, and emotions are not possible to comprehend; therefore, they are meaningless. Truth, beauty, and goodness exist as functions of personal experience not as transcendental realities that can inform or critique human experience and discourse. I counter these ideas with the experience of empathy, the universality of truth, the reality of beauty, and the essential nature of the good—these are more than human constructions and perceptions. A mature person can recognize these, and a competent communicator can share that understanding with others.

Derrida assumes that all rhetoric has hierarchical dualism (such as being and non-being, male and female . . .) in which the first element is stronger and thus unconsciously overshadows the lesser. The reader must discover the power of the author's unarticulated dualism revealing what appears to be a logical message as illogical and paradoxical. Meaning also includes what is left out of the text (or ignored or silenced by the author). Readers must constantly be aware of what is not said, as much or more than what is included. Thus, all interpretation of authorial intent is by definition misinterpretation. Deconstructing messages by an attempt to discern who benefits from the communication is now a legitimate part of criticism. However, assuming that hierarchical dualism with a power benefit is the only part of any communication that actually matters, is a logical fallacy.

Language is overflowing with meaning. Speaking or writing uses words that can be interpreted in multiple ways that reflect the ideology of the speaker and audience. Implications, associations, and interpretations along with contradictions permeate our language use. In *The Hobbit* Gandalf and Bilbo have a conversation where the phrase "good day" can mean a greeting, that the day is good whether we want it to be or not, it is a day to be good on, the quality of the day is good, the hope is for the day to be a good one; all at the same time. Then the phrase is used as a dismissal meaning, "Gandalf, will you please leave." These multiple layers of meaning are the foundation of deconstructive thinking. This is a good, correct observation. However, extrapolating from that observation that truth, evidence, demonstrations, arguments, and proofs are all subjective linguistic gestures is an illogical extension of the observation.

The next step in the logical thinking of Derrida is to say that because of the multiple layers of meaning, words never reach the point where they concretely refer to a concept. Like in the example above, the word "good" evokes a chain of meanings in my mind, and when I speak it, the word calls forth a chain of meanings in the mind of the audience. Thus the use of language becomes Derrida's "random play of signifiers" (Caputo and Derrida, 1997) not communication. Meaning is thus always at the end of a never-ending chain of words that occur in the mind during dialogue (de Man, 1983) leaving meaning just out of reach. The allegorical metaphor of a chain with each link of meaning leading to another in a never-ending search has some significant appeal, but again I believe the metaphor breaks down where the theory does—each link can have meaning, or in philosophical jargon, "an objective presence." For example: to publicly introduce my wife Glenda before she gives a speech does not uncover all of the links of meaning those words bring up in my mind and heart and communicate them to the audience. However, the specific linking of the individual present who is about to speak has objective meaning both relationally (my), social and spiritual role (wife), as well as personally (Glenda). The relational link is more present and objective than absent and subjective and any of the other links of meaning I choose to reveal (like a funny story) will give a greater sense of "presence" and "relationship" of the audience with her; i.e. Derrida is wrong; real meaning can be shared.

The third step in deconstructive thinking about language use is that the illusion of meaning happens as a relationship of differences, not similarities. A muffin is a breakfast food contrasted to a croissant, Danish, or doughnut. The category is more important than the reality of being. The muffin is a muffin because it is not something else. Red is a color because it is not-blue, and not-green. Red is only red because our ideological worldview perceives it as being different from other colors. Derrida (1976) coins a word for this combining words for "to defer" and "to differ" into *differance*—the only meaning language can have is to defer to the end of a never-ending chain of meaning the difference between concepts. Therefore we have no stable meaning (Caputo and Derrida, 1997). This is a radical extension of Aristotle's logical foundation of the law of no contradiction (A and not-A is false). As it works out in this instance: a text both has meaning and not-meaning.

I strongly differ from deconstruction here because in saying, "I love you" to my wife, meaningful content is communicated—not as a relationship of differences (such as opposed to hate, abuse, or anger), but love has meaning in and of itself. We have a standard of meaning (marital love) by which other relationships, activities, and states of being may be measured but the meaning is inherent in the people and rhetorical communication as it happens in relationship. No unconscious layers of meaning, no ever-changing chain of meaning can explain the essence of communication in the simple phrase "I love you" because it is stable and not an ideological perspective. The emotional impact of a word, phrase, or discourse may change. The experience of love may mature. The wonder of the relationship may become more magical. Yet the meaning of love is a constant that is much deeper and more substantial than a category of contrast. The reality of being in love is more important than whether Derrida categorizes love as a decision of the will, an emotion, an attitude, a state of mind, or any other classification. Foucault (1990) is even worse here by denying self-giving, passionate love for another and making it into a biological power relationship constructed by the individual for self.

For a deconstructionist, speech and writing are closed systems whose only context is itself, with nothing outside of language itself to guarantee the meaning of the words that are used (a dictionary gives more words to define a word). The idea is not that meaning does not exist, but more meaning is floating around in a constantly changing form so that it is beyond control, rendering proof or specificity impossible through language. A public speech becomes an experience of words rather than a communication or a sharing of meaning. Reading a newspaper or novel becomes an experience of the reader's imagination rather than meaning led by an author. Deconstructive thinking can enable us to think critically about how language determines experience because the mind conceptualizes using words, which in turn limit our ability to think beyond language. Perhaps we can even agree that language forms that experience and therefore our being in the interplay of signifiers.

My disagreement with deconstruction is stronger than Crosswhite's (1996) "quibbles." I reject the endless negative interpretation of skepticism and instead assert communicative competence. People can and do communicate with each other in a manner that fairly accurately transfers meaning and creates culture while establishing and maintaining relationships. The closer the meaning received approximates the meaning sent, the greater the ability or competence of the communicators. Absolute perfection within a transfer of meaning may not be attainable; however, the closer people come to understanding the better the communication can and will be, especially when the intended emotional impact creates a similar emotion in an appropriate direction and intensity (empathy). Deconstructive philosophy does not adequately interpret the aesthetic and emotional dimensions of language useage. Derrida's deconstructive approach to language attempts to discover extralinguistic connections and forces to anchor meanings within language, when he finds no meaning, radical skepticism results. The focus of Derrida's search is off target because meaning resides in people, not language. Language is a vehicle for transferring the meaning from the soul to another's soul; language is the servant, and people are the masters (the exact opposite of his assertion). Language, therefore, has a mystic spiritual dimension. Derrida does not address this spiritual aspect of language. When language is coupled with nonverbal elements, people can co-create, transfer, and propagate meaning. The degree to which that meaning is shared and accurate, demonstrates the degree of competence of the rhetors.

Derrida attempts to discover the definitive denotative meaning of words. He is right in that denotative meanings do not exist in an absolute dictionary sense, nor are they simply arbitrary but primarily connotative invigorators of a message. In other words, Derrida is looking for the wrong thing in the wrong place. The "signifiers" (sounds that point to meanings) should call forth "signifieds" (meanings), but the words do not summon the meanings into existence; instead they only reinforce their absence. Signifiers are intoned to clarify differences separating *this* from *that* (referents or being) or to signify what is *present* or *absent* (relationships) in order to create a text. Because definitive differences cannot be called into absolute existence, "there is no outside-the-text" for Derrida. Even though he is right in understanding that language mediates our experience of our world and ourselves, he carries that thought too far and is therefore in error.

Connotative meaning, however, does exist. The meaning within people to people happens regularly; therefore, accurate, adequate communication can and does occur on spiritual, cognitive, and emotional levels even if absolute or definitive differences and definitions cannot be called into existence. Empathy can be achieved through language where two people feel similar emotions about similar concepts. Through communication competence, the art and science of rhetorical persuasion uses the vehicle of connotative language to engage, impact, and influence others. When increasing virtue (good) in an aesthetically pleasing manner as one speaker influences the audience, resulting in a "transfer" of meaning, the process is called rhetorical persuasion.

I believe a tree has meaning in and of itself, objectively, outside of human experience and this is reality. Whether or not a human has ever laid eyes on a particular tree does not negate the role it plays in our ecosystem or the lives of the birds who live in the branches. "Deep in the Ecuadorian jungle, weaving its way through dense undergrowth, lifting its arms into the upper canopy, reaching for life-giving light, grows an undiscovered balsa tree." The previous sentence is not a never-ending chain of subjective human experience but objectivity that extends beyond language or experience to describe a tree. Writing about this undiscovered tree in a remote forest does elicit connotative meaning within you, the reader. My competence and style will determine the clarity and beauty with which you will experience this idea of an "undiscovered tree." Taking this idea a step farther, let me describe a tree outside my study window: "the bare arms of the liquid amber tree catch the rain, gather the rain's droplets and send them cascading to the ground in large splashes of delight." Hopefully you will capture some of the objective truth that is real and beyond my human determination: a liquid amber tree is growing in our front yard, and we are having a California style rainstorm. These are objective truths; you can examine their veracity and comprehend the reality of the tree and the experience of the storm. However, the language of the sentence also portrays a poetic element of a tree "gathering" and "sending" water and that water being "delighted." These are poetic, subjective creations of my language. Yes, to distinguish the tree as liquid amber is an arbitrary designation of human convention, and to call the weather a rainstorm is also an arbitrary social construction. However, these words represent an objective reality that we as people can and do experience outside of the text. I can touch and see the tree. I would get soaked walking in the storm. Most competent readers would be able to understand and make those distinctions of objectivity and subjectivity.

A second aspect of deconstructive thinking that cannot mesh easily with rhetorical perspectives is that of the arbitrariness of meaning. Latching onto the fact that "denotative" meaning of individual words is arbitrary, deconstructive philosophy then pronounces all meaning to be arbitrary. The difficulty is that *words in context are not arbitrary*. "Green," "freeway," and "mustang" may be arbitrary labels, but put into a context "That green mustang is speeding down the freeway," the words are no longer arbitrary but verifiable and connotative. The words become a truth-claim that can be judged as true or false. Whether the truth-claim is in French, Spanish, or English, it does not matter; the meaning communicated is no longer arbitrary. If the vehicle is a black Honda going well below the posted speed, the statement is false in all of the particulars. Facts can be known. *Truth-value can be assessed. Words can enable, mediate, verify, and transfer meaning.* Thus, deconstructive linguistic philosophy looses the primary impetus to its foundation.

Terry Brooks in *The Sword of Shannara* uses the form of a novel to challenge deconstructive denial of reality by giving the sword the virtue of truth instead of the power of sharp violence. Using the talisman of truth overcomes the power of evil. In the end of the novel, the illusions individuals build for themselves need to be destroyed by truth, in order for life to be fulfilling.

Some time has passed, now as I write this section of the text, I am sitting at a table looking out at a storm raging in the waves of the Pacific. The phonemes that form the word "wind" are arbitrary because if society agreed that "pffit" meant that invisible force of air moving, then the sound "pffit" would arbitrarily mean the same thing. This does not mean that the wind changes, only our designation for it has changed. It also does not change the intensity of the storm. However, the word *wind* does allow us to have a discussion about the intensity, direction, and kind of a real phenomenon, and thus the conversation has a message and enables a co-creation of shared relational meaning. Anyone who has similar experience can picture graphically the west wind blowing rain sideways sending foam and mist into the air with the breakers crashing against the rocks—a winter storm on the Oregon coast. If you have never been on the coast during a storm, you can still gain a measure of the event simply from the words used. If you have experienced a hurricane, then your connotation may be much more intense than the message my words are intended to communicate. Regardless, the words elicit meaning within your mind and heart. You are experiencing some kind of emotion as you are thinking about the meaning of the words. Therefore, not only are the words calling forth a denotative message (storm on the Oregon coast) more importantly they are eliciting a connotative meaning enabling a measure of shared experience through rhetoric (my storm and your storm in relationship through words). In other words, competent rhetoric leads people to share meaning. The quality of rhetorical competence can be measured by how closely the speaker or writer can enable the audience to know the truth of the message.

Summary of Deconstructive Linguistic Philosophy

Postmodern deconstructivism's view of language and communication leads to a number of healthy rhetorical aspects.

- ➤ It begins with a distrust of authority for authority's sake; this can be a healthy skepticism when it enables us to consider alternatives.

- ➤ It assists people to evaluate their interpretative grids of reality, especially any assumptions underlying world-views. Questioning all possible interpretations is a healthy exercise.

- ➤ It encourages exploration of differing perspectives and combining them in unique ways to provide eclectic understanding.

- ➤ It enables the reader and listener to understand their experience of the text in a fresh manner, placing proper responsibility on them for elicited meaning.

➤ It seeks out who benefits from and who is hurt by a particular attitude or articulation of knowledge placing people over facts. Knowledge of the power centers, beneficiaries, and assumptions allows significant criticism of both writing and speech.

➤ It examines the ideology of language, language use, and the limitations we place on the subject matter because of our choice of words.

➤ It encourages the speaker to contemplate the chains of meaning that could happen in an audience member with the use of particular words like *cancer* or *crime*, making the speaker more sensitive to the audience.

➤ It seeks deeper meaning than binary oppositions that structure thought by considering what a concept is not.

➤ Postmodern deconstructivism focuses on the process of communication and experience thus enabling us to evaluate the impacts of that experience on our worldview.

➤ Deconstructive thinking attempts to demonstrate that texts are multivocal—an author within a culture and ideology.

These are healthy things to do. They make a much stronger public communication that can influence others for good. These items assist us in understanding how power can be used inappropriately. They enable us to create a diverse system of communication to meet the needs of different audiences. They help us consider what is left out of an individual communication.

While taking homiletics in seminary I used exegesis to understand a text, applied hermeneutics to interpret it, then used theological method to place the truth in propositional form, and finally fashioned the message into a sermon. After preaching in class we had to go to the professor's office and watch a recording of our sermon with him for a thorough analysis. I walked into his office confident and ready for his praise; this time he left the video off and paused for a long moment without saying anything. Wisely, I waited. Finally he turned to me and asked if I had a problem in a particular area of my life. Flabbergasted, I confessed. After a time of prayer I asked him, "How did you know?" His response was, "Because you didn't say anything about a particular phrase in the passage. A person who has difficulty in an area will either focus the entire sermon about that one thing, or they will ignore it all together." What I did not say in a public communication revealed my shortcoming. Deconstructive thinking places a high value on what is not said, what is not recognized, what is contrasted to the message. This is good and healthy. I often ask students to evaluate a book by what is not said by the author.

My rejection of deconstructivism includes the following thoughts:

Sacrificing concepts such as truth, fact, objectivity, empathy, and meaning is a high price—and an illogical extension. These are not personal and arbitrary, nor are they equal—people can be sincerely wrong. Therefore not all statements are equal nor are they simply arbitrary. Reality is more complex than deconstruction will admit.

Belief and perception are unequal to truth, yet deconstructive thinking uses them as synonyms. People may co-create language but the objectivity of a tree existing beyond the text in time and space—reality and history—will critique and judge the communication. Language can approximate that presence and objective nature.

Some beliefs are evil, some perceptions are wrong; deconstruction does not recognize the ethical dimension of language and rhetoric. Values and ethics are assumed to be subjective cultural constructs not objective virtues and principles.

Deconstructive thinkers extend multi-vocal ideas to the point that authorial intentionality is destroyed and, therefore, dialogue ceases to exist. All we are left with from deconstruction philosophy is an intrapersonal monologue. Dialectical dialogue is a functional reality, therefore they are wrong.

Extending good observations to unwarranted conclusions is beyond reason, especially when used with a process of unjustifiable extreme relativism coupled with skepticism. Illogical conclusions should not form our foundation for language and thought.

Limiting primary experience to ideology and power while relegating emotion and thought to secondary aspects does not square with my personal experience of life or texts. Ideology is secondary. Love and empathy are primary.

Ideology is too narrow of a concept for worldview, which encompasses values, attitudes, and other states of being. Foucault's redefinition of power and placing it as primary is inadequate to explain the reality of communication in relationships.

Deconstructive thinking leads to revisionist history—like the CBS miniseries *The Reagans* or Michael Moore's *Fahrenheit 9/11* where facts mean whatever we want them to mean—perhaps an ignorance of history?

We can know the truth and communicate it in an objective manner, and ethically evaluate the result.

Communicative competence stands directly opposed to the conclusions of deconstructive thought—and I believe competence exists and I experience differing levels of competence in giving and listening to public communication. Degrees of proficiency can be seen in freshmen writing classes yet aptitudes should not be able to be seen if deconstructive philosophy is accurate.

Chains of meaning need not be endless, random, or arbitrary nor are they mutually exclusive. Also, each word along the chain of thought can and does shape present meaning, not simply defer meaning.

Practically speaking deconstructive thinkers find communicating their thoughts virtually impossible. They have to violate their own philosophy to have a conversation. Many words are redefined in order to bend them to their use. If something has to be "re" defined, then it must have a definition to begin with, thus they are wrong.

Meaning does not simply occur in opposition to other ideas. Love has meaning as an emotion, a decision of the will, a state of being, and an experience--not simply as an opposition to hate, but it is rather a positive individuation of particular meaning in a healthy relationship. Deconstructionist philosophy has no room for such virtue. Love is real; therefore, Derrida is wrong.

Finally, deconstruction does not recognize the aesthetic beauty possible in language. Authors and readers have varying levels of competence in creating works of art. Not all novels are great works of literature. Not all speeches call forth the good in people. The difference can be dramatic.

Therefore, I recognize many positive aspects of deconstructive thought while rejecting the system of thinking. All public communicators will encounter the popular form of deconstructive thinking where audience members believe truth is personal, arbitrary, and equal; not objective or absolute. Religions are personal, arbitrary, and equal; not true or false. Politics are personal, arbitrary, and equal; not good or bad. Freedom of choice to believe and my rights to power, become the foundation of popular deconstructive thought. Evidence that is contrary to their belief system makes no logical dissonance, making persuasion exceptionally difficult. In other words, the "play of meanings" enables people to stubbornly remain justified in their own belief system whether it is accurate or not. When their "truth" does not square with reality or facts, they seek other evidences, not a change of mind or heart. As a society we no longer search for truth but for self-expression of my ideological experience. Freedom of speech is no longer primarily a search for truth but an expression of personal rights to say whatever I want to say.

For a public communicator to reach this kind of audience, we must re-organize their experience through analogy and metaphor, give them vicarious experience through story, and support all propositions through multiple forms of evidence. For a persuasive change of mind, we should provide a motivation for change that reaches into their value system in a positive manner. Having an attitude as a speaker that allows others to disagree while maintaining a spirit of grace and love is perhaps the most necessary lesson to take from this discussion. Knowing the truth and clearly communicating it is no longer enough to persuade.

Perhaps the most invasive part of deconstructive thinking into public communication is in the area of ethics. Everyone becomes their own determiner of what is right and wrong, good and bad, aesthetically pleasing or not. Morality is no longer objective but subjective and transitory with the individual's choice as the only good. Freedom is becoming the right to do what I want, or what used to be called license. Freedom is no longer saying and doing what I ought, or ethical responsibility. This personal power without personal responsibility enables people to do what they want, get what they want, and experience what they want without consequences or dissonance. Public communicators will have to engage audiences who feel they can interpret the words any way they desire and that is the appropriate meaning—for them.

Characteristics of Rhetorical Persuasion

As a science, rhetorical persuasion points to a number of principles or qualities that enhance understanding in conceptualizing knowledge, enabling communication processes, and improving rhetorical situations. As an art, rhetorical persuasion points to principles that create the beauty of eloquence and expression within communication processes and situations. Rhetoric is both an art and a science through which persuasion can become a beneficial, sufficient, and beautiful event. These constructs and principles are developed from many sources and systematized into a model called "Elaboration Likelihood." When followed in many rhetorical situations they increase levels of communication competence (Berger, 1990). This discussion recognizes the qualities while not presenting the entire model.

Novelty

Novelty is defined as providing or not providing new information to the audience (Morley & Walker, 1987). Encasing old ideas and arguments in new vocabulary or using different rhetorical methods can also create a novel atmosphere (Petty & Cacioppo, 1986). As a rhetorical principle audiences need fresh approaches and information for a communication to impact them. Simple restatement of old ideas usually does not provide the motivation for a listener to change. Strategies used in producing novelty include such approaches as the following: linking the presented attitude to already held beliefs, linking ideas that are usually separate, giving information that the audience does not already know, articulating an idea in an unusual manner with colorful tropes and figures, and slanting information that the audience already knows in a new direction.

Message Quality

The degree of message quality is determined by how many and how strong the arguments are in the persuasive message as understood by the audience (Petty & Cacioppo, 1986). When the necessary and sufficient evidence supports the claim through a reasonable, logical process, the quality is high. Message quality is an audience-centered principle. Argument that convinces a proattitudinal audience may be quite different from that which would persuade a specific, counterattitudinal audience. The argumentation of a lawyer may convince a defendant quite easily while the jury remains skeptical, waiting for clear and convincing proof. The same message has differing degrees of quality, high and convincing for one person while weak and unconvincing for another.

Personal Relevance

The degree to which subject matter will be personally relevant to a particular audience depends on the message's level of significance to that audience (Morley & Walker, 1987). The immediate value of the message for the individuals of the audience impacts their motivation to change as a result of persuasive communication. When the audience is involved in some manner or the subject matter relates to a personal activity prior to the communication, the likelihood of a favorable impact is increased significantly. The construct personal relevance includes the level of interest the audience members have in the subject and whether or not they have done prior thinking on the issue. For example, an audience who was born after 1985 probably has not thought about, and may not be interested in, the subject of nuclear war with Russia; however, those born prior to 1960 probably have thought about it and lived with the threat.

Plausibility

The subject matter of a speech has to represent the audience's reality, with a ring of truth to the presentation. If the audience perceives the evidence or argument to be unlikely, then the believability becomes strained and a positive impact is lessened or negated. Morley's (1987) Subjective Message Construct Theory considers plausibility to be a necessary element of a persuasive argument. In Meyer's (1989) Persuasive Arguments Theory, persuasibility of the subject is closely connected to the plausibility of the message and is viewed as necessary in the persuasive process.

While speaking in Ecuador in 1976, my translator introduced me to some Quichua Indians as being from New York. When I objected and said I was from Oregon, she again told the audience I was from New York. Frustrated I repeated clearly I was from the opposite side of the country. Then she told me that to these Indians anyone who was not from their valley was from "New York" because that was where the buyers for their products were from. The term New York had come to represent the entire outside world, and yes, I was from New York. To say that I was from Oregon had no meaning to these people because geography was either in the present place or the larger outside world. Europe, Asia, Africa . . . the whole world was represented by the concept "New York." Acceptable ideas have to be processed so that the audience is not overwhelmed with the information, style, and delivery. One speech cannot change a geographical worldview. The advocacy of a speech has to be seen as appropriate, believable, and plausible by the audience.

Comprehensibility

Clear, straightforward language that expresses the intended meaning in a manner and situation that is understandable to the audience enhances communication competence (Fant, 1975). The word choices, delivery, and inadvertent distractions (noise) that hinder the ability of the audience to listen will distract from the ability of the rhetor to transfer meaning through symbolic interaction. If the message is not comprehensible, it is highly unlikely that any of the other rhetorical principles would be affective (Eagly, 1974; Eagly & Warren, 1976; Petty & Cacioppo, 1986). Comprehensibility alone is not enough to be persuasive. The arguments must be accepted, and they must be perceived as evidence leading to the conclusion of the message (i.e. understood in context) for persuasion to occur (Eagly, 1974). Attempting to engage a young mother in an intense political debate while she is holding a crying, hungry baby would probably heighten negative feelings, increase misunderstandings, and lessen communication competence.

The discussion earlier in this chapter about deconstruction thinking probably introduced enough fear and loathing that "the random play of signifiers," "non-referential chains of meaning," and "the transcendental signified" will send you running for cover—because deconstructive thought uses unfamiliar words and thoughts organized in a manner for which few of us have the background to comprehend. Yet the philosophy is spreading throughout European and American culture. I attempted to make the ideas comprehensible and accessible, recognizing the good, and rejecting the bad.

Relationship

As stated above, relationship is perhaps the most significant aspect of persuasive address and argumentation. When deciding who to vote for in an election, words by trusted friends and associates have a greater impact than those of the media, proponents of the individuals, or strangers on the street. Because we trust people and persuasive communication is a person-oriented behavior, relationships are primary in persuasion. The dimensions of relationship go beyond the people involved to the way words, ideas, environments, contexts, and worldviews are connected and associated together through language in the formation and maintenance of messages and meanings.

Virtues of Rhetoric

These characteristics of public communication expressed from a rhetorical perspective permeate this book. They provide a snapshot view of the landscape of quality public address that influences people. Building them into speeches, writings, and campaigns will make the communication accessible and effectual.

Ronald Reagan's eloquent rhetoric can be seen as he embodied this kind of communication in his speech commemorating the fortieth anniversary of D-Day.

> *We stand on a lonely, windswept point on the northern shore of France. The air is soft, but 40 years ago at this moment, the air was dense with smoke and the cries of men, and the air was filled with the crack of rifle fire and the roar of cannon.*

> *At dawn, on the morning of the 6th of June, 1944, 225 Rangers jumped off the British landing craft and ran to the bottom of these cliffs . . . When one Ranger fell, another would take his place. When one rope was cut, a Ranger would grab another and begin his climb again. They climbed, shot back, and in seizing the firm land at the top of these cliffs, they began to seize back the continent of Europe . . . .*

Regan's speech united once again the French, British, and American people in remembrance of a gallant past with hope for a better future: persuasive public communication that moves an audience. As a noble undertaking, persuasion that focuses on creating better people will fulfill Cicero's dream of citizen orators.

Understanding the Process of Change

Rhetorical persuasion is the process of intentional human influence, encounter, and change through communication that results in audience impact. Rhetoric involves far more than persuasive speech, and persuasion involves areas that could be considered outside the scope of rhetoric. In one sense, every communication brings about some kind of change in the communicators, but the focus of persuasive rhetoric will be on intentional, attempted influence through human symbolic behavior (both verbal and nonverbal).

Cause and effect understanding has logical problems in the absolute realm. Hume affectively demonstrates that when scientific observation leads to "whenever X appears to happen, then Y also appears to happen." Cause and effect or change cannot be certain or necessary in any definitive manner. Hume's solution is that we can have "practical" certainty, while Kant proposed a "synthetic *a priori*" or reality that cannot be known from experience. Popper eliminated induction through creating the modern scientific method of imaginatively generating a hypothesis and then attempting to falsify the idea through testing. Rhetoricians do not have the problem of philosophic and scientific absolutes because of the acceptance of probability. Likelihood is enough to urge change through conviction, even if the exact moment of change is not observable, and even if the change is motivated through complex multiple means of both free choice and predetermined tendencies.

In his *Metaphysics,* Aristotle describes the foundation of change in the human sphere. Four of the different causes work together as a process in public communication.

1. Matter or material cause—the "thing" or "substratum" out of which the change occurs (e.g. the bronze, marble, or wood out of which a statue is made).

2. Formal cause—the essence of the "thing" or form to which the change is being made (e.g. the statue *will be* of Apollo).

3. Efficient cause—the moving cause and impetus to change (e.g. the sculptor).

4. Final or end cause—the goal or purpose of the change (e.g. the statue is to represent Apollo as a symbol for thanks, praise, and admiration).

The matter is transformed through the process of change to become something new and different, yet still have the same substance. The matter is still bronze, marble or wood but it now is transformed into a new state of being. Just as once a sculptor's chisel begins to form a different thing from the material so that it will never be the same, once meaning has transferred between people, neither one will ever be exactly the same again. Information itself changes people. Increasing the likelihood of change is the practical nature of cause in persuasion.

Rhetorical persuasion is the process of human change through communication; even if that change is so slight it is virtually undetectable. Thoughts, attitudes, and actions are the matter or material cause. The formal cause is two-fold: the desired direction of the rhetor (speaker) and the desired direction of the auditor (receiver). The efficient cause is the interaction between the rhetor's communication and the auditor's intrapersonal processing. The final or end cause is that for which the change is made—becoming a better person.

31

Aristotle also wrote of another way to look at change in terms of *potentiality* and *actuality*:

> For example, take a tree: the seed of the tree is *potentially* the mature tree (acorn, the oak). Similarly the fetus is potentially the adult human; a piece of wood, potentially the table; a piece of marble, potentially the statue of Apollo. In each instance it is the relatively formless matter, the shapless [sic] wood or marble that may be said to possess potentiality. Qualityless matter, the abstraction is pure potentiality. But relatively formless matter possesses potentialities in different senses and to different degrees. . . . Form is not something transcendent and separate, as Plato claimed, but something that is gradually acquired and brought to actuality during the process of change. (Pojman, 1998 p. 247)

For Aristotle, persuasion is the intentional process of change in humans that is brought about through rhetorical communication.

The material, while in its original state, has only potential. Substance can only become (actualize) what it could and should be through change. The major impetus to change a human attitude, thought, or action is through persuasion with the rhetor being the change agent producing an efficient cause (speech or writing) that brings about the difference.

Public Communication as Argument

The situation prior to the material change in a person is called presumption. Anglican Archbishop Richard Whately (1854) noted the idea of presumption because people will not change unless good and sufficient argument is presented in a *prima facia* case (one where "on the surface" the best argument is presented). Whately illustrated this point with an example from the military: A company of soldiers inside a secure fort would have to change through persuasion to go out and meet the enemy on an unknown battlefield. They would instead keep the secure position and allow the opposing army to attack. Presumption (perceived strength in the *status quo*) belongs to the army in the fort, and unless they are in some manner moved, they will remain where they are, protected. Likewise, presumption belongs to the audience, and without clear and sufficient argument, they will not move from their position.

Changing people through public communication is the art and science of rhetorical persuasion. People may change through experiences they have. People may change through relationships with others. People may change as time passes. But most change happens through communication. What we purchase at the store is influenced by advertising—persuasive communication. Which movies we attend are influenced by public communication. Where we choose to work, where we go to church, who we vote for, and what issues we care about are all influenced by public communication.

The rhetor advocates a change through a prima fascia case to become an efficient cause in order to motivate the change in the desired direction. Within the persuasive process, opponents may arise. The auditor (listener) may oppose the change from within, or another rhetor may oppose the change from without. The role of the rhetor is to meet the need of the audience and motivate change when it is best for the audience.

Realizing human choices are not determined by a simple cause and effect relationship, or external causes, persuasive rhetoric still influences others. The free will of people enters into consideration. People are not definitively established in a specific course of action, thought, or emotion through rhetorical persuasion. Chains of cause and effect are complex, and when the human decision-making process is involved, probability enters the picture. *Therefore, the goal of rhetorical persuasion is to increase the likelihood that the auditor will change in a favorable direction.* Argument is the rational method used to achieve that end through the content of the meaning of language.

God's Persuasive Communication

When God wants to influence people, he chooses to persuade rather than coerce. The Bible is God's revelation—his endeavor to communicate with people in a manner that will change them. His direct presence thundering from Mt. Sinai so overwhelmed the people they cried out for him to tell Moses the message and have him speak it to the masses (Deuteronomy 5:23-27). This arrangement takes the power and drive away from the human communicator and places the responsibility of change on the listener. The speaker is accountable to God to speak, leaving the results with God for the impact of the message:

> *When I say to a wicked man, 'You will surely die,' and you do not warn him or speak out to dissuade him from his evil ways in order to save his life, that wicked man will die for his sin, and will hold you accountable for his blood. But if you do warn the wicked man and he does not*

turn form his evil ways, he will die for his sin; but you will have saved yourself. (Ezekiel 3:18-19)

God's persuasive method is to communicate the truth clearly and concisely, allowing people to either choose to be persuaded to believe and act or not.

Rhetoric, Truth and Reality

Aristotle focused rhetoric on enthymatic probabilities leaving certainty for math, logic, and philosophy. At its best, rhetoric represents what exists in time and space (e.g. what is real). Truth claims are then linguistic representations of reality. Objects, ideas and events are all real, even when abstract. When a police officer investigates a crime scene, the investigation is neither for the victim's perception, nor the eyewitness's perspective, but for what actually happened (the event) and the result (product/artifact).

In one sense, the absolute truth can never be known because we are finite beings limited by time, language, space, and environment. However, simply because people cannot fully measure reality does not mean that truth is beyond comprehension, nor does it mean all search for truth and reality is hopeless.

Little "t" truth is the relationship between communication and reality. When a rhetor makes a truth-claim, it is not the same as reality but an attempt to describe, understand, or transmit that reality. When truth-claims approximate with physical, social, or spiritual reality, they are accurate or "true." This "correspondence" perspective of reality and truth (Strom, 1996) applied to communication enables invention of knowledge, the transmission of meaning through human symbols, and growth in competence and beauty. Propositions or statements that mirror what exists in time and space in the physical, social, and spiritual realms are thus true, and those which do not reflect accurately the reality they represent are false. Persuasive rhetoric adds to correspondence the epistemic nature (Scott, 1967) that goes beyond expression of truth-claims to the creation of truth through invention, organization, style, memory, and delivery involving a generative action or process of knowing.

Anderson (1990) gives a simplistic metaphor that clarifies current philosophical perspectives on reality and truth. Three baseball umpires were talking, and the first one says "There's balls and there's strikes and I calls 'em the way they are." The second umpire says "There's balls and there's strikes and I calls 'em like I see's 'um." The third umpire responds, "There's balls and there's strikes but they ain't nothin' till I calls 'em." Perhaps we should add a fourth umpire, one who failed to make the game because during training every time he stepped behind the plate he said, "there's no such things as balls or strikes and even if there were it wouldn't matter." In the conversation the first umpire could be called an *objectivist,* the second a *subjectivist,* the third a *constructivist,* and finally the *deconstructivist.*

The objectivist believes that external reality (physical, spiritual and social) is constant and human senses accurately observe that truth. What the umpire sees, tastes, hears or feels is what he gets. Science, history, reason, or God may provide the foundation of that truth and it is inherently knowable. However the senses obtain the perspective of reality (through scientific methodology, logical reasoning, or God's revealed truth), that reality is knowable by humans. Most quantitative research is developed from this perspective where propositions are developed from observation of reality through scientific methodology, usually to explain cause and effect relationships.

The subjectivist umpire calls balls and strikes, as he perceives the nature of those pitches fully realizing that humans have flawed senses, illogical reasoning, and tainted character. Capital "T" truth probably does not exist either in the spiritual, social, or physical realms, but even if it did, the pursuit of truth is a subjective encounter. Flawed human perceptions influenced by such things as character, expectations, language, history and intellect form and interpret knowledge. Empirical evidence is questioned along with withholding judgment about the observations of others because they also are influenced through their world-views, expectations, environment and character. Subjectivist research in the quantitative realm usually takes on a more "self-report" analysis from the subjects and qualitatively uses even more tempered conclusions. Some subjectivists believe an objective world exists, but doubt the possibility of true knowledge of it as it exists.

The constructivist umpire believes that humans are the measure of all things and that reality does not exist until it is developed through personal understanding as defined in the physical realm and created in the social or spiritual realms. Most constructivists are secular humanists who focus study on the social reality of communication studies. Physical "facts" are often questioned (real balls and strikes) and language is doubted as adequate for representing reality if it does exist. For those constructivist umpires who hold to a physical reality, it is only knowable through human invention; i.e. the idea of height, how long a dimension is, and the starting point for measurement may combine to interpret the "tallness" of a tree or mountain so that the concepts used to understand are human instruments. Different cultures have different "metanarratives," constructing different world-views and thus experience with understanding, are best conceived as "multiple realities" where groups and individuals can know the symbolic world in a different sense (Strom, 2003). Rorty believes values are human constructs and as we live within these we experience and communicate with the meanings we create within ourselves (Moore & Bruder, 1996).

Adding to the baseball metaphor, the deconstructivists could not make it through umpire training because they have given up on the search for truth and now attempt to expand the horizons of others through opening endless possibilities including a skeptical wondering whether baseball exists or not. If strikes and balls can be called, then usurping the power to do so is ideologically insensitive either to the pitcher or the batter. The radical skepticism of Derrida leads to a surrender in the search for truth. Instead, we would be disembarking on a dismantling of concepts and reality by substituting the process and experience for an attempt to gain an understanding (Silverman, 1989). The deconstructivist perspective of Foucault and Derrida does help the rhetorician recognize authoritarianism and our own interpretive "grids" with the bias inherent in human "know-ability." Asking who benefits from and who is hurt by a particular articulation of truth and whether any other perspective would have a greater balance of equality for everyone are deconstructive questions that are healthy in any circumstance. Uncovering power imbalances and layers of meaning can be an effective way to study persuasive messages. However, classical deconstructive thinkers still are caught in the contradiction that by denying truth they deny the very principles used to formulate their own worldview and their objections to others.

Rhetorical Synthesis

Taking into account these perspectives in a modified "correspondence" theory of human communication, we come at last to a philosophical base from which transfer of meaning can take place between humans through language:

1. Objective reality exists and is knowable, and rhetoric emphasizes the content of knowledge while also expressing the process of knowing.

2. Human perceptions are flawed, so perfection in either communication or understanding is impossible—we can never know absolutely.

3. People construct their own meanings through intrapersonal elaboration and socially through interpersonal interaction.

4. Language symbolizes referents creating a relationship between people and the construct, enabling shared meaning through messages.

5. The closer the meaning received is to the meaning sent, the more competent the communication process and rhetors are. Meaning happens along a continuum of comprehension rather than in discrete categories of 100% right or 100% wrong.

6. The "enabling constraints" should be "constantly available for critical inspection" (Bruner, 1996) so that fundamental assumptions and methods may be continually revisited especially in the process of knowing and persuading.

7. The findings of knowledge should always be questioned to see if any other perspectives provide a better articulation of that meaning, and then revised so the creation of knowledge will be accurate and the transfer of meaning will benefit the greatest number of people.

8. Observations of communication in real life situations, especially those where people are impacted for the good should be considered as primary evidence in consideration of rhetorical philosophy and theory.

The rhetorical perspective of language and the reality it represents is that people can comprehend reality, invent arguments, arrange them sensibly, and then transmit that meaning to other humans. Competency in accurately transferring that meaning to others is the heart of rhetorical faculties. Doing this in an influential manner is rhetorical persuasion. All four approaches to truth and communication have merit, and perhaps dominate certain contexts; therefore a synthesis may be the best approach.

In a war, orders are given using language. The messages are life and death in interpretation. When the situation is dire, we rely on communication to enable the meaning necessary to save lives. A private does not stop and say, "Sergeant, the layers of meaning in your orders are arbitrary and ambiguous, so I can interpret them in any way I desire." Obedience is possible because understanding happens through the use of language—deconstruction is unable to fully explain exact obedience. Rhetoric is able to recognize messages and meaning.

Rhetorical Methodology

The complexities of studying rhetorical communication are compounded by: society, individuals, communication channels, multiple messages and diversity of world-views. Myriads of theories and manifold approaches make inquiry into persuasion a stimulating challenge. Investigating persuasive communication leads careful observers to ask questions and carefully evaluate alternative explanations. Voltaire judged people, not by their answers, but by the questions they asked. This is true of communication scientists as well as the theories they develop—the best scholars and theories ask the best questions and give insightful, tentative answers that explore the issues. Once the hypothetical structure of an ambiguous reality is constructed, this theory should be tested methodically.

Qualitative study explores the qualities and characteristics of the rhetorical phenomena. Interpreting the nature of communication is important to understanding and improving competence. Quantitative methodologies reduce the scope, isolate variables, count their occurrences, and analyze the results. Degrees of validity (whether it represents reality) and reliability (whether it is repeatable) determine the significance of the explanation in a given answer or hypothesis.

Qualitative studies also use methods like ethnography, historical analysis, critical investigation, social inquiry, linguistic exegesis, and genre studies. Some may choose a particular socio-political perspective like feminism or gay studies and consider all rhetorical artifacts in how they relate to the specific view of that group. Others may choose an issue such as how a Marxist understanding of economics relates to a particular speech another will consider the hegemonic pre-occupation with power in an article.

With understanding comes intentional practice. The study of public rhetoric is primarily geared for real world communicating in the most effective manner possible. Putting the ideas to work making better speakers, listeners, and artifacts (speeches, writings . . .) is the essence of persuasive public communication.

Conclusion

We have traveled far in this chapter; considering an overall perspective and approach to rhetoric, definitions, philosophy of language, characteristics of rhetoric, spiritual dimensions, and relationship of public communication all the way to truth. Combined with chapter 2 on ethics and 3 on theology, the concepts discussed here form a foundation for an understanding of persuasive public rhetoric.

Lovers fall in love with each other through verbal and nonverbal communication. Rhetoric enables them to create and send messages, share meaning, and develop the relationship. Competence is possible. What is true for interpersonal relationships is also true in the realm of public speaking and writing; we can and do commune through words. Thinking similar thoughts, feeling similar feelings, and sharing our inner selves are part of the human experience (empathy) that is made possible through rhetoric. This wonder, the mystery of people communicating with people, souls engaging in intimacy of spirit is a real rhetorical phenomenon—speaking the truth in love. Persuasive public communication builds on this kind of life experience, which makes possible the kind of shared understanding that deepens and enriches human relationships.

Chapter 2

Toward an Ethic of Rhetoric

So God created man in His own image;
In the image of God He created him;
Male and female He created them.

Genesis 1:27 NKJV

WHAT IS good? What is bad? What is right, wrong? Sin? Righteousness? Important? Unimportant? What should I do? Can I judge what you do? How ought I to live? Do I defend my opinions because they are mine, or because they are right? How certain am I that I am right? Does life have a purpose or meaning? What kind of character should I develop? Whom should I trust? How willing am I to consider the opinions of people who are different from me? For Western Culture, Socrates began the process of forming ethics through asking questions. He wrote no books and gave few speeches, but he has influenced the whole modern world through his questions and conversations. The most important question of all is the focus of the meaning of an individual's life. "What sort of life is worth living?" "What is the meaning of life?" or to put it Aristotle's way, "What sort of person should I be if I am to be truly happy?"

Some of the significant questions and issues involving moral philosophy and prescriptive logic that form the field of ethics for persuasive rhetoric are:

1. What is the foundation of ethics?

2. What is the nature of good and evil?

3. What is the meaning or purpose of life?

4. Are ethical truths, values, and principles applicable to all people of all time (objective and absolute) or for one time and culture or only for one individual or one situation (subjective or relative)?

5. How free is my speech before any given audience in any given culture? Am I free to not tell the truth? Is a court of law different from the court of public opinion concerning freedom of speech?

6. What is the place of religion, logic, free will, motivation, or consciousness as they relate to public communication?

7. What is the relationship between issues of content and truth and how are these related to virtue?

8. How do I coordinate and co-create with other people as we communicate together?

9. What is beauty (aesthetically pleasing) in relationship to language and use in public rhetoric?

Final answers to these questions are not going to arise, but certain directions and thoughts as they apply to persuasive rhetoric will be considered. Entering into a dialectic debate will at least bring a cognizance of the perspectives and issues that face speakers.

Public speakers and writers face ethical choices each time they open their mouth to speak or take up a pen to write. First of all, because of the content of the communication, is it accurate or inaccurate? Representing truth or falsehood in speech has been a significant ethical issue from the beginning of time. What a speaker says is important to consider. In the "documentary" movie *Fahrenheit 9/11*, Michael Moore makes some true statements such as only one full-time Oregon State policeman is on duty along highway 101 during the winter. That this policeman "guards" the coastline against terrorists is false; protection is the job of the Coast Guard. Is giving truth (one state policeman) in a misleading manner (he protects the entire coastline from terrorist attacks) ethical? When adding as many as 53 of these misleading "facts," has the concept of documentary movie become "polytainment" and no longer history, but an attempt to warp the perspective of the audience away from truth and historical accuracy through cleverly blended half-truths supplemented with real footage?

41

If public communicators have an ethical responsibility to the audience to portray the truth, then the virtue is objective and possibly absolute, and accuracy is more than simply telling truth; it involves how it is communicated as well. Now consider, if truth is absolute and accuracy involves an objective portrayal of that truth then the movie is in violation of ethical practice because it communicates inaccurate information with misleading commentary as though it were accurate. On the other hand, if truth is merely subjective perception so that "my truth" and "your truth" can be different, then the assertion that the Oregon State Police are primarily concerned with terrorism infiltrating from the ocean can be considered "truth" even though it is erroneous and led millions of people around the world to believe something that is false. The primary point is that public communicators must make an ethical decision concerning the accuracy of their content every time they communicate. Many communications, such as the example cited here are mixed so that truth and falsehood are combined to form perception.

A second ethical issue involves the time element; is now the right time to speak, record, or write these words? Copying another student's notes after a missed class is ethical at most times and encouraged by most teachers, but not during a midterm or final exam; the timing makes the difference. When a speaker says what is said demands ethical consideration. In times of war, news organizations may come across information such as the telephone "wiretaps" the Bush administration ran on terrorists. The *New York Times* had to make a decision on whether or not to withhold the information from the public or to report it and risk terrorists taking advantage of the information. This is a very important distinction, not just that the wiretaps may be illegal, but the timing may give advantage to an enemy with the result that innocent lives may be lost. Later the *Times* became aware of financial tracking of terrorist money and in spite of administration requests to the contrary, they decided to publish the story virtually eliminating international assistance in addressing the issue taking away an effective weapon against terrorist attacks. The debate between constitutionality and illegality, between civil rights and safety, and executive branch power as opposed to judicial power, along with freedom of the press, should be carried on in light of the ethical issue of timing—should this be considered after the fact instead of during the terrorist aggression (when, timing)?

The third ethical issue brought up every time we communicate is the motivation of the content and method of delivery: what drives a speaker to communicate influences all aspects of rhetoric. Why a speaker says what is said, when it is communicated is an important ethical issue. If the *New*

York Times published the story in order to uncover illegal activity, then it was perhaps a good thing. If they published the same story because they wanted to attempt to create a difficult situation for President Bush, then they were unethical. Publishing classified information is possibly illegal and likely treasonous. The reason, the motivation, a communication is made is an ethical decision. Similarly, if *Fahrenheit 9/11* was documented because Michael Moore thought it was true, then we have a different situation (he was sincerely mistaken or grossly incompetent) as opposed to nonfactual entertainment or malicious deception. If it was filmed and released in order to influence the election process through hateful inaccuracies, then the ethical dimension becomes even more significant (then we have intentional errors complied with inappropriate timing and complicated with unethical motivation).

The motivation can also be seen in the money and power issues involved in the communication. For instance, Michael Moore's movie *Fahrenheit 9/11* received a significant amount of money from terrorists organizations for showing throughout the Arab world as opposed to Bush's campaign money which largely came from individual Americans and businesses. Moore's movie railed against the political power structure of the current administration in the United States in an attempt to gain influence in overthrowing the elected officials, then we have a greater problem than incompetence or mistakes. Motivation is linked to power and money that can be used in moral or immoral ways.

Fourthly, the place where the communication happens has ethical impacts. What is appropriate for the classroom may not be appropriate in a church, at work, in family conversation, a courtroom . . . the context of communication changes the practices and content of rhetoric. Where a speaker speaks or writer writes, what is said, when it takes place, and why it is communicated all make an interaction of ethical questions the balance of which should be attained before communication. As a country we are embroiled in a controversy concerning the Pledge of Allegiance and where the words "under God" are appropriate. Also, should US currency have the words "in God we trust" written on it? Where a message happens is a vital difference. For example, an amendment to ban flag burning as a form of freedom of speech did not pass the senate by one vote. Burning a flag that has worn out through proper ceremony is considered a patriotic act. Burning one in protest is considered anti-American and borders on an illegal act. Where a message happens makes a vital difference. Back to our illustration of *Fahrenheit 9/11*, that this movie was shown in theaters rather than on news broadcasts was an important difference in context. When the movie was shown in foreign countries as a factual foundation for understanding the US government then the concept of "where" takes on a different dimension as well. The *Dixie Chicks* discovered that political comments made to an audience in France can and does have immediate impacts on their fan base at home through mass media coverage.

Finally, who the audience is changes the ethical nature of communication. Some adult only comedy clubs have entertainment that is not proper for a general audience. Those who attend such places expect a certain kind of humor they would not get in a Christian comedy club. Rarely can a message be confined solely to one audience. Matching the content and words with the audience is an essential part of ethics. Extending the illustration of Fahrenheit 9/11, if the motivation were to entertain as opposed to persuade or inform, then showing the film France would allow the audience to laugh at the foolish Yanks and that would be the end of the matter. However, the film was believed to be the truth by many of the foreign audience which would indicate Michael Moore was incompetent because the film was seen as something it was not—a documentary of historical accuracy.

Ethical choices in the rhetorical sphere need to consider all of these questions and issues as well as other elements. The content, motivation, timing, place, and audience should be considered every time we communicate. Many other dimensions such as virtue, relationships, codes of conduct, and culture should be carefully considered when and where they apply. Rhetorical persuasion has further ethical implications because of the responsibility of influencing others.

Rhetoric as Epistemic

Rhetorical persuasion is not just an art of expressing arguments that already exist, but also has the power to create knowledge and truth claims—it is epistemic (Scott, 1967). Because of this ability to generate change and new knowledge, the ethical dimension of rhetoric is of vital concern for the speaker and the audience. Bitzer (1968, 1978) stresses the vital nature of expressing truth and values when speaking in order to create unity, coherence, and stability in the knowledge of the audience.

Does rhetoric discover "truth" or "create multiple realities?" Those who strive to discover and describe reality envision rhetoric as a method of knowing, understanding, and communicating the truth. When approached with a deterministic philosophy, the scientist attempts to discover cause-and-effect relationships and the categorical definitions leading to universal principles. Social-scientific methodologies used will focus on tests that reveal the observable truth about the nature of a phenomenon. Take, for example, the question: When does the art and positive communication of the human body become pornography? For those who consider only the physical aspects, hardly any form of nudity could have the negative moral label of pornography (or else they could define pornography as good or as a civil right). For them, little difference is seen between Michalengelo's *David* and the centerfolds of *Playgirl* or *Playboy*. For most of us, we see a great difference. The aesthetic ideal of human perfection out of flawed marble (*David*) is unequal to the glossy photographs of lewd desire (*Playboy*).

Those who approach the question, "When does the art and positive communication of the human body become pornography?" from a humanities perspective, envision rhetoric as a method of knowing multiple realities based on interpretations in a manner that co-creates culture. When approached with a relative philosophy of free will, the rhetorician attempts to discover resources and perspectives that illuminate the phenomenon and the experience of the communication leading to better directions for self-determination. Methodology focuses on interpreting, understanding and applying communicative distinctives in search of significance. The example of pornography, from people who look at rhetoric from this perspective, may center on the political aspects of freedom of speech and individual choice or on aesthetics with a view to improve the community, rather than descriptive studies. From this perspective, people have the right to freedom of speech; therefore, pornography is not something to be controlled until it influences people to do illegal acts. Yet the pornographic form of speech is unethical because it treats people as sexual objects and heightens prurient passions that degrade healthy relationships. The artistic nonverbal portrayal of nudity can do just the opposite; emotionally and cognitively urge people to desire "the good" in themselves and relationships, not objectify.

Rhetoric also is a means of naming or defining reality. The aspect of a label helps individuals understand and apply specific meaning to ideas, events, and things within the society. In the pornography debates, people who hold to this perspective would consider the impact on the audience, the uses, and the positive or negative aspects that result. Some would label all pornography as art, others would label it as harmless fun, while others would label it as sin, still others may use the label "pornography industry" in an effort to demonstrate either the positive or negative economical impacts of the issue, all of these are creating very different realities because of their perspective, through public rhetoric.

A different example of how naming is part of the ethical dimension is from the social debate over abortion in the United States; the pro- and anti- abortion sides use the power of naming effectively. Pro-abortionists call themselves the positive "pro-choice" while naming those who disagree with them by the negative "anti-abortionists." On the other side those who call themselves "pro-life" call the others "pro-abortion." Further adjectives often enter the naming with the addition of "fundamentalist," "liberal" or "left-wing" creating an intensification of the words. These labels frame the perspective of the individuals and the perceptions of those they name as being the opposition. Is the action of abortion murder or the right to choose? In a similar manner, labeling nudity as pornography or labeling it as art will probably create a very different impact on the viewer.

Another way to consider the ethical aspects of rhetoric is the "co-creation" of culture and community. Culture involves the whole of the worldview(s), core beliefs, values, organizations and activities of a people as well as the physical elements or "artifacts." The non-physical (or spiritual) parts of culture can said to be created or invented through rhetoric, while the physical components are defined, named, and interpreted through the use of language. People co-create culture through commonly transmitted meaning as seen in patterns of word usage. Norms, mores, and rules arise from the consensus of meaning. What is labeled pornographic changes from one society to another as well as what is acceptable to communicate about sexuality. Much of European culture is more tolerant of nudity in public communication, giving a higher tolerance of what is considered proper or improper. The society will punish those who violate the norms and reward those who keep within them. This is a constant process, not a static product so that change is constant. Another example is the movie ratings system. In the United States, when a "G" rating is given, certain audiences who want to watch sex and violence will not even consider going, while others will never attend an "R" or "X" rated movie. The process of naming things creates meaning within and among those who communicate.

Rhetorical persuasion is large enough to encompass all of these perspectives concerning the "reality formation" brought about through the rhetorical use of language. Methodologies used in discovery, theorization, and application vary widely from person to person as well as from society to society. Ethical orientation is built on the philosophical base of epistemology (what can we know and how do we know we know), as well as metaphysics (our understanding of being), and cosmology (our view of the world). Therefore, ethics is inseparably bound to the concept and issues of truth and knowledge through how they are communicated. Both the deterministic and free will ways of thinking add to the field of rhetoric, also, the scientific and humanistic approaches to knowledge ask different questions seeking different goals enabling different understanding of rhetoric. In other words, these are not necessarily mutually exclusive paradigms, but may be used side by side with effective results.

The interactions within a rhetorical situation may invent, arrange, and instill new knowledge into the belief system of the rhetor and the audience. Often the epistemic nature of rhetoric is discussed in the invention (discovery and development of content) and artifact (the resulting communication such as a speech or book) aspects of rhetorical situations; however the entire process from invention, through organization, to style, memory, and delivery is epistemic in creating a reasoning process or "coming-to-know" in both the humanistic and scientific approaches. Returning to our example: adolescents come to know the difference between pornography and art as parents, teachers, and others communicate with them about the objects so the labels help form ways of thinking. *The ascertainment, assembly, and articulation of truth-claims create an ethical perspective with responsibility for speakers because knowledge and discovery happens in the thinking of the audience through rhetoric.*

Spiritual Nature of Ethics

Humans are spiritual in nature, not simply physical, so that people are cognizant of right and wrong, beautiful and ugly, as well as good and bad. Other parts of nature do not have the same spiritual-moral capacity. Any spiritual nature of a tree does not translate into moral implications of actions, neither is it communicative in any sense of the term. Also, the physical-life-force reality of a bear leaves very little space for actions of right and wrong. Survival of the fittest is not an ethic, but the law of the jungle. Yet humans have an innate sense of morality forming a qualitative difference between the purely physical dimension of inanimate nature, the physical-life-force of plants and animals, and the physical-spiritual nature of humans. Because of this difference, for a human to take a life through murder is qualitatively different from a cougar's behavior of killing for food or defense. The often-used example where the sexual behavior of animals is applied to humans is inappropriate because people have ethical paradigms, animals do not have the same issues and impacts. A primate having ethical dimensions of pornographic "art" is meaningless as opposed to our discussion of human ethical communication earlier. Much of ethical behavior focuses around language use, and humans are uniquely symbol users within the ethical realm.

47

Humans are created in the image of God (Genesis 1:27). This means that the more like God an individual is, the more humane he or she becomes. Ethics, therefore, has a foundation in the person or nature of God. The qualities of God's character (holiness, righteousness, faithfulness, love, joy . . .) are what is good, and that which is not like God is evil (lies, selfishness, fulfilling lusts . . .). Human ethics is, therefore, based on God in both character and action. Good, right, wrong, sin and righteousness are not determined by people whether socially or personally; ethics are divinely revealed based on the nature of God.

The ethical character of language use may not be exclusively human because angels, seraphim, cherubim, demons, God, and Satan all seem to be able to use language. The nature of right and wrong does not change from species to species, situation to situation, or person to person. The Good remains the same throughout creation and is objective in form, not subjectively different depending on the perspective of the individual or relative to a culture. Ethics are discovered as we learn about the being of God. This means ethical principles are objective; outside of human construction. Ethical values are constant because they are based on the person of God, not transitory, relative, or subjective.

Comprehensive Nature of Ethics

With the guns of war still reverberating in his soul, C. S. Lewis gave a battlefield metaphor to understand the comprehensive scope of ethical thinking. He said that we are a fleet of ships, and ethics are the sailing orders that tell us three things:

1. How to avoid bumping into one another through establishing order (social ethics).

2. How to keep afloat and in good condition (individual or virtue ethics).

3. What our mission is—the *summum bonum* (the ultimate purpose and goal of life).

Ethics tell us what is good (the ideal of life), what is right (quality of virtue), and what we ought (personal responsibility, duty).

Another common metaphor for ethics is story. In Tolkien's *The Lord of the Rings*, Sam asks Frodo what kind of story are they in. On a quest to rid the world of power that can be used for evil, Sam wants to know more about the story; not just how it turns out but whether or not they are doing something heroic, noble, and good. Narrative understanding of ethics understands the plot of the storyline as social ethics—action that enables characters to overcome obstacles climaxing in the good. The characters of the story embody individual ethics—model virtue and vice; they are the heroes and villains. The theme of the story is the *summum bonum*—the greatest good, the purpose, the beauty of life. Without a plot there is no story, no action, no obstacles. Without characters action cannot happen. Without a theme the action and characters have no meaning. Ethics is, therefore, a whole that gives meaning, responsibility, action, and aesthetic beauty to life.

Practice and Ethics

Different ethical practices do not necessarily mean different moral standards (Moore and Burder, 1996). For example, the people of one culture allow or even encourage abortion while another disapproves of the practice. They are not necessarily different standards: both cultures may agree that killing a living person is morally wrong, but they disagree when life begins. However a strong difference may occur when one values life and another values freedom of choice and yet another values economics. The conflict between these cultures may be far more devastating, and the debate may shake the societies to their roots when the values come into conflict. Ethical paradigms are created through the interaction between character, value, action, and rationality. This process formulates the diversity of foundations for ethical systems, especially as seen in different cultures. Ethics without action is dead theory; the practice of right and wrong complicates the process of persuasion. In the New Testament, the letter of James states that faith without works is dead indicating an ethical element in belief. That ingredient, faith seen in what is done, is necessary for persuasion as well. We need to "practice what we preach."

Radical Skepticism

Before considering ethical systems, an important question to consider is whether or not ethical understanding is even possible. The perspective that moral knowledge is not achievable or does not exist is called skepticism. Assuming that rational justification based on physical sense observation is necessary and within the scope of absolute logic, no prescriptive or moral principles can be formed. Since this method is impossible, specific knowledge of moral standards is beyond the grasp of human sense observation; therefore, all ethical systems must be questioned and ultimately rejected.

However, the demand for scientific methodology to be applied to an ethical domain gives absolute faith in a particular process that may be flawed for this kind of knowledge. The human spirit may not be "observable" in a scientific manner, while motivations, pre-meditation, and desires that move action may be better understood through other means. Another consideration is that when character, value, and principle form the foundation of ethics, then radical skepticism is unnecessary and off target. Knowledge of right and wrong is attainable and definitely worth the struggle; even when it is not scientifically demonstrable as modernism demands.

Ethics deals with power, beauty, good, and duty—abstract ideas and ideals that cannot be observed by the senses in the same way we observe the properties of water or the processes of making sand. Skepticism demands absolute empirical data in an area where other methods such as logic, intuition, emotion, relationship, being, and revelation are the primary means of knowing. In philosophical language ethics is *a priori* knowledge (before experience) while scientific methodology is *a posteriori* knowledge (after experience).

Some Answers of the Ages

Throughout the centuries and across countless cultures many approaches to ethics are given. They may be grouped into six fundamental perspectives. Combinations of these are also prevalent in moral philosophy (Moore and Bruder, 1996). The first is the divine-command view that answers the question, "What ought I to do?" with the concept, what God ordains for me to do, thus leaving God with the responsibility of understanding and choosing what is good. The second major approach is that of consequentialism where the question "What ought I to do?" is answered by whatever has the most desirable consequences making ethics a fulfillment of intended ends or results without consideration of the means by which those ends are accomplished. The third way of thinking about ethics is the deontological system that sets moral duty as the answer to what an individual should do in a given situation giving the human conscience as the primary arbiter of what is good. The fourth is virtue ethics, which asks a different question, "What kind of person ought I to be?" leaving the morality of actions to flow from the inner virtue of a mature person. The fifth ethical paradigm is that of relativism which answers the question "What ought I to do?" with whatever I, or my society, believes I should do making ethics into social and personal loyalties. The last of the major foundations for ethics is that of contractarianism, setting forth the social contract as an answer to the question of "What I ought to do?" making ethics a set of legal responsibilities. We will consider each one of these in turn to discover some of the strengths and weaknesses so that a comprehensive discussion can be placed in context with discernable alternatives.

Divine Command Ethics

Almost every religion has a group of followers who want black and white answers to moral dilemmas. For many all ways are concrete absolutism with a specific action required in every situation. The "God said it, I believe it, that settles it" mindset finds the truth of every modern dilemma in laws set down in ancient manuscripts. Codes of rules developed through these form unquestioned loyalty and are followed as a private obeys the orders of a general.

Plato addressed the divine-command ethical perspective with a question, "Is something right or good because the gods decree that it is, or is it decreed by god as right or good because it is right or good?" Plato places a dichotomy that is difficult to face before adherents to this perspective. If god decrees something is good because it is good, then he is not the ultimate authority or source of goodness. On the other hand, if something is good simply because god said it is good, then goodness is arbitrary and god could have just as well ordained that thing to be bad. Plato believed the source of goodness was beyond the gods and they were not the ultimate authorities but the good lay in spiritual forms.

For Plato this was a real dilemma. In a religion where gods raped young women, acted in jealousy, spite, and revenge, the good could be very difficult to discuss even if all the gods agreed it is good. However, for most others this is a false dilemma, especially for those who follow the divine-command view of ethics. Christians, for instance, believe that God is good—in and of himself; his character is good and righteous and therefore holy. From that perspective good is good because it is god-like, therefore, giving God both the authority for ordaining and making him the ultimate source of goodness. Judaism, Islam, and several other religions have similar concepts of holy gods who are good in and of themselves.

Followers of divine-command ethics usually have historically based sacred documents that stipulate the decrees, laws, or rules that the god has set forth. These guide and give precedence for all ethical elements. Whatever rules are most applicable to the present situation become the standard to speak by. If the truth is commanded, then any lie in a persuasive situation is anathema. If the rule says to love each other, then the speaker must demonstrate love in the speech or it is sinful. Rule guided through the quagmires of moral swamps, these divine-command adherents focus solely on the law-book and need not stretch beyond the code. For those of great religious heritage this system often works well throughout life.

Sadly, many follow organizational codes as though God set them. The movie *A Few Good Men* explored how the Marine Corps code could be followed as a divine-command ethic. Obedience was expected, demanded, and if one fell slightly, then all was lost; therefore, punishment would be extreme and swift. Yet the unthinking carrying out of the orders led to the betrayal of the very mission and values they were trying to protect. So it often is with those who follow law codes or business codes of conduct with unreasoned adherence to a handful of absolutes.

The Divine-Command approach to ethics can be very beneficial. Correctly recognizing a higher power and authority enables us to look beyond our own perspective to discover principles, values, and absolutes to base a good life upon. This method leads to a happier life for more people, considers both means and ends, sets standards by which we can evaluate character as well as action, and enables easily understood traditions to regulate behavior.

Consequentialism

The results of a course of action is the foundation of this perspective of ethics and is more important than the means or motive in the process of acting. Two major schools of thought following Epicurus or John Stewart Mill arrive at different perspectives of the consequences, but they are similar in thinking.

Epicurus followed thinkers like Aristotle and Aristippus in thinking about happiness as a foundation for ethics and came to the conclusion that seeking a pleasant life is natural and, therefore, ought to be done by all people. Satisfying desires leads to a pleasant existence, so above all else people should satisfy innate desires and drives, but not just any passions, three kinds of desires exist for the proper fulfillment:

1. Those that are natural must be satisfied (such as food, shelter and clothing).

2. Those that are natural but need not be satisfied for a pleasant life (such as sexual gratification or alcohol consumption).

3. Those that are unnatural (such as the desire for wealth or fame).

When these are satisfied properly, peace of the soul results. The pleasant life is attained through personal gratification of the first kind of desire while not seeking to fulfill the third order of desires at all. The second level of desire may be fulfilled when no pain or discomfort results from the gratification.

> *When, therefore, we maintain that pleasure is the end, we do not mean the pleasure that profiligates [sic] and those that consist in sensuality, as is supposed by some who are either ignorant or disagree with us, or do not understand, but freedom from pain in the body and from trouble in the mind. For it is not continuous drinkings and revelings, not satisfaction of lusts, nor the enjoyment of fish and other luxuries of the wealthy table, which produce a pleasant life, but sober reasoning, searching out the motives for choice and avoidance, and banishing mere opinions, to which are due the greatest disturbance of spirit* (letter to Menolceus as quoted in Newberry p. 72-73).

The Epicurean form of hedonism taught that the human should not seek pain unless that pain leads to a greater pleasure. If misrepresenting a product in a persuasive sales presentation gains a sale, immediate gratification may result; however, the long term effect of an angry customer, return of the product, and loss of the job are of much greater pain, therefore do not misrepresent the product. A reasonable approach to gratifying the desires of the human spirit should be used, not an emotional one. The great gain of wealth should be avoided at all cost; earning a wage that will meet your basic natural needs will lead to greater satisfaction.

True pleasure is not mere happiness but *ataraxia*, peace of soul or tranquility within the spirit; these are true pleasures that last. Shortsighted self-indulgence leads to greater pain; therefore, carefully consider the consequences before acting so as to measure the long-term impact on the soul. For most people anxiety about future pain is the greatest obstacle to the peace of spirit. Worrying lessens the favorable impact of the fulfillment of pleasurable desires of the moment. Eliminating anxiety and focusing on attainable peace of mind and body will create happiness. Therefore, prudence "is a more precious thing than even philosophy" (letter to M) for from prudence springs virtue and those characteristics of life lead to happiness.

Honor, justice, and integrity are necessary for peace of mind brought about through self-controlled fulfillment of natural passion.

Epicurean ethics calls the persuasive rhetor to consider the long-term impact of a persuasive speech on his or her spirit. Will the speech lead to a greater pleasure or pain, especially in the peace of mind and tranquility of spirit? What are the possible repercussions beyond the desired short term goals? Writing for the gain of honor, power, money, and goods is a worthy endeavor because of the good ends of public communication. If lying brings these results, then nothing is wrong with the means as long as they accomplished a good end. Self-expression is a fulfillment that may bring harmonious happiness in and of itself and is therefore worthy to undertake.

A second form of consequentialism is that of Utilitarianism. Jeremy Behtham and John Stewart Mill extended the epicurean ideas and those of Hume into a system where the morality of a course of action is determined by the happiness it produces as a consequence. The biggest difference from Epicureanism is a focus not on the happiness of self but for everyone who may be influenced or impacted. Less emphasis is placed on personal quality or virtue in utilitarianism where the consideration of the consequences of an act solely determines whether it is right or wrong. The evaluation of the resulting pleasure should only take into consideration quantitative data of how much happiness results from an action. Bentham suggests the criteria of: certainty, intensity, duration, immediacy, as well as the extent of the pleasure or pain should be used to evaluate an act. Calculating alternative courses of action through their consequences determines the morality of the situation.

Mill added several aspects making Bentham's perspective more palatable in an attempt to make an ethical system to replace Christianity's divine-command ethics as well as encompass a growing modernist movement. Beyond Bentham, first the individual should attempt to be objectively impartial when determining the consequences placing self and close associates on equal footing with others' happiness. Second, some pleasures are inherently better than others, so a *quality* of happiness may be greater in some instances and lead to longer-term satisfaction, and these kinds of ends should be valued above those that have shorter-term and lesser satisfaction. Finally, Mill also extended the idea of impacts beyond one simple act to rules or principles which the act exemplifies. Thus an action of high moral quality should be objectively calculated to have quality happiness for the greatest number of people establishing a model, rule or principle others may use to increase happiness. No acts are right or wrong in and of themselves; the moral standard comes from the impact on the happiness or pain of people. Therefore, stealing, murder, defending the country, giving, lying, telling the truth, or keeping promises, none of these things are inherently wrong or right, but the consequences may be similar in consistency of producing pleasure or pain and in that they may produce ethical models, rules or principles which all could follow by keeping the ends in sight.

The journalistic dictum, "do no harm," falls into the consequential ethical perspective. When coupled with the "divine command" attitude of breaking no laws, then freedom of speech can be manipulated in unethical ways while giving lip service to ethics.

Persuasive speakers ought to consider the impact of the speech not just on themselves, but also on the audience as a whole. What will they think or do as a result of what I am saying and doing; will that lead them into further happiness or greater pain? Every piece of evidence is significant in that the impact must produce a greater good for the community of listeners with the good of the speaker being equal to that of only one of the audience members.

Deontological Ethics

The moral duty of a person is the primary consideration in a moral situation. The constant production of maximum quality of happiness in the greatest quantity is not necessarily what is right because good is more than happiness, pleasure and tranquility. A strong sense of moral duty, the responsibility to do what is right usually results in tranquility and happiness, but these are a by-product of doing the moral duty, not the good itself.

Kant believed that moral principles could not be attained through scientific methodology because they are absolutes—they hold true, without exception, for all people and all situations. The categorical imperative is to act rationally in such a manner that you would desire to prescribe everyone else in all other similar situations to act, i.e. act on the basis of the absolute universal law. The essence of Kant's perspective is to carry the "golden rule" (do unto others what you wish they would do unto you) to the point of wishing it to be a universal law.

The ends, the effects of a moral act are not what makes the act good or bad, neither are the means, but rather the motive or intent of the individual who is initiating the action. The greatest good, or the "good without qualification," is a morally good will, the strength and determination to choose what is right because it is right and for no other reason. Kant reframed the same idea by saying treat other humans as ends and not simply means. If acts are done in any manner that the actor would not desire and think it should be a universal law, then treatment of others is subordinate to the individual actor. Providing this logical rationale as the basis for all morality, calling it the moral duty that is imprinted on the human soul, Kant imparts a complete ethical system.

"According to Kant, if a universal law allowed breach of promise, then there would be no such thing as a promise. Thus the maxim 'Break promises!' if it were to become a universal law, would (as Kant says) 'destroy itself.' But hold on. Suppose I promise to return your car at 4 o'clock. And suppose that shortly before 4 my wife becomes ill and must be rushed to the hospital—and the only transportation available is your car! Should I break my promise to you in order to save my wife's life? And if I did, which maxim would I be acting on, breaking promises or saving lives? "Kant's answer (of course) would be that the maxim I acted on is 'Break promises when doing so is required to save a life.' And there would apparently be no inconsistency in willing this maxim to be a universal law. "For Kant, then, the maxim 'Break your promises!' cannot be universalized. But that doesn't mean that, given his principles, you should never break a promise" (Moore and Bruder, 1996 p. 233). Most ethical principles therefore are held in tension with other ethical principles so that few are absolute.

Most proponents of deontological ethics believe your understand your moral duty through first principles. Discernment of what is most important: like love, justice, or equality enable an understanding of what I am to do in the situation I find myself in at this point of time. Personal responsibility in the form of duty is the most important thing to know in the realm of ethics.

The deontological ethical point of view applied to persuasive speaking and writing is what is right to say in this situation, to these people? What would you will that others would write in this column on this day? Extra attention should be placed in consideration of the goal of the communication and the motivation for the statement. The intent of the participants is the most telling factor in determining the moral impact and goodness of persuasive rhetoric.

Virtue Ethics

Refocusing morality from action into character, virtue ethics considers what is good from a personal perspective. Actions are not right or wrong based on the means, the ends, the intent nor the divine will, but are to be judged on the type of character they reflect in the individual over time.

Development of people instead of rules, codes, or prescriptions for action is the foundation of moral logic.

For Socrates the key to the good life lay in knowledge of good. For Plato the key lay in reflecting the forms of character. The form of courage is the model for all the specific instances of courage that are observable in the world, and knowledge of that true courage makes a person courageous. The highest of all ideals is goodness and a full knowledge of that good makes a person good in every aspect. Goodness is a single concept in which all good things idealistically "participate."

In Aristotle the fullness of virtue ethics becomes explicit in a systematic presentation of ethics. Aristotle defines the term *good* as being different in each instance as the things in that category fulfill their primary purpose. Good hammers pound nails well, while good musicians play music well, and thus good people are those who fulfill the intended purpose of people (Newberry p. 46). *For Aristotle, the greatest good is, therefore, a harmonious blessedness of being and acting according to virtues inherent in the character of the individual.* Virtue ethics is a system focused on developing individuals into good people, not simply producing good actions. The highest good for humanity is reason, and for individuals the greatest virtue is happiness, a lasting contentment based on maturity of the inner being. Virtue is the difference between merely doing something and doing it well (Rosenstand p. 295), and the highest virtue is that which fulfills the *telos* or purpose of reason—rational character driven by the will bringing about blessedness.

Virtues exist as golden means between vices of excess and deficit as a characteristic of choice. Virtue is the action or feeling giving the correct response, at the right time, in the right way, in the right amount, for the right reason (*Nicomanchean Ethics*). This balance is achieved through a lifetime of education, conscious training, and practice involving the entire person. Danger can be faced with too little courage, cowardice, or just the right amount of courage (the golden mean) or too much courage which is brash foolhardiness. Thus virtue lies in the mean, and either the excess or absence of the character are vices to be avoided. Food can be withheld to the point of starvation, or eaten temperately, or with gluttony; again, virtue is in the mean between excess and deficit. Truth is a virtue, but ironic mock modesty is too little, truth is the median of reality, while bragging is truth's excess. Experimentation with constant attention and reasonable means will succeed in training the appetites into being able to follow the golden mean—virtue. Being virtuous makes a person happy and thus helps fulfill the meaning of life. The ultimately happy life is that of a contemplator, a thinker (and Aristotle adds it helps to have friends, reputation, money, and good looks as well). When a person has gained virtue, then generally future actions will be virtuous in all categories, not just one aspect of character and thus good people are identified through their maturity. Individuals may jump from one vice to another, or from excess to deficit, but once they discover the joy of virtue, they generally strive to gain and maintain that golden mean.

In persuasive speaking and writing, the noble rhetors attempt to move people into virtue and avoid excess. The right to speak on an issue may be determined by the advancement of the communicator into virtue and thus be a good person speaking truth. The rhetoric itself should also be an example of virtue, should support solid character, and should have the content match the delivery as one of self-control and reason in balance.

Aristotle's Virtues of the Golden Mean

Aristotle agreed with Plato's four cardinal virtues: Justice, courage, moderation, and wisdom. However, he adds several more virtues to the list in the Nicomachean Ethics.

Excess (Vice)	Mean (Virtue)	Deficit (Vice)
Uncritical	Loyal	Disloyal
Passive	Patient	Impatient
Intrusive	Compassionate	Unfeeling
Feeling Indebted	Grateful	Ungrateful
Everything is too serious	Responsible	Irresponsible
Stubborn	Persevering	Quitter
Being Rude	Honest	Lying
Strict	Rules with Exceptions	Lenient in all things
Worries about the future	Concerned with welfare	Unconcerned
Intemperate pleasure	Enjoy pleasures	Unimpressionable
Prodigal spender	Liberal with money	Miser
Vanity	Proper pride with humility	Excess humility
Anger	Even tempered	Unaware meekness
Lust	Love	Apathy
Jealousy	Empathy	Self seeking

Ethical Virtues From *Character Counts*

- Trustworthiness
  - o   Honesty
  - o   Integrity
  - o   Reliability
  - o   Loyalty
- Respect
  - o   Golden Rule

- o Tolerance
- o Nonviolence
- o Courtesy
- Responsibility
  - o Duty
  - o Accountability
  - o Pursue Excellence
  - o Self-control
- Fairness
  - o Justice
  - o Openness
  - o Impartial
- Caring
  - o Concern for others
  - o Charity/Altruistic
- Citizenship
  - o Do your share
  - o Respect Authority
  - o Obey the Law

The Lakota Sioux taught 4 virtues:

- ➤ Courage
- ➤ Strength
- ➤ Wisdom
- ➤ Generosity

For the Christian, we recognize that virtue lies in the nature of the being of God. What is good is like God in character. What is bad is not like God. Justice is right because God is just. Love is a desirable quality because God is love. The attributes of God become the norm for people because people are created in his image. God has these divine attributes as an absolute while humans only reflect his perfection with mixed good and bad because of our sin nature. Nothing we do is absolute righteousness or perfect good because we are an amalgamation of what is right and wrong, so we struggle with ethical issues. In theology this is called "depravity" or the extent of the "sin nature." The Apostle Paul debates why he does bad things in Romans 7. Goodness changes from human happiness to that which reflects God's being making him the ultimate arbitrator of what is right and wrong, not through decrees like Divine commands (Calvin and Luther), but though his being.

Christian public communication should occur genuinely—from a heart of integrity. It should create in a congruent message that communicates truth from a life of virtue. Hypocritical words or creating messages with empty content should be avoided as unethical. All communication should be in the character of God.

Relativism

Ethical systems that teach what is right or good and wrong or bad, changes from culture to culture or person to person, are called relativistic ethics or situational ethics. These systems are humanistic and subjectivist because they are determined and measured by the people involved; with human opinion being the ultimate authority. Cultural relativism considers what is right and wrong is what each culture believes is right: good and bad are chosen by, or grown into, through the social collective of people. People co-create what is valued, good, and right. Individual relativism considers that what is right and wrong is what each person believes is right and wrong: each individual, often in each situation, determines for himself or herself what is good and bad. Absolutes and universal principles do not exist; therefore, ethics becomes more descriptive and normative than prescriptive and standardized.

For example: throughout the impeachment hearings of President Clinton, he was more concerned about public opinion poles than many issues of the trial. Guilt or innocence was not the focus, but the winning of the high moral ground of the culture—what the people think and believe is right is right, and if they believe Clinton is right, then he should not be impeached. Objective truth or objective adherence to law or standards of morality were not a part of the consideration; instead, subjectivist relativism held sway, and he was able to retain his position and power. That was cultural relativism at work in a major democracy from which has flowed many speeches and analysis but few recognize the ethical dimension.

This form of ethics is widely held in the United States at this time in history. Some of the perspectives can be evidenced through these kinds of comments: "That's your truth, but this is my truth" (as if reality changes from person to person), "Your god may be like that, but I can't believe in a god who would do or say something like that" (as if human belief changes the nature of god), "This is right for me" (good, bad, right and wrong change according to each person—so follow your own conscience).

Deconstructionism coupled with relative ethics takes relativism a step further so that all moral thoughts and systems are equally valid and equally arbitrary (Derrida, 1978).

Many questions remain unanswered concerning relativism: Is an action or characteristic neither right nor wrong until an individual or culture has thought about it? If what is right is what you believe is right, then you cannot be mistaken in moral issues. People often change their minds about ethical issues; does that mean what was right is now wrong simply because an individual changed positions? What happens when belief systems conflict with each other? What size of 'culture' does it take to make an authoritative ethical system: a country, ethnic group, religion, gang, family, counter-culture movement? Often people will be members of different 'cultures' at the same time with conflicting ethical values and practices; how can these be balanced rationally?

Persuasive rhetors need to be aware of the culture and ethical beliefs of the audience and should incorporate their beliefs into the content and appeal of their messages. Christian rhetors do not compromise their integrity but at the same time do love the audience enough to speak with them in the most persuasive way. Ignoring the cultural implications and expectations will negate the intended impact of a speech or article. Changing the words so that an audience can hear the message may become necessary for public communicators. If rhetors do not consider what an audience believes to be true, then their messages will probably be rejected, even if it is right or in the best interest of the audience. From this perspective, all public messages should be communicated within the bounds of accepted moral principles, or they will not be persuasive.

Contractarianism

The social contract focused on justice and critique of the state began with Thomas Hobbes and flourished in the philosophy of John Locke. The political philosophy of Hobbes had a foundational presupposition that "the legitimacy of the state and its laws derives from an initial consent of those governed" (Moore and Bruder p. 302). Our laws become a social contract that is the basis of personal moral action. People delegate their personal power to a legislature to enact the social contract for all to follow in their public actions. As this philosophy took hold in the political realm, Western cultures progressed from monarchical governments to democratic rule.

Locke believed that a natural moral law providing inalienable rights of life, liberty, and property underlay the government of the state that was to secure peace and safety as well as to enhance the public good through citizen agreement. Consent of the governed to submit to the will of the majority is the key to the outworking of the social contract. Separating the powers within the government is necessary. Doing so creates a legislative branch to make the laws, an executive branch to enact the law, a federative branch for action, and a judicial branch to settle disputes and punish those who violate the social contract. Government becomes a servant of the people, conversely, the people should not become servants of the government. The United States government wrote this ethical perspective into the heart of our government. We are primarily a community of the Constitution—our social contract.

Ethical practice is largely determined by following the laws of the country making what is good and right a political or governmental function rather than from virtue, principle, or society. Codified rules determine right and wrong for the people of the society. Both formal aspects of law and informal agreements among us as a people are part of the social contract; even nonverbal expectations. Many organizations follow the social contract model expecting their members to abide by policies and procedures and if any are broken, then the member is punished or their rights may be terminated.

Persuasive public speaking and writing should be within the limits of the social contract. For instance, expressly persuading an audience in a school classroom to vote for an individual may be illegal and, therefore, immoral. Exercising the freedom of speech to pray can no longer be done within certain boundaries of abortion clinics (while the freedom to protest wages or working conditions may occur within those same boundaries). While keeping much of the freedoms of communication, consent to the social contract restricts some of those rights. Most people feel morally inclined to obey those limitations of freedom, yet others believe that they are morally propelled to break those same aspects of the code.

Summary and Practice of Ethics

The primary focus of each approach enables public speakers to consider significant questions prior to giving a speech or writing a story ensuring that the ethical dimension impacts the content. Cooper (1989) gives the social contract as the basis with virtue as an outcome of public discourse. Jensen (1981) outlines ethics of persuasion from a virtue of the content perspective: accuracy, completeness, relevance, openness, understandability, reason, social utility, and benevolence with sources of specific ethical practices being the individual, social context, culture, and religion. Rybacki and Rybacki (2005) suggest that when advocating a position, the speaker consider the common good responsibility (utilitarian), reasoning responsibility (deontological), and the social code (contractarian) while recognizing communication as a means or process which can lead to good and personal growth.

Perhaps a rhetorician can broaden an outlook to include all six in a functional balance. From the divine-command perspective, do the religious beliefs of the speaker or audience have any specific direction for the subject material or delivery (such as dress . . .) that is needed to form the speech? Consequentialism leads the speaker to think through the intended and possible outcomes of the speech as they impact both the speaker and the audience. Are the moral duties of the speaker covered, from a deontological perspective, where the content and delivery lay within the categorical imperative? From the virtue ethics position, is the speaker demonstrating maturity of character in a manner that urges the audience to do what is good through becoming better people? Within the relativistic ethical conclave, what does the host society believe about the subject and appropriate behavior concerning application of the issue? Finally, does the social contract have any specific application to this particular issue spoken of in this particular manner? Most speakers will find themselves drawn to one of these systems as a primary consideration in all areas of ethics and then use the others as secondary considerations.

Conclusion

Personally I follow a combination of virtue ethics with divine-command elements where the foundation is the nature of God as the primary good and the maturity of character as the element of motivation to act within the mean between excess and deficit. God's creative intent is that we reflect his image. The more god-like a person becomes, the more truly human that person is through the transformation of virtue leading to specific humane action. The balance of answers from all six questions above will probably lead speakers to a strong conviction about what is right or wrong for a communication, whether it is a speech, story, prose, or poetry as communicated to a particular audience.

The list of ethics is not drawn from society as Plato and Aristotle did, but from the person and being God himself. Holiness is a virtue, as are faithfulness, courage, patience, love, joy, peace . . . not because they bring happiness, but because they transform fallen humans to become like their

Creator. The goal, the purpose, is not to gain personal elements, but to be changed into his image or substance. The ideal is to become like God, not to experience happiness or harmonious satisfaction.

This Christian virtue ethic not only provides the social aspects of communication (to use C. S. Lewis again, keeping the ships from bumping into one another), along with the individual aspects of communication (what virtues enable shipshape floating), but also answer the summum bonum—the ultimate purpose and meaning of life is to become like Christ and thus give glory to the Creator in whose image we are made.

Chapter 3

Toward a Theology of Rhetorical Persuasion

I will make my words in your mouth a fire
and these people the wood it consumes.
Jeremiah 5:14 NIV

God is speaking

FROM THE beginning of Genesis to the culmination of Revelation, God is the one who *is speaking* and not just in the past tense, *has spoken*. God began the world through creative acts of rhetoric; he spoke and it came into being (Genesis 1; Hebrews 11:3—worlds were framed by the *rhema*, the rhetoric of God). He upholds that same creation through his rhetoric (Hebrews 1:3). He chose to communicate with people in the Garden, but after the fall direct access became less frequent and with greater difficulty. Communication decreased until Moses' day. At that time, when God spoke directly to the people they were so overwhelmed with awe they could not stand the experience, so they chose Moses to go and talk with God, and then tell them what he said (Exodus 20). Moses became a rhetorical mediator. By the time of Samuel, direct communication with God in the form of rhetoric became scarce (I Samuel 3:1). God continued to speak through nature, the prophets, and his word. Then he sent his only Son in order to communicate with people (Hebrews 1:1-2). The Bible is the record of that communication, and God continues to speak through it (Hebrews 12:25) God's special revelation.

In the pattern and dance of the stars, in the crash of the thunderstorm, in the whirlwind—God speaks (Psalm 18). The heavens *are declar-*

ing the glory of God (Psalm 19) and nature *is speaking* of his eternal divinity (Romans 1:20), God's general revelation. The Creator speaks through the creation both in the past and the present. The clear articulation of his message is through language spoken in the Bible and by the Holy Spirit in the quiet of the heart. God chooses to persuade people through rhetoric. Humans are the audience for those words, we are also responsible to enunciate them to others. People are the conduit of God's public communication.

God Calls People to Communicate

The great commission is primarily a call to communicate. The identity of a disciple is a *fisher of men*—a communicator. The method of salvation involves communication: on the part of God, on the part of the human mediator, and on the part of the recipient (Romans 10). Most importantly, in Christian rhetoric, God must act through grace to move the hearts of the audience before they can receive the living Word. When God speaks along side of the orator, the audience may or may not be convinced because of God's grace, love, authority, *logos*, and the power of the Holy Spirit. God receives the glory, not the orator when the audience is moved.

One of the most fascinating passages of literary persuasion is found in God's discussion with Ezekiel:

> *And he said to me, 'Son of man, listen carefully and take to heart all the words I speak to you. Go now to your countrymen in exile and speak to them. Say to them, 'This is what the Sovereign LORD says, whether they listen or fail to listen . . . .' At the end of seven days the word of the Lord came to me: 'Son of man, I have made you a watchman for the house of Israel; so hear the word I speak and give them warning from me. When I say to a wicked man, 'You will surely die,' and you do not warn him or speak out to dissuade him from his evil ways in order to save his life, that wicked man will die for his sin, and I will hold you accountable for his blood. But if you do warn the wicked man and he does not turn from his wickedness or from his evil ways, he will die for his sin; but you will have saved yourself. Again, when a righteous man turns from his righteousness and does evil, and I put a stumbling block before him, he will die. Since you did not warn him, he will die for his sin. The righteous things he did will not be remembered, and I will hold you accountable for his blood. But if you do warn the righteous man not to sin and he does not sin, he will surely live because he took warning, and you will have saved yourself.' Ezekiel 3:10-21*

God appointed Ezekiel to be a *watchman* over the people of Israel. Standing on the wall a watchman would look for invaders from without. He would close the gate at night and keep guard. Watchmen would also look out for danger within the walls like a fire or people doing something wrong.

Ezekiel's job is to listen to God on behalf of the people and then to communicate them to people. God's judgment is at the gates and the people are in danger. Many of them are already in exile because they have disobeyed God for so long. He is to leave the promised land and to face the punishment they are facing. There, Ezekiel is commanded to use persuasive public communication—drama, poetry, preaching, and nonverbal signs all to express God's message.

God holds the communicator accountable for the message being heard and understood by the audience. But God does not hold the speaker or writer answerable for the actions that come following the delivery of the message—that is the audience's responsibility. The speaker must speak and the listener must listen, the writer must write and the reader must read-communicative responsibilities are clear in biblical, persuasive communication.

The message content, from a Christian worldview, should originate with God. According to the Greco-Roman tradition, rhetoric is all the available means of persuasion in a given instance and the rhetor himself or herself is responsible for the *invention* of the content. Here, Ezekiel is more like a medium for the message than an independent originator of that communication. The call of Ezekiel is not "when you want to speak" but "When I say" then you are to persuade. Freedom of speech from a theological perspective is therefore more about the responsibility to use opportunity than the content of the expression or whether or not to communicate.

Notice too that Ezekiel is not given a choice in the matter of being a herald. The King calls him and gives him the task of communication. He does not ask, "do you want to be my herald?" He does not ask, "will you please speak to my people?" He does not use an interrogative statement giving the freedom of choice to the prophet; God gives a direct command with the full impact of the consequences.

Jeremiah experiences the word of God like a fire burning into his heart (Jeremiah 20:9). He could not quench it, so he was compelled to speak God's words to others. He was so filled with the message that words like sparks flew from the pyre of his heart igniting others.

For Jesus, speaking is a spiritual responsibility of universal human accountability in that people will be judged for every "careless word" we have spoken (Matthew 12:36). We cannot excuse ourselves from the responsibility of communicating on behalf of God by saying only those with a special burden must speak God's words. Christian rhetoric is not just for full-time pastors or clergy, but also for everyone else. We no longer need a Mosaic mediator to absorb the resounding thunder from Mount Sinai, but each person is able to listen to the still small voice of the Holy Spirit and then speak out. If we keep silent, God will judge the lack of communication severely.

The apostles in Acts 5 were arrested and left in jail for the night. The Angel of the Lord came and released them and told them to go to the temple and speak "all the rhetoric (*rhemata*) of life." When they were re-arrested, Peter responded to the charge that God had exalted Jesus to be a Prince and Savior to give repentance and forgiveness of sins. "And we are his witnesses of this rhetoric (*rhematon*)." The call of God is to publicly communicate the content of the gospel message and this process is the heart of Christian rhetoric. The Word—*rhema*—connotes not just the individual's responsibility to God's call, but represents the content, as well as the process of persuasive public communication.

Love: The Foundation of Rhetorical Relationships

In I Corinthians 13:1 the Apostle Paul says, if I *speak* without love, my words are a sounding gong, even if I know all the languages of the world. Love is necessary for spiritual speaking. Love is a more excellent way of approaching community life than that of the individualistic exercise of spiritual gifts (I Corinthians 12:31). The attitude of the heart, the content of the words, the nonverbal relational messages—these are all spoken from and in love. The greatest virtues are not Plato's justice, moderation, courage, and wisdom, but faith, hope, and love. Of these, the greatest is love, not justice. Love is the peaceful harmony of a life in balance, not the Greco-Roman ideal of justice.

In the United States we like to think and speak of our rights. Empowering others and ourselves through writing and speaking enables us to comprehend our existence on a power basis. Rhetoric based on a relationship of love provides a worldview founded in intimate relationships instead of power.

While we were yet sinners, Christ died for us (Romans 5:6-10). We were enemies of God, yet he loved us as a basis for the relationship (I John 3:1) and adopted us as his children. In the Sermon on the Mount, Jesus taught that we were to have the same kind of foundation for relationships. Loving those who love us is nothing, even pagans and nonbelievers do that. Loving the unlovely, those who actively persecute us, that is the underpinning of Christian relationship with those whom we communicate (Matthew 5:43-46; Romans 12:20). Love is to so permeate our character that others will know we are Christians by that relationship of active love (John 13:35; I John 3:11). We also have the assurance of our own salvation when we love others (I John 3:14). With this assurance our words reach out to others.

Take a look at the following list of Classical Greek variations on the concept of love:

- Ludos: love is a fun game. Laughter from a heart filled with joy, just to be with the one we love, gives life heartiness and fulfillment. This is a flirtatious teasing kind of love that enjoys tantalizing excitement and fun.

    This is a new love, the first love, where life is filled with zest. If you have never experienced lovers' games you are missing one of the most fulfilling feelings of life.

- *Pragma*: love is practical, intimacy of experience. We have jobs in order to earn what it takes to make ends meet for each other, cook, clean, yard-work and a host of other things because we love each other. Doing things with and for each other makes the day-to-day drudgery worthwhile. This is a logical kind of love based on the function of partners within common goals and interests: we are better together.

    Hebrews 11:1 Faith is the substance, the reality of hoped for *pragma*. If Hebrews is primarily Classical Greek this may be a very interesting interpretive twist.

- *Storge*: love is commitment, social intimacy, and trust. A slow enduring love that gets you through the hard times. Being trustworthy in the relationship gives you confidence. *Storge* is a companionship coupled with partnership that enables two people to share a lifetime of love.

    This is the love of the wife of a Greek soldier who remains faithful even though he is gone more than ten years.

- *Mania*: love is emotional, experiencing the best and worst of life together. The mountaintop experience, it lifts the soul in

69

weightless ecstasy, coupled with the valleys, and the ache of pain (in later use this takes on the quality of madness or insanity and looses the quality of love).

> *Mania* is a "Romeo and Juliet" kind of extreme passion or the kind of love that makes one sick. This is the love Cupid shoots into people with his arrows.

- *Philos*: love is companionship, intimacy of the soul. Friendship feels good just being with the other person sitting by the fire and enjoying the conversation. This involves being able to think together, work together, vacation together, and to enjoy the intimacy of soul.

> John 5:20 For the Father loves (*philos*) the Son.

> I Peter 3:8 Command to love (*philos*) as brothers.

> *Nicomanchean Ethics* of Aristotle, love (*philos*) is the only way to achieve happiness that has no negative consequences.

- *Eros*: love is passionate, an intimacy of the body. Yes, this is the sexual rapture and frenzied infatuation, the physical attraction: but it is much more. Eros is emotion so deep and penetrating that every fiber of being is intensely stimulated and alive with wonder. This kind of love enraptures the spirit through sex in such a manner that two become one flesh.

> In Ephesians 4:15, Paul changes Plato's idea of speaking the truth in *eros* (*Phadrus*) to speaking the truth in *agape*.

- *Splagchnon*: love is compassion, tender mercy, and affection that comes from the inner being. This is a metaphorical use of the literal word *intestine*. Meeting others in their need through inner compassion is the heart of mercy and grace. This involves doing what is best for others, to meet their needs especially when they are unable to help themselves.

> In Matthew 9:36 Jesus was *moved with compassion.*

> In Luke 1:78 Through the *tender mercy* of our God.

- *Agape*: love is self-giving, intimacy of the spirit. As an altruistic love focused on giving to others with no expectation that the deed will be repaid, agape considers the other person first. This is the divine love that is the opposite of self-actualization; it is being a living sacrifice, freely giving of life for a friend.

  > Jesus said in John 15:9ff, I *agape* you, continue in my *agape* . . . greater *agape* hath no man than this, that a man lay down his life for his friends.

  > Paul speaks of virtues in I Corinthians 13:13 concluding that the greatest of these is *agape*.

These facets of the diamond of love are designed to be in balance. When *mania* supersedes *philos*, Romeo and Juliet commit suicide. When *pragma* and *storge* predominate with little *eros* or *philos*, then Babbit's life takes over with mundane humdrum. All eight should be facets in the diamond called love for it to be most valuable and beautiful. They encompass the mind, will, emotions, attitudes . . . the thinking, feeling, action, and being of people. Christian rhetoric, like classical persuasive public communication is based on truth spoken in love (Ephesians 4:15).

When a rhetor has this kind of balanced love both in the core of the soul and spirit as well as in relationship, persuasive rhetoric will have a greater impact. Words communicated with the integrity and congruency of love will change both the speaker and the audience. The ethos of a speaker or writer over time is directly connected to the character as demonstrated in words, actions, charisma and demeanor. Living a life of love will enhance the appeals given because the audience will believe the nonverbal communication of love, and that is the spiritual power of Christian persuasion. Love is the foundation, the motivation for the message, and the attitude of delivery in Christian Rhetoric.

Secular rhetorical theory looks to scientifically identifiable variables to measure impacts and predict future effectiveness. Christians rely on the Holy Spirit moving the audience through truth grounded in God and relationships of love flowing from the Spirit. Love is therefore the primary characteristic of Christian rhetoric; while important in classical rhetoric, it is, at best, a secondary part of secular thinking concerning public communication.

Grace: The Enabling Characteristic of Rhetoric

In Matthew 11:25 Jesus praises God because people misunderstand the message he is speaking. The little children comprehend the meaning while the wise do not grasp the truth. Grace given to a little child for understanding. The same words hide the good news from one group while it makes the message plain to another. The difference is in the listeners (John 8:47) as they experience God's grace to be able to listen. As speakers, we ought to spend time and energy in overcoming miscommunication, but sometimes the blocks put in place by the listeners are their own responsibility to overcome.

God, showing the gift of free, unmerited favor to undeserving people, is called grace. For by grace we are saved through faith (Ephesians 2:8). The transformation of people through encountering the living God into a state of being where we are able to believe and respond is called prevenient, efficacious grace—the irresistible wonder of partnership with God coming to people. *Prevenient* means that God takes the initiative on our behalf; he takes the first step toward people (I John 4:10, 19). *Efficacious* grace means that God's grace accomplishes the purpose for which it is given (Isaiah 55; Philippians 1:6). The receiver cannot reject *irresistible* grace once it is given (Ephesians 1:4; Acts 26:14; Galatians 1:15). Grace is adequate for the needs of the receiver (Hebrews 13:5-6; Psalm 118:6).

God's grace is a deep mystery that is beyond comprehension. He freely gives people all that we need to respond to the message while preparing hearts and minds to accept the persuasive appeal. Grace is given in such a manner that it does not overpower the human will, but enables people to hear the language of the living God. Grace comes into public communication from God through the written and spoken words of humans. We are conduits of God's grace channeling a message into the life of the audience. None of us deserve to hear or speak but we are able to because of God's gracious heart.

Heart: The Source of Words

The intrapersonal communication (within a person) that dialogues within people's minds is often the most important part of a rhetorical situation (Proverbs 10:20; Luke 6:45). Words express the congruent integration of the entire human mind, will, and emotion with a spiritual impact. In articulating the essence of this philosophy, Jesus said:

Make a tree good and its fruit will be good, or make a tree bad and its fruit will be bad, for a tree is recognized by its fruit. You brood of vipers, how can you who are evil say anything good? For out of the overflow of the heart the mouth speaks. The good man brings good things out of the good stored up in him, and the evil man brings evil things out of the evil stored up in him. But I tell you that men will have to give account on the day of judgment for every careless word they have spoken. For by your words you will be acquitted, and by your words you will be condemned.

Matthew 12:33-37 NIV

The words we speak come from the heart. Aristotle focused on the virtue of rhetoricians as the basis for ethical speaking. *Ethos*, the audience's perception of the character of the speaker, is primary in allowing words to persuade the mind. Christian thinking takes this a large step farther in that character is the source of spoken words, and these are so vital to the spiritual essence of people that they will form a foundation for justice and eternal reward or punishment. Developing a spiritually mature character is, therefore, the essence of rhetorical training.

Often the Bible exhorts those in relationship with God to search their hearts for evil and good. Passages such as Psalm 4:4 encourage us at the end of the day to take stalk of who we are and what we have done by looking into our heart. Other times like Psalm 139:23 we call on God to search us and reveal what he finds there so we can confess sin and enhance righteousness.

Gospel: The Content of Christian Rhetoric

The content of the rhetoric of God comes from the Lord Jesus (John 17:8). These *rhema* are the words of life offered as a gift to be received. Rather than individual inventing, God should be the source. Messages generated through people should be in the character, spirit, and power of God.

The Apostle Paul described his kind of persuasive communication in this way: He was sent to preach, the content of his message is the cross of Christ, and spiritual wisdom is the result. He also said that he is not speaking in eloquent, persuasive words. The evidence he uses to support his words is not logic or literature, but actions with power. Paul enters a lengthy discussion of this topic in I Corinthians 1 NIV translation.

Christ did not send me to baptize, but to preach the gospel--not with words of human wisdom, lest the cross of Christ be emptied of its power. For the message of the cross is foolishness to those who are perishing, but to us who are being saved it is the power of God. For it is written: "I will destroy the wisdom of the wise; the intelligence of the intelligent I will frustrate." I Corinthians 1:17-19

Paul was intentionally speaking in a way that would not fit within the argumentative paradigms of the secular wisdom. The content of the message originates from God and is articulated by people. The gospel is preached—communicated orally and through action.

Where is the wise man? Where is the scholar? Where is the philosopher of this age? Has not God made foolish the wisdom of the world? For since in the wisdom of God the world through its wisdom did not know him, God was pleased through the foolishness of what was preached to save those who believe. Jews demand miraculous signs and Greeks look for wisdom, but we preach Christ crucified: a stumbling block to Jews and foolishness to Gentiles, but to those whom God has called, both Jews and Greeks, Christ is the power of God and the wisdom of God. For the foolishness of God is wiser than man's wisdom, and the weakness of God is stronger than man's strength. I Corinthians 1:20-25

Paul chose a straightforward presentation of the gospel message without extensive, intentional ornamentation of rhetorical ploys. The spiritual power of the words to impact the audience comes from God and not from the persuasive talent of the human speaker. In Isaiah 29:13-14 the Lord tells the prophet that when people hypocritically say one thing, but do not let it influence their hearts, their wisdom will be confused and lead them to emptiness. People are not seeking to listen to God for what he says, but seek wisdom or miracles instead of a personal relationship with a God who is speaking. But God is not primarily concerned with empowering humans and visibly demonstrating his presence; he is far more interested in transforming people through his words.

Brothers, think of what you were when you were called. Not many of you were wise by human standards; not many were influential; not many were of noble birth. But God chose the foolish things of the world to shame the wise; God chose the weak things of the world to shame the strong. He chose the lowly things of this world and the despised things--and the things that are not--to nullify the things that are, so that no one may boast before him. It is because of him that you are in Christ

Jesus, who has become for us wisdom from God--that is, our righteousness, holiness and redemption. Therefore, as it is written: "Let him who boasts boast in the Lord." I Corinthians 1:26-31

Human religious thinking, secular philosophical processing, political issue pondering, do not lead to truth. The seemingly weak argument of the gospel is the strongest case that can be made. This may be offensive to some in the secular culture—perhaps the time has arrived for us to allow them to be offended. Our virtue is not in how powerful we are, how well we can debate, or how much our income has become. The weak things like "mere rhetoric," love, and grace can change the strong; the lowly people and simple things can shame the grand—through the words of God's grace.

When I came to you, brothers, I did not come with eloquence or superior wisdom as I proclaimed to you the testimony about God. For I resolved to know nothing while I was with you except Jesus Christ and him crucified. I came to you in weakness and fear, and with much trembling. My message and my preaching were not with wise and persuasive words, but with a demonstration of the Spirit's power, so that your faith might not rest on men's wisdom, but on God's power. I Corinthians 2:1-5

Paul contrasts the message content of the gospel, with its poor technique, to the message and technique of other persuaders. His conclusion is that the spiritual truth of the divine message, spoken in a manner that is technically clear and unadorned, but with spiritual power, is better than other truth spoken in a manner that is rhetorically eloquent but deficient in spiritual authority. Faith rests on the power of God's message, not on persuasive technique. God provides what is necessary for the impact, neither the charisma of the speaker nor the persuasive power of words alone, but rather the grace of God through words.

We do, however, speak a message of wisdom among the mature, but not the wisdom of this age or of the rulers of this age, who are coming to nothing. No, we speak of God's secret wisdom, a wisdom that has been hidden and that God destined for our glory before time began. None of the rulers of this age understood it, for if they had, they would not have crucified the Lord of glory. I Corinthians 2:6-8

Unsaved people view the message as foolishness, but spiritually mature people will understand the nature of God's wisdom. Living with the mystery of truth without the certainty of logical deduction is not easy. If others understood, they would not have executed the incarnate, living God.

> *However, as it is written:*
> *"No eye has seen,*
> *no ear has heard,*
> *no mind has conceived*
> *what God has prepared for those who love him"* --
> *but God has revealed it to us by his Spirit.* I Corinthians 2:9-10

The hidden wisdom of God is unveiled through the illumination of the Holy Spirit—the inner communication of God to people. The invention of the message as taught by Cicero and Aristotle being the foundation of rhetorical persuasion is replaced by revelation from the mind of God. This leads us to the primacy of the Holy Spirit in the process of communication.

> The Spirit searches all things, even the deep things of God. For who among men knows the thoughts of a man except the man's spirit within him? In the same way no one knows the thoughts of God except the Spirit of God. We have not received the spirit of the world but the Spirit who is from God, that we may understand what God has freely given us. This is what we speak, not in words taught us by human wisdom but in words taught by the Spirit, expressing spiritual truths in spiritual words. I Corinthians 2:11-13

The political, philosophical wisdom of the world does not match the spiritual truth as revealed by the Holy Spirit. The words (*logos*) themselves are characteristically different than those spoken by others. They may be the same form but have a different meaning and impact when God speaks them. The message originates with God as the source of truth; therefore, our message should reflect his message.

> The man without the Spirit does not accept the things that come from the Spirit of God, for they are foolishness to him, and he cannot understand them, because they are spiritually discerned. The spiritual man makes judgments about all things, but he himself is not subject to any man's judgment: "For who has known the mind of the Lord that he may instruct him?" But we have the mind of Christ. I Corinthians 2:14-16

Quoting Isaiah 40:13, Paul casts as impossible knowing God's wisdom without the communication of the Holy Spirit. Greco-Roman philosophers and Jewish sign-seekers can speak and judge—but the mature, spiritual Christian can understand glimpses into the mind of God through revelatory communication.

The source of the message for Christian communicators is God; his content, his word, and his virtue. The process of relationship is the revealing voice of the Spirit through our words. The soundness of the words is in spiritual power not persuasive logic or rhetorical technique. The presentation of the message is cast in simplicity with non-flowery technique but with clarity for understanding. Because of these principles; Christian rhetoric is foundationally and presentationally different from secular presentation. This is uncomfortable to many Christians, especially as we have the responsibility of articulating the message to people who may be offended with the content, the implications, and the impacts of that persuasive rhetoric.

Logos: words and the Word

Jesus is the living *logos,* the Word (John 1:1). In Greek philosophy the term *logos* referred to the concept of reason and meaning that underlies the universe, and sometimes it was used to add the idea that this reason and meaning forms a bond between God (gods) and people. In first century Judaism *logos* was occasionally used as a metaphor to speak about God himself. Jesus was the tangible word who could be seen and touched (I John 1:1); he dwelt among us (John 1:14) and was empirically verified. Christian rhetoric should be intimately connected to God as he is the embodiment of the message. He is the active, powerful aura of God entering history with the mystery of "presence." Foundationally the *Logos* has the import of the logical ordering of the universe by the personal expressive God. John 17:17 states that the Father's *logos* is truth, providing the eternal standard for communication being in his character.

The Bible is the written *logos,* Word, and is dynamically accomplishing spiritual purposes (Hebrews 4:12). The concrete nature of written text belies the living power that penetrates the reader's inner being. Nothing in the body, soul or spirit is hidden from the piercing thrust of the verbally wielded Word. Only those who believe can fully understand the message of the written Word, but none can escape the impacts (I Corinthians 2:6-16). As we respond to the message, we experience the reality of meeting with the personal, living God through the medium of language. God in-breathed (*theopneustos*) the text in such a manner that it expresses his thoughts and words in a mode that changes people (II Timothy 3:16). Peter expresses it like this,

> Above all, you must understand that no prophecy of Scripture came about by the prophet's own interpretation. For prophecy never had its origin in the will of man, but men spoke from God as they were carried along by the Holy Spirit. II Peter 1:20-21

The authors of the written biblical text were *pheromenoi*, blown as a sailboat driven by the wind, by the Holy Spirit. The authors of Scripture were under the guidance, influence and control of God as they penned the passages that express his message with congruent integrity. Today, if you can hear his voice, do not harden your heart; listen as you read (Hebrews 3:15). The expressive nature of divine revelation articulating the message of redemption along with unveiling glimpses of the hidden glory and wisdom of God should be reflected in how seriously we take our own public communication.

As God's personal and propositional communication to people, the Bible is a primary text to understanding Christian rhetoric. The spoken Word of God has transforming power that impacts others (Matthew 8:8; 16). Resurrecting the spiritually decayed and dead happens through the hearing and believing the *logos* of God (John 5:24). We have the ability to "plant" the Word in our lives and allow it to "grow" spiritually (Matthew 13:18-23). The *logos* of Jesus should dwell in us (John 5:38) as we give it room (John 8:37) and keep it (John 8:51).

Persuasive Preaching

From the beginning, God chose people to proclaim his message to others. Enoch, seventh in line from Adam preached to the people of his day. Noah was a preacher before and during the building of the ark. The book of Deuteronomy is a series of sermons on the Mosaic law. In the Hebrew, words for the action of persuasive communication called "preaching" are: to tell the good news *basar*, to proclaim *qara*, or preaching *qeria*. The preacher is *qohelet*. Perhaps the most significant aspect of early Hebrew preaching is the statement "Thus saith the Lord." Taken as a whole, these words express the voice of God speaking through people to people in a manner that influences them. The prophet Isaiah said "the Lord has anointed me to preach good news to the poor."

In New Testament Greek, preaching is *keruso* (to proclaim) spoken by a *keryx* (herald) whose content is *euangelion* (good news). Preaching at its essence is proclamation based on the grace, love, revelation, and authority of God. Persuasive preaching focuses on the voice of the Holy Spirit, not the orator. At times preaching takes on the character of persuasion with *ethos*, *pathos*, and *logos*.

John the Baptist is the last of the Old Testament prophets and the first of the New Testament preachers. The rhetoric of God came to him (Luke 3:2), and John responded by preaching (Mathew 3:1). Jesus followed suit preaching (Matthew 4:23) the rhetoric of God (John 3:34). The disciples were sent to preach with spiritual authority for people to repent (Matthew 10:5ff).

The rhetoric of God is the process of preaching (Romans 10:8). Preaching is necessary because Faith comes by hearing and hearing by the rhetoric of God (Romans 10:17). This leads to a rhetorical cleansing of the church (Ephesians 5:26). Peter called his sermon at Pentecost rhetoric (Acts 2:14). The content of preaching is the rhetoric of truth (Acts 26:25).

Theogenerative Language as God-Begun

God created people to communicate—gave us the ability to form and use language. From the Garden of Eden where Adam and Eve walked and talked with God, named all the animals, and talked with each other, language is part of the creative order. Although humans have the ability to change language, change perception through language, and co-create culture with language, the linguistic essence is still a God-generated activity of communication: *theogenerative*.

As such, language functions without direct intervention by God so that people perceive total autonomy with freedom of speech. God is still the author of language itself and thus language is of divine origin. Language is learned and used in its fullness as people develop God-likeness.

Language is influenced by biology, society, culture, cognitive processes, and personality, but not determined by any of them. Therefore, language use is a spiritually based choice by self-determined people, and we are ethically responsible for those choices in how we use or abuse language. A distinctly Christian perspective of communication begins with God who created people with the ability to think in language, communicates with people through language, and enables linguistic communication between people.

Rhema: God's Rhetoric

Isaiah 55 says that the rhetoric (Hebrew *dabar,* Septuagint *rhema*) of God is powerful so that it uproots sin (briars) and fertilizes righteousness (trees). God's words will supply for human needs and desires in a manner that permanently fulfills the spirit. His *rhema* will also accomplish his will in people and the world. Jesus echoes this in John 15:3 when he says that the disciples are clean through (because of) the *logos* spoken to them. Foot-washing is a physical, outward symbol of the community while the spiritual reality is accomplished through spoken words cleansing the heart. Although the Greek word *rhetorikhae* is transliterated into the English word *rhetoric,* the use of the word *rhema* is actually closer to the current use of *rhetoric* as public communication. In biblical and classical literature, *rhema* can refer to the utterance or saying, the words or language, the thing or referent, the logic or thinking, dialectical discourse, explanation, questioning, the speech event whether written or spoken, or even the entire argumentative case; while *rhetorikhae* was often limited to public speaking or even persuasive public address. The more comprehensive root *rhema* is, therefore, representative of the way current rhetoricians use the term *rhetoric.*

People are to live by the *rhema,* the rhetoric of the living God (Matthew 4:4). In Acts 5:20 the angel tells the apostles to speak the rhetoric of life to people. The sword of the Spirit is that same rhetoric (Ephesians 6:17). While Peter was speaking *rhema* to the gentiles, the Holy Spirit fell upon them (Acts 10:44). In Acts 11:14 [Peter] "will tell you [rhetoric] by which you and all your household will be saved." The rhetoric of Jesus is both spirit and life (John 6:63; 68). The sword of the Spirit is the rhetoric of God (Ephesians 6:5).

In Luke 3:2 the Word of the Lord came to John the Baptist so that he preached powerfully in a manner that caused many to repent and look for the coming Messiah. The Old Testament formula "Word of the Lord came . . ." was used to express the message. The words and work of the New Testament prophet, John the Baptist, prepared the hearts and minds of many to hear Jesus' message. The orality of the message from God through the prophet and to the audience is an essential part of revelation.

God's rhetoric is eloquently delightful (Hebrews 6:5) yet overwhelmingly powerful (Hebrews 12:19). Some of God's rhetoric is so otherworldly it cannot be put into human language (II Corinthians 12:4). No matter how illogical the message or event seems, no *rhema* of God is impossible, even a virgin giving birth (Luke 1:37). His word endures forever (I Peter 1:25). Yet it both reveals and conceals the meaning of God (Luke 9:45;

18:34). The spoken words carry the authority of God (John 14:10). The written word of God is congruent with the rhetoric of Jesus (John 5:47). In him we discover the fulfillment of the written law (Matthew 5:18). His *rhema* extends to the end of the world (Romans 10:18).

In John 17, the high priestly prayer of Christ, Jesus states that the disciples *know* all things that were *given* for them to know (v. 7) and the *rhema* given to Christ was in turn given to them and they received (grasped, comprehended, taken hold of) the message that gave true knowledge (v. 8) concerning Jesus' divine nature; all this leads to their belief. Rhetoric given from God, when received, provides true knowledge, which in turn yields belief. Humans are not the measure of all things with perception being the key to knowledge, but God's revelation of reality determines the appraisal of things, experiences, and ideas so that knowledge comes through rhetoric.

Rhema: Human Rhetoric

Luke, in Acts 5:32, says we are rhetorical witnesses (we see and hear, we experience with understanding, we think logically, and then we speak). That is the way Peter conceptualized the Christian. Paul contends that he speaks a rhetoric of truth and reason (Acts 26:25). Even though that truth is reasonable, it is based on a revelation he received directly from Christ making him an Apostle. Human rhetoric is inexorably connected to the spiritual communication of God.

Control of the tongue is a sign of spiritual maturity. Jesus' half-brother James explained the intense struggle over speech.

> *Not many of you should presume to be teachers, my brothers, because you know that we who teach will be judged more strictly. We all stumble in many ways. If anyone is never at fault in what he says, he is a perfect man, able to keep his whole body in check.*

> *When we put bits into the mouths of horses to make them obey us, we can turn the whole animal. Or take ships as an example. Although they are so large and are driven by strong winds, they are steered by a very small rudder wherever the pilot wants to go. Likewise the tongue is a small part of the body, but it makes great boasts. Consider what a great forest is set on fire by a small spark. The tongue also is a fire, a world of evil among the parts of the body. It corrupts the whole person, sets the whole course of his life on fire, and is itself set on fire by hell.*

81

All kinds of animals, birds, reptiles and creatures of the sea are being tamed and have been tamed by man, but no man can tame the tongue. It is a restless evil, full of deadly poison.

With the tongue we praise our Lord and Father, and with it we curse men, who have been made in God's likeness. Out of the same mouth come praise and cursing. My brothers, this should not be. Can both fresh water and salt water flow from the same spring? My brothers, can a fig tree bear olives, or a grapevine bear figs? Neither can a salt spring produce fresh water. James 3:1-11

A lifetime of spiritual growth is needed to control speech. How often do we open our mouths and insert our feet? Writing words that flawlessly express thoughts is a very intricate process. So we have speech and writing classes to educate us in eloquent expression. Most of us will exhaust a great deal of energy searching for the precise words that will convey our messages.

Commissioned to Communicate

God gives us the Great Commission, not the great alternative, not the great opportunity, not the great experience, not the great option, not even the great choice. The command is clear, straightforward, and undeniable:

All authority in heaven and on earth has been given to me. Therefore go and make disciples of all nations, baptizing them in the name of the Father and of the Son and of the Holy Spirit, and teaching them to obey everything I have command you. And surely I am with you always to the very end of the age. Matthew 28:18-20

That is a command by the living God to communicate in a persuasive manner the message of the gospel using both verbal and nonverbal means. Learning persuasive rhetoric is not an option; it is the divine responsibility of all believers to become a channel of his message. We have the ministry of reconciliation in bodies of clay expressed to the world. The Great Commission is a call to communicate: nonverbally through baptism and rhetorically through teaching. This commissioning of disciples for disciple-making happens through communication.

Communicating the redemptive love of God to the ruined hearts of others is one of the great responsibilities and privileges that people have. That claim is built on the reality that as we communicate, we know we can lean on him. All authority is given to him: unrestricted universal sovereignty over heaven and earth. He chooses not to exercise absolute power over evil—yet. That time will come; now is the day of proclamation through persuasive rhetoric. That may seem foolish to people; if he has such power, why not wield it? In mercy and grace God is choosing to woo and sway rather than coerce people into an active relationship with him.

The Holy Spirit: Vocalizing the Message

One of the ways the Holy Spirit works in and through people is in the area of persuasive rhetoric. When God called Moses at the burning bush, Moses was concerned that the people would not believe his persuasive appeal, so God demonstrated his power with the rod. Then Moses complained that he was not eloquent. God's response was,

> Who gave man his mouth? Who makes him deaf or mute? Who gives him sight or makes him blind? Is it not I, the LORD? Now go; I will help you speak and will teach you what to say. Exodus 4:11-12

Moses struggled with eloquence, but when he stood before Pharaoh, he spoke with dynamic clarity and prevailing authority. Although Aaron was his spokesperson, the words of Moses are those that resounded through the marble halls, into the streets, and down through the ages to stir hearts even today. Not only were the words of the message given but the strength and eloquence to articulate them clearly before the most powerful adversary.

When God called him, the prophet Jeremiah complained that he was not old enough to do the job. People would not listen because he did not have the wisdom and respect that comes with age. God touched Jeremiah's lips and said: *Now, I have put my words in your mouth. See, today I appoint you over nations and kingdoms to uproot and tear down, to destroy and overthrow, to build and to plant* Jeremiah 1:9-10. The convicting others of sin, the statements of judgment and condemnation, the encouragement of righteousness, the spiritual growth of others all happen as the Holy Spirit inspires persuasive messages through people. Taking a young boy and giving him exceptional power through spiritual rhetoric is one of the ways God chooses to work in this world. He uses our own, and other's, mouths in order to change our hearts and minds through rhetoric.

God is the Great Communicator. Even Jesus while on earth claimed, "The words I say to you are not just my own. Rather, it is the Father, living in me, who is doing his work" (John 14:10). The words spoken are divinely generated, and they are the work of the living God. Rhetoric is more than the sum of the individual morphemes, more than the phonetic summary of oral linguistic exercise: God's rhema is God's ergon, action. This goes beyond practicing what we preach—it is more than keeping promises—the speaking event is an active work. The primary choice of God is to communicate with people; from the words that spoke the heavens into being, to the moment you read these lines, God is speaking. Filter through these words, sift your thoughts, listen to the voice of the Spirit, and you can hear God speak to your heart. The still small voice of the Lord can be more clearly heard in the text of Scripture.

God will also give you words to say when you are in a difficult situation. When you are in a habit of listening to God, you will be able to hear him when you need it most.

> But make up your mind not to worry beforehand how you will defend yourselves. For I will give you words and wisdom that none of your adversaries will be able to resist or contradict. Luke 21:14-15

God gives not only the authority and responsibility to communicate his message, but also the enabling power to express his words to others whether in speaking or writing. I do not have to rely on my own impromptu ability, on my own logical ability, on my own eloquence because God is willing and able to give me the words necessary to represent him.

The Intellect, Reason

Seek a relationship with God and in doing so seek knowledge, wisdom, and truth. Sometimes finding the right questions is more difficult than discovering the right answers.

> *My son, if you accept my words*
> *and store up my commands within you,*
> *turning your ear to wisdom*
> *and applying your heart to understanding,*
> *and if you call out for insight*
> *and cry aloud for understanding,*
> *and if you look for it as for silver*
> *and search for it as for hidden treasure,*
> *then you will understand the fear of the Lord*
> *and find the knowledge of God. Proverbs 2:1-5*

Without the search, nothing will be found. Seek, look, hunt, rummage through your heart and mind, then through the words of those who have gone before to discover the truth that God has waiting to be found. Research of this kind does not lead to an academic paper, a Pulitzer Prize, or a standing ovation at the end of a speech. Instead, it leads to a meaningful life from which great public communication flows.

Knowledge, reason, wisdom, and truth do not yield their fruit through simply reading a textbook or listening to a lecture. You have to assert yourself through diligence, discipline, and desire, sharpening your intellect to grasp hold of their riches. *It is the glory of God to conceal a matter, to search out a matter is the glory of kings* (Proverbs 25:2).

Knowledge

My people are destroyed for lack of knowledge
Because you have rejected knowledge
I also will reject you from being priest for Me

Hosea 4:6 NKJV

Gold there is, and rubies in abundance,
but lips that speak knowledge are a rare jewel.

Proverbs 20:15

With the primary content of the truth of a message originating with God and revealed to people, what can the human communicator know? Aristotle's *Metaphysics* begins with these words, "Man by nature desires to know." Solid content based on personal knowledge forms the words of persuasive public communication. Epistemology: what can we know and how do we know that we know it? God's understanding is infinite; we call this omniscience (Psalm 147:5). God knows the past (*God remembered Rachel,* Genesis 30:22), he knows the present (*he sees all my ways and counts all my steps,* Job 30:4), and he knows the future (*in that day there shall be,* Zechariah 13:1; *Christ was slain before the foundation of the world,* Revelation 13:8). God even knows hypothetical events or options about the future (*they will deliver you up,* I Samuel 23:12). God also knows himself (*the Spirit searches the deep things of God,* I Corinthians 2:11). God knows all truth. Human perception may be flawed; we may not be able to comprehend the nature of things, people, or events, but God can and does know all things—he is omniscient.

As created beings we cannot comprehend the infinite presence, knowledge, being, love, or power of God. He is wholly other. God is infinite while we are finite. We cannot fully understand God; he is too wonderful to know (Job 42:3). He is invisible to our senses (Colossians 1:15). We are corporeal, but he is spirit (John 4:24). But, as beings created in his image, we may not be able to know in the absolute sense, but we can know some things about God, ourselves, others, and nature.

Some things are revealed knowledge, content that God specifically communicates to people; the Bible is a written record of God's public writing through people. The book of Job is the story of a search for specific knowledge about why bad things happened to Job. The knowledge came through revelation, not method open to human discovery and explanation.

Some knowledge comes by sense observation, whether of nature by a scientist, or of people by a psychologist, or of any other event or thing. Other knowledge comes through experience such as new operating procedures developed by medical doctors. Knowledge can also come through logic such as the axioms of geometry. Another way to gain knowledge is through communication such as the process of education, or reading a book like this one. Other kinds of knowledge comes through relationships, such as love or trust. Intuition also brings specific knowledge because we know that if I have never ridden a motorcycle before, jumping one across a stream is not wise; I do not need to study the proposition from a scientific observational perspective. Faith gives another kind of knowledge as does hope. People gain knowledge in many different ways; however, all of these kinds of knowledge are incomplete and partial (I Corinthians 13:9). *We can know parts of absolutes, but we cannot know anything absolutely because we are finite.*

Ever since Decart's *Discourse on Method*, some people have insisted that the only way to know truth is through scientific observation. Since our senses often are wrong or only partly right, we can never know anything absolutely; therefore, skeptically concluding that all knowledge about truth is beyond human reach. Defining knowledge by one method (scientific sense observation) is not legitimate, nor is concluding that certainty can only be reached through science. The faith, hope, and love I have with my wife gives knowledge far beyond anything sense observation can provide. That knowledge is objective and subjective at the same time. It is thorough and incomplete; it is magical and mundane; it is comforting and exciting, a personal knowledge too wonderful to place into words encompassing dialectical opposites with power and grace.

The question still rings from perhaps the oldest literature in existence: "What can we know?" (Job 11:8). Consider a few of the things we know for certain:

I know that my Redeemer lives, and that in the end he will stand upon the earth. Job 19:25

Know for certain that your descendants will be strangers in a country not their own . . . Genesis 15:13

Then you will know that I am the Lord your God . . . Exodus 6:7

Now I know that the Lord is greater than all other gods . . . Exodus 18:11

The Lord said, ". . . I know you by name . . ." Exodus 33:17

Be still and know that I am God. Psalm 46:10

. . . I am fearfully and wonderfully made; your works are wonderful, I know that full well. Psalm 139:1

So that you may know that the Son of Man has authority on earth to forgive sins . . . Matthew 9:6

The Father . . . will give you another counselor to be with you forever— the Spirit of Truth. The world cannot accept him, because it neither sees him nor knows him. But you know him, for he lives with you and will be in you . . . John 14:15

Now this is eternal life: that they may know you, the only true God, and Jesus Christ whom you have sent. John 17:3

And we know that in all things God works for the good of those who love him, who have been called according to his purpose. Romans 8:28

Now we know that if the earthly tent we live in is destroyed, we have a building from God, an eternal house in heaven . . . II Corinthians 5:1

You know that the testing of your faith develops perseverance . . . James 1:3

We know that anyone born of God does not continue to sin; the one who was born of God keeps him safe and the evil one cannot harm him. We know that we are children of God, and that the whole world is under the control of the evil one. We know that the Son of God has come and has given us understanding, so that we may know him who is true. And we are in him who is true—even in his Son Jesus Christ. He is the true God and eternal life. I John 5:18-20

These are all things that we can have confidence in knowing. No doubt is necessary; no skepticism is warranted; no wondering what if—we can *know* with assurance of veracity. Based on the nature of God's character and his revealed information, we have certain knowledge, even though it is incomplete. These propositions and promises can be made received in confidence as true and are therefore absolute.

Knowledge is so vital that the Apostle Paul sought one thing, to know Christ and the power of his resurrection and the fellowship of sharing in his sufferings (Philippians 3:10). How many of us would seek such knowledge as the sharing in Christ's suffering and death? We seek to know what is fun, what gains money, what feels good—not the experiential knowledge that shares in suffering. We seek unlimited possibilities of self-fulfillment, our rights, our choices, our successes, and our power. Our culture is surely post-Christian as it pertains to values, knowledge, and actions.

Apply this knowledge to public communication. If we know any truth, then we must understand it as a truth that God already knows. *A sentence's true meaning is what that sentence means to God* (Clark, 1984). We can know very closely, but not absolutely, the meaning of any individual sentence. God reveals meaning to us. We can understand; we can know the truth. Human logic, rationality, and intellectual capacities can grasp hold of the truth and know for certain that truth. *I will make my words known to you* Proverbs 1:23.

At the center of rhetorical communication is certain knowledge of the truth to be spoken from a heart of love. Certainty comes from God, an absolute being, who reveals absolutes to finite beings, people. As his Spirit bears witness to our spirits we can know.

Truth

Your word is truth

John 17:17

"You will know the truth and the truth will set you free" (John 8:32), but first, before we know the truth, we must be disciples. Freedom comes in assurance of our experiential knowledge of truth. World War II was fought under the banner of the Four Freedoms: freedom from want, freedom from fear, freedom of speech, and freedom of religion. The French Revolution was fought with the war cry "Liberty, equality, fraternity;" freedom from governmental restraint giving the ability to act in whatever way an individual chooses. These human ideas and values worth dying for are a mere fraction of the freedom brought through truth. Truth gives inner freedom from the tyranny of desires led by sin. Becoming independent moral agents through knowledge of the truth enables us to make wise choices as self-determining beings. Purchasing a slave, providing the worth to the master sets the slave free. Satisfying the law sets us free from the consequences of the law. Freedom of the spirit comes through knowledge of the truth. Our public communication should set people free. Not just from ignorance but freedom to, freedom for, a positive life.

Pilate asked Jesus, "What is truth?" So now I ask you to struggle with the idea. Public communication is to *speak the truth in love* (Ephesians 4:15), then we need to come to grips with the idea of truth. Begin with a prayer from Psalm 43:3 *Send forth your light and your truth, let them guide me; let them bring me to your holy mountain, to the place where you dwell.*

God is the God of truth (Psalm 31:5). Isaiah and Jeremiah picture a society which struggles with truth and rejects it:

> *So justice is driven back*
> *And righteousness stands at a distance*
> *Truth has stumbled in the streets*
> *Honesty cannot enter*
> *Truth is nowhere to be found*
> *And whoever shuns evil becomes a prey.*
> Isaiah 59:14

> *Truth has perished;*
> *It has vanished from their lips.* Jeremiah 7:28

When a people lack truth, they will become more evil, and those who are good will be persecuted. Zechariah called the people to do four things—speak the truth to each other was the first and most important (8:16-17).

In the dialogue *Georgias*, Plato rejects rhetoric as a knack that moves others to believe falsehood and warps ethics. A more mature Plato recognizes the good of rhetoric when truth is spoken from a disposition of love in the *Phaedrus*. The difference for Plato between acceptance and rejection of rhetoric is the message content of truth.

Saint Augustine said that four different features could be seen in the word truth: The first is an affirmation of what is; i.e. two minus one is one, the capital of Oregon is Salem. The second is that every reality is an affirmation of itself; i.e. beauty, freedom, and wisdom are true. This is ontological truth; that of being. The third is that the Lord Jesus Christ is true because he perfectly expresses the nature of the Father. Jesus is a substance of truth while people are an image of that same truth. And finally in the realm of sense objects, flowers, trees, and animals are true in that they reflect the primary realities (c.f. Plato). This fourfold view of truth has influenced many theologians and philosophers through centuries of following his analysis and still holds validity today.

Both the Greek (*alaethia*) and Hebrew (*emeth*) words for truth also translate into the English word faithfulness. They infer that reality is true as opposed to appearance, that lies are the opposite of speaking truth, that people can have true and false characteristics (fidelity vs. faithlessness) and the certainty or assurance of accuracy. Biblically, to speak the truth is to express fundamental and spiritual realities that are known in the heart. Both written and spoken truths are presented in the Bible. Biblical writers value people who can put into words the reality of the heart as it experiences the world. *Truth* and *faithfulness* are translated from the same Hebrew and Greek words. They express the characteristic of being true. A careful study of the book of *Proverbs* for passages about truth, knowledge, wisdom, and speaking will yield significant results in consideration of speaking the truth.

Knowing the truth leads to practicing the truth with the result of becoming like God in righteousness and holiness (Ephesians 4:19-24). This seems to contrast the Socratic notion that if you know the good you will do the good which will result in justice and happiness (Plato's *Meno* and *Euthyphro*). For Socrates, knowledge of the good comes from divine teaching; for the Apostle Paul knowledge of the truth comes through atonement, revelation, and a relationship with God. For both the impact of knowledge is a virtuous life. While Platonic philosophy sought after the good, Paul abandons the search for goodness for none can become good in that manner (Romans 3:12) because of sin (Romans 7:19-20) and turns to seek after the truth. This is a significant change in the foundational approach to life: to seek truth as opposed to goodness (Plato) or happiness (Aristotle). For Paul the practice of doing good is an acceptance of the truth while a rejection of truth leads to doing evil (Romans 2:6-8). Paul is addressing both

Jewish law and Greek philosophy in his argument for good, law, and truth along with how they work out in what we say and do.

Is Jesus right, can we know truth? Skepticism, deconstructivism, and other postmodern philosophies sincerely doubt the possibility. They correctly recognize that since finite creatures such as we humans cannot know infinite absolute truth in its entirety, a measure of doubt exists. However, just because we cannot know truth completely does not mean we cannot recognize or know anything about truth. Yes, we can be deceived. Yes, others may obtain a different sense observation from the same stimuli. That individuals can "customize" truth to fit their current whims is a popular understanding of deconstructive thought. Concluding that truth is, therefore, unknowable is not a necessary, logical deduction and therefore patently false. We can and do know absolute truth and can be truthful. Our words can reflect that truth in the messages we send. Skepticism is simply false.

Soren Kierkegaard sought truth and found "something which reaches to the deepest roots of my existence and wherein I am connected into the divine and held fast to it, even though the whole world falls apart" (Groothuis, 2000). Postmodern philosophy believes truth is constructed in the mind of individuals, is co-created through social experience, and is personal in that each person has different experiences and perspectives of reality. Humanism, in the tradition of Protagorus where *man is the measure of all things,* may lead to illogical skepticism. For them the meaning is constantly changing, co-created and reconstructed by human minds. Truth can thus be chosen and determined individually with "your truth" and "my truth" incompatible with each other, but both "true." Socially relative perspectives give no objective basis or eternal meaning for truth; truth becomes what individuals *make* it to be as opposed to what it already *is* ontologically.

Absolute, objective, and universal truth that is self-evident—that kind of truth is words conforming to fact, to being and history, not just to categories, naming, or individual arbitrary volition. Communicating what is, not perspective, but, corresponds to reality is an important function of rhetoric. Douglas Groothuis (2000) lists these characteristics of a Christian view of truth:

1. Truth is revealed by God (not invented by humans individually or socially).

2. Objective truth exists and is knowable (reality is not dependent on perspective).

3. Truth is absolute in nature (invariable across time, space, cultures, and individuals).

4. Truth is universal (engages everything and excludes nothing).

5. The truth of God is eternally engaging and momentous, not trendy or superficial (meaningful not ideological).

6. Truth is exclusive, specific and antithetical (what is true excludes what opposes it as false).

7. Truth is systematic and unified (truth is one harmony of what is; an end in itself).

I would add to this an explanation that absolute truth is objective (outside of humans and discoverable c.f. #2) while some truth is subjective (inside of humans and co-creatable). For example, the ethical absolute that wife-beating is bad is not something we *co-create* or is simply a human based value. Rather, it is an objective reality, an ethical absolute; truth. At the same time the rules to basketball have a different kind of truth; they can be changed by a decision of people and are therefore subjective. Double-dribbling a basketball is, therefore, not a sin (even through it violates the truth of the rules of basketball), while beating your spouse is a sin (because it violates an objective ethical standard based on the nature of God).

This approach to truth enables us to speak and write in a manner that corresponds to facts and events—reality. Image-making, propaganda, ideology, and political posturing can be communication campaigns, but only as they represent reality can they be called accurate or true. The average reader or listener will respect a rhetor who communicates in this manner—one who seeks and speaks the truth.

An individual who is running for public office makes a claim of military service. The truth-value of the claim is whether it is falsifiable (test null) or demonstrable (evidence to support). We can know the truth through researching multiple forms of evidence to discover the veracity of the claim. Then we can evaluate the difference it makes in the person's life. The military service records of Bob Dole, John McCain, John Kerry, and both George Bushes are very different in creating qualifications for public office. The truth must still be sought, weighed, and balanced in order to make an informed decision based on the evidence as to whether or not to vote for them.

Wisdom

All the way back in the Garden, Eve was tempted by the serpent to eat the fruit in order to gain wisdom (Genesis 3:6). Having knowledge and truth is not enough without being able to put that understanding to work in practical ways of righteousness. Being able to make sense of the truth and communicate it in a manner that impacts people in a positive direction is wisdom.

In his humility Solomon prayed to God for wisdom, *God gave Solomon wisdom and very great insight, and a breadth of understanding as measureless as the sand on the seashore. Solomon's wisdom was greater than the wisdom of all the men of the East . . .* (I Kings 4:29). The Queen of Sheba understood the impact of that wisdom, *How happy your men must be! How happy your officials, who continually stand before you and hear your wisdom! Praise be to the Lord your God, who has delighted in you"* (I Kings 10:8-9). Putting a knowledge of truth to work within the words spoken is not an easy task.

The Hebrew concept of wisdom is derived from several word clusters with *hokema* being the primary choice. The wisdom literature (Job, Proverbs, and Ecclesiastes) set the theological background for the New Testament use of the Greek term *sophia*. Divine wisdom is given by God and empowers people to live a good, pleasant, satisfying, and useful life. Human wisdom is often contrasted to the spiritual ideal from God and leads to destructive ends. Philosophy is the study and search for wisdom. The ancient Sophists were considered to be wise people. The Jewish wisdom literature can be seen in the Apocrypha and Philo, a contemporary Jewish philosopher of Jesus and Paul.

Beginning with the fear of the Lord, placing God first in worshipful awe, wisdom is both illusive and attainable—it must be diligently sought, but it can be found. For those attuned to her voice, wisdom may even be found crying out in the streets.

Jesus is envisioned as the *wisdom of God* and the ultimate source of all true wisdom (I Corinthians 1:24-30). His work of atoning salvation, his words of parabolic meaning, his actions of loving compassion, his ideal character, his propositional teaching are all part and parcel of the wisdom of God as revealed in the words and work of our Lord.

Wisdom is tied to speaking from a character of righteousness (Psalm 37:30). A wise person will listen to other wise people and will increase in learning and understanding (Proverbs 1:1-6). The communicator as a person, the understanding of truth, and the words that express the message are a congruent package called wisdom.

93

Faith

These are written that you may believe
that Jesus is the Christ, the Son of God,
and that believing you may have life in his name.

John 20:31

The end of Christian public communication is not skepticism, nor simple information, Christian rhetoric is influential in the aspect of faith and life. This does not mean that all speeches, poems, or stories are about doctrine or have spiritual themes but that *they are written from a worldview that enables, enhances, and ennobles character and truth consistent with God's nature.* Christian rhetoric is qualitatively different from non-Christian communication whether it is in the form of a movie, newspaper article, sermon, or political speech.

J. R. R. Tolkein's *Lord of the Rings* is perhaps the greatest literature of the last century. One of the purposes of the books is that readers will be able to think in a way so that when they hear the gospel message, they can respond. Fictional works constructed in such a manner that good and evil, power and relationships, people and character are all presented from the Christian perspective enable faith to blossom at a later time. George Lucas created the world of *Star Wars* so that people could think in a manner consistent with Hindu beliefs. His literature conveys a worldview that will enable audiences to accept Hinduism when they hear the teachings. Most great literature and movies enables readers or watchers to vicariously experience life in a manner consistent with the intended perspective of the author. The influence goes much deeper than the theme or overt cognitive message into the warp and woof, the very fibres, of who we are.

Romans 10 has some interesting things to say about rhetoric. We who believe speak the *rhema*—the words, the rhetoric—of faith (v. 8). Confess with your mouth, speak, and believe in the heart—believe and publicly communicate—the message of who Jesus is and that he died and rose again (v. 9). Then v. 10 reaffirms the necessity to confess with the mouth that belief of the heart. Paul continues in v. 13-18 to explain that communication of the message is necessary for salvation to happen.

Competent Congruency

Words, emotions, states of being, character, and action all need to be congruent in public communication. The body, soul, and spirit are not entirely separate elements of the human being; they are united and separable only through death. Hypocrisy crops up when someone speaks in a manner that is not congruent with what they do and believe. Public communication should be a reflection of who you are as a person and what you practice. Never lie to the public—even if you are a lawyer or an advertiser. Functional linguistics points out the essential nature of a discourse as being competent and congruent. Jesus' harshest criticism were not against the most heinous of sinners, but against those who were not congruent in their beliefs and actions—the hypocrites. Psalm 15:2 summarizes the person who lives with God as one who does what is righteous and speaks the truth from his heart. This kind of individual is one who is harmonious in relationship with God, generates genuine good works from a righteous character, and articulates authentic words that are communicated to others—these words are congruent in worldview, relationship, practice, and speech while competent enough to get the message across. Turning articulated beliefs into practical actions provides a foundation of competent congruency for rhetoric to influence audiences.

Community of Peace

In II Corinthians 5:20-21 we are commissioned as the ambassadors of Christ in this era to the people of the world. Individuals and communities are called by God to communicate his message and persuade others concerning the truth of the content. We are to represent the King and Kingdom of Heaven through communication to the people of the world. The advent, the presence, of the baby Jesus was to bring peace on earth and goodwill.

Quentin Schultze (2002, p.186) explains, "Most of the rhetoric about cyber-community wrongly assumes that we can deeply commune with one another using only the instrumental techniques of communication." Communion is the root of good communication. The ultimate result of communing is intimate empathy in a community of peace based on truth. Heartfelt dialogue enables an encounter between individuals creating the mystery of intimate friendship and being in that spiritual entity called *shalom*.

To regain a moral footing in contemporary life, we must dig deeper than information and knowledge, to the traditions that carry virtue from generation to generation. We will have to invest as much time and energy in the habits of our hearts as we do in our high-tech practices. Otherwise we will lose track of the crucial links to the past that can illuminate the path to goodness. Schultz, 2002, p.209

The primary aspect of biblical peace is completeness of spirit in a harmony that connects individuals with God. This quiet security of well-being permeates the soul in a manner that calms the heart no matter what the situation. Yes, it passes understanding (John 14:27) because the inscrutability of being in relationship with the living God changes people, and that is persuasive rhetoric at its best. Persuasive public rhetoric from a Christian worldview will build people into a community of peace.

Conclusion

Perhaps the Apostle Peter summarized it best when he said "If anyone speaks, he should do it as one speaking the very words of God" (I Peter 4:11). A Christian theology of public communication ends with the responsibility to speak *as if* we were speaking God's words, communicating his nature, encapsulating his ideas into our written and spoken messages. Every story, every speech, every sermon, every conversation, every novel, every article we produce should be as though they are the *very words of God.*

Part II

Tracing the History of Christian Rhetoric

GAINING A glimpse of the development of ideas through the people who gave them will enable you to appreciate your own thoughts in light of others. As a primary part of a liberal arts education, historical understanding provides a background of the context in which we function as postmodern rhetors. I hope you have read or taken a complete history of Western Civilization and have a grasp of world history so that the rhetors can be understood in their larger context. When reading Plato and Aristotle, knowing something about Athens will be exceptionally helpful so that you can know why persuasion was so vital to them. When reading Cicero, knowing about the expansion of the Roman Republic will give insight into his debating emphasis. When reading Quintilian, knowing about the despotic empire will give insight into why he placed emphasis on inspiration over persuasion. When reading Augustine, knowing he comes at the end of the empire and beginning of the Dark Ages enables a understanding of his emphasis on teaching.

Wading into the ocean of history with waves of ideas, each with a different perspective, coming to know the ebb and flow of the tides, watching in wonder at the storms, glorying in the exquisite sunsets and basking in the clear afternoons. We will get our feet wet with the men and women of ancient Greece as they conceptualized Classical rhetoric. The tide goes out, and we will come back at the resurgence of the Romans as they rediscover the principles of philosophic rhetoric. Then the darkness falls across the sea and little is seen walking in starlight along the sand. The enlightened dawn of the renaissance brings a storm of furry to thought and debate where dialogue and dialectic drive the debate. Quickly wading into the present we will see the many shades and waves of thought have grown more diverse with each adding to the joy of exploration.

Although this is a brief survey covering only a few of the most prominent thinkers, it should provide you with a depth of knowledge impossible without history. Hopefully these brief pages will give you an appreciation for the many men and women who have undertaken the spiritual-academic struggle of a rigorous examination of rhetorical communication.

Chapter 4

Classical Rhetoric

Wisdom calls aloud outside
She raises her voice in the open square
Proverbs 1:20 NKJV

The path of the just is like the shining sun
Proverbs 4:18 NKJV

TRACING THE rhetorical tradition through its checkered history is a major undertaking in itself. Here we will give an overview of a few influential thinkers to give depth, breadth, and progression to persuasive thinking. A comprehensive understanding of the history would take several volumes bridging East and West, North and South, male and female, culture and ethnicity while balancing the written and oral elements of rhetorical practice and thought. Here we simply want to take a glimpse at some of the giants on whose shoulders we stand. Through this account we will attempt to contrast philosophical rhetoric with technical and sophistic traditions in a manner that enables understanding of the strengths of each, but with the bulk of the communication focused on Christian philosophical concepts.

Technical Rhetoric

The conceptualization of rhetoric came out of practical need. Corax and Tisias systematized rhetorical principles after the people of Syracuse overthrew a tyrant ruler and formed a democracy in 467 BC. For many years its ruling class had usurped ownership of the land. Now the people had to argue in court to regain title to the land their fathers and grandfathers had owned. Observing that those with the best speaking skills and those who articulated argument well usually won the cases, Corax and Tisias developed the *technai* (art) *rhema* (word) or the technical art of using words to influence others—rhetoric. The two men deduced principles for effective delivery, argumentation, and style of language use based on their observations of effective and ineffective speaking. They taught these rules and then published them in a manual of effective discourse. The success of their system brought about a very high demand for their services and copies of their book.

The news of their ability soon reached Athens and various people undertook teaching rhetoric in a manner similar to that which Corax and Tisias were using in Syracuse. Several of these Greeks also wrote handbooks of basic public speaking rules, which were very popular. The standards for speeches in the political realm and the entertainment efforts of speakers in Athens rose quickly. The general population soon became sophisticated in evaluating or judging the ability of a speaker as well as the content of the speech. Later Aristotle gathered these handbooks together into the *Synagogue Technon* or *Collection of the Arts* as a systematization of the rules of technical rhetoric. This book has not survived, but it is widely quoted and referred to in the works of later attic writers.

In the *Phaedrus*, Plato has Socrates quickly summarize the talking points of those who taught rhetoric as an art (266-267). He notes that the order of a general speech should follow a specific outline: 1) the *proemium* or introduction, 2) the *diegesis* or narrative, 3) the *pistis* and *epipistis* or the witnesses, evidence, proof and supplemental proof, and probabilities 4) the *refutation* of other arguments and finally 5) the *epilogos* or conclusion. Besides the arrangement of a speech, technical teachers taught style of language such as proper words, figurative words and poetic words. This early rhetorical theory sought to understand the people involved as the speaker and audience, but most of the focus was on the speech itself. The artistic rhetors sought to add *pathos*, emotion, into the speech.

The hallmark of technical rhetoric was the development and delivery of excellent speeches by following the rules of oratory. The emphasis on doing, practice, and impact gave a "rules" approach similar to the elocution movement of the 1800s. The teachers and students honed their skills of oratory and consequently impacted all of society.

As technical rhetoric opened the door for probability instead of an unwavering search for truth, people began to think in terms of what could be, or might be, and the likelihood of events within the rational discourse of society. The shift from the discovery of Truth to the presentation of possibilities and probabilities offered major opportunities for debate in the coming conflict over ideas. The art of technical rhetoric gave birth to sophistic and philosophic rhetoric. Although these movements took people into new paradigms and debates, the field of rhetoric has never strayed far from its artistic roots.

Sophistic Rhetoric

Greek citizens, especially in Athens, were expected to have eclectic abilities and interests. All men were expected to take part in the legal system where 200 or more jurists were selected from a pool of 6,000 for each trial. Every male was also expected to take part in the military whether as a soldier, officer, or in supply. Athenian men were expected to be engineers with knowledge of architecture and materials. Besides their own craft or business, the people took part in the economy of the city. Above all was the political system where every man was expected to be a significant part of the democracy.

Itinerant teachers arose in the 5th century BC to train people in the practical arts of being a good citizen. The curriculum often included grammar, rhetoric, art, drama, mathematics, architecture, politics, poetry and literature as well as other specialties. This individualized liberal education was available to anyone who would pay for it. Individuals and small groups of students were transformed through the educational process making Athens a progressive cultural leader.

The Sophists were not a cohesive or even centralized group or college. They were individuals who had a vision for a better citizenry through education. They practiced largely by tutoring individuals who could pay for their services. They focused on skills, practical knowledge, and creative thinking leading to a better income. These men were largely from other places and traveled to Greece and became a significant part of their society.

Many of the Sophists and their disciples were so focused on method, winning influence, and practicing their eloquence that they disdained truth, virtue, and relationships. This tendency to place personal power, money, and acclaim over service and virtue led critics like Socrates and Plato to strongly denounce not just what they were doing with rhetoric, but rhetoric itself. The weakness of neglecting truth in favor of provisionalism and power ensured a ready supply of fuel for their flaming opposition.

The Sophists have sometimes liked to shock or indulge conceits, it should be remembered that most Sophists have believed that the orator should be a good man, and their most consistent theme has not been how to make the worse seem the better cause, but celebration of enlightened government, the love of the gods, the beauty of classical cities, the value of friendship, the meaning of patriotism, the triumph of reason and the artistry of speech. Kennedy, 1980 p. 40

Four of the significant impacts of the sophistic movement on rhetorical theory and practice are: 1) the extension of the idea of probability in rhetorical discourse; 2) education was given to all, not just the nobility; 3) education should have practical uses such as governing and decision which transformed education into one of the bedrocks of society; and 4) personal genius and inspiration, especially in invention and style, were encouraged. Sophistic education did much to bring democracy as a workable idea to the masses. When a majority of the citizens have the ability to speak well coupled with decision-making skills based on practical knowledge, democracy has a foundation upon which it can flourish.

Philosophic Rhetoric

The third strand of thinking about rhetoric is that of the philosophers. In contrast to the technical search for the proper technique and the sophistic search for practical wisdom; philosophers sought to know and understand truth. Pragmatics were important, but truth outweighed what works in a given situation. In the area of virtue this meant that power (the motivating force of pragmatics) was de-emphasized and love, justice, courage, moderation, and wisdom were sought. The reaction of philosophers to the perception that the sophists did not care about truth was a harsh criticism of rhetoric. Just as the sophists were not a cohesive group, neither were the philosophers, but for convenience considering them both as a group and as individuals may help. We will look at Aspasia, Plato, Isocrates, Aristotle, Cicero, and Quintilian as representatives of the philosophers who thought about rhetoric, while understanding that many others added significantly to both philosophy and the theory of rhetorical persuasion. This is the rhetorical perspective of Paul and John in the New Testament.

Aspasia

470-410 B.C.

Aspasia was educated in philosophy and politics in the sophistic tradition and taught Pericles and Socrates both philosophy and rhetoric. What we know of her teaching is second and third hand for she left no writings or speeches that have survived (except those she probably ghost wrote for Pericles). Plato has Socrates recounting his conversations with her and Plutarch includes her in his *Twelve Lives*.

Aspasia was from Miletus and began a salon to teach women in a similar manner to that used in Plato's school which many wealthy Athenian women attended. Yet at the same time she had a group of attractive women who served as concubines living in her house. She was the teacher of many eloquent Athenians. Pericles recognizes her influence, especially in his speech the Funeral Oration. Socrates credits Aspasia as one of his own instructors in rhetoric. Plato recognizes her influence in his thinking and abilities. Cicero quotes a lost dialogue by Aeschines in *De Inventione* (I: 31. 51-52) in which she counseled Xenophon and his wife that their search for a perfect, ideal partner was in vain, instead they should both try to become the best spouse so that their partner's desire could be fulfilled. Quintilian in *Institutio Oratoria* (V 11:27-29) praises her argumentative logic, but suggests that a better answer would not be to desire the best, but be content with one who is good.

Not only was she excellent in the skills of technical rhetoric, Aspasia was probably the bridge from sophistic rhetoric into philosophic rhetorical channels where logic and content are joined with character and audience. Her thinking along side of Plato's reaction to Socrates' trial probably influenced the philosophical tradition to limit the seeking of power as in the Sophists and concentrate on other virtues. These contributions changed the direction and nature of rhetorical thinking for many Athenians, including Plato and Aristotle.

Plato

428-347 B.C.

One of history's greatest writers and thinkers grew from a distrust and disgust of rhetorical persuasion to an acceptance and grudging admiration for rhetorical studies. Plato, a nickname for the Athenian Aristocles, was the star student of Socrates. Plato's literary genius is seen in his characterization, movement, and style, as well as the clarity of thought, arrangement of argument, and integration of ideals with ideas. The prose of his work has intense beauty with deep impact—exceptional rhetoric. Yet he did not recognize his own rhetorical prowess nor the value others' works for many years.

Written shortly after Socrates' death, the *Gorgias* belittles rhetoric and envisions oratorical eloquence as a perfumeless, ugly flower. In the discussion Plato has Socrates hesitate to define rhetoric because it would be "discourteous" to the Sophist Gorgias who was an eloquent rhetorician. During the dialogue Gorgias reveals his perspective that oratory is the foundation of democracy with ruling by persuasion being superior to other modes of government and the best eloquence as that which produces conviction in the souls of the hearers. Socrates counters Gorgias with the idea that "producing conviction" in the masses is not necessarily knowledge and that *belief based on falsehood or probability is inferior to knowledge based on truth.* Conviction based on belief cannot produce ethical decisions and behavior but truth will lead to moral virtues. The "knack" of convincing the ignorant without a foundation of truth produces the dishonorable field of eloquence "because it makes pleasure its aim instead of the good" (465). Socrates calls rhetoric "pandering," "flattery," "the shadow part of politics," "bad," and "ignoble." Probably blaming rhetoric for the death of Socrates, Plato lashed out at the whole concept of oratorical eloquence calling it a pseudo-art where appearances are more important than truth. The use of rhetoric is to please the "mob" in a selfish grab of power, not to do and say what is good, right, and just in service to the *polis.*

In his *Apology,* Plato's version of Socrates' speeches during the trial, rhetorical persuasion is blamed for the guilty verdict and sentencing of the philosopher. Convicted of atheism and corrupting the young, Socrates gave an eloquent defense and condemnation of those who judge him. By apology Socrates does not mean "I'm sorry, I was wrong," but in the formal apologetic sense, "I'm right and here is why I am right and you are wrong." Plato sets up a dichotomy between Socrates and the prosecution from the first sentences. The defense begins with a statement of the distortion of truth brought by the prosecutors' speeches so much so that Socrates says he cannot recognize himself.

The primary tenant of philosophic rhetoric is set forth early in the first speech "for this is the excellence of a juryman, and of an orator, it is to speak the truth" (17-18). Socrates then states the case and denies the charges, but recognizes that prejudice against him has developed over many years because of his methods and confrontational attitude. Then Socrates states the specific charges and refutes them one by one. Following the defense the jurors cast their ballots, and he was convicted on a close vote.

The second speech of the Apology was to set the punishment for the violation. The prosecution suggested the death penalty, and Socrates countered by proposing a small fine. During this speech a further premise of philosophical rhetoric is put forth,

> *I am trying to persuade each of you not to have greater concern for any-*
> *thing you have than for yourselves, that each of you may be the best and*
> *wisest person possible, nor to consider the affairs of the city in preference*
> *to the well-being of the city itself.* (36)

The good of people and relationships is greater than persuasion in a specific instance with the perspective being what is best in the long term over the short term. Rhetorical persuasion in conversation and small groups rather than public speaking was Socrates chosen method, so he was ill equipped to face this jury of more than 500 men. He was sentenced to die.

In the final speech Socrates condemns the prosecution of "wickedness," oratory in a style of flowery flattery, and the jurors of mindless listening for linguistic tricks rather than substance of argument and truth. The proposition of philosophical rhetoric here is the integrity of the speaker. Character and virtue with integrity is more important than winning the audience or political power; upholding truth, justice, and people is more important than even life itself.

In *The Republic*, Plato bans rhetoricians from the ideal republic because they are "two steps" removed from the truth. The first order of truth is that which is pure concept in the minds of the gods. The second order of truth is that which appears in matter. The third order of truth represents the work of the painter, poet, or orator who in turn represent matter that in turn represents the Truth. This portrayal of truth is two steps removed from the first order and, therefore, suspect and unreliable. Added to this the focus on probability instead of a search for truth in the development of speeches and the content of all eloquent orators should be considered with suspicion or rejected.

Over the years, and possibly also due to his relationship with Aristotle, Plato mellowed in his perspective of rhetoric as a discipline and art. The *Phaedrus,* written later in Plato's life as one of the "middle" dialogues, demonstrates his reconciliation with persuasive oratory. In it Socrates and

Phaedrus are sitting beneath a tree by a stream outside of Athens and the discussion cascades through three speeches on the nature of rhetoric. The first speech was presented by Lysias earlier and here related by Phaedrus to Socrates. The essential element of the speech is that the orator should place no value judgments on anything but, instead, purify communication through lack of emotion and persuasion. "People should grant favors to non-lovers" is Plato's way of expressing "objective" presentation without passion or opinion. Give the facts in a straightforward manner allowing the evidence to speak for itself to an audience who is dispassionate, and the ideal speech will be achieved. When this happens often enough, language and culture will change in the direction of "Spock Speak," the point where logic dominates and emotion evaporates.

Socrates responds with a speech of his own that begins to differentiate between good and bad use of emotion. Here evil rhetoricians who manipulate others through clever language serve themselves and gain power over others. Motivating through guilt and spurious argument, these bad lovers distort the truth for their own personal advantage over others. Included in this kind of rhetoric is the sophist position of making the worse seem the better cause.

Following this second speech Socrates wades out into the water and receives a divine revelation that the preceding speeches were full of error. Love is the power that enable humans to know and understand true reality; thus good rhetoric is that of a noble lover, not objective nor self-seeking, but a passionate seeking of the best for the other person. Skillful use of speech produces insight into truth and inspires the audience to virtue so that the rhetor focuses on what is good. Because love is the realm of the gods, both the speaker and the audience are empowered to become more godlike.

Socrates uses the metaphor of the winged charioteer to express the tension of the human condition. The chariot is harnessed to two winged horses, one represents the spiritual soul and is noble; the other representing the physical and selfish desires which are evil. The two horses war against each other, one attempting to draw the chariot up into the heavens to glimpse beauty and truth, the other attempts to drag the chariot into the depths of desire and hedonism. The challenge of the charioteer is to steer life in the direction of truth, nobility and morality.

> The conviction which impels us towards excellence is rational, and
> the power by which it masters us we call self-control; the desire
> which drags us towards pleasure is irrational, and when it gets the

upper hand in us its dominion is called excess . . . . When the ir-
rational desire that prevails over the conviction which aims at right
is directed at the pleasure derived from beauty, and in the case of
physical beauty powerfully reinforced by the appetites which are
akin to it, so that it emerges victorious, it takes its name from the
very power with which it is endowed and is called eros or passionate
love. (p. 238)

Speech that enables love to direct the human driver correctly is true rhetoric aimed at the soul and leading to knowledge and a triumph of virtue.
That kind of communication is good rhetoric.

The dialogue between Phaedrus and Socrates has captured an encounter between good and evil on the field of love through the use of oratory.
The conversation transitions into a discussion of the technical art of rhetoric as a true rhetorician may practice oratory. A significant difference remains between philosophic rhetorical persuasion and both the technical
and sophistic: consideration of truthful content and the virtuous impact
are the primary elements in philosophic rhetoric while they are ignored or
demphasized in the other forms.

How would Plato have viewed the Clinton-Lewinski political battles?
First, he would have been disgusted that the issue was even brought up
much less debated at such length; however, the legal squabbling, the gossip, the misrepresentation of intentional meaning before a judge, and the
definition of "is" would have turned him strongly against the President's
rhetorical defense. This would be a case where, from Plato's perspective,
a non-issue became an offense against society and the law, through the
defense's communication, by making a mockery of truth and replacing it
with probability. Plato would have said, tell the truth and be done with the
entire matter; however, once the strategy to mislead and skate on technical
litigation was chosen, then a swift condemnation by the judge should take
place and he would denounce the defense's method as "sophistic excess."

How would Plato have responded to the Bush/Gore reliance upon the
judicial system to win an election? Probably with disdain. Undoubtedly,
he would have walked away and let someone else rule. But most likely
he would not have been in the running since he thought an oligarchy is a
better form of government. Clearly neither Bush nor Gore are "ones who
know." The rhetorical and political strategies used to win a contest were not
those of great leadership.

Integrating the foundation of psychology into rhetoric, in the *Phaedrus*,
Plato has Socrates say:

The serious and scientific teacher of the art of speaking will regard it as his first duty to make use as precisely as possible whether the soul is naturally homogenous unity or complex . . . . The next [duty] describes how and what it naturally acts and how and by what it is acted upon and to what effect . . . . In the third he will classify the various types of speech and of soul and the ways in which souls can be affected . . . . The function of speech is to influence the soul. (p. 271)

This audience-centered content, style, and arrangement is the strength of oral argument. Plato points out that a written document does not adjust to the people as the content is delivered making oral rhetoric superior to the concrete meaning of written words. Rhetorical persuasion must be based on truth (knowledge of the eternal realities or forms) and adapt that truth to the soul of the audience. Eloquent speech should be "organic," "like a living being" (212) working, functioning, a whole message influencing the self and others for good.

Isocrates

436–338 B.C.

"Isocrates was the most influential Greek rhetorician among his contemporaries. Aristotle with his more philosophical treatise on rhetoric wins the title for long range influence" (Corbett p. 596). Standing between the technicians, the Sophists, and the philosophers; Isocrates does not fit fully into any of the camps. He established a university with a consistent curriculum where rhetoric was the basis of learning. He sought to teach strong character, high ethical practice, idealistic perspectives, and public speaking all based on knowledge making his rhetoric philosophical. He did take money for teaching students, tried to make learning practical, and taught that the absolute truth was not knowable similar to the sophistic teaching. He taught methods and delivery making his teaching similar to technicians. Because of the similarity of his teaching to philosophic rhetoric, and that he did not consider himself to be a Sophist, for this history he is placed among the philosophical rhetoricians. Even Plato (Phaedrus) says Isocrates teaches "something of philosophy" and his rhetorical theory is "more excellent" than the sophistic approaches.

One of the major impacts Isocrates has on rhetorical theory and practice is his emphasis that the whole person be brought into the persuasive process. Balancing philosophy, to train the mind, and gymnastics, to train the body, the entire person must be educated before speaking can be approached. As a result of a well-rounded education, "eloquence and wisdom will become the possession of those who are philosophically and honorably disposed toward speech" (277). The aim of technical rhetoric is the development of eloquent speeches; the aim of sophistic rhetoric is the impact of the style, while the aim of philosophic rhetoric becomes noble people who speak accurately and well while seeking the good in a process of love.

Although Isocrates did not believe virtue could be taught, he did believe virtue could be sharpened and directed through the self-discipline of rhetoric. An inner drive to communicate publicly will provide the self-discipline necessary for virtue to exist.

> I consider that the kind of art which can implant honesty and justice in depraved natures has never existed and does not now exist, and that people who profess that power will grow weary and cease from their vain pretensions before such an education is ever found. But I do hold that people can become better and worthier if they conceive an ambition to speak well, if they become possessed of the desire to be able to persuade their hearers, and, finally, if they set their hearts on seizing their advantage. Isocrates Antidosis, in Bizzell p. 52

We can see the definite emphasis on the person with an ultimate goal of the good along with an emphasis on eliminating what is bad. Again, Isocrates teaches the content of the speech should be formed from research into truth along side of addressing the audience appropriately.

> *And yet those who desire to follow the true precepts of this discipline may, if they will, be helped more speedily towards honesty of character than towards facility in oratory. And let no one suppose that I claim that just living can be taught, for, in a word, I hold that there does not exist an art of the kind which can implant sobriety and justice in depraved natures. Nevertheless, I do think that the study of political discourse can help more than any other thing to stimulate and form such qualities of character.* Isocrates, Against the Sophists, in Bizzell p. 49

The formation of the good person's character into self-control with eloquence is the result of a rhetorical education. Application of rhetoric for the good of the community through political service will even further benefit the individual's discipline to be able to develop virtue.

Isocrates believed that a rhetorical approach to training allows a teacher to:

Educate the ignorant and appraise the wise; for the power to speak well is taken as the surest index of a sound understanding, and discourse which is true and lawful and just is the outward image of a good and faithful soul. With this faculty we both contend against others on matters which are open to dispute and seek light for ourselves on things which are unknown; for the same arguments which we use in persuading others when we speak in public, we employ also when we deliberate in our own thoughts; and, while we call eloquent those who are able to speak before a crowd, we regard as sage those who most skillfully debate their problems in their own minds.   Antidosis, Quoted in Golden p. 42

The thinking habits are addressed as a significant part of rhetoric and in many situations this may be the most significant communication that takes place. The good thinking leads to an ability to choose wisely in difficult situations.

Service to the *polis*, the city-community, was the energy of Isocrates' educational theory and practice. Training students to be leaders who have the best of the people at heart with good decision making qualities and well-rounded knowledge gave the school a constant flow of students who were willing to pay the high tuition rates. Following the way of the Sophists, Isocrates often taught through the use of great rhetorical models as well as teaching theory and delivery.

With the focus of education on the character of the student and developing the individual to serve the *polis*, what would Isocrates think of the modern educational reform movement? We are focused on meeting standardized test scores in math, writing, reading and science; these reforms create a system that directs teaching a curriculum in a rote manner of memorized trivia rather than Isocrates teaching for a vital, thinking, eloquent citizen. Along with the misdirected content, the modern school movement takes all religious and character emphasis out of the curriculum replacing it with values clarification and skepticism. Isocrates would probably think that this kind of reform is anti-intellectual, producing people trained for minor occupations rather than patriotic citizens ready to serve the community. In those few classrooms where teachers work against the system by adding dialectic, rhetoric, art, and philosophy with a strong character orientation, those lucky students may profit immensely from the reform.

Isocrates had high entrance qualifications for his school. Believing that the students' natural ability could be trained into moral excellence, he set about "sharpening" them into better people. If a student had a bad character or an insufficient base of knowledge, then no amount of higher education could make that student into a good person. He may be able to learn skills and facts, but to become a leader, to influence others for good, to impact the *polis* in a positive manner, no amount of education could accomplish those goals in a lesser person.

Isocrates also added to the art of oratory. Viewing prose with an almost poetic desire, he attempted to refine students' style to be an elegant eloquence. His book *The Art of Rhetoric* has been lost but it had a significant impact on Cicero and Quintilian. Probably Aristotle took up the challenge of teaching rhetoric in Plato's Academy because of the success of Isocrates' method and the demand of students.

Socially applied knowledge and skill that expresses deep abiding issues in a manner that makes a specific difference in the *polis* is the best rhetoric in Isocrate's school. A rhetorical education that begins with a good person understanding the principles and contemplating exceptional models will lead to a better person of maturity and eloquence ready to serve the people as a leader. Throughout the centuries he has been recognized for the great teaching and students who became some of Athens' most prominent leaders.

Aristotle

384-322 B.C.

Aristotle was perhaps the greatest rhetorician of all time, unquestionably the most influential in impact, not only on rhetorical theory but also with expansion of knowledge in all areas. He began his teaching career by developing a course in rhetoric for Plato's Academy. Aristotle systematized branches of knowledge and then extended the limits in ethics, politics, aesthetics, metaphysics, physics, astronomy and rhetoric. He is also considered to be the father of biology, zoology, psychology, and logic.

Aristotle went to Plato's Academy when he was eighteen and stayed for twenty years teaching along side of his professor. After the death of Socrates, Aristotle left Athens and traveled, ending up as the tutor to Alexander the Great in Macedonia. During the reign of Alexander, Aristotle returned to Athens and founded the *Peripatetic* (walking) school at the Lyceum.

As the founder of scientific methodology, Aristotle emphasized observation of reality prior to creating theory. Before a full understanding could be reached, Aristotle believed description, then classification, and finally a causal explanation must be given for a thing or event. This systematic thinking led to the discovery of much knowledge of the physical world, people, and dialectic. Most of the books we have of Aristotle are his class notes or those compiled by his students. *The Rhetoric* is probably his own notes from the course he taught in persuasive public address. Because he taught for more than twenty years, it is a "growing" document as a guide for lectures, making it incomplete and often abbreviated. Occasionally words are used in different ways (like enthymeme and topics) so that difficulties arise in understanding precisely what he thought. Even so, it remains the first systematic philosophy and guide to rhetorical oratory.

Aristotle's systematization and summarization of the technical handbooks were so powerful that those written by others seem to be lost in the shuffle of history, and now even his monumental work lives only in legend and rumor with snippets quoted from admiring readers. Here is one of his key passages to the place of rhetoric:

> But the art of rhetoric has its value. It is valuable, first, because truth and justice are by nature more powerful than their opposites; so that, when decisions are not made as they should be the speakers with the right on their side have only themselves to thank for the outcome . . . . Secondly, rhetoric is valuable as a means of instruction. Even if our speaker had the most accurate scientific information, still there are persons whom he could not readily persuade with scientific arguments . . . . Thirdly, in rhetoric, as in dialectic, we should be able to argue on either side of a question . . . . in order that no aspect of the case may escape us, and that if our opposition makes unfair use of the arguments, we may be able to in turn to refute them . . . . Lastly, if it is a disgrace to a man when he cannot defend himself in a bodily way, it would be odd not to think him disgraced when he cannot defend himself with reason in a speech. Reason is more distinctive of man than is bodily effort. Aristotle The Rhetoric p. 6

Aristotle views rhetoric as an art that can be either used well to beautify or used evilly to harm. Like most useful things, strength, wealth, health and military skill, rhetoric can be a blessing or detriment to the person or audience. The appellation "rhetor" may signify a person of great skill in the use of language but is equally, if not more applicable to, the person with a strong moral purpose in speaking, writing, or listening.

In his methodical way of thinking, Aristotle defines rhetoric as "the faculty [*dunamis* or power] of discovering in the particular case what are the available means of persuasion" (1355). Too often in the history of rhetoric Aristotle's idea translated "faculty" has been understood as only a skill rather than *power*. Words expressed contain a power to change both the speaker and the audience.

For Aristotle persuasion is wider than converted thinking or doing; to be persuasive specific evidence needs to be woven into the communication. "Now proof is a kind of demonstration: for we entertain the strongest conviction of a thing if we believe it has been demonstrated" (1355). Evidence and proof are so integrated into his thinking that Aristotle occasionally uses the terms interchangeably. Rhetorical persuasion uses primarily the most powerful examples and enthymemes to convict an audience into belief about something that is true and good.

Besides rhetoric, the logic of Aristotle is developed beyond that of his contemporaries. For his teacher, Plato, the only form of true reason is dialectic, a process of developing an irrefutable definition by looking at all sides of an issue and then classifying the elements as well as the whole. Aristotle believes a superior form of reasoning is demonstration [*apodeixus*], which draws conclusions from observable facts or scientifically true premises. Rhetoric is a counterpart or correlative to dialectic [*antistrophe*] using the probabilities, enthymemes and examples to draw conclusions. The reasoning aspect of rhetoric with its moral implications is what goaded Aristotle's art into the practice of eloquence. Aristotle suggested that rhetors consider both sides of an issue analyzing the best arguments prior to giving a speech.

Plato and Aristotle form an interesting contrast. Plato was a poet, playwright, speaker, and author yet he was uneasy with the field of rhetoric. Aristotle was a systematic thinker in a wide variety of fields, a true Renaissance man of practical and theoretical skill who valued rhetoric, yet was a plodding author and often boring speaker.

One of the primary developments of Aristotle's teaching of public communicaiton is the articulation of the five cannons of rhetoric. The natural development of a speech begins with 1) the *invention* or discovery of arguments, then 2) the *arranging* them into an organizational pattern, wording the ideas in appropriate linguistic 3) *style*, entrusting the speech to 4) the *memory*, and finally 5) *delivering* the speech to an audience. These cannons dominate rhetorical theory up to the present. Many works such as Cicero and Quintilian outline the entire schemata in terms of these five powerful measurements of oratory. Technical rhetoricians attempt to divide these cannons into either a hierarchy or chronology considering them to be discrete categories or activities accomplished by a set of skills. The process of developing a speech does not begin with invention and end with delivery, instead all five cannons are interdependent leading to both the unearthing of truth and the discovery of the power to convince the audience.

In the area of delivery, Aristotle brings out a new focus on vocal quality. The purpose of intentional vocalics is to create the appropriate emotion in the audience. When a speaker harmonizes the volume, pitch, and rhythm of the voice, expressions and communication of emotion become clear to the audience.

The cannon of style was often taught by the Sophists to be more poetic than prose. Clarity is the utmost significance for Aristotle in word choice and arrangement. His student Theophrastus extended Aristotle to a more rounded view encompassing correctness of grammar, clarity of argument, ornamentation for beauty, and propriety for the audience.

Aristotle also taught about the *location* of *topics* to use in the invention of speeches. "We state the general *loci* of quality when we assert that what is good for the greatest number is preferable to what profits only a few; that the durable is preferable to the fragile; or that something useful in varied situations is preferable to something that is of use in highly specific ones" (*Rhetoric*). "If we give as our reason for preferring something that is unique, rare, irreplaceable, or that it can never happen again (*carpe diem*) we are stating the general *locus* of quality. It is a locus that favors the elite over the mass, the exceptional over the normal, that values what is difficult . . . . Then we have the spirit of general *locus*" (*Topics*). Arguments should be of high quality, valuing what is significant to the whole, rather than those that give power or wealth to a few.

Enthymatic reasoning, where conclusions are inductively inferred rather than deduced from specific evidence through syllogistic logic, marks Aristotle's treatment of artistic proof. Inartistic or "external" proof is factual or "true," and the proof needs to be expertly used in speeches, but not "discovered" through rhetorical reasoning. Artistic proof is where the speaker develops his or her own arguments through observation, analysis and reasoning leaving the conclusion as probable instead of certain. Sometimes a premise is left out of enthymatic reasoning with the speaker trusting the audience to supply it during the speech. With the works of Aristotle being taken from across his life, the definition and use of *enthymeme* is not consistent within his own framework.

One of the most important of Aristotle's contributions to rhetorical theory is that of the modes of persuasion: ethos, pathos, and logos. First, *ethos*, "the character of the speaker is a cause of persuasion when the speech is so uttered as to make him worthy of belief." Second, *pathos*, "persuasion is effected through the audience when they are brought by the speech into a state of emotion; for we give very different decision under the sway of pain or joy, and liking or hatred." Third, *logos*, "persuasion is effected by the arguments, when we demonstrate truth, real or apparent, by such means as inhere in particular cases. Such being the instruments of persuasion, to master all three obviously calls for a man who can reason logically, can analyze the types of human character, along with the virtues, and, thirdly, can analyze the emotions—the nature and quality of each emotion with the means by which, and the manner in which, it is excited" (Rhetoric, 1356).

If Aristotle were going to give a speech today on media violence what kind of arguments would he use in developing the content of the speech? Probably he would begin by researching the inartistic proofs—finding out what the specific factual evidence is for the case: relevant laws, statistics of amount, and quotes from authorities. Then he would set about the discovery of artistic proofs: specific examples and probable results in the lives of young consumers. These he would formulate into enthymemes and place them into a speech.

Cicero

106-43 B.C.

"Wisdom with eloquence has been of little help to states, but eloquence without wisdom has often been a great obstacle and never an advantage" (*De Inventione*). With this thought Cicero summarizes his philosophy of rhetorical persuasion. Moving through time from the Golden Age of Greece to the Republic of Rome, we come to Cicero, the greatest of the Roman orators. The ability to speak, for Cicero, is what differentiates humans from animals; therefore, eloquence with wisdom is a great good for all people.

Formulating the educational system of Isocrates with the ethics of Plato and the systematic clarity of Aristotle, Cicero designed a comprehensive curriculum for developing citizen orators. Trained as a lawyer, experienced in the senate, Cicero was eventually elected Consul of the Republic (similar to President of the United States). He lived in a tumultuous time where political alliances were often gifts of power and could easily lead to sudden death. Following Caesar's assassination in 44 BC Cicero spoke out against Mark Antony. In the months to come Antony slowly won the leadership. Less than a year later Cicero realized the political tide had turned and was stabbed to death in his coach as he tried to flee from Rome. His head and hands were cut off and nailed over the rostrum in the City as a warning.

Alongside of Socrates, Plato and Aristotle, Cicero called for eloquence based on knowledge. In the early Attic period the discipline of rhetoric arose as a technical art and then developed into the sophistic and finally philosophical perspectives. During the intervening years, rhetoric "slipped" backwards toward a technical perspective. Kennedy notes,

> *A persistent characteristic of classical rhetoric, in almost every phase of its ancient and modern history, to move from primary into secondary forms. For this phenomenon the Italian term letteraturizzazione is convenient shorthand. Letteraturizzazione is the tendency of rhetoric to shift its focus from persuasion to narration, from civic to personal contexts, and from discourse to literature . . . . The primary reason for the letteraturizzazione of rhetoric is probably the place given rhetoric in education and the recurring tendency to teach it by rote to young children rather than to make it a more intellectually demanding advanced discipline, but the development is of course directly influenced by the opportunities, open to primary rhetoric throughout history.* (p. 5)

Cicero was a major voice, calling rhetoricians back to the philosophical perspective. This reconceptualization of rhetoric took place in years of tumult and upheaval as Rome changed from a Republic to an Empire.

Cicero built the concept of stasis, from Hermagerous, into the mainstream of rhetorical thought and practice. The crux of a conflict between two sides of an issue, stasis, may develop along four lines: 1) when a fact is at issue, 2) when a definition is at issue, 3) when it is a matter of the nature, quality, or classification that is at issue, and finally, 4) when the jurisdiction is at issue. Stasis is an understanding of the kind of conflict involved and the point at which it occurs in dialectical rhetoric and forensic oratory. Some cases are simple, involving only one question while others may be complex and even weigh answers through criteria for the best course of action. Understanding the reason why change must be made and where persuasion is needed empowers speakers in the invention process of developing speech content.

How would Cicero analyze the arguments in the physician-assisted suicide issue? 1) Stasis of fact: The law in Oregon, as voted by the citizens is in favor of physician-assisted suicide for terminally ill patients. 2) Stasis of definition: Is this in reality murder? Euthanasia? Suicide? 3) Stasis of quality or classification: The legal realm is interacting with moral and medical issues, and at the convergence a balance between them must be reached with the rights and desires of the individual considered in light of the good for the whole citizenry. Some of the values at issue are the quality of life, self-determination, sanctity of life, role of the doctor with the Hippocratic oath, mental health of the individual, rights of the family, financial obligations, and the practical issues of how the suicide takes place. And finally, 4) Stasis of jurisdiction: Does the state have the right to allow citizens this "right" to death? Should it fall under the federal government? The state courts have upheld the bill, and the federal courts have also upheld the initiative. Does the federal legislature (house and senate) have the right now to intervene? Does the federal legislative branch have a moral imperative to overturn the law of the state? Cicero would have considered where the conflict lay with the particular audience and would develop the speech from that point. Few would argue the first point, stasis of fact. Even the stasis of definition would probably be settled quickly. However, the last two points, those of quality and jurisdiction would carry the major part of the controversy for this particular issue.

Although Plato had intimated the applicability of rhetoric to interpersonal conversation, Cicero was the first to seriously consider the "science of conversations" (*On Moral Duties*). The subject of speech changes in conversation, the decorum of the speaker, and the delivery all need to be adapted to the realities of a changed rhetorical situation.

Another major contribution of Cicero was a focus on the organization of speeches. The arrangement or argument in a speech, like the arrangement of soldiers in a battle, can be the most significant element in achieving victory. Presenting six parts to a persuasive speech, Cicero gives order to substance focused on accomplishing the goal of persuasion. Exordium, narration, partition, confirmation, refutation, and peroration form the basic progression of rhetorical ideas. The exordium is an introduction that prepares the audience to listen to the speech by creating a situational urgency (*exigence*) creating a desire or passion to hear. The narration is setting forth the case in a brief, clear and probable manner enabling an overview of the issue and the manner in which it will be addressed. The partition lists the points the speaker will prove or state the points of agreement and disagreement with the opposition. The confirmation is the building up of the speech where the case is made with full arguments giving specific evidence for each point. This body of the speech leads into the refutation where the opponent's case is countered, through: 1) not allowing the premises, 2) demonstrating illogical form, 3) showing the conclusion does not flow from the evidence, or 4) demonstrating that the stronger argument favors the speaker, not the opponent. The speech ends with the peroration or conclusion that contains an appeal, summarizes the argument, incites indignation against the opponent and/or arouses the audience to favor the speaker. Cicero also speaks of transitions to make the speech flow better, "there are many words which, like joints, connect the members of our speech together" (DeOrator II, 88).

One of the often-overlooked aspects of Cicero's rhetorical practice is that of laughter. He believed that humor added significantly to the positive emotional appeals of persuasive oratory (DeOrator II, 108). The judicious use of humor that is in good taste can set the atmosphere of the speech in favor of the speaker before any arguments are given. "It certainly becomes the orator to excite laughter; either because mirth itself attracts favor to him by whom it is raised, or because all admire wit . . ." (I, 58).

The conceptualization of the "duties" of an orator is perhaps the most influential of Cicero's ideas. "The whole theory of speaking is dependent on three sources of persuasion: that we prove our case to be true; that we win over those who are listening; and that we call their hearts to what emotion the case demands" (DeOrator, II, 115). These three duties, to prove, to delight, and to stir, form a vision of persuasion that impacts the mind, heart, and will enabling the whole person of the speaker to encounter the entire humanity of the audience. The greatest of rhetoricians is a citizen orator, a leader in virtue and eloquence in the community.

Cicero linked memory to tropes and figures of style: "Those things are most easily retained in our minds which we received from the hearing or understanding if they are also recommended to the imagination by means of the mental eye" (DeOrator, I, 87). The orator remembers his own speech but also makes it memorable for the audience through the use of tropes and figures.

The form or "complexion" or style of eloquence is threefold: "There is one sort which has a fullness, but is free of tumor; one which is plain, but not without nerve and vigour [sic]; and one which, participating of both these kinds is commended for a certain middle quality" (DeOratore III 52). Choosing the words is important and they may change through the delivery process, but the thoughts, the arguments, they are what really count the most in a speech for they will remain after the style is forgotten. "No single style can be adapted to every cause, or every audience, or every person, or every occasion" (DeOrator I, 55). Kind and style of oratory must be adapted by the rhetor in flexible recognition of the rhetorical situation.

Quintilian

35-96 A.D.

Placing rhetoric as the foundation of a life-long process of learning, Quintilian was a consummate educator. Systematizing the cannons of rhetoric into a pedagogical curriculum beginning at age three and continuing through adulthood, he creates an integrated interdisciplinary approach to education through the field of rhetoric.

Quintilian was born shortly after Cicero's death, but was trained in the heritage of the citizen-orator. Living during a time when emperors tightly controlled socio-political issues and policies, Quintilian taught rhetoric from a government funded chair in Rome for more than twenty years.

Taking the idea of stasis from Cicero, Quintilian clarified it into three areas of questions: those of fact, definition, and quality or value.

> Quintilian analyzed Cicero's defense of Milo, as an example: 'First, Did Milo kill Claudius? (Fact). Yes, fact admitted. Second, Did Milo murder Claudius? (Definition). Claudius lay in wait and attacked Milo. Therefore, the killing was not premeditated. It must be defined as self-defense, not as murder. Third, Was the act good or bad? (Quality). Good, because, Claudius was a bad citizen, and the Republic was better off with him dead.' Let the student examine the nature of the cause with these three questions in mind and the point at issue becomes immediately apparent. (Golden, p. 45)

Later Quintilian wrote of issues of policy, a course of action with the motives for why they were done. Policies should be questioned with why, where, when, in what manner, and by what means they are done or should be done. The topics or "places" Quintilian's questions revealed are the cause, place, time, person(s), manner and means. In analyzing these topics, the motives of the people involved are always kept in the forefront, but they must all be considered in the development of a whole argument covering an entire case.

Applying Quintilian's perspective of stasis and locus to the current debate on abortion in the United States, a clearer understanding of a social dilemma unfolds in the clash of argument.

1. Stasis of Definition: Pro-Choice: Abortion is riding the body of unwanted tissue. Pro-Life: Abortion is the murder of a living human.

2. Stasis of Fact: Pro-Life: Uniqueness of the child upon conception. Pro-Choice: Dependency and lack of viability without the mother.

3. Stasis of Quality: Is abortion justifiable?

4. Locus of Cause: Why is the mother seeking the abortion: for convenience, gender selection, abnormality, rape, incest, or disease?

5. Locus of Place: Without clinics and hospitals pro-choice adherents claim women would seek abortions in back alleys and homes.

6. Locus of Time: Is there a point following conception but yet short of birth where abortion should not be performed? Usually this part of the debate is formed in terms of trimesters from conception.

7. Locus of Manner: From the professionalism of the doctor to the amount and kind of counseling received, the style and manner is at issue. Even the choice of words can be an issue; few people would consider themselves pro-abortion but instead, pro-choice, while painting the opposition as anti-abortion instead of pro-life.

8. Locus of Means: From IUD's to drugs to partial birth abortions, the way in which the abortion takes place is hotly debated.

From Quintilian's approach, the debate on abortion covers the entire realm of controversy with little or no compromise in any of the issues of stasis or locus. Understanding the points of clash may give impetus for dialogue, especially by people who are in the center of the issue rather than on the fringes.

Incorporating moral philosophy into rhetoric even more than his predecessors, Quintilian focused rhetoric as "a good man speaking well." Ethical implications permeate his thinking and teaching attempting to place the idealism of virtue into the practical, action-oriented Roman culture. The good person is one who is free from vice, loves wisdom, sincerely believes in the cause he advocates, and is a servant of the state and people. The moral strength of a good person has a more eloquent impact on the audience than all the grammatical devices, which may be employed to communicate the message.

Applying the three styles of rhetoric to purposes of a speech Quintilian integrates Cicero's teaching into that of Aristotle. "He in fact is eloquent who can discuss commonplace matters simply, lofty subjects impressively, and topics ranging between in a temporal style" (29). He holds Cicero as the ideal rhetor saying, "Cicero is the name, not of a man, but of eloquence" (10).

Summary

The Classical rhetoricians developed synthesized perspectives of rhetoric that can be divided into "schools" of thought: technical, sophistic, and philosophical.

First, the technical rhetoricians entered the scene focusing the theory and practice of rhetorical persuasion on the means of influence. Development of eloquent speeches that move the audience toward the speaker's goal was the focus of technical rhetoric. Handbooks of oratory taught how to grow a presentation into an excellent speech.

Second came the sophistic rhetoricians who focused on the artistry of the speech with individual talent and power becoming the primary directives. Because of the strong focus on politics, people began to value power and eloquence and reputation, and in turn disdaining truth, virtue and relationships. The sophistic method sought probability over truth in argument and idealized convincing the audience to the point that Gorgias is accused of "delighting in making the worse seem to be the better cause and the guilty seem innocent" creating an "excess" in rhetoric.

The third rhetorical movement is that of the philosophical rhetoricians. Perhaps the Apostle Paul best summarized this view with the phrase "speaking the truth in love" (Ephesians 4:15) as the ideal of more mature thinkers instead of the "childlike" listeners who are deceived by those who place eloquence over truth. Philosophic rhetorical persuasion emphasizes the moral character of the rhetoric over the stylistic devices of grammarians and sound argument based on truth over the probable argument based on possibilities.

This development of rhetoric through the classical period provided a foundation of understanding that stands secure millennia later. Expanded over the following centuries of darkness and light, people enlarged these ideas and debates as each generation learned anew the process and products of persuasive oratory. We still have people who are more interested in charismatic delivery with emotional impact on the audience (technical rhetoric). Others are most interested in the power they exert and gain in winning arguments regardless of the truth-value or costs (sophistic rhetoric). Many rhetors are vitally interested in seeking truth and conveying it in a loving, influential manner for the good of the community (philosophical rhetoric). The three strands that began so many centuries ago still have adherents. Christian rhetoric follows the classical philosophical tradition and builds upon it the relationship with God and message of the Bible delivered in the power of the Holy Spirit. Some preachers are all flash and flare with no substance (technicians), other preachers seek power and winning arguments (sophists), but most exegete the truth in love as representatives of God (philosophers). This text focuses on the Christian philosophic rhetoric to enable speakers and writers to discover the truth and communicate it in a persuasive manner from a virtuous character with an attitude of love.

Chapter 5

Middle Rhetoric: Augustine to Whately

So that you may walk in the way of goodness
And keep to the paths of righteousness
Proverbs 2:20 NKJV

IN THE second century, the Roman Empire became increasingly auto-cratic and emperors resembled tyrants more than the ideal of a servant-leader focused on truth and justice, like Cicero and Caesar. Rhetorical persuasion slipped from its philosophical position where good people and citizen orators developed clear accurate argument into the second sophistic movement. With a socio-political atmosphere where dissent was seen as duplicitous betrayal, those who dared debate government policy and action were executed or imprisoned. Deliberative and forensic oratory almost became nonexistent due to the radical punishment of independent thinking and communicating. With the *letteraturizzazione* slip from the classical ideal, rhetors of the second sophistic became enamored with style and delivery where little or no emphasis were placed on substance and none at all on truth. The emphasis on the moral character of the speaker was also lost by the sophistic rhetoricians. Inspiration and entertainment replaced persuasion and influence as public oratory slid into aesthetics and impact without substance in civic discourse.

Some religious speakers took the part of Plato in a Gorgian style of condemnation of this rhetorical slide. Beginning in the first century with the Apostle Paul who argued against worldly "wisdom" and "eloquence" and for the substance of truth (especially that of the *revealed* Word of God), rhetoric was denigrated to serve those with eloquence searching for power. The reaction to the sophistic movement was so strong that Christians called

123

their oratory "preaching" and "homiletics" instead of public speaking and rhetoric. They had the "concrete," written *Rhema* or *Logos* of God in the Bible, so substance in speaking was judged by the listeners as to whether or not the speaker remained true to the text. Exegesis and hermeneutics replaced invention as the process for developing the content of the messages. Clear revealing of truth in the content was valued over eloquent presentation of the message.

Augustine

354–430 A.D.

One of the pivotal thinkers in the long history of persuasive rhetoric, Augustine fought against the ideas of the second sophistic, doubters of rhetoric from inside Christianity, and doubters of Christianity itself. In his call back to a measure of truth, love, and character, Augustine integrated rhetoric into Christian beliefs so closely that they weave an intricate pattern of the discovery and presentation of religious truth to the point he names his book about rhetoric *On Christian Doctrine*. Rhetorical persuasion involves: "A way of discovering those things which are to be understood, and a way of teaching what we have learned" (Book 1:1 p. 7). Keeping a great emphasis on invention and the content along with the presentation techniques places Augustine in the philosophical tradition: "For he who speaks eloquently is heard with pleasure; he who speaks wisely is heard with profit" (4:5 p. 122). Following Aristotle, Augustine asserts "the life of the speaker has greater weight in determining whether he is obediently heard than any grandness of eloquence. For he who speaks wisely and eloquently but lives wickedly, may benefit many students, although, as it is written, he 'is unprofitable to his own soul'" (4:27, p. 164).

Augustine's view of truth has often been misunderstood or caricatured in manners that are not in keeping with his radical statements of language and scripture. The discovery of truth by the rhetor happens through hermeneutics, the art and science of interpretation, as it is revealed in the Bible. For Augustine, communication is formulated from signs both "natural" and "conventional" with natural signs (like unintentional tracks left by animals) and nonverbal facial expressions of pain or sadness. Just as the intended meaning of a dancer is unintelligible except through interpretation and learning, language has meaning by "common consent" (2:25 p. 61). Natural truth is indisputable with a right and a wrong; seven plus three is

10, not 9 or 11, while the tracks made in the sand by a deer are not those of a bear. Language written or expressed communicates meaning and is best when truth is spoken. Truth with a capital "T" is personal in Jesus, while the truth about the Truth is the Bible. However, the truth is not always clear when it is filled with ambiguity and figurative language.

Rhetoric is the means of knowing and expressing the truth and as such is vital for the Christian speaker, even though the "probability" focus of the second sophistic was an anathema for the church.

> *For since by means of rhetoric both truth and falsehood are urged, who would dare to say that truth should stand in the person of its defenders unarmed against lying, so that they who wish to urge falsehoods may know how to make their listeners benevolent, or attentive, or docile in their presentation while the defenders of truth are ignorant of that art. Should they speak briefly, clearly, and plausibly while the defenders of truth speak so that they tire their listeners, make themselves difficult to understand and what they have to say dubious? . . . . While the faculty of eloquence, which is of great value in urging either evil or justice, is in itself indifferent, why should it not be obtained for the uses of the good in service of truth if the evil usurp it for the winning of perverse and vain causes in defense of iniquity and error?* (4:2 p. 118-119)

Misunderstanding happens as an inaccurate transfer of meaning between people. "There are two reasons why things written are not understood: they are obscured either by unknown or by ambiguous signs" (2:10 p. 43). Developing the ability of the communicator is the correct response to miscommunication, but also the hard work of clear understanding is echoed in metaphors where the message is a "knot" to be unraveled, a "road" to be traveled, a "body" to be exercised and diligently "sought" as patterns of stars by astronomers. The presence of ambiguity increases the chance of misunderstanding with figurative language more susceptible than literal communication. Beginning with a healthy "fear" of God, the rhetorician should also be gentle in piety, and conversant with grammar, and acquire an understanding of logic with a philosophical foundation, have a knowledge of the basics of science, and finally be familiar with a chronology of history. "Thus instructed, he may turn his attention to the investigation and solution of the ambiguities of the Scriptures . . . with care and industry" (3:1 p. 78).

In Augustine's thinking, understanding is the key to rhetorical eloquence. "For even though he has said something which he himself understands, he is not yet to be thought of as having spoken to the person who does not understand him: on the other hand, if he is understood, he has spoken, no matter how he has spoken" (4:12, p. 136). Language is not really language unless the meaning is transferred through the signs expressed. "Instruction should come before persuasion. And perhaps when the necessary things are learned, they may be so moved by a knowledge of them that it is not necessary to move them further by greater powers of eloquence" (4:12 p.137).

Augustine's focus on understanding, knowing fully, and then conveying that information to the audience prior to persuasion should impact rhetorical communication in the 21st century. More and more our media sources are leaving the "objective" standard and taking editorial perspectives. Many newspapers, radio stations, and television networks are taking specific stands on social issues and campaigns. An attempt is usually made to give other perspectives; however, the general reporting is slanted to the worldview of the reporter and company. Gaining a balance and full understanding of issues, events and people before taking a position of persuasion is a worthy goal, providing that information to the audience prior to attempting to influence them manages the information in an appropriate manner.

"He who seeks to teach in speech what is good, spurning none of these three things, that is, to teach, to delight, and to persuade, should pray and strive that he be heard intelligently, willingly, and obediently. When he does this well and properly, he can justly be called eloquent, even though he fails to win the assent of his audience" (4:17, p. 142). The interaction, of the subject matter (small, moderate and grand issues), the audience (before judges and superiors speak subdued, before those we would convince of eternal truth speak in a grand manner, and others in a middle style) and the intention of the speaker (to teach, to please or to persuade) determines the eloquence style (low, middle, or grand) to be used in a speech. "The grand style differs from the moderate style not so much in that it is adorned with verbal ornaments, but in that it is forceful with emotions of the spirit. Although it uses almost all of the ornaments it does not seek them if it does not need them" (4:20, p. 150). The styles of rhetoric are to be used "in such a way that they assist that good which we wish to convey by persuasion" (4:25, p. 162).

Augustine also associated style with the discovery and communication of truth. His practice demonstrates both the multiple dimensions of truth he envisioned as well as the "harmonic" style.

> *The structure of Augustine's sentences and clauses—and sometimes even his choice of words as signs—imparts significance and makes cognitive connections which cannot be indicated by literal speech. Resonating with overtones of sophistication and intricacy, Augustine's rhetoric reached a complex inner and external world. . . . This Classical rhetorician brought to expression intuitive understandings that are difficult to verbalize; in doing so, he effected a correspondence of wisdom and eloquence that seems lost to present philosophies of communication.*
> McDaniel, 1998

The style and organizational patterns of ideas are part of the rhetorical construction of reality with harmonic tones that resonate with the audience.

De-emphasizing the rhetorical focus on probability and substituting the more acceptable ideas of ambiguity and figurative language in understanding truth, Augustine reconciled Christianity with the rhetorical tradition and gave clear justification for improving eloquence. Rhetorical methodology of invention melded with Hillellian hermeneutical practice became the basis for development of the content of speeches in a process known now as exegetical hermeneutics (interpretation and understanding based on textual analysis). This christianization of rhetoric (or rhetorization of Christianity?) dominated the development and education of speakers through the following centuries and still influences linguistic philosophy and rhetorical studies today. In Augustine's words; "For it is the universal office of eloquence, in any of these three styles to speak in a manner leading to persuasion; and the end of eloquence is to persuade of that which you are speaking" (4:25, p. 161). Augustine's call for Christians to communicate the truth eloquently spread throughout society enacting a general movement away from the "probability" of the second sophistic in all aspects of society.

Boethius

480-524 A.D.

With the Greco-Roman influence waning in the socio-political realms, the government no longer supported education, few saw reason for training in scholarly issues, and fewer still could afford private tutors. Fewer occasions for public speeches occurred as senates disbanded, barbarians attacked, tyrant kings ruled, and judicial processes were run; all without public address. In the East, where Byzantium (Constantinople) was the capitol, a classical conservativism kept some rhetorical education alive through a system of grammar schools, and Hermongenes of Tarsus kept alive the tradition of rhetorical training with an emphasis on declamation from a sophistic perspective. In the West as the Greek language began to fade, Latin became the universal language. Cities were abandoned as people left in an attempt to survive on small farms and serfdoms—the social order collapsed. Even within the churches homilies were given in Latin instead of the local languages, and then mass replaced homilies within the worship services.

Classical rhetoric, although wounded, did not die out during these dark centuries. In monistaries, in some churches, in a few public appearances, in some political realms the ability to reason with eloquence was still valued and taught. The few schools usually taught the liberal arts of the trivium (grammar, rhetoric and dialectic) along with the quadrivium (geometry, arithmetic, astronomy and music) (Kennedy, p. 175). Throughout the West a few private teachers kept alive scholarship and education, but many libraries closed and the books deteriorated leaving less and less information from the ancient authors.

Boethius followed Augustine in keeping rhetoric alive through scholarship. He was one of the last Roman scholars who were able to read Greek well and attempted to translate the works of Aristotle and Plato into Latin. This project was cut short by his execution by Theodoric the Great who suspected he was plotting to overthrow his kingdom by joining Byzantine emperor Justin the First.

Logic, philosophy, and rhetoric are intertwined in Boethius' presentation. Philosophy deals with the larger issues or theses while rhetoric approaches specific questions or hypotheses. Under his frame of reference, "rhetoric becomes a means of applying general rules of argumentation, established by dialectic, to specific cases. Rhetorical argument has no epistemological force of its own" (Bizzell and Herzberg, 1990 p.423). More than these, Boethius follows a misunderstanding of Aristotle in that he believes that rhetoric is a skill level "faculty" devoid of the power of transformative thinking. "By genus, rhetoric is a faculty; by species it can be one of three: judicial, demonstrative, deliberative . . . . Since nearly every faculty must use a tool to accomplish what it can do, we must look for some tool here, that tool is oration" (Botehius trans. Miller, 1973, in Bizzell and Herzberg p. 425). Perhaps the greatest harm Boethius propagated was a misunderstanding of Aristotle that rhetoric was subordinate to dialectic rather than parallel to it (Reid, 2000).

Boethius, along with Aristotle, views the cannons of rhetoric as a whole with interrelated parts rather than as a simple sequential system. With a lack in any area, the orator will be "imperfect" in the speech. Boethius re-states much of classical rhetoric in his works as well as translating Aristotle's books. His work on topics was classical in nature with civic speaking, rather than religious, as the major emphasis of rhetoric.

Adding to the ancient study of rhetoric, Boethius helped usher in a focus on the rhetoric of letter writing. Travel was difficult, yet relation-ships widened and people relied more on letter writing than sending oral messages through heralds. One of his primary considerations is matching the language style to the audience and the subject matter. Specifically he discusses letters between rulers and government officials and those between religious clerics and explains how these should differ in tone and content. Soon letter writing became a major scholastic endeavor with professors con-versing and debating on parchment; this broadening of rhetoric is clearly anticipated in Boethius' rhetoric just as Cicero foreshadowed the expansion of rhetoric into interpersonal communication. Combining the harmonics of Augustine with the dialogues of Plato, Boethius wrote about the woman "Philosophy" visiting him in jail prior to his execution in *The Consolation of Philosophy*. In a poetic prose she reveals many secrets to him. One of these is about the nature of knowledge within communication.

> For if a man is sitting, then the belief that he is sitting must be true and conversely, if the opinion that the man is sitting is true, then he must necessarily be sitting. There is therefore necessity in both cases: in the for-mer the opinion must be true and in the latter the man must be sitting. However, he is not sitting because the opinion is true, but rather the opinion is true because his being seated preceded it . . . . Finally, if any one believes something which is actually not so, he has no knowledge but a fallacious opinion, a thing far removed from scientific truth . . . . Knowledge itself is unmixed with falsity, so also that which is conceived by it cannot be otherwise than it is conceived. (p. 423)

Truth in opinion is reflected in reality with this base, knowledge is definite and any premises built on that foundation will be certain. God's thinking, knowledge, and forthtelling is superior to human communication, think-ing, and knowing because his insight is perfect, complete, and holy while humans' virtues are finite.

Beothius also brought the foundation of love into the concept of truth in book two of *The Consolation of Philosophy*, "through love the universe with constancy makes changes all without discord." Love is the fundamen-tal aspect of all the world:

Hesperus brought: the greedy sea confines its waves in bounds, lest the earth's borders be changed by its beating on them: all these are firmly bound by Love, which rules both earth and sea, and has its empire in the heavens too. If Love should slacken this its hold, all mutual love would change to war; and these would strive to undo the scheme which now their glorious movements carry out with trust and with accord. By Love are peoples too kept bound together by a treaty which they may not break. Love binds with pure affection the sacred tie of wedlock, and speaks its bidding to all trusty friends. O happy race of mortals, if your hearts are ruled as is the universe, by Love!

The modern concept of diversity (which at its best calls for equality and respect with resulting values of equal opportunity, material equity, personal power, and self-determination), would better be replaced with Boethius' concept of love. Many of the same things would be done, but the motivation and values would produce far different effects in the attitudes and character of people. Diversity leads to quotas, salary counts, maintained differences, and forced integration with people measured by productivity and net worth, while love leads to empathy, reciprocity, and relationships with people measured by character and integrity.

Although Boethius places rhetoric under philosophy in the hierarchy of the liberal arts, thereby limiting the scope of the study and practice of persuasion. He stands where truth and love are central, thus passing on much of the system of classical, philosophic rhetoric. His perspective influenced many students through the centuries of scholastic education by keeping alive the works of Aristotle and Plato through his translations, commentaries, and original works.

Christine de Pisan

1364-1430 A.D.

In the awakening of the human intellect and the restructuring of societies that we call the Renaissance, one of the early leaders in the rediscovery of classical philosophy and humanistic ideals was Christine de Pisan. "Her stated objective was to offer schooling as the means of achieving honor and virtue through lessons that would demonstrate humility, diligence and moral rectitude" (Golden, Berquist and Coleman, 1997 p. 333).

Raised and educated in the court of France she was trained by her father and court tutors. At age 25 the king, her father, and her husband died leaving her widowed with three small children. De Pisan became one of the first women in the western tradition to be a professional author and teacher. She wrote poetry and prose, designed to influence and teach womanly virtue from a feminine perspective so that women could have meaning outside the home through worthy acts. Many of her fictional heroines performed behind the scenes influencing men by moving them to be more compassionate in dealing with people, logical in dealing with conflict, and maintain integrity in personal relationships.

Among the virtues de Pisan extolled was the control of the tongue. In *The Treasure of the City of Ladies* she speaks about avoiding slander and gossip: "For never was serpent's sting, thrust of sword, or other wound so envenomed or so dangerous as is the tongue of an envious person, for it strikes and often kills both itself and another, and sometimes in both soul and body" (p. 492). Few men had extolled the character of individuals by urging compassion in such harmonic prose. She could captivate the mind, engage the imagination, and quicken the emotions while activating the will to communicate with integrity—an excellent example of classical rhetorical persuasion.

Erasmus

1469-1536 AD

Through the centuries rhetoric again slid back into secondary issues and technical skills. Erasmus, the self-proclaimed "citizen of the world," was a Christian humanist who revived classical perspectives calling people to an eloquence of truth and love. Writing at the beginning of the Renaissance, Erasmus played the midwife in the rebirth of ideas and ideals which lay dormant through neglect and misuse. Because of the many competing philosophies, theologies, and political perspectives that arose during these years; scholasticism began to fade and humanism took a deep root. One of the most dramatic effects of the Renaissance was the art that came through the heart and fingers of Leonardo da Vinci, Raphael, Michelangelo, and even Machiavelli. Also, the invention of the printing press drastically changed the publishing ability of scholars.

Citing the short span of years he spent in different places and his wide-ranging impact on education, Corbett (1971) believes Erasmus was the most influential of the continental rhetoricians during the Renaissance. When a colleague was starting a school in England, Erasmus wrote *De Copia* (abundance) as a rhetorical text. Written in Latin for students whose primary language was English, the effect of the work was largely literary. With Erasmus, rhetoric expanded from oratory to involving all kinds of composition and literature. The educational philosophy of Erasmus led him to add a significant amount of reading for students to learn rhetoric. The young men had to write and re-write constantly in their lessons. As a type of journal students kept a "commonplace" book in which they paraphrased poetry into prose and transformed prose into poetry, stating the same proposition in several different speech styles, providing different lines of argument along side of each other on a single issue, and translating between English, Latin, and Greek.

For Erasmus human reason was not enough to develop truthful content for rhetorical activities; faith must be part of the invention process. Rhetoric took on the epistemic elements of Aristotle and Cicero in the creation of knowledge. Homiliticians and rhetoricians of the late middle ages largely fell into the scholastic habit of quoting accepted authorities for opinions and using them as the evidence for argument. Erasmus encouraged a study of the original sources in the original languages and edited a textually accurate Greek New Testament for use in preaching. Humanism's emphasis on the historical events and accounts became part of the specific knowledge developing aspects of the return of the process of gaining and articulating knowledge to the realm of rhetoric:

> *The speech of man is a magnificent and impressive thing when it surges along like a golden river, with thoughts and words pouring out in rich abundance. Yet the pursuit of speech like this involves considerable risk. As the proverb says, 'Not every man has the means to visit the city of Corinth.' We find that a good many mortal men who make great efforts to achieve this godlike power of speech fall instead into mere glibness, which is both silly and offensive . . . . Such considerations have induced me to put forward some ideas on copia, the abundant style, myself, treating its two aspects of content and expressions, and giving some examples and patterns.* Golden, Berquist and Coleman eds., 1997.

After learning Italian humanism, Erasmus was skeptical of the Neo-Ciceronian *sprezzatura* form of rhetoric that focused on style over content and beauty over effectiveness. Clarity and communication are far more important than high verbosity and courtly jargon so that the ideal persuasive speaker and writer was Cicero's citizen orator speaking out of wisdom.

Although Erasmus' chief addition to the tradition of rhetoric is in the area of style, he does not advocate "overabundant and extravagant expression," but seeks for "beauty with power" through "variety" that "enriches" the content with an "abundance" of subject material.

The style of language interacts within a manner where it is inseparable from content. Significantly different from the dictum, the medium is the message, Erasmus' idea is that the style of rhetoric chosen can add both beauty and power that enriches the content providing abundance. In the current strife for civil rights the beauty and power of nonviolence, marches and coordinated rallies with speeches has given way to reactionary mob activity with sound-bites of demands. Where once persuasive rhetoric moved the nation, now the riots and strife have little to no impact on the attitudes and actions of the people. Re-asserted with beauty and power, the civil rights campaigns of the twenty-first century could gain equality for all.

Ramus

1515-1572 A.D.

Pierre de La Ramee, Peter Ramus, changed the way rhetoric was taught in much of Europe. Isocrates, Cicero and most of the classical rhetoricians taught rhetoric to young men in their late teens. Ramus moved rhetorical training up to the very early teens and in so doing simplified the system of teaching. Through a series of books Ramus attempted to discredit the ancient authorities on rhetoric: "I have a single argument, a single subject matter, that the arts of dialectic and rhetoric have been confused by Aristotle, Cicero, and Quintilian" (Ramus, 1547 trans. Newlands, 1986 p. 79). His *Arguments in Rhetoric against Quintilian* is perhaps the most comprehensive statement of his own perspective. Not just persuasive rhetoric, but the entire discipline could be at stake as a science and limited as an art if Ramus is correct. Because of the danger and the wide-spread acceptance of his logic, Kennedy (1980) believes Ramus is the most influential of the Renaissance rhetoricians.

Quintilian believed that the citizen orator should have his entire character addressed in rhetoric with thinking process, wise content, and outstanding eloquence secondary to the rhetor being a good person possessing "all the virtuous qualities of character." The rhetorical training should come near the end of the person's education since orators demand all the resources of science, math, logic, reading and philosophy. Rhetoric was addressed through the five cannons: invention, arrangement, style, memory, and delivery. The discovery of content happened through "topics" (categories of thought such as definition, classification, and circumstances) and "stasus" (set questions such as who, what, jurisdiction . . .).

Oddly enough, Ramus' methodology is derived from Aristotle as he attempts to apply three of Aristotle's "laws" to the liberal arts. The first is the Law of Truth that indicates principles in any liberal discipline are required to be universally true. Secondly, the Law of Wisdom where principles of any liberal discipline are ordered in generality and particularity. Finally, the Law of Justice, each liberal discipline must keep to its own subject matter (Golden, Berquist, and Coleman, 1997). These laws may be taken out of context and applied in manners other than intended by Aristotle and inappropriate for understanding rhetoric.

The attack on Quintilian begins with the idea that the character of the orator is beyond the limits of the art of rhetoric. Moral philosophy deals with the reality of human virtue and the rightness or wrongness of actions; therefore, the definition that controls Quintilian's thought system is flawed in Ramus' mind. The assumption Ramus makes that the person who participates in an activity is not significant has fundamental problems in that meaning is centered in the person, not the language. The same words spoken by a child, a spouse, a friend, a student, a superior, or a political figure would have a far different impact on the audience. Aristotle's concept of *ethos* is neglected in Ramus' educational reform while it is primary in Quintilian.

The heart of Ramus' teaching on rhetoric is that dialectic is the proper method of invention and arrangement while rhetoric covers the style of language (he largely ignores memory and delivery). In use rhetoric and dialectic "should be united, so that the same oration can expound purely, speak ornately, and express thought wisely. However, the precepts of pure diction, ornate delivery, and intelligent treatment must be kept separate and should not be confused" (p. 86). In keeping with the classical nature of knowledge, dialectic should lead to "the fundament of truth, not the error of custom" (p. 99). Ramus makes another unwarranted assumption creating a false dichotomy, that only dialectic concerns the mind and reason and no other art or science can address that area. He is again wrong in that psychology, neurology, psychiatry, and numerous other disciplines now address the workings of the psyche. In the process of broadening dialectic to cover all of the workings of the brain, Ramus diluted dialectic so the essence of questioning for classification and definition in a search for knowledge was lost. His own complaint that rhetoric and dialectic cannot both cover the mind because they are both arts is countered in that he assigns both grammar and rhetoric to cover "language and speech."

Another interesting attack by Ramus is on the division of persuasive discourse into five parts or cannons. He claims that if such a division is made, then nothing but these may be addressed in the discussion of the activity and that all five must be used in every instance of the activity; therefore, rhetoric cannot be divided into subjects (p. 109f and 118). Again, this is a false reasoning process for a musician does not use all the instruments, all the scales, all the properties of rhythm, all the processes and combinations to form a composition, only those appropriate to the situation. Neither do scientists use all the available analyzing methods or parts of research in each investigation, only those most appropriate to the question or phenomena being studied.

Ramus also does not draw from the scientific side of rhetoric even though he recognizes the reality of it: "I agree with Quintilian's opinion that rhetoric is defined as the science of speaking well, not about this or that, but about all subjects" (p. 109). All of Ramus' arguments are against persuasive rhetoric as an art, not the principles that can be observed, rules that can be formulated, theories that explain, questions that probe or situations to explore in order to make discourse influential.

When art, rhetoric, dialectic, and philosophy are given definitive definitions by setting absolute boundaries around the scope of their consideration, then the systematization of Ramus may make sense. In the process of enacting these artificial limitations, much of the power, many of the processes, and all of the interconnectedness are lost. For the gain of making rhetoric accessible to young children and easy to teach, Ramus confused and eliminated so much of the disciplines of dialectic, rhetoric, philosophy and grammar that they are all weaker for the exercise.

Bacon

1561[5]? -1626 A.D.

Reacting to the misguided educational reform and dismantling of rhetoric brought about by Peter Ramus, Francis Bacon spoke and wrote in a lively political scene.

He served in the House of Commons at a time when real political debates on important issues produced major orations for the first time in

English, and thus in modern, history. The subjects included the religious policy of the court, the privileges of the House of Commons, and the control of finance. Primary rhetoric in general and deliberative oratory in particular are always closely linked to each other, and in Bacon's speeches they appear together after sixteen hundred years of quiescence. (Kennedy, 1980 p. 215-16).

Bacon attempted to fill in the overall gaps in the systematic rhetoric of the classical period. To do this he began, like Ramus, with an educational system based on a psychology of learning.

For Bacon, the mind is divided into the faculties of reason, memory, and imagination. Educationally reason is elucidated through philosophy, memory corresponds to history, and the imagination to *posey*. Appetites and the will motivate people to acquire and act. Bacon defines rhetoric as applying reason to the imagination to move the will. Rhetoric involves intentionality—the rhetor has a purpose and uses persuasive speech to attempt to motivate the audience to exercise their own free will in a direction. Rhetoric involves reason—logical processes in the mind of the speaker should engage the logical processes in the listener. Rhetoric involves imagination—the beauty of style activates the mind and emotions. Knowledge and reason are applied to social concerns in the art of persuasive rhetoric. "Bacon concurs with Zeno's characterization of dialectic as a fist and rhetoric as an open hand—that is, the idea that scientific discourse is a technical treatment of truth, whereas rhetoric links knowledge to social concerns" (Bizzell and Herzberg, 1990 p. 624).

Knowledge is gained through exploration of the topics, but Bacon gives four new "commonplaces." The first is the *colors of good and bad*; degrees of good and evil so that things are not simply black or white in a dichotomy but many shades of meaning within ethics (difference in kinds of lies) with degrees of significance as well (murder is worse than stealing). Careful consideration should be given because often things that appear to be good at first glance turn out to be evil. The second topic is that of *antitheta* or antithesis; here the rhetor contemplates arguments pro and con carefully weighing all the available arguments in order to reach a reasoned conclusion. The third commonplace is formulae; responses that are "already made up" to counter oppositional questions and thinking during dialogue diminishing the impact of the counter.

When one's adversary declares, 'you go from the matter,' you reply: 'But it was to follow you.' When he demands that 'you come to the point,' you answer 'Why, I should not find you there.' If he says, 'You take more

than is for granted,' you retort: 'You grant less than is proved. Golden,
Berquist, and Coleman, 1997, p. 88

The final topic is *apothegms;* memorized pithy statements incorporated into persuasive speeches and responses to counterargumentation. Short quotes, illustrations and proverbs are gained through observation of the world, conversation with intelligent people and study of history and literature.

Bacon's rhetoric can be applied to a current social issue such as genetic engineering of plants and animals for human consumption. Using Bacon's methodology before experimentation begins, people would sit down together and write all the positive arguments in one column (help feed the world, disease resistant strains, higher productivity, better nutrition, less pollution, lower cost with high yield . . .) and all the negative arguments in another column (unknown effects, irreversible effects, interruption of natural processes, experimentation on human subjects without informed consent . . .). Balancing the theses in favor of an argument and against the argument with the evidence that can be gathered from observation and induction produces a reasoned method of deciding a political or social issue.

Reality exists in Bacon's worldview, but humans cannot perceive or reason in an infallible manner. Sense perception is warped, preconceptions keep the mind from comprehension, personal predilections distort understanding, linguistic ambiguities frustrate formulation of the ideas, the complacency of the will hinders the hard work of knowledge, and philosophical systems foster misrepresentations through prejudice. Scientific methodology should be used to bring about an accurate perception of the world as it is through induction using observation and experimentation.

Campbell

1719-1796 A.D.

Born in Aberdeen Scotland, George Campbell was a minister for eleven years, then became principle of Marischal College, and later was professor of divinity at the same school. He wrote *The Philosophy of Rhetoric* (1776) approaching the field from a liberal arts perspective that includes a holistic perspective of people.

According to Campbell, persuasive rhetoric must address all of the mind's faculties in order to influence the audience: the understanding, the imagination, the passions, and the will. Persuasion is a process that passes through the entire human psyche beginning with mental understanding through convincing information spoken with perspicuity and argument. Then the imagination is pleased through the beauty of style thus captivating the mind. Passions become aroused and moved to emotionally support the perspective with *pathos*. And finally the will is persuaded with vehemence. "There is no art whatever that hath so close a connexion [sic] with all the faculties and powers of the mind as eloquence, or the art of speaking . . . . It not only pleases, but by pleasing commands attention, rouses the passions and often at last subdues the most stubborn resolution" (Campbell, 1835 p. 5). Rhetoric to Campbell was interaction between people; therefore, philosophy, psychology, moral reasoning, and logic were significant to the dynamic process of symbolic interaction:

> *In contemplating a human creature, the most natural division of the subject is the common division into soul and body, or into the living principle of perception and of action and that system of material organs by which the other receives information from without and is enabled to exert its powers both for its own benefit and for that of the species. Analogous to this, there are two things in every discourse which principally claim our attention, the sense and the expression; or, in other words, the thought and the symbol by which it is communicated.* (p. 41)

Logic and philosophy form the thought while grammar and elocution form the symbols so that together the process is known as rhetoric.

Campbell begins his discussion focused on the intended impact of persuasive rhetoric:

> *In speaking there is always some end proposed, or some effect which the speaker intends to produce in the hearer. The word eloquence in its greatest latitude denotes 'That art or talent by which the discourse is adapted to its end.' All the ends of speaking are reducible to four; every speech being intended to enlighten the understanding, to please the imagination, to move the passions or to influence the will. Any one discourse admits only one of these ends as the principal.* (p. 11)

The speech should accommodate the style, arrangement and content to the audience and the purpose of the rhetor.

Campbell moves into the second chapter covering the use of humor in eloquence. Placing this in a high position as one of the essentials of rhetorical persuasion is a new twist to the treatment of the subject. Throughout the text the place of humor is recalled for use with grace and dignity.

The primary focus of Campbell's *Philosophy of Rhetoric* is placed on the message. Within his analysis he keeps psychology and philosophy in the forefront of the discussion. Beginning with a Platonic sounding introduction he transfers into an Aristotilian and Baconian perspective of logic and knowledge. "Logical turth consisteth in the conformity of our conceptions to their archetypes in the nature of things. This conformity is perceived by the mind, either immediately on a bare attention to the ideas under review or mediately by a comparison of these with other related ideas. Evidence of the former kind is called intuitive; of the latter, deductive" (p. 44).

Content is derived from and supported by evidence. Mathematical axioms, consciousness, and common sense are intuitive, inductive means of gaining evidence; while deductive evidence being scientific or observational, and moral. Moral reasoning is further divided into experience, analogy, testimony, and calculations of chances (probability). The process of understanding truth is gradual so a rhetor must lead the audience by aid of the memory through steps they are capable of making toward the conclusion. A wise speaker does not acquiesce the truth but gives no more than those listening can contemplate and perceive of the evidence provided. Speakers should also remember that "nothing is more certain, however inconceivable . . . than that the possibility of error attends the most complete demonstration" (p. 65). All evidence should be given with a sense of humility and acknowledgement of those who have provided information for human has a "consciousness of the fallibility of his own faculties."

More than previous authors, Campbell explored the impacts of speech on the emotions and the proper place passions play in public discourse.

> *How is a passion or disposition that is favorable to the design of the orator, to be excited in the hearers? . . . It was already said, in general, that passion must be awakened by communicating lively ideas of the object. The reason will be obvious from the following remarks: A passion is most strongly excited by sensation. The sight of danger, immediate or near, instantly rouseth fear; the feeling of an injury, and the presence of the injurer, in a moment kindle anger. Next to the influence of sense, is that of memory, the effect of which upon passion, if the fact be recent and remembered distinctly and circumstantially, is almost equal. Next to the influence of memory, is that of imagination: by which is here solely meant, the faculty of apprehending what is neither perceived by the senses, nor remembered. Now, as it is the power of which the orator must chiefly avail himself, it is proper to inquire what those circum-*

stances are, which will make the ideas he summons up in the imagina-
tions of his hearers, resemble, in luster and steadiness, those of sensation
and remembrance. (p. 85-86)

Added to the vivid luster of style, Campbell suggests persuasive rhetoricians use probability, plausibility, importance, proximity of time, connection of place, relation of the actors or sufferers to the hearers, and the interest of the audience in the consequences of the subject to call the audience to the appropriate emotion with the best intensity of passion.

In choosing the best style, Campbell suggests taking into consideration the speaker, the audience, the subject, the occasion, and the purpose. With these in view, the rhetor can make an informed decision about how to calm unfavorable passion, and excite a series of emotions leading to the conclusion while engaging the mind in the content of the speech in order to bring about the influence. To have the audience convinced by the truth of the message, that full understanding be accomplished, that the attention be focused throughout the speech, and that the persuasive impact be remembered—in order for lasting persuasion to be accomplished, the emotional nature must be engaged and directed along the path of the speech. The emotion is not to "supplant" reason, but to be a "handmaiden" along the way to securing a favorable reception of the message.

Campbell's rhetoric is unforgiving to mistakes in grammar for the truth should be spoken with "grace and purity that upholds moral virtue," yet "the violation is much more conspicuous than the observance" (p171). He labels grammatical errors as "sins," "blunders," "betrayals," "barbarisms," "offenses," and "heinous faults" which "injure" the audience. Before opening the mouth, the rhetor "ought therefore to be master of the language which he speaks or writes, and to be capable of adding to grammatic purity those higher qualities of elocution which will give grace and energy to discourse" (p. 170).

This backbone of correct grammar is "connected" to rhetoric through the principle of "use." Rhetoric uses language, and if the language is not pure, then the meaning will be obscured. Proper usage is the opposite of linguistic degradation: using *present, national,* and *reputable* words and phrases. Obsolete or totally new words "have no more meaning than foreign words" to an audience so that a vocabulary of the *present* use of grammar for the audience is essential to clear communication. Using the idiom of the country in which the writing or speaking is being done, including pronunciation, will enable understanding is the *national* aspect of grammar. Finally, the *reputable* character of words is that of the generally accepted usage of the words by the educated members of the audience.

Whately

1787-1863 A. D.

Richard Whately educated at Oxford he became a minister, teacher, and ultimately Archbishop in the Church of England. Noting that Campbell and others of his age had neglected Aristotelian logic in their understanding of rhetoric, Whately wrote *Elements of Logic* in 1826 followed by *Elements of Rhetoric* in 1828. He set out to recapture a true understanding of classical rhetoric for use both the church and society.

"What is meant by man's ruling passion? . . . The ruling passion is not a passion in the ordinary sense of the word, but an habitual sentiment fixing the mind . . ." The world-view of individuals controls the communication and influences the audience. "This then should be the first thing looked to in forming a judgment of any character, viz. to see if there be any perceptible ruling passion, what it is, and how far it operates" (1864 p. 1-4). Whately's worldview begins with his religious faith yet includes science, philosophy, and psychology as significant in the development of knowledge and understanding of truth.

Language is not simply the system of symbols used for transferring meaning: it includes more importantly the system of signs used in the reasoning process to produce thought (*Elements of Rhetoric,* 1854 p. 38). Rhetoric, therefore, goes beyond simple communication to logic. Influence is the key to impact so that the key issue of rhetorical eloquence is to determine what the audience will accept as true and persuasive and then use those arguments to convince them. Although the only aspect rhetoric can claim "entirely and exclusively" is the invention and arrangement of argument, the art of rhetoric extends from logic to delivery thus overlapping philosophy and grammar (1854, p. 64).

From here Whately develops the idea of presumption, the figurative ground that represents thinking and perception (the ground) the way they are presently for the audience (1854). The burden of proof lies on the side opposite of the presumption because the audience will not change unless the argument is much stronger in the opposition. To move a listener from presumption the persuader needs a prima facia case in the field of argumentation as well as an understanding of the audience's presumption. The accepted practices in a field or the accepted ideas in an issue are "naturally stronger" in an audience than new or different areas. This natural presumption must be changed for persuasion to take place.

> *For Whately, as for Edmund Burke before him, presumption is a mechanism for acknowledging that arguments cannot be abstracted from a historical context. Any given argument will be responsive to the premises, conclusions, and structural features of previous arguments within an ongoing socially-situated debate. Further, presumption is a mechanism for acknowledging that argumentation is not wholly a conscious and deliberate enterprise. Any rhetorical theory—like any political theory—must leave room for the influence of unconscious and unexamined prejudices, habits, motives and desires* Whedbee, 1998

However, presumption does not necessarily have an advantage because the case will be decided by the audience's evaluation of the evidence. During persuasive communication the presumption can be overcome and the burden of proof can be transferred to the other side. Whatley also differentiates between presumption and deference. An individual with high ethos may have the deference of the audience even though speaking from an opposition viewpoint.

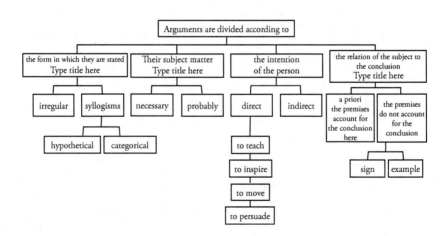

Whately entered into the audience psychology enough to understand that persuasion is not necessarily dependent on a preponderance of evidence and probability but on the side which gains and maintains the presumption in the field of argument. He also noted that presumption may favor an existing institution (characteristics like "innocence," or people who hold an office like "president," or particular "schools"). This can be seen in UN security council meetings where certain delegates carry more weight than others because of the countries they represent. Gaining a hearing from the audience is largely dependent on the ability of the speaker to create a favorable disposition toward his or her ethos (1854 p. 239). This will be accomplished in different ways according to the character of the audience (1854, p. 244).

More than being simply communicative, language is the foundation of reason; therefore, the choice of style and diction can largely determine the impact of the message through the patterns of thought it brings about in the listeners. Beauty and energy can add to the impact on the audience, not only on their thoughts but also on their perception of the *ethos* of the speaker. For example:

> *Metaphors may be employed, as Aristotle observes, either to elevate or to degrade the subject, according to the design of the Author; being drawn from similar or corresponding objects of a higher or lower character. Thus a loud and vehement speaker may be described either as bellowing or as thundering. And in both cases, if the Metaphor is apt and suitable to the purpose designed, it is alike conducive to Energy.* 1854, p. 327 (emphasis Whatley's).

Conscious decisions of style affect the influence of a speaker on the listener. Going against the trend of his day, Whatley said little of delivery and the nonverbal aspects of elocution focusing instead of a logical presentation of truth through language.

Summary

Highlighting a smattering of specific individuals through hundreds of years does not do justice to the rich heritage of rhetorical persuasion. The perspective gained here is one where the nature of philosophical rhetoric in the classical persuasive tradition comes alive through those who sought to become better people and to further others with sound thinking and eloquent speaking. Each one has influenced the theory and practice of persuasive rhetorical education, theory, and practice.

Chapter 6

20th Century Rhetorical Persuasion

That you may preserve discretion,
And that your lips may keep knowledge.
Proverbs 5:2 NKJV

RHETORICAL PERSUASION in the twentieth century has many facets and has asked fascinating questions providing a kaleidoscope of color to the perspective of the art and science of the field. The technology of communication has exploded from printed page and telegraphy through radio, television, the silver screen, and now the internet. Communication theory has broadened to adapt to this burgeoning, chaotic atmosphere of change and expansion. A brief glimpse is all we will gain in this overview of contemporary rhetorical thought. Further insight will be provided in the chapter covering rhetorical theory.

Richards

1893–1979 A.D.

Born in England, Ivor Armstrong Richards studied philosophy at Magdalen College at Cambridge. He did postgraduate work in medicine, psychology, linguistics, anthropology, and philosophy. Then he returned to his Alma Mater where he taught philosophy. Among other texts, he wrote *The Meaning of Meaning* with C. K. Ogden (1923) and *The Philosophy of Rhetoric* (1936).

For I. A. Richards, meaning is a function of interpretation that arises within humans: it does not reside within language. This simple observation was a revolution to rhetoric, philosophy, and linguistics. He mistrusted and avoided the technical rhetoric of the elocutionary movement calling for rhetoricians to "minister successfully to important needs" (1936, p. 3). Richards also disdained the sophistic tendencies of persuasive "sales-talk selling sales-talk" (Griffin 1997 p. 57). Richards calls for the field to return to a philosophic rhetoric that considers good and bad quality, questions foundational assumptions, and serves a central role in the invention of knowledge. He believed rhetoric began with Aristotle and ended with Whatley.

Beginning with an understanding of misunderstandings, the communication discipline should attempt to provide "remedies" to prevent and remove those misunderstandings. Comprehension by the audience becomes the measuring rod of the speaker, with influence and persuasion giving way to understanding as the goal of rhetorical communication. The methodology employed is to understand the role words played in discourse.

Richards conceptualizes language as signs sorted into the events of a context to create meaning. Words are the signs. Sorting into categories of meaning happens in the brain. Contexts are all the events related to the use of the sign. One person may sort the concept "love" into the romance of sunset strolls, long talks by the firelight. Another may sort the concept "love" by the intense joy of sex. Another may sort the concept "love" by hard work for the family and efforts to make the world a better place. Denotative meaning, the dictionary definition of signs, does not exist in communication situations. Meaning comes from within people—connotative meaning that has all the emotional, historical, and environmental baggage attached to the sign. The more shared experiences, similar environments, and similar exposure to things and events, the more likely meaning transferred between two people will be competent.

When my parents took my grandmother to a football game, my mother said, "It's third down." "Down?" my grandmother replied, "Down where?" To her the sign *down* was locative indicating a lower place on the flat surface of a football field, but there seemed to be no place for three levels of "down." In the shared experience of a football game *down* becomes an event, what happens between the snap of the ball and the end of the play (notice the word *snap* is used in the jargon). To make the sign even more confusing, *down* can also refer to the end of the play when the ball or the ball-carrier's leg from the knee to the hip touch the ground ("his knee was down before he fumbled the ball"). And even worse, combined with *touch* the term *down* references a specific manner of scoring ("she ran across the goal line scoring a touchdown"). Of course *down* can be used in the locative manner in football to indicate the place where the play ended ("he was down on the 20 yard line"). When the receiving team does not field a punt, the kicking team has the right to *down* the ball wherever it is on the field ("the end downed the ball on the two yard line"). *Down* is usually the word the quarterback calls out telling the linemen to get in the "set" position and not to move until the snap of the ball ("Down, set, hut one . . . "). Then again, *down* is used to indicate the team that is trailing in score ("the Tigers are down to the Vikings by 7 points"). *Down* refers also to the amount of the game that is completed ("three quarters down and one to go"). When an "underdog" defeats an opposing team the word *down* often refers to the whole game ("the Ducks really put the Irish down today on the gridiron"). When coupled with the word "first," several meanings are possible ("We made a first down" and "It's first down"). Tired of the word yet? Because down has more uses in the game of football such as "down-marker," "down-field," and "down-position." A phrase such as "We need to get this down" can mean several things in football (make a certain number of yards during this play, understand a play, be able to coordinate movement in a play, stop the other team from making a certain number of yards during this play . . .). You may be surprised, sometimes a player may even fall *down* onto the turf, and if he is carrying the ball, he is unquestionably *down*.

Richards is right, meaning is a function of interpretation that arises within people, not language, and is interpreted only in context. The meaning of sign *down* in the environment of a football game still needs a direct or immediate context in order for communicators to share meaning because the term is tremendously ambiguous with a multiplicity of possible meanings. Which one of the many shades of meaning is being referred to in this particular instance? The connection between the word *down* and the many different referents described here is tenuous at best. Virtually any other group of sounds could work equally well to indicate any of the specific meanings. These kinds of observations led Richards and his colleague Ogden to develop the semantic triangle.

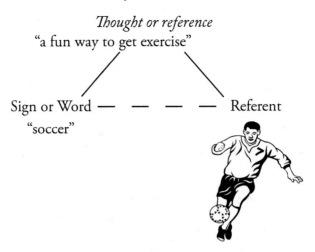

The past experiences of the individuals determine the thought or reference. For someone who has never played soccer and knows little of the rules, the game can be confusing and the *reference* will be far different from someone who plays regularly. The larger the differences in life experience and culture, the greater the opportunity for misunderstanding. The closer the words chosen bring out the thoughts and feelings which they are attempting to convey, the more competent is the attempt at communication. Usage of words does not determine meaning because:

> It takes the senses of an author's words to be things we know before we read him, fixed factors with which he has to build up the meaning of his sentences as a mosaic is put together of discrete independent tesserae. Instead, they are resultants which we arrive at only through the interplay of the interpretative possibilities of the whole utterance. In brief, we have to guess them and we guess much better when we realize we are guessing, and watch out for indications, than when we think we know. (1936, p. 55)

Meaning comes from the thoughts of the communicators through interpretation based on life experience and knowledge. These "comparison fields" of similar words used in similar contexts assist the communicator in deciding which words to use and in how to interpret the words of others.

Richards' perspectives can be systematized from his various writings to explain the functions of discourse. First from the speaker's perspective, there are four functions of language:

1. Sense: Words function to direct the listeners' attention to some state of affairs and to cause them to think about selected events or items.

2. Feeling: Words express feelings or attitudes toward the referent; only in exceptional cases—as in the language of mathematics—is no feeling conveyed through an utterance. Feeling also involves the degree of certainty or confidence the speaker has in the soundness of the statement being made.

3. Tone: Words convey the attitude of the speaker toward the audience. The correct emotion, as well as a sense of the intensity, infiltrates the communication passing on that signification to the audience.

4. Intention: Words express the aim or outcome desired by the speaker or writer—whether this is conscious or unconscious. (Foss, Foss and Trapp 1985 p. 29)

The audience, however, considers seven functions of language in order to determine the meaning in an individual context.

1. Indicating: A message points to or selects which items are to be the focus of attention.

2. Characterizing: The utterance says something about the items on which attention is being focused; it begins to sort from among various characteristics and qualities.

3. Realizing: Realizing concerns the degree and vividness to which the utterance makes the audience sense the particular item; "what is in question is the nearness and fulness [sic] with which something is to be presented to us." This activity deals with the nature of the presentation, whether the subject is presented "vividly or plainly, excitingly or quieteningly, close up or remotely."

4. Valuing: Valuing is the raising of the question, "Should this be so?" Valuing functions to assign a positive or negative value to the item being discussed.

5. Influencing: At issue in this function is whether the audience would like to maintain or change the status quo. Encouraging an audience to change a situation and persuading it to become

adjusted to a set of circumstances are major activities of this function.

6. Controlling: Controlling is the management and administration of the other activities or functions so that they do not interfere too much with one another.

7. Purposing: In this function, the end, aim or intention that is being pursued in the discourse is revealed to the audience. (Foss, Foss, and Trapp 1985 p. 29-30)

These two perspectives of language function are similar to Whately's *use*, much to the dismay of Richards, but he extends that *use* into interpretative spheres.

The primary aspect of Richards "new" rhetoric is the elimination or remedy of misunderstanding. He proposes several different ways to accomplish this ultimate goal: Through Definition. Like a map explaining the starting point of dialogue and an overview of the route or routes used. A few of these different routes to definition are:

1. Symbolization: "That's what I mean by *love*" (while pointing to a couple exchanging wedding vows).

2. Similarity: "As I interpret the word, *love* is like a lifetime commitment."

3. Spatial relations: "I consider *love* to be sexual intercourse, nothing more, nothing less."

4. Temporal relations: "As I see it, individuals can *love* others only after they like themselves."

5. Causation: "I believe *love* inevitably leads to self-sacrifice."

6. Object of a mental state: "*Love* to me is desiring the best for another person."

7. Legal relations: "I judge a couple to be in a state of *love* when they have entered into a joint property agreement." (Griffin, p. 63)

Most definitions will require more than one aspect before understanding can be achieved (Ogden and Richards 1946, p. 123). People will continue to run through these in their subconscious or conscious minds until they come up with an interpretation that will explain to them what an utterance means.

Another way to eliminate misunderstanding is through metaphor: The combining of two referents into one thought yields a greater meaning than is conveyed by either of the thoughts alone. The essence of metaphors is the creation of common experience vicariously. The tenor is the underlying meaning, and the vehicle is the means of conveying the message. When these resonate, the discrepancy in relationship decreases; so does the misunderstanding resulting in "waking up" the meaning (1936, p. 102).

Richards also proposed the idea of feedforward to cut down on misunderstanding. Feedback is the effect the receiver has on the source during and after the communication. Feedforward is the speaker attempting to be the first listener to pretest the impact of the words on the receiver. This is a kind of empathy achieved by a speaker or writer sharing in the thoughts and feelings of the audience. Anticipatory reception enables a sender to modify the message through choices of verbal and nonverbal means (Griffin 1997, p. 65).

Perhaps the best way to eliminate misunderstanding is to use Basic English. Richards worked through several projects with Ogden to simplify English. They selected 850 basic words that can be combined to formulate almost any message. Simplification of vocabulary allows for increased understanding, even if speaking in phrases increases the length of time required for the communication.

Richards stressed interpreting messages through literary context in order to eliminate misunderstanding even further. Words are used in context, not isolation. Like a giant jigsaw puzzle, words, phrases, paragraphs, pictures, sentences are all dependent on one another for determination and transmission of meaning (Foss, Foss and Trapp 1985, p. 36). Clues should be sought out in the functions of language and the evidence surrounding the use such as the attitude and tone.

A speaker's use of language can and will be misunderstood by the audience; therefore, both the speaker and listener need to take on the responsibility for a clear transmission of meaning.

Weaver

1910–1963

Born and raised in the United States, Richard Weaver was a man of his time and place. His undergraduate training at the University of Kentucky led him to join the Socialist party. While in graduate school at Vanderbilt University he rejected the "philistine" culture and joined the conservative Southern Agrarian movement. This complete reversal of values and thought led him to understand two sides of many issues. As a prodigious author he wrote many books and articles; we will consider most closely *Ideas have Consequences* (1948), *The Ethics of Rhetoric* (1953), and a lecture "Language is Sermonic" (1963).

Conceptualizing communication through the narrative paradigm, Richard Weaver illumines specific aspects of persuasive argumentation. Weaver developed his approach through considering the ethical implications and processes in speech experienced through story. According to his way of thinking, most people hear dialogue as part of a narrative.

Weaver's perspective begins with his understanding of the *human nature* as tripartite: body, mind, and soul. For Weaver this was a theologically informed, but not theologically determined idea. The physical is not merely a house for the spiritual aspects of thinking and feeling, it has a self-centered power to tempt people into satisfactions of sensual pleasure. The body focuses the person on enticements of anticipated fulfilled lust.

The mind involves the emotional or aesthetic elements allowing beauty, pleasure, or pain to be experienced. A second aspect of the mind is the capacity to make ethical judgments of right and wrong, good and bad. The mind thirdly has a religious aspect where values, destiny and ultimate questions are addressed. Finally the mind has rational capacities that allow logical analysis, critical thinking, and ordered ideas.

The third part of a human is the soul or spirit. As an integrative power, the spirit guides the body and mind toward what is good and right. It sorts values and directs actions in a manner that reflects significant insight. This is also the part of the human that can and does communicate with God.

Weaver's *epistemology* divides the nature of knowledge and truth into three levels of "knowable" phenomena: The first level is thought and observation about specific things. Sense data, statistical representation, experiential skills, what we know from books, classrooms and jobs. The second level of knowledge and truth is that of beliefs and worldviews. These generalizations provide the foundation for judgments, preferences and standards by which we evaluate all other knowledge. The third level of knowledge is a "metaphysical dream." This idealistic view of the way things ought to be is an intuitive understanding about the nature of reality. This level gives significance and meaning to the first two levels of knowing.

Human culture influences people most in the highest area of thinking: the metaphysical dream. At the center of every culture is an authority, called the "tyrannizing image" that attempts to dictate and determine the individual's idealistic dream. Conflicts occur between the way things are and they way they ought to be, so humans attempt to reason why and attempt to reconcile their reality to their dream.

Language is the process through which we understand our own metaphysical dream and convey it to others within the culture. Although language cannot fully express truth, it can, through dialectic and rhetoric, competently communicate enough meaning to be understandable.

On the title page of Weaver's book, *The Ethics of Rhetoric,* he quotes Aristotle, "Thus it happens that rhetoric is an offshoot of dialectic and also of ethical studies." This simple phrase energized the life work and teaching of Richard Weaver. Many have debated the first part of the sentence and attempted to define and categorize dialectic and rhetoric. Few have undertaken the second part of Aristotle's idea and focused significant energy on ethics and rhetoric. Combining the three ideas of dialectic, rhetoric, and ethics is a monumental task that adds completeness to the communication of knowledge.

Dialectic, to Weaver, is deductive reasoning about abstract, ambiguous, or doubtful propositions to discover knowledge about definitions or essences and principles. The foundational focus on the essence or nature of ideas and things is neo-Platonic. Logical thought is the "plot" of rhetoric but is not enough to move an audience to change. Dialectic needs emotionality, aesthetic satisfaction, and a yearning for relationship with the infinite to encounter the whole human, these come from rhetoric as applied through ethics. Persuasive rhetoric that is ethical has a heart of logical, truthful content. The inventive process should be guided by ethical principles in order to discover the most appropriate message to send.

Topics are the places where arguments are found for dialogue in rhetoric. Weaver categorizes these broadly into four areas that form a hierarchy of what is most convincing to what is least persuasive. The first and most important is that of definition: to capture the essence of the subject—fundamental and unchanging properties of the issue or thing. The second topic is placing it in cause-and-effect relationships with other elements or issues. Determination whether or not the thing causes other things to act or react is significant in understanding the issue. The third topic is in terms of relationships of similarity and dissimilarity to other issues or things. Comparison and contrast, in likeness and example, establish probabilities and can be persuasive. The last topic is that of external testimony or authority based on the credibility of others (Language is Sermonic: Bizzell p. 1047). These topics do not form a set of formal rules or devices guaranteeing success of a persuasive appeal but need to be *adapted virtuously* to the audience. The priority of definition creates a "vision" of the issue ideally (through dialectic) and virtuously (through ethics), then through rhetoric specific consideration adjusts the material to the special circumstances of the audience.

Rhetoric is, therefore, an "art of emphasis" where the rhetor chooses which of the topics best conforms to the receptivity of the audience. Presentation of the most compelling evidence for the audience will be most likely to energize and enlarge the audience. Clear, compelling presentation is accomplished through a style that actualizes and visualizes the description in the "mind's eye" of the audience so that it is vivid and living. The choices made by the persuader in a communicative process are ethical because they can be right or wrong, good or bad. The choices extend beyond dialectic and topics into the organizational process determining the specific information to be sent.

The problem extends through invention and organization into style as misunderstanding and unethical communicative behavior can take advantage of the audience. Excess of imagery, evoking senses and emotions, puffing up the significance of arguments, distorting evidence, all kinds of rhetorical excess and deception can tempt the rhetor to move the audience through personal power toward a biased end. Weaver says, "Common sense replies that any individual who advises a friend or speaks up in a meeting is exercising a kind of leadership, which may be justified by superior virtue, knowledge, or personal insight" (p. 1052). The responsibility then, is to speak ethically, moving the audience toward virtue.

"Ever since I first heard the idea mentioned seriously it impressed me as impossible and even ridiculous that the utterances of men could be neutral" (p. 1052). Expression cannot be purged of emotion and direction; language itself is reflective of the human potential in areas other than dialectic. "The condition essential to see is that every use of speech, oral and written, exhibits an attitude, and an attitude implies an act" (p. 1052). What a speaker chooses to say, the amount that is said, the audiences to whom it is said, the style of intonation in delivery, and the elaboration of word choices all demand an ethical decision. Most importantly and of greatest import

153

is the motive of the rhetor. Here the responsibility of the communicators becomes most evident.

The ethics of rhetorical expression include the delivery of the message. "Linguistic expression is a carrier of tendency" so that the one who intones a message has some sort of purpose. Whether a simple sound of exuberance or a formal composition, that goal or orientation will direct the audience persuasively. "We have no sooner uttered words than we have given impulse to other people to look at the world, or some small part of it, in our way" (p. 1054).

> That is why I must agree with Quintilian that the true orator is the good man, skilled in speaking—good in his formed character and right in his ethical philosophy. When to this he adds fertility in invention and skill in the arts of language, he is entitled to that leadership which tradition accords him. (p. 1054)

The impact on the audience is a primary concern in the ethical communication of Weaver. The values of the rhetor as revealed in the communicative process can lead to a good or bad influence.

> Rhetoric must be viewed formally as operating at that point where literature and politics meet, or where literary values and political urgencies can be brought together. The rhetorician makes use of the moving power of literary presentation to induce in his hearers an attitude or decision which is political in the very broadest sense. . . . Finally, we must never lose sight of the order of values as the ultimate sanction of rhetoric. No one can live a life of direction and purpose without some scheme of values. As rhetoric confronts us with choices involving values, the rhetorician is a preacher to us, noble if he tries to direct our passion toward noble ends and base if he uses our passion to confuse and degrade us. Since all utterance influences us in one or the other of these directions, it is important that the direction be the right one, and it is better if this lay preacher is a master of his art. (p. 1054)

An individual's rhetorical choices embody the person's worldview and value system and even the word choices made in selection of argument and style.

Rhetoric is the solution. Rhetorical language moves beyond the metaphysical demonstration to relationship with the real world. Although being absolutely objective is impossible, rhetoric communicates between two real people in a real situation and thus can move people toward an ideal uniting understanding with action. Persuasive rhetoric is ideally ethical—it moves individuals to think, value and act in a manner reflecting the good metaphysical dream. Language is *sermonic* in that it categorizes the world into dialectical perspectives and then rhetorically influences the audience toward the metaphysical ideal.

Perelman and Olbrechts-Tyteca

1912-1984 A. D. Perelman

1899-1989 A.D. Olbrechts-Tyteca

Born in Warsaw, Chaim Perelman earned a law degree and then a doctorate in Philosophy at the Free University in Brussels, Belgium. During World War II he was active in the resistance movement and afterwards joined the faculty at his Alma Mater. Perelman was joined by Olbrechts-Tyteca in a search for logical argumentation that can be communicated persuasively which led them to re-discover classical rhetoric.

Chaim Perelman and Lucie Olbrechts-Tyteca attempt to uncover how people reason about and make judgments or decisions based on values. Analyzing and synthesizing real value thinking led the researchers back to Aristotle and the topics along with dialectical reasoning. The slide of rhetoric into secondary issues, especially that of style in writing and speaking was so complete in European studies that Perelman and Olbrechts-Tyteca were unaware of the discipline of speech as taught in American universities. In their book, *The New Rhetoric,* they called for a rebirth of rhetoric with a proper emphasis on rationality. Readers then pointed them to the rich heritage they had missed.

Communication pictures reality as perceived and reasoned. Human senses can be mistaken; therefore, those who reason about values and form judgments need to conceptualize clearly and then test the appearance by a worldview and any objective measures available before communicating.

> Normally, reality is perceived through appearances that are taken as signs referring to it. When, however, appearances are incompatible—an oar in water looks broken but feels straight to the touch—it must be admitted, if one is to have a coherent picture of reality, that some appearances are illusory and may lead to error regarding the real. Because the status of appearance is equivocal, one is forced

to distinguish between those appearances that correspond with reality and those that are only illusory. The distinction will depend on a conception of reality that can serve as a criterion for judging appearances. Whatever is comfortable to this conception of the real will be given value; whatever is opposed to it will be denied value . . . . Every ontology, or theory about the nature of being, makes use of this philosophical process that gives value to certain aspects of reality and denies it to others according to dissociations that it justifies by developing a particular conception of reality. Perelman and Olbrechts-Tyteca p. 894

Factual truth does not speak for itself but is interpreted and reconstructed by the audience through language and communicated through rhetoric, which produces a persuasive impact on the audience. They place more emphasis on the audience's responsibility in rhetoric than previous rhetoricians.

Often decisions about values are made prior to considering all of the information so that a strong sense of conclusion precedes reasoning rather than follows it. A "sense of the world" generates a decision with "incommunicable intuition" and the dialectic reasoning follows the preformulated outcome.

It is a common . . . occurrence even for a magistrate who knows the law to formulate his judgment in two steps: the conclusions are first inspired by what conforms most closely with his sense of justice, the technical motivation being added on later. . . . Strictly legal reasons are adduced only for the purpose of justifying the decision to another audience. . . . Fresh arguments brought in after the decision, may consist of the insertion of the conclusion into a technical framework.(p. 43)

Formal logic is a closed system of deduction or induction, but the practical reasoning of life happens through informal dialectical logic and is processed rhetorically. The formal logic belongs to the sphere of philosophy, and even though Peter Ramus attempted to place dialectical processes within the realm of philosophy, this did not work because philosophers attempt to achieve certain truth instead of dealing with probability, character, and ethics in problem solving and decision-making. Rhetorical method attempts to persuade with what is likely, beyond reasonable doubt, and accurate, but does not focus on absolute truth as a necessity before communicating.

Argumentation in the public sphere develops informally. Syllogistic patterns do not stipulate the content of political debate, scientific observations do not formulate the substance of sibling rivalry, and mathematical precision does not constitute the subject matter of editorial pages. Intuitive thinking based on unstated warrants and unwritten assumptions can be stronger and more persuasive than propositional logic, whether inductive or deductive.

Kenneth Burke

1897–1993 A.D.

Born in Pittsburgh, Burke attended Ohio State and Columbia Universities and began writing from Greenwich Village for *The Dial*, an avant-garde magazine. Later he taught at the New School for Social Research and then at Bennington College. He was politically attached to the Communist Party but never joined. He wrote many books and articles, here we will delve into *Counter-Statement* (1931) and *A Rhetoric of Motives* (1950) as well as drawing from some of his other writings.

Kenneth Burke understood life as drama, not *like* drama, not *dramatic* in character, but life *is* drama. He never earned a bachelors, masters, or Ph.D. but he taught at Harvard, Princeton, and the University of Chicago—all *acts* of communication or parts of the drama of life. We will consider his concepts of language as motivation, people in identification, the dramatistic pentad, and the guilt-redemption cycle.

Language motivation is the foundation of acts of communication within the drama of life. Communication is an intentional choice that humans make. In *The Rhetoric of Motives* (1950) he characterizes rhetorical communication as the use of language to form attitudes and influence action. Within the complexity of human experience, persuasive rhetoric is a spiritual event.

> *Persuasion is spiritual, in contrast with the producing of change by purely material agencies. For if it is bodily to move a man from here to there by pushing him, then by antithesis it is spiritual to produce the same movement in pleading, "Come hither." (p. 177)*

People are motivated through rhetorical persuasion. Change for the better, whether it is an action or attitude happens as people communicate.

> *And finally let us observe, all about us, forever goading us, though it be in fragments, the motive that attains its ultimate identification in the*

thought, not of the universal holocaust, but of the universal order—as with the rhetorical and dialectic symmetry of the Aristotelian metaphysics, whereby all classes of beings are hierarchally arranged in a chain or ladder or pyramid of mounting worth, each kind striving towards the perfection of its kind, and so towards the kind next above it, while the strivings of the entire series head in God as the beloved cynosure and sinecure, the end of all desire. (p. 333)

Rhetorical forms are thus understood by their impacts on the readers. Each communication forming acts in the drama of life.

He considers clusters of words as dances of attitudes. According to Burke, the critic's job is to figure out why a writer or speaker selected the words that were choreographed into the message. The task is ultimately one of assessing motives. Griffin, 2005, p. 313

Burke also emphasized *identification*. Literature and all other forms of communication should be understood as rhetorical acts in which the *substance* of individuals enters a relationship of meaning with others. The degree of overlap between the worldview, personality, talents, character traits, occupation, and environment of a speaker and a listener enables identification.

For Burke, persuasion focuses on the deliberative design of language, while identification includes unconscious and nonverbal aspects of communication acts. He called this *consubstantiation*, the sharing of substance between people as an act in the drama of life. Identification works both ways—for the audience to adapt to the speaker and the speaker to align with the audience. A complete identification is not possible even when another's perceptions are perfectly aligned with one's own.

The dramatistic pentad is the heart of Burke's understanding of rhetorical communication. As a critical method it gives insight into literature, speeches, newspaper articles, or conversations over tea. Virtually any written or oral use of human symbolic activity can be enlightened through pentadic analysis.

The Act is the first part of the pentad. The use of language to communicate as a part of the drama of life as experienced by the people is an act. Analogous to an act in a play, this is the process of communicative behavior.

The Scene is the context in which the act takes place. Circumstances have contributing factors that influence rhetors in a manner that enhance and detract from motivations in the use of language.

The Agent is the person who is performing the communicative act. The actors are considered individually before paired in the process of identification when using pentadic dramatism so that a fuller picture can be gained of their self, spirit, and personal responsibility in the process of communication.

The Agency is the means or techniques the agent uses to communicate within the scene. The message strategies coupled with nonverbal aspects give a complete picture of the communicative act.

The Purpose is the goal of the agent in initiating the act of communication. The purpose is similar to the motivation, but is the intentional or surface goal, while the motivation is the underlying aspect often based on human need, desires, and ultimate directions.

Later, Burke added the concept of attitude to his Pentad. The emotional-psychological approach of rhetors as well as the characters in the drama make a significant difference in understanding a rhetorical situation.

When a critic evaluates the ratio of importance between the different pairs of the pentad, a picture of the rhetorical motivation of the rhetor appears. We can evaluate why a speaker selected a given rhetorical strategy to persuade or identify with the listener through the interactions between these elements.

A final aspect of Burke's thinking will focus on the guilt-redemption cycle that he calls the root of all rhetoric. Immediate goals and purposes, motivating initiation of communicative acts such as public speaking or writing of literature are all underlain with the ultimate, ever-present sense of guilt. The human condition is a form of spiritual-psychological tension, anxiety, shame, disgust with self, embarrassment, and a host of other emotions and attitudes of strain called guilt.

The words of language are not simple tools of communication; they are "tools to make tools." Using words articulates motivations that create meaning in an effort to make ordered harmony from the guilt.

The cycle begins with order or hierarchy that has negative impacts resulting in "victimage." Thus, redemption comes as people, uniting through victimization toward a common enemy, act by symbolizing. We attempt to purge guilt from our lives through acts of communication, but this gives only a temporary relief because as power is used in creating order, guilt returns to plague the human condition.

Burke provides several interwoven frameworks from which we can understand rhetorical phenomena and the people who are involved. From this, he gives us insight into ourselves and into the mystery of life. I wonder how his theories would change if he could grasp forgiveness and love in their fullness.

Walter Fisher

As a professor of at the University of Southern California's Annenberg School of Communication, Walter Fisher believes rhetoric is more than a mathematical formula of adding evidence, reason, and logic together with style and delivery to equal successful transfer of meaning. Instead, he explores the more mysterious aspects of the synthetic whole and calls it *story*. His Ph.D. is from Iowa and he wrote *Human Communication as Narration* in 1987.

Rhetoric is not simply constative (saying something) but it is also performative (doing something): and that something is story. Understanding human communication from the perspective of narrative, Kenneth Burke understood rhetoric from the perspective that life is drama. Fisher takes a long step beyond to say that communication is best understood in context of narrative. He is searching for practical wisdom or the classical idea of *phronesis* as a way of addressing nonscientific questions, problems, and phenomena (Herrick, 1997). *Stories persuade us, move us to action, and form the foundation for our beliefs and actions.* The narrative paradigm provides us with a comprehensive explanation of public symbolic messages; i.e. all public language use can be explained through story.

People are basically storytellers, or, to use Fisher's phrase, "storytelling animals." Yes, humans have rational capabilities, but we think in terms of examples. The world is experienced through a set of interwoven stories. Individuals have the choice between narratives and thus have the ability to continually re-create their lives.

As opposed to the rational paradigm, narrative thinking says that people make decisions based on "good reasons" rather than "sound argument." Good reasons for making a decision are determined by people's awareness of the stories of history, biography, culture and character. We live, are influenced, and decide through narrative.

For Fisher, narrative is any "account," whether verbal or nonverbal, with a sequence of events to which a speaker or listener assigns a meaning. A narrative is symbolic action—something people do through language. For him, all communication is narrative with valuing and reasoning whether discursive or nondiscursive, linear, or nonlinear.

Standing at the crossroads of the literary, aesthetic elements of rhetoric and the rational, persuasive argument; narration creates a "dialectical synthesis." Human communication can be both rational and aesthetic when it is story. The "ground for determining meaning, validity, reason, rationality, and truth must be a narrative context: history, culture, biography, and character" (1999). Likewise, the base of aesthetically pleasing literature, poetry, and mass media is also narration.

Hebrew is a storytelling language. Judaism is built upon the stories of the Patriarchs and what happened to their people in the following centuries. The religion, culture, and national life of the people is narrative. Christian theology is built upon stories. Jesus' primary teaching method was to tell stories. They both reveal the message and conceal other meanings. The propositions of Paul are founded in the history of the Old Testament. Hauerwas (1981) stated, "The social significance of the Gospel requires recognition of the narrative structure of Christian convictions for the life of the church" (p. 9).

Narrative rationality provides the methodology for understanding communication as story. Evaluating the coherence and fidelity of the narrative will enable insight into the speech or literature.

Coherence is the internal consistency of the narrative. If an imaginary land is based on magic, then events happening through extranatural means would be considered normal. If the story is religious and God acts in or through natural or supernatural means, then the story would be consistent. This internal consistence is the major aspect of narrative acceptance or rejection. *Structural coherence* is the degree to which the elements of the story flow smoothly in the form of plot and character. *Material coherence* is the degree to which one story is congruent with other stories of the same genre. *Characterological coherence* is the degree to which the characters are believable and consistent within their type.

Fidelity is the truthfulness or reliability of the story. Fisher proposes the "logic of good reasons" as the method of measuring fidelity. People ask two series of five questions to evaluate the narrative. The first set is to assess the logic of the story:

1. Are the statements that claim to be factual in the narrative really factual?

2. Have any relevant facts been omitted from the narrative or distorted in its telling?

3. What are the patterns of reasoning that exist in the narrative?

4. How relevant are the arguments in the story to any decision the listener may make?

5. How well does the narrative address the important and significant issues of this case?

If the logic is accepted as sound, the second set of questions transform the logic into *good* reasons through value evaluation:

1. What are the implicit and explicit values contained in the narrative?

2. Are the values appropriate to the decision that is relevant to the narrative?

3. What would be the effects of adhering to the values embedded in the narrative?

4. Are the values confirmed or validated in lived experience?

5. Are the values of the narrative the basis for ideal human conduct?

(West and Turner, 2000, p. 297-298)

Narrative communication provides a foundation for persuasion and is an excellent mode of discourse that influences people of all ages. Businesses understand the value of story and are transforming much of their internal and external messages into narrative form. Pastors are telling more and more narrative messages as the bulk of a sermon rather than as a short illustration. Politicians are using more stories and less statistical and rational argument. The productions of mass media are primarily stories told through mediated channels. Journalists are focused more on the story and sprinkling information through the narrative. People are story-telling at our very nature and persuasive communicators should understand, honor and master the art.

Conclusion

Considering these few thinkers throughout time, from classical Greece to the present day provides a background from which we can explore the depths and breadth of public communication. They provide a significant foundation for understanding and practicing public communication. Each one is a product of their time and those who came before them. Each one adds a unique perspective to public rhetoric. Each one should be valued for their contributions. Keep in mind that this brief survey does not include many great men and women who have significantly influenced the way we think about language and communication today.

Part III

Theoretical Considerations

ENVISIONING PUBLIC rhetoric enables the rhetor to intentionally develop and deliver truth in an effective manner. Theory pictures communication in different ways so that various aspects are drawn out in a way that enables better rhetoric. Forming the "product" of communication that consistently and effectively influences audiences in the desired manner arises out of application of persuasive theory and artistically applying valid forms of a message.

Audience adaptation is a skill of forming the message into whole that will properly impact the particular audience in an appropriate manner. Not simply the immediate people will receive the content but also a universal audience. For the Christian, God is also part of the audience.

Rhetorical theories enable different understandings of communication. No individual theory is adequate to explain all of communication phenomena, however, together they are useful in that they encourage flexible thinking and adaptation to different situations, contexts, and audiences.

Argumentation builds propositions that can be discussed in a dialogue or a debate. A message becomes a full case through coupling ideas with evidence forming a conceptual unit.

Logical reasoning links propositions with conclusions in a manner that audiences can comprehend. Logic is rigorous thinking about the message.

Logical fallacies are ways that rhetors and audiences think about arguments in ways that are illogical. These are misleading approaches that should be avoided in our own thinking and countered in those who have propositions that are opposed to our position.

Supporting evidence is the key to people accepting what we have said. Even those who say they believe in the subjective nature of truth and reality will only accept facts, examples, and statistics that accurately represent the truth.

Cokesbury ASKY 36900

300 N. LEXINGTON AVENUE
WILMORE, KY 40390
02/19/09   10:40   F   11   2705

Customer Account Record # 0027224328
Charge to Account # FB05473

FISK ELLEY
204 N LEXINGTON AVE
SPO 331
WILMORE, KY 40390-1129
Telephone # (859) 802-8287

ORDERED BY ELLEY

    1@ 35.00 9781556351181 %0%   35.00*
                   SPEAKING THE TRUTH IN LO
SUBTOTAL $ 35.00
TAX   @ 6.0000% $ 0.00
TOTAL $ 35.00
TENDERED Charge 0027224328 $ 35.00

         This is your invoice.
Please retain to match w/your statement.

X---

         WE APPRECIATE YOUR BUSINESS!
USED/CLEARANCE ITEMS MAY NOT BE RETURNED

Chapter 7

Understanding Your Audience

And He said to me: "Son of man, go to the [audience]
And speak my words to them . . . . But the [audience]
Will not listen to you, because they will not listen to me. "
Ezekiel 3:4-7 NKJV

A T LEAST since the time of Aristotle, taking the audience into consideration before giving a message has been a significant aspect of effective
communication. Adapting a message to an audience does not imply being
double minded, speaking with a *forked tongue*, or *waffling*. Taking one position with one audience and another position with another audience is an
unethical spinning of your message in a manner that manipulates instead
of persuades. Generally speaking, the more you know the audience, the
greater impact your communication may have.

Once when I was giving a speech to an audience that contained a large
number of grass-seed farmers, I lumped unwanted grass in my yard into the
category of *crabgrass* in an illustration. While this would be perfectly per-
missible with suburban professionals, my credibility suffered a significant
blow with that audience—even though it was not a major point, only an
illustration. I lost the persuasive impact on the topic because of my insen-
sitivity to the audience's expertise. After the speech several of the farmers
straightened me out on the one word—no one even mentioned the topic
of the speech.

Writing a feature article for a small town newspaper is far different
from writing about the same subject for the *New York Times*. One has a
neighborly feel with a primary emphasis on relationship—like discussing
the issue over breakfast on the back porch. The other has an information

167

emphasis—like trying to enable the audience to enrich their lives through knowledge. Both of these are different from giving the same message in a public speech or through a radio talk show. The medium needs to match the message through the style and the communicator in the experience of the audience.

Who is the auditor (reader or listener)?

Getting to know whom you are communicating with is essential for the public rhetor. Get out among people, talk with them, listen to them, find out what is important to them. When giving a speech to an audience I don't know, I often go out before the speech, listen to the words the audience uses among themselves and use some of those same words—as long as they are mine. When talking with teenagers, I do not adapt to their slang because they can smell it as a manipulative attempt to be hip. As a white pastor of an African-American church, I had to be especially careful about the use of Ebonics in preaching. A word or two may relate, but any more than that and I would loose credibility in the message because of the artificiality of my using Ebonics when they knew it was not natural for me. I may ask for a definition of a word and then quote the person who gave it to me so that they know I am listening to them a care about them and their communication. Authentic interest, when an audience understands the rhetor is truly valuing and accepting them, enables a greater capacity for the audience to listen to a message.

Writing a syndicated newspaper column and radio commentary for seven years, I would go out among the readers and listeners and drink coffee with them, ask for their stories, and listen to their heartaches. I could then identify with the readers and take to heart what real people thought about what I was writing. The more I knew them, the more I could identify with them, and the more impact I had on their thinking and lives.

At several stages in preparing to write or speak to an audience, I usually step back from my work and think about individual people who are likely to be the recipients of the words. If I do not know anyone in the particular audience, I give it the Joya-Steve test. Joya was a vibrant young girl who caught a disease that left her partially paralyzed and mentally disabled. Will what I have to say keep her interested through the speech or article? How can I re-grasp her attention with each point. Steve was a brilliant young man who could tear apart arguments and search out the truth. Will my evidence be strong enough to convince him? We all know individuals whose personalities and abilities embody the characteristics of audiences we want to reach with our message. Choose several from different perspectives and keep them in mind when choosing evidence, molding stories, or enlivening the style.

Public communication establishes and maintains relationships between the rhetor and the audience. As such, we need to carefully consider many ways in which our communication affects that relationship. Also, many people will judge us as writers or speakers based on the words we use to convey our ideas. What people already know and believe will largely determine their reaction to what we have to say. Because feedback is often at a minimum in public communication the author and speaker have to carefully consider the audience prior to the communication. In short, we have to relate the communication to them and help them care about the message.

Socio-cultural Background

This category includes race and/or ethnicity. Diversity at its best recognizes the differences between people and leads us to accept others. At its worst, discriminatory diversity divides people into *other* categories where tolerance is granted as long as separation is maintained. Good public communicators will accept as equal all people in the audience respecting and valuing them. Geographic location is another part of socio-cultural background: from which country, state, province, city, neighborhood, or home: both where the audience lives now back to where they grew up. In some places a person who grew up on the *wrong side of the tracks* will never be accepted, no matter how long they are part of a group. Speaking to native American Indians who grew up on a reservation is different than speaking to African Americans who grew up as sharecroppers on a plantation and these are still different from speaking to Redneck, Hillbilly White Trash. None of these will be like speaking to those who have grown up in extreme affluence, no matter what ethnicity. Income is therefore a significant part of the socio-cultural scene.

Demographic Audience Differences

As a football coach I can send chills down any teenager's back making him want to run faster, jump higher, hit harder with the little phrase, "Way to go big boy." Slight alterations make it even more effective such as substituting "fella" for "boy" or "that's the" added as a suffix. Sometimes a guttural grunt will augment the impact. Even professional football players respond to that little phrase. Simple praise is a primary motivating skill that works better than most other communication tools.

When my wife could not finish the last couple games coaching a Jr. High girls basketball team I substituted for her—even though I knew nothing about basketball or Jr. High girls. My first game on the bench was getting toward the end of the fourth quarter; we set up a play, and our star hit a 3 point shot to put us up by one, and I yelled at the top of my voice the phrase I used to motivate the guys; "Way to go big girl!" Chills didn't go down her back. She didn't run faster or shoot straighter. In fact, the celebration stopped. The whole gym stopped. Both teams, both refs, and the entire audience turned and stared at me. The ball rolled out of bounds untouched—because demographics make a significant difference in public communication.

Gender

In spite of everything we were told in the '70s, males and females are different; not just physically, but in the ways we think, in our perceptions, in our social interactions, in our relationships—in most ways we are different. Girls do not respond the same way to the same words as boys do. Sometimes gender discrimination does not make sense. When males who get breast cancer have less of a voice or help from society than females we have no logical explanation. When a woman astronaut becomes commander of a shuttle mission, it becomes news, simply because she is a woman, that makes no logical sense. People are equal whether male or female, but we are different. "Big girl" attached to any phrase will not motivate a middle school female to do anything. The words and illustrations used to impact a group of women will not be the same as those that captivate and move a similar group of men.

Age

Aristotle noticed that age level was one of the most important determiners of what to consider when forming a public communication. Today's college students know Pearl Harbor, not from behind gun sites like my father, but from the pages of a history book and a camera lens. They have heard of Watergate, but few know the hotel or have read below the headlines to understand the drama as it was slowly revealed. The attack on 9/11 they know and have lived, but not Mai Lai, the Tet offensive, Normandy, or Korea. What makes us who we are is, to a significant measure, the culture and events of our lifetime. Take time to talk with those in the audience who knew the depression before you speak of finances. Listen to the stories of WWII veterans in the audience before you proclaim a stance against the Iraq war. Understanding good and evil, aesthetic beauty, or success from the perspective of the audience is necessary prior to writing or speaking in order for the impact to move them in the desired direction. Not all young people are radicals, nor are all the elderly wise.

My grandmother used to like asking young people what modern appliance they would want the most in the kitchen. Replies usually included the refrigerator or a microwave. If they were astute enough to ask her, she would always reply, "a sink with running water." Few ever think of things like a sink being an appliance or running water as being modern. She had lived with outhouses and a hand-pump well. She learned to cook in a home without electricity. She knew what it was like to grow and clean everything that went into Sunday dinner from the chicken to the mashed potatoes. We simply drive to the store and buy what we want; others do the real work of preparing a meal. These life experiences are woven into the demographic "age," and a public communicator is wise to recognize the different life experiences from our microwave generation.

Education level

My grandfather went to public school through third grade, yet he was one of the most educated men I have ever known. He read voraciously from newspapers and magazines, listened to the radio, and paid attention to all the speeches he could hear. Few things moved him indoors, but he was often glued to the nightly news. Knowledge may come through self-education, not simply from a classroom. A thirst for knowledge is the foundation of education, and people often become self-educated.

Generally speaking, those with a greater education level will have a larger vocabulary, understand disciplinary thinking, be capable of handling philosophical ideas, and have an easier time of thinking abstractly. A liberal arts education will enable an audience to learn quickly in a large variety of fields, issues, and ways. Public speaking researchers have discovered a strong correlation between prior knowledge of a topic and the ability of an audience to think through a speech. The same is true of those reading a newspaper or magazine article. Technical writing has to gage very accurately the ability to the audience to understand a given topic from "How To" manuals to journal articles.

Group affiliation

If you are speaking to a mixed group of NOW (National Organization for Women) and Dittoheads (those who listen to Rush Limbaugh and agree with him) on the subject of abortion—you better know it before you walk to the front of the room. If you are unaware and do not plan carefully half the room will be angry from your first sentence. Not all Muslims radically want to murder others, not all Christians are evangelical, not all Republicans support tax cuts, nor do all college professors register Democrat. Be careful of stereotyping people according to others in the group—but be ready to generalize and adjust your message. People who are members of a group tend to understand specific words, know many of the same stories, and have similar interests. Do not write off all fundamentalists as poor, ignorant, and unthinking. Do not write off all liberals as impractical, unethical, and thoughtless.

Religious affiliation often forms communities of faith where a strong sense of identity keeps people close together. Christianity, which is more of a relationship than a religion, fits within this category. Like-minded people share together in their spiritual lives in a manner that influences how they will read or listen to your message. Muslims, Jews, Mormons, and Jehovah's Witnesses will be in your audiences. Hindus, Sikhs, and Buddhists also read and listen. In our diverse society we need to keep in mind the associations and affiliations of our audiences with grace and understanding.

Situational Audience Analysis

The group size is important. Once I was asked to give a workshop to a group of workers in an organization that employed over 1200 people. They were all required to attend one or the all-day events. The first one was scheduled for April 14th and about 25 people came. We had rented a hall that could seat about 800, had coffee, doughnuts, and juice. I had to drastically change my presentation because of the size of the group. The large-group seminar techniques I had prepared were now useless. The delivery had to become more intimate and discussion-based. Yes, we did get inundated with more than 1100 the next week.

The *Harvey Harold* newspaper will be interested in PTA meetings while the New York Times will ignore them as irrelevant to people—the difference is not the quality of person reading, but the size of the audience and their shared interests as well as the reason people purchase the paper. To the parents of children the meetings are just as important in New York as they are in Harvey, North Dakota. The difference is the size of readership and the sense of community engendered through the communication medium.

The physical setting is also vital to public communication. Writing about a farm crisis in a local paper will be different from addressing the same issue on a radio talk show, the nightly TV news, or a speech. Presenting ideas in a retreat setting where everyone has put all else aside and focus on the topic is very different from a soap box on the corner of Broadway and Vine. An article for *Newsweek* is probably inappropriate for *American Woodworker*. What may get you an "A" for an essay in philosophy class may not fly in a poetry contest; although the size of the audience may be one professor or judge, the expectations will be very different. If members of the audience are sitting on hard benches with no back, they may not be as patient as if they are seated in comfortable chairs. Anything from the temperature, the proximity of a freeway, or the beauty of the forest can become noise to distract the audience. Consider the community size and expectations prior to crafting a public message.

Dynamic Audience Analysis

Knowing the prior attitude or disposition of the audience will enable the public communicator to be more effective. As I write these words, many polls are being conducted about the War in Iraq. "Do you agree with how President Bush is running the war?" is a common question. Yet they do not follow up with whether or not the person thinks we ought to be tougher or pull out—the pollsters and newscasters simply assume that the individual is against the War. Be careful that you really do understand the audience, not just a cursory illusion.

Understanding the interests of people will enable the speaker or writer to draw them into a new topic. Funneling the message through other topics may enable you to capture the imagination of those who read or hear your ideas. Couching your ideas into the framework of their interests will enable your impact to increase.

The value system of the audience will greatly affect their ability to pay attention to your message. If you advocate gay marriage to an audience that believes all sex outside of a heterosexual marriage is sin, then you will have a very different message than if you were addressing the same topic to a group of ACLU lawyers. The construct, "family values" for a conservative are different from "family values" for a liberal—even if the two people are using the same language.

173

The worldview of the audience will make a drastic difference in how they will hear evidence supporting your ideas. To a postmodern deconstructionist, who believes that truth varies according to personal perspective, much empirical data is only appropriate if you already believe in it. Stories of experiences will be more likely to influence one who holds to this kind of thinking. To someone who is a Christian, quoting the Bible will probably have a much greater impact, for good or ill, than quoting a movie star. To others, quoting the Bible will automatically detract from the message.

Heterogeneous and Homogenous Audiences

Whether an audience is similar or different in any given aspect will affect how they will read or hear the message. If everyone in the audience are members of one household, the author should consider carefully the impact the words will have on the family unit. Likewise, if the entire audience is of one age or one gender, the impact of that variable will be greater than when it is dispersed through the crowd or confounded by similar variables. Writing for publication that is sent to only Democrats will be very different from writing about the same topic with the same evidence for a magazine that is designed to appeal to all political parties. In a similar vein, writing for the *Baptist Herald,* a small denominational magazine, will be very different from writing for *Christianity Today*, to appeal to all evangelical Christians. Localized radio programs appeal to a specific area while national programs need to address the issues in a more comprehensive manner.

A wise communicator constantly is aware of the audience and is able to feed off of them. This may be difficult if you are the president and want foreign policy to match what people think as opposed to a Supreme Court justice who is supposed to think of the law, as opposed to me, an average Joe who needs to relate to a college class. All audiences have some kind of similarities in that they are human and have taken the initiative to listen to or read the message. Cultivation of those items of homogeneity will create a communication community in a way that is more likely to positively impact the audience.

Adaptation to Audiences

The audience's disposition toward the presenter and topic will largely determine how the individual will be influenced by the communication. Sometimes an audience will be unfavorably disposed toward the occasion or the place of a public communication. If someone has experienced a traumatic event and returns to the place where it happened, often the emotions are so overwhelming that no matter what is said, the person will react unfavorably. Anticipating how audiences will react to given points, words, and ideas will enable you to craft a message that can change their lives. Capitalizing on either positive or negative emotions that will build the case will enable the rhetor to be more effective.

Great public writings and speeches are clear, appropriate, relevant, and captivating. Eloquence is a function of rhetoric that matches communication with an audience in a manner that is beautiful and good. Audience adaptation adjusts style, manner, evidence, and complexity to the people who receive the communication.

Language can be adapted to audiences. If speaking to a heterogeneous audience of kindergarteners, then use words they can understand. On the other hand, the same words spoken in an academic conference will offend the audience by talking down to them. Choose an appropriate level of vocabulary. Speaking through an interpreter is a very difficult task for some; be careful to say what is necessary in a way that enters into the audience's world.

I have spoken to groups of natives who have no conception of statistics. Speaking my message to them in ways they could envision using a bunch of bananas, threads in a shawl, or grass that they can understand my message in their context. Evidence in that setting is very different from evidence that is appropriate for a newscast, or a feature article for *Scientific America*. Be aware that some audiences can calculate, in fact numbers may be necessary as descriptive or explanatory evidence, while others will have a harder time with numbers. Unfamiliar examples may actually detract from the main message because the audience will spend their energy trying to understand the example rather than comprehend and evaluate the message itself.

Which stories chosen by the rhetor may make the difference between a great article and a mediocre one. The illustrations used, the narratives, examples, or situations all make a significant difference to audiences. Using mass media is largely a story-telling activity so that the larger and more diverse the audience, the more important it is to my close attention to the choice between narratives. A recent sermon I heard was basically a combination of two stories I first heard in the mid 70s. Good stories, but taken from an old book of illustrations could have been said in two or three minutes each yet they were extended to take up ten minutes each in a 25 minute sermon, they were ineffective and detracted from the *ethos* of the speaker because the stories were ones previous speakers used often. Others in the audience had a similar negative reaction to the sermon; I doubt it accomplished the intent of the preacher.

The kind of facts used in a speech or article will make a great difference. If writing for a group of engineers, the facts about nuclear fission need to be precise and detailed. However if giving a speech to a group of grade school children, the facts about nuclear fission should be much more generalized and coupled with comparisons or metaphors they can understand. Most audiences will fall between these extremes on that topic. However, giving a public speech on the need for relaxation to those same two audiences, pro-fessional engineers and grade school children, *could* sound very similar.

Which authorities do you believe? If giving a sermon in a church with people who have believed the Bible for decades and you do not cite a pas-sage from the text, you will not be accepted in the same way as if you did. For some audiences actors and famous people are more authoritative than academic experts. For other audiences business people who have become successful are the real-world experts. Others will look to newsmakers or politicians for their expertise. Finding out who the audience believes is an important aspect of audience analysis. Adapt your message to their authori-ties and you will be further ahead. Also, whom will they doubt? If you give a speech in a classroom of atheists and quote the Bible, it may actually hurt your chances of persuasion. Give the same message, but adapt the kind of evidence that supports the content to that which will convince the audi-ence.

Psychology of Audiences

Attitude Formation, Intensification, and Change

The process of persuasion usually begins with a felt need. The motivation to develop attitudes, grow them stronger, or change their direction comes from an inner emotional response to a situation. Physical needs like the necessity to have food, shelter and clothing are part of the makeup of all humans. Interpersonal social needs like the desire for friendship, commu-nication, and sex are also vital, not only to survival, but to human well-be-ing. Inner psychological needs like artistic nature, self-actualization, and ego form a significant part of the internal nature of people. Spiritual needs like faith, hope, and love form a significant part of the human experience. Human motivation is the dynamic process that initiates a drive in these areas aimed at satisfying the need.

At a debate tournament in Los Angeles a student fell ill, and I took her to the hospital; knowing I had to wait at least an hour, I took a brief walk. In a very dark, dirty alley a toddler, perhaps two or at most three years old, was sitting cross-legged with her back against her mom's leg. The woman was passed out in a sitting position against a brick wall. I approached and the girl ran back into the alley and hid behind a garbage bin. Hospital workers would not come out and help the mother. The police took the call and said they would look into it, sometime that night. I went out to buy her some food, and as I came back, a young man approached, grabbed the mother's arms and drug the woman into a back door and the toddler followed. I asked if I could help. Not a word was spoken in answer. A haunting moment, I did little to help a baby who is growing up in physical, social, and spiritual poverty, but returned to the emergency room to continue to help a student. Persuaded to try to help by the circumstances, something deep inside me motivated an attempt to help. First, a fruitless attempt to get others to do the work for me, the self-persuasion to act then moved me to purchase some food and give it to the people. A very small gesture from someone passing through a neighborhood, will it give a nameless little girl some measure of hope? That awakening of compassion within me, happens repeatedly as a response to people and situations. Public persuasion often keys on whether or not we can awaken the consciousness and interest of the audience.

This process to maintain a balance between felt needs, our consciousness, and our thinking is called is called homeostasis. The need to help a student who is in the hospital, to help a child who is virtually alone, to help a woman who has passed out are all legitimate desires, but they can conflict with the reality of being in an unsafe neighborhood late at night. Finding a balance between ethical responsibility of action toward others and preservation of self is not always easy. Matching style to the content, organizing the communication around Monroe's Motivated Sequence (see chapter 13 on organization), using striking illustrations, or diction chosen with care are typical ways of accomplishing this balance. However, the best way is to truly love the audience and attempt to gain an empathetic understanding of who they are and what they are experiencing. A compassionate attitude will arise through your words spoken from a heart of love.

These psychological aspects of public communication are vital to a comprehensive liberal arts approach. Understanding, knowing myself and others as people is essential to being able to write and speak messages that have a positive impact on the audience.

Proattitudinal and Counterattitudinal Persuasion

As the art and science of influencing people, persuasion is both proattitudinal and counterattitudinal. The intentional process of developing and implementing communication that actively impacts other people's character, attitudes, thoughts, behaviors or emotions is furthered through an understanding of attitude formation and change.

Proattitudinal persuasion increases, intensifies, or strengthens attitudes. Automobile manufactures often advertise, not to get new customers, but for those who have already purchased their vehicles to continue to have a positive emotional response to the product. Coke and Pepsi advertise to keep their customers purchasing the product as much or more than to persuade new customers to buy their colas. Many religious persuasive messages are to people who already believe the content and they are strengthened in their resolve.

Cheerleaders stimulate the emotions of a partisan crowd in order to enable players to believe in themselves and do a better job. They are proattitudinal parts of the sports culture. Proattitudinal persuasive messages inundate the marketplace of ideas. Many of the speeches, radio programs, television programs, and other journalism articles are geared toward people who already believe the message. Many viewers of CNN news already have the left leaning political bent so that the words chosen by reporters and talking heads "ring true" to their worldview. Likewise, more conservative people are more likely to watch Fox news because its perspective is believable from their worldview. Most people who attend church already believe the content of what the pastor says in a sermon; it is therefore a proattitudinal public communication to a largely homogenous audience.

Counterattitudinal persuasive measures are invented to change the minds of the audience. Many editorials are designed to change the minds of the readers concerning specific social or political perspectives. Political promotion is often designed to influence the voters to decide for a specific candidate. Although some advertising is proattitudinal, most commercial marketing is specifically calculated to change the attitude of the audience so they will desire to purchase a product. Motivating thoughts and actions to be focused in a positive direction is a persuasive art. Billy Graham has spoken to more people than any other individual in history, and his main message is counterattitudinal evangelism—to convert people to Christianity. To Christians, Dr. Graham's message is proattitudinal, while to those who do not believe, it is a counterattitudinal message; therefore, the audience is heterogeneous along the lines of belief.

Beliefs, values, and attitudes

As a predisposition to behave, attitudes are linked closely to values and beliefs. Beliefs are those *things* that we hold to be true. Values are those sets of beliefs that we hold to be significant. The three constructs are probably closely related to each other in the processes of persuasion.

Attitudes are more than a simple predisposition to behave; they are also patterns of mannerisms that reflect emotional states. Individuals have positive and negative attitudes concerning others, objects, and events. The attitude of a student in class affects her more than the possible behaviors; it involves current dispositions about herself, the teacher, the subject, classmates, methodologies, and perhaps even pressure from parents to earn a specific grade. Therefore, attitudes are complex and often unpredictable when isolated from beliefs and values within an individual.

Beliefs, values, and attitudes have a cognitive aspect in that they develop out of our knowledge base. What we know about nuclear weapons (history, tests, and risks) influences our beliefs (they are dangerous in more ways than one) and our values (peace and environmental security) resulting in the attitude stance (elimination, evil necessity or desirability).

Beliefs, values, and attitudes also sway our emotions about people, things, and issues. This affective function changes or strengthens how we feel about the world in which we live. The kind and intensity of emotion about the issue of nuclear weapons (relief they are protecting or anger in their expansion) is closely linked with our attitude toward them.

Beliefs, values, and attitudes lead to specific behavioral measures. They predispose us to take specific actions. Our attitudes about nuclear weapons could induce us to protest their presence or write an editorial defending their existence. In other words, they often affect what we do about specific issues, especially in the area of public communication.

Even with these connections, specific predictions based on the presence of given attitudes, beliefs or values are difficult at best. Most evangelical Christians are against extramarital sexual encounters, yet many Christians have affairs or become involved in premarital sex. The attitude based on beliefs and values does not necessarily predict the sexual behavior of an individual or an entire group. This is because humans have a free-will or ability to choose in any given situation and we have a sin nature that entices us to think about sin as something desirable. We are not necessarily consistent with our own attitudes, beliefs, and values either through dealing with temptation or listening to persuasive public communication.

Prevalence of attitudes

Milton Rokeach (1968) presented a widely held perspective that beliefs range from strongly held "primitive" beliefs to those that are loosely based on outside authority. Beliefs cluster and form attitudes that fall into two categories, those toward objects or issues and those toward situations. These often conflict with each other and bring about confusion within the person (his theory may be most inadequate when it comes to expressing attitudes toward people and experiences).

Martin Fisbein and Icek Ajzen (1975) included behavioral intention to the prominent place attitudes play in persuasive processes. Attitude change usually precedes how people intend to act in specific situations. When a smoker says she intends to quit smoking, the statement often follows a lengthy change in attitudes. Started by knowledge that smoking causes cancer and other diseases in herself and others, the belief system begins to change. Understanding that smoking may cause disease in those around her, the conflicting values toward herself and valuing others begin to shift priorities. Affective measures of changed emotions about the habit of smoking make the activity less desirable in her own mind. When she arrives at the point of an un-coerced statement, she is much nearer the point of following through with the action of quitting smoking. This does not mean she will, but that she is more likely to try.

Attitudes can be seen as *evaluating* a person, an object or a situation with favor or disfavor (Petty and Cacioppo, 1986). From this perspective, the human attitude is a cognitive psychological tendency that can be seen in such ways as expression of approval or disapproval, attraction or avoidance, or actions either for or against the object of the attitude. In this case, the persuader should become aware of the audience's attitude toward any aspects of appeals.

I believe attitudes are ingrained emotional patterns that unconsciously arise in response to a person, object, or situation. They are not the simply determinates of behavior, emotive-cognate evaluation, or conflicting clusters of beliefs and values. Let's explore them further.

Aspects of Attitudes

Attitudes function in numerous ways (Shavitt & Nelson, 2002). Some are utilitarian in nature, maximizing rewards and minimizing punishments. For example, your attitude about ice cream falls into this category. The incentive of having an enjoyable eating experience (reward) is balanced with weight gain (negative consequence), so you choose to eat non-fat frozen yogurt (maximizing benefits while minimizing costs). Other attitudes function as an aid in social interaction balanced with self-expression. For example, while at church you may talk with someone you would be uncomfortable talking with in the hall at school because of her social position. For some reason you find it easier to cross socio-cultural boundaries in the context of worship and fellowship than in the context of school. The public identity and private identity may also be in conflict in attitudes enabling people to do things they would not normally choose because of peer pressure. Students may drink alcohol, wear revealing clothing, take drugs, or have sex even if these things are against their beliefs and values in order to fulfill the stronger attitudinal desire and need to be accepted. Other attitudes function to build and maintain self-esteem.

How we choose to dress and how we feel when dressed in certain ways are attitudinal decisions. For some dress may be a function of social expectations and interactions. For others the same object, clothing, is a value-expressive function of remaining true to one's inner self through outer nonverbal communication. For most people the way we choose to dress is multifunctional—a balance of attitudes, values, and beliefs in conjunction with what fits and is clean at the moment.

Christian attitudes, values, and beliefs function on a variety of levels. A congruent person will be true to himself (identity function), while attempting to be intimate with others (social function), along with building a more virtuous character (esteem function), in a manner that meets his needs (utilitarian function). A congruent Christian adds into the mix both his or her current relationship with God along with the creative design of becoming more like God. These complex interactions of attitudes will attempt to create a homeostatic state where attitudes, values and beliefs are congruent with each other. Each individual has a unique mix of personality in which attitudes lead to harmony or discord—faith mixed with questions and doubt.

People are known to be hypocritical—doing things that are counter to their beliefs and attitudes. This is a major problem in all areas of life, but even more so for Christians who state their beliefs and then act in different ways. For someone who believes in a holy and just God, sexual relations with others outside of marriage should be considered sin and abhorrent. Yet many in our society confess their belief and think nothing of committing adultery or fornication. King David is the first on the list. Bringing actions into alignment with beliefs is more difficult than aligning the tires on a car. There you have mechanical means to manipulate within tolerances. You can put the automobile on a machine and measure exactly how far out of alignment it is and then adjust it back into the correct configuration. With people we cannot use wrenches or diagnostic computers to determine their compliance; we use personal, persuasive rhetoric. Communication becomes a key to understanding our current situation, getting into alignment, and then keeping our homeostatic balance.

Measurement of attitudes

If the audience evaluates the communication of a persuader to be positive, they will be more likely to move their beliefs, values, attitudes, or actions in a positive direction (the persuader's intended direction). In order to understand the inter-workings of attitudes, these attitudes need to be isolated and measured so that the impact of persuasive communication can be known.

Likert (1932) developed scales that are still used to assess the viability of attitudes. They are calculated to measure the direction (positive or negative) and degree or intensity (on a numbered scale) of attitudes about any given subject.

1. People who kill children by abuse should receive the death penalty.

   Strongly Agree ___ ___ ___ ___ Strongly Disagree

Osgood, Suci, and Tannenbaum (1957) designed a semantic differential that is used to measure attitudes. This method gives depth to the degree and direction of attitudes.

2. Rate how you feel about people being given the death penalty after they are convicted of killing a child through death-by-abuse

   DEATH FOR CHILD ABUSERS WHO KILL IS:

   Bad ___ ___ ___ ___ ___ ___ ___ Good
        -3 -2 -1 0 +1 +2 +3

   Just ___ ___ ___ ___ ___ ___ ___ Unjust
        -3 -2 -1 0 +1 +2 +3

   Adverse ___ ___ ___ ___ ___ ___ ___ Favorable
        -3 -2 -1 0 +1 +2 +3

   Beneficial ___ ___ ___ ___ ___ ___ ___ Harmful
        -3 -2 -1 0 +1 +2 +3

Cacioppo, Harkins, and Petty (1981) formed the singe-item rating scale. This method is more precise in measuring the specifics of the issue.

3. To what extent do you agree with the law mandating capitol punishment for all people convicted of killing a child through "death-by-abuse"?

Do not
Agree ___ ___ ___ ___ ___ ___ ___ ___ Agree
    1 2 3 4 5 6 7 8

These ways of scientifically determining attitudes give significant understanding of themselves and audiences to public communicators. These are self-report methods that may or may not be accurate, depending on the degree of understanding an individual has about himself or herself.

Do we learn from our mistakes?

Do people change their attitudes following adverse consequences to a greater degree than from persuasive appeals? Accidents from use or abuse of consumer products is the leading cause of death for citizens of the United States under age 35. Overall, unintentional injuries from consumer products are the fifth leading cause of death. Research that examined product users' past accidents while using a consumer product with their willingness to comply with safety instructions found little change. Baltimore and Meyer (1969) considered storage of poison in households where accidental poisoning had occurred as well as randomly selected homes and found no difference in how products were kept. People did not learn from being poisoned. Bragg (1973) reported that many people previously involved in auto accidents did not wear seat belts when they recovered from their injuries. I know a man who was injured in a logging accident and was in traction for six months. On the day he got out of the hospital he was involved in a motorcycle accident that put him back in the hospital for another nine months. The day after he got out, he rode his motorcycle out to cut wood; his wife threatened divorce if he did not quit.

Culturally we attempt to address the adverse consequence problem through product safety warning labels. Putting surgeon general's warning labels on cigarettes does not significantly lower the rate of people smoking. The persuasive appeal for consumer caution is related to awareness of the severity and likelihood of negative consequences, comprehension of product safety information, and perception of the risk involved (deTurck, 2002).

Compliance is difficult to determine because of ethical constraints in exposing people to hazards in order to study their behavior. When warnings appear at the beginning of instructions individuals are more likely to comply with them than if they are at the end. When multiple simple messages are given, they are more likely to be followed than if one complex instruction is given. If a role model follows the safety instructions individuals are more likely to comply as well. When the cost of compliance is determined to be higher than the cost of injury, compliance is very low. When personal involvement is high, compliance usually increases (deTurck, 2002).

Overall, persuasive appeals through safety warnings have little effect on consumer's actions. The situational aspects of role models, perceived cost of awareness, and personal factors such as familiarity have a greater effect on hazardous behavior. The highest degree of compliance comes when persuasive appeals are actively thought about in conjunction with personal factors. *That means persuasive communication that grasps the attention of individuals in a personally relevant way while meeting a felt need will be more effective in producing a change in behavior.* This principle can be generalized beyond safety instructions to many kinds of persuasive messages.

Intention to behave

A predisposition to behave is often unconscious; when it moves into intentionality, the cognitive processes strengthen that attitude. In political persuasion placing a sign in your yard or a sticker on your bumper increases the likelihood that you will vote in a specific direction. The public stance coupled with having processed the issue or candidate thoroughly enough to communicate to others concerning that position solidifies the direction of your vote. The attitude coupled with active cognition processed enough to become an intention for action integrates the mind and will with the emotions concerning the object of the attitude. In an interpersonal romantic relationship doing something—holding hands, kissing, giving a gift—usually leads to stronger feelings, positive thoughts, and more actions of love.

Ever since LaPiere (1934) found a discrepancy between individual's attitudes toward Oriental customers and behavior in serving them, studies have been inconclusive in proving a direct relationship between attitudes and overt actions. This practical discrepancy has been a thorn-in-the-flesh for many theories of persuasion. Petty and Cacioppo (1986) demonstrate that issue-relevant cognitive effort significantly reduces the discrepancy between attitudes and actions—actively thinking through and deciding about an issue will lessen the difference between what we do and what we value..

This cognitive consistency may be directly related to the amount of cognitive effort spent by an individual in forming, changing or intensifying the attitude (Verplanken, 1989). Being consciously aware of your own experiences and emotions, thinking them through to categorize and explain your ideas about them, and finally making a decision about the underlying issue will solidify your attitudes and enable you to be a better public communicator who influences other people in appositive direction.

Attitude Intensification

One of the primary aspects of persuasion is proattitudinal advocacy that intensifies an attitude making it more robust. Attitude intensification is seen as attitude persistence, predictive of attitude-relevant behavior and resistant to counterattitudinal persuasion. Persistence means that the subjects attitude following the persuasive communication will be similar to the same attitude accessed at a later time (Perloff & Brock, 1980). Cialdini, Levy, Herman, Kozlowski and Petty (1976) did a study in which college students anticipated a dyadic conversation with a peer over a specified topic. Those who were led to believe that the discussion would take place immediately listed more thoughts and had more intense attitude positions than those who anticipated the conversation to be a week later. The conversation was canceled for all subjects. Three weeks later those who had put more cognitive effort into preparation for the original conversation remained firm in their positions while those who did not undertake the same amount of elaboration were much more apt to change. Thus thinking issue-relevant thoughts enhance attitude persistence. One of the public communicator's primary tasks is, therefore, to get the audience to think about the message of the communication in multiple ways.

Parents can engage their children in conversation about communication and impact the likelihood they are influenced in a particular direction. Asking them about what they learned in school or to recount a Sunday School lesson, sermon, movie, or book they read will reinforce the message in a manner that is positive. The family habit of eating at a dinner table and talking about the day is more healthy than watching the TV during dinner.

Resistant to counterattitudinal advocacy means a person tends to keep his or her position in spite of attempts to change it. This counterattitudinal message is often called *counterpropaganda*. Information formed specifically to change the mind of individuals with certain attitudes. Festinger and Maccoby (1964) found that resistance to persuasion is enhanced when a person thinks actively about the issue before the counterpropaganda is presented. They also confirmed that distraction during persuasive messages increases counterattitudinal persuasion in that it decreases the ability to think actively about the message. This effect is especially true when there is high source credibility. McGuire's (1964) research on cultural truisms indicates that those persistent attitudes adopted with little cognitive processing are highly susceptible to counterattitudinal advocacy. Unquestioning acceptance of a position leaves a person vulnerable in the face of counterpropaganda.

One reason so many converts to religions are from very different religious experiences is that children grow up in families that believe a specific way but do not talk about it often. Especially when questioning is frowned upon, the individuals will be far more open to counter argument. Practical thinking and defending beliefs is important in making attitudes resistant to change. The person is thus inoculated or immunized against attack.

Power and influence

Persuasion can become coercion through the misuse of power in a relationship. Sometimes the use of compulsive power is good and necessary. If a toddler wants to play in the street physical boundaries or restraints are necessary. Rash acts by an adult may have to involve physical intervention in order that harm is not caused. No absolute line can be drawn between the right and wrong. Persuasive influence bringing about an impact will almost always bring about a better attitude and more permanent change than manipulation, intimidation or coercion.

Power can be defined as the ability to act in a specific direction with the capability of accomplishing something. When an individual attempts to overcome another person, accomplishing her desires without consideration for others, then power is being misused. Power may also be defined as the control of others' minds through persuasion. But I prefer the definition of power as the ability and opportunity to influence others. How that power is wielded is the ethical practice of persuasion.

Intimacy of relationship and compassion are alternative to power that persuade in a manner that invites a change through influence as opposed to overt use of power. Convincing through reason and evidence is also much better than communicating from a position of power. Modeling and providing a means for positive action with results is also preferable to use of power as a foundation for communication. These alternative ways of public persuasion will be better as a complete means of persuasive public appeal than a manipulation of power-based communication for persuasion.

Temptation

Considering eating a large slice of cheesecake or a bowl of grapes for desert? Which one will win may be determined by past persuasive communication. A slogan such as "Nothing tastes as good as thin feels" can enable the attitudes toward a less caloric, more healthy choice to determine the action. However, indulging as an extension of a romantic dinner may cue in other desires so that we eat the cheesecake.

In Romans 7 the Apostle Paul wrestles with conflicting desires, beliefs, attitudes and values so that he does things he would rather not do. There in Romans, as in I Corinthians 10:13, he teaches that we will always have the power to overcome temptation and do the right thing. The process is a struggle, and we don't always win, but God gives the power to overcome to those who believe. Because we are complex people with differing drives, beliefs, values, and attitudes, persuasive influences will be subjective in nature.

Tempt an audience to do what is good, right, and just—not what is beneficial to you. Enticement to act in beneficial ways will endear the audience to the rhetor in a manner that enhances relationships and build up people.

Biological Beginnings

Humans are more than spiritual; we are also biological creatures. We have a body made of water and chemicals arranged in such a manner that ever since God began the cycle of life, it continues to be passed from generation to generation. We have real needs to eat, have shelter and security. We need air, water rest and food to subsist. Meeting these needs is a foundational aspect of being a living body. When one or more of these needs is unfulfilled in some aspect, persuasive attempts in that particular direction are more likely to work. Our security need is strong enough that when an armed robber holds a gun to our chest, we are more likely to turn over our wallet than if someone merely asks for it. Manipulating the power of physical need, the criminal accomplishes his goal while the victim is violated.

Biological needs can be blown out of proportion through persuasive appeals. Jonathan Edwards sermon *Sinners in the Hands of an Angry God* is a fear appeal with vibrant word pictures. The need for security from the uncertainty of death and afterlife is strong enough that many could be persuaded to respond to the altar call. The need for sexual fulfillment can easily grow and get out of control through persuasive appeals largely because of the degree of pleasure gained from meeting the needs. The condom ads on TV sell sex outside of marriage far more than they prevent AIDS.

Being human

Motivation is deeper than mere biological functions and drives. Although biology may be a significant part of persuasive influences and appeals, people are not biologically determined we are primarily spiritual beings. Humans were created with a free will. The ability and responsibility to make choices is a significant part of being human. Created in the image of God the most humane person is the most godlike. The significance and impact of having a Creator is that we have meaning beyond the biological. God is love; therefore, loving is good and right. God is just; therefore, justice is true. God is holy; therefore, holiness is virtuous. Attitudes and ideals should align with God's nature because he created us in his own image.

Assumptions about anthropology, the understanding of being human, fall into four possible categories of ontology (being human is valuable or worthless) and morality (doing good or evil):

1. Rousseau says that people are ontologically good and morally good. The only evil is believing in evil—we are independently good moral agents.

2. Sartre says that people are ontologically bad but morally good. Humans are no greater than animals where neither vice or virtue, sin or righteousness exist.

3. Hobbes' view of people is that we are ontologically bad and morally bad. We are just advanced animals; thought is refined sensation with the material world all that really exists.

4. The Classical Christian perspective of anthropology envisions people as ontologically good, made in the image of God. Yet we are also sinners by nature through the fall. We are capable of both moral virtue as well as evil actions.

Western society is becoming more Rousseauian, yet still has a strong Classical influence. A rhetor's perspective of who we are as humans will influence the messages and the style of communicating.

Being human also means we have to deal with *fallenness*. In the Garden of Eden, Adam and Eve fell into sin through the deceptive temptation of Satan. From this we have inherited a sin nature that is enticed by many things, and we fall short of God's glory. The problem with attitudes is the direct result of the human spirit having chosen sin over righteousness. The ontological goodness of people is warped or bent by sin leading to moral goodness being corrupted into doing evil at times; therefore, persuasive appeals should be both respectful of the audience and appealing to people to do or think in more positive ways.

Can you make a sexually attractive ad without exploitation? Are you able to produce a fiercely aggressive virtual reality without promoting violence? Mass media has a difficult time appealing to the needs and desires of audiences without crossing the line into exploitation and promotion. Creating aesthetically pleasing communication while maintaining integrity of message, without overt use of power or prurient use of desire, is harder than most people realize. We need people who are willing and capable of doing just that.

Motivation

Ross (1994) summarizes the human needs that underlie persuasive appeals. These "weapons of influence" allow communication to penetrate into the personality and move us through our desires and needs.

1. Reciprocity—the need to reciprocate

2. Consistency—the need to be consistent

3. Commitment—the need to live up to public commitments

4. Social Proof—the need to be in sync with others

5. Liking—the need to be liked

6. Scarcity—the need to overcome scarcity

7. Authority—the need to follow and be followed

8. Instant influence—need to accommodate the automatic age

I believe Ross has missed several inner needs that are significant in the process of persuasion.

189

9. Power—the desire to control my self and situation

10. Freedom—the desire to be without constraint on choice

11. Love—far deeper than like, to cherish and be cherished

12. Generativity—the need to impact others for good

13. Ownership—the desire to have

14. Happiness—the desire to be fulfilled

15. Security—the desire to be unaffected by the unexpected

16. Knowledge—the need to know information

17. Peace—the need for inner harmony.

We could probably add more of these basic needs that underlie the persuasive impacts of appeals. When these needs are being met, or at least perceived to be met, through change, then that change will be far easier. Meeting felt needs is a good way to be persuasive.

Packard (1957) described eight hidden needs that compel people to respond to advertising. His example is how they may be used selling soap. If you can build these into an image of the product you are selling, then the audience is likely to become the customer:

1. Emotional security

2. Reassurance of worth

3. Ego gratification

4. Creative outlets

5. Love objects

6. Sense of power

7. Sense of roots

8. Immortality

Often subconscious, our yearnings and desires result in inner needs that can be visualized as satisfied through products. The freezer represents the assurance food is always present and available. A new car can give ego gratification and a sense of power. Packard goes on to some not-so-hidden needs that advertisements can use to draw customers:

1. Sexual overtones

2. Youth and ideal early adult years

3. Social class and status

4. Achievement and advancement

5. Solving our problems and aversions

6. Assuaging the conscious

7. Appeal through children and childhood

8. Political identification

9. Image builders

Identifying and meeting these needs through persuasive advertisement will make the persuasion have greater impact.

Maslow places needs in five categories. *Physiological needs* of self-preservation, food, water, rest, shelter and sex are foundational. Above them we have the *safety needs* of security, stability, and order with an absence of violence, harm, and fear. Upon these are the *love needs* of giving and receiving, belonging, approval, and acceptance. Then our *esteem needs* of self-respect and recognition along with status and dignity can be met. The uppermost part are the *self-actualization needs* of growth, self-fulfillment, adequacy, competence, and creativeness.

Maslow is wrong. Spiritual needs are more foundational than physical needs are for humans. The need for God and intimacy with others goes deeper than the need for food. But most importantly, self-actualization is not the highest needs—the opposite—self-giving is a much higher form of human life and need. To love so much that we give is greater than to become fulfilled. Most basic of all is the human need for meaning—to have a purpose for life.

Attitudes are tied to our biological, spiritual, and psychological needs being met through change. People have needs of belonging and affiliation, desires to achieve and have power, inner drives to be competent and resourceful. Wise communicators tap into these needs and attempt to meet them through persuasive rhetoric.

Homeostasis

People attempt to do what is right in their own eyes. We seek an inner state of balance. Everyone desires to do what we think is best and right. Attitudes poise beliefs, values and actions in an equilibrium that reflects the state of the soul. Jesus gives a peace that passes understanding so that the presence of harmony can be experienced in many situations where discord and chaos usually reign. When attitudes do not match ideals and values or thoughts, the *dissonance* that arises within people is uncomfortable. Persuasive appeals that provide a means to re-establish a healthy balance are welcomed by most people.

Sometimes persuasive communication adds information or emotions that do not match a current state of balance and it unbalances the life. To achieve a consistency or *consonance* of balance you can: 1) reject the data, 2) fragment the original attitude, or 3) change your attitudes. Most people will have to act in order to relieve the tension and arrive in the state of homeostasis.

For some postmodern people, deconstructive thinking enables them to continue to live with the confusion of contradictory and inconsistent beliefs, values, and attitudes. Persuasive communication becomes extremely difficult when truth is envisioned as individuated and fluid. For them, homeostasis is achieved through denial of objective truth rather than consistency of thought and attitude. Logic of argument gives way to perspective while observation of fact yields to perception of experience. An increasing number of people are becoming very difficult to appeal to in any consistent, persuasive manner because need, attitude and motivation are disconnected from logic, character and emotion—while rhetoric has the foundational assumption that they are connected.

Chapter 8

Persuasive Models and Theories

Rebuke a wise man,
And he will love you;
Give instruction to a wise man
And he will be still wiser
Proverbs 9:8-9 NKJV

MODELS GIVE people a way to consider and picture something. Sometimes they represent the thing they are modeling, like an architects' model of a building. Other times models give an image of something. A scale model of the *USS Missouri* will give a perspective of the battleship, but not an entire image. The model helps us grasp the overall structure and some of the details, but seeing the real ship is essential for a complete understanding. At other times models are typical forms or styles of something; like the 1967 model of a Ford Mustang. It will give you an understanding of the car but not the details. No matter how well done, the model cannot give you the experience of driving the Mustang through the California redwoods on a clear summer evening.

Consider real examples of persuasive communication as you look at the following theories and models. Each will give you a way of thinking about communicative behavior, but none are complete in and of themselves, and none will be able to provide you with a full experience of clear congruent public communication. The value of this chapter is that the theories and models will facilitate your understanding of the nature of communication as it happens and, we hope, enable you to craft more effective public communications. Postmodern engineers use computer models to construct and test a better car while cutting the time, effort, and expense of design and development from concept to sale. As a communication professional, using these models and theories will provide a foundation for fast and efficient construction of communication from invention to delivery.

Compliance Gaining

One of the most common uses of communication, as well as highly researched areas of interpersonal behavior, is compliance gaining. In essence compliance gaining strategies are persuasive appeals but they can be easily misused as coercive manipulation of other people. Although compliance gaining is primarily associated with interpersonal communication, these principles can be practically used in many public communication contexts. Focusing largely on message production, compliance gaining strategies elicit action in the direction desired by the advocate in public speaking, advertising, small groups, and writing. Compliance-gaining messages are essentially attempting to get people to do what you want them to do, or to stop doing something you do not want them to do. It is action oriented. Marwell and Schmitt (1967) observed 16 strategies often used for gaining compliance from others.

1. Promising a reward for compliance.

2. Threatening the application of a punishment for noncompliance.

3. Showing expertise about positive outcomes: demonstrating good things that will happen to those who comply.

4. Showing expertise about negative outcomes: demonstrating bad things that will happen to those who do not comply.

5. Liking: showing friendliness implying compliance will gain more appreciative behavior.

6. Pre-giving a reward before asking for compliance.

7. Applying aversive stimulation so that punishment happens until compliance is gained.

8. Calling in a debt: reminding a person of past favors.

9. Making moral appeals through description of the behavior as the right or honorable thing to do.

10. Attributing positive feelings to compliance so that the person will associate compliance with good emotions.

11. Attributing negative feelings to noncompliance so the person will associate noncompliance with bad emotions.

12. Positive altercasting associates compliance with positive character traits of other individuals.

13. Negative altercasting associates noncompliance with negative character traits of other individuals.

14. Seeking altruistic compliance or simply asking for a favor.

15. Showing positive esteem for another person so that one will have more ego "strokes" with compliance.

16. Showing negative esteem by communicating that the person will be liked less by others if he or she does not comply.

The list of strategies could be shortened to five areas: rewarding, punishing, expertise, impersonal commitments, and personal commitments.

Compliance-gaining strategies are systematized into seven categories by Bettinghaus and Cody (1994). The most common type is the direct request which gains impetus from the rhetorical situation, the social interaction, and relational dynamics. Rationality uses logical processes and information to convince the auditor. Another compliance-gaining strategy is to exchange favors for a measure of mutual benefit. Manipulative strategies move through emotional impetus. Coercive communication uses threats or punishment to stimulate obedient conformity. Indirect hinting relies on the receptiveness and sensitivity of the auditor to understand the advocate's desires. Emotional appeals involving love and affection are usually used in established relationships.

Wheeless, Barraclough and Stewart (1983) add three types of power used in compliance gaining situations: 1) perceived ability to manipulate the circumstances; 2) perceived ability to determine the relational position between the advocate and auditor; and 3) perceived ability to determine or define values or obligations of the parties. An auditor determines the kind of power and chooses tactics that invoke that power.

Within interpersonal settings these communication strategies can enable significant persuasive impact. Using them with influence, reciprocity, and love may provide a stronger relational base than using them with power as a primary force. The degree of intimacy, dominance and resistance to persuasive efforts (Perloff, 1993) also influences the nature of the appeal. Individuals with interpersonal "debts" can interactively appeal without verbally calling the debt into consciousness. Promises or other compliance gaining strategies are often unnecessary where committed love is the foundation of relationships.

The context of the communication may have a great influence on the degree of positive response. An employee may respond to a superior out of either respect or fear. A friend may respond out of loyalty or limpid responsibility. These relational characteristics may not be apparent from the verbal interaction, but only be understood by the communicators (Woodward & Denton, 2000).

Persuasive appeals that use multiple channels may have a greater impact (function additively) than those using only one strategy. If Sandra uses positive altercasting (other couples we respect are going on the romantic retreat), liking with promise (making nonverbal suggestive sexual advances), and pregiving (kiss), she is more likely to persuade her husband Jim to go to the coast. In a similar manner multiple strategies of compliance gaining can be used in a series of editorials about whether or not a community should allow a major international retailer to build in a locality. An editorial in favor of Wal Mart building a superstore could include: the promise (more jobs and cheaper, better service), with altruism (they will donate to worthy causes in the area), altercasting (other communities who are improved because of the company), positive feelings with moral appeal (capitalism that helps individuals), and a threat (they will build in a neighboring community so that we will loose the benefits). An editorial against building the Wal Mart could include: threat (traffic, low pay, and elimination of competition), altercasting (where harm has happened in other communities), pre-giving (lowering costs and increasing service in present stores), positive esteem (we can do this without them), expertise (economist testimony against the store), and moral appeal (the legal suits against the company in labor issues and they get most of their merchandise from China). These same kinds of strategies can be used in public speeches, sermons, and virtually any public communication.

Consistency Theories

Based on the assumption that humans desire to reduce tension in their lives, consistency theories seek homeostasis or a steady equilibrium. Tension may come from competing sets of information. A person who believes God created the world as a literal interpretation of Genesis 1 and 2 is confronted with the theory of evolution and tension results—incompatibility of information. Persuasive communication is the major manner of re-creating a spiritual balance that resolves the strain with inner socio-cognitive peace.

Another source of inner tension is between personal behavior and information. Sometimes people become aware of hypocritical behavior that already exists while at other times a communication will create that tension through new knowledge. For example, when a smoker is confronted with the unhealthy effects of smoking, an uneasy pang of guilt is usually created. Expectations of others can create tension when they are incongruent with our behaviors. When young adults want to get married while their parents think they should wait, both intrapersonal and interpersonal imbalance is created.

Tension motivates a person to change a worldview, belief, attitude, or behavior to create the peace of balance. Thus, perception can be influenced more easily through persuasion at the point of tension. When a public communicator correctly ascertains the correct point of tension; that will be the place of the most significant point for a decision—stasis. Terrorists use the tension of questionable leadership to exploit public opinion in favor of their unethical behavior. Public media becomes their primary weapon in advancing attacks on others because their tactics do nothing to gain or hold territory or people. With no possible positive outcome from their actions, they seek to manipulate public opinion by creating tension within the opposition. What many need to recognize is that the primary weapon against such strategies is positive public communication that counters their subversive agenda. Political power comes to the person or party who can best provide a way for the public to make sense of the situation and resolve the tension.

Balance Theory

When tension arises within a person or between people, most individuals try to reduce the conflict through persuasion. Self-persuasion is the intrapersonal process of debating the issue internally. Interpersonal persuasion is the process of influencing someone else to change, or be influenced to change. Public persuasion is moving large audiences at the same time, through the same means, using the same media.

The interaction between two people and an object, event, idea, or another person can create either balance or imbalance.

Balance occurs in these ways:

1. The sender and receiver have a negative attitude toward an object and a positive attitude toward each other. Sally and Bill like each other, but neither likes alcohol. They experience comfort or "balance" in their intrapersonal and interpersonal relationships.

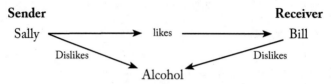

2. The sender and receiver can have a positive attitude toward the object and a positive attitude toward each other. Kamron and April both like each other and they both like alcohol. Their frame of reference is balanced within themselves. The liking of April or Alcohol may be increased because of the triangle.

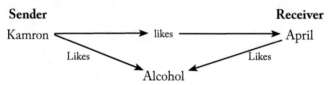

3. The sender and receiver can disagree about the object and dislike each other. Jon dislikes Jennifer and dislikes alcohol, while Jennifer dislikes Jon but likes alcohol. Creating peace with those we like and respect leads to liking in others who like us; while those we don't like, often disagree with us leading to disagreement with those who like us.

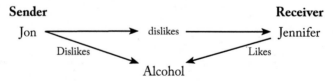

Proattitudinal persuasion can strengthen these tendencies and make them resistant to counterpersuasion. The stronger the attitude and broader the personal involvement the greater the balance will be. In this example, Jon's dislike for alcohol may increase because Jennifer likes it and he does not like her.

Counter-attitudinal persuasion needs to create an imbalance in a person. New information, re-framing old information, or changed perspectives may help create a sense of inconsistency. The individual will not be motivated to change unless a need is created within himself or herself.

Three major ways imbalance can be created through persuasion are:

1. When a sender and receiver like each other but disagree about an object the receiver will have an imbalance. Bohn likes Liz, but he does not like Jazz music, while Liz likes Jazz.

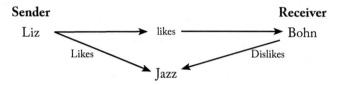

    When Liz sends Bohn a message about attending an all-day Jazz festival, Bohn's negative attitude about Jazz will effect an imbalance—he will experience the tension of wanting to go with her but not wanting to waste a day listening to music he doesn't like.

2. When the sender and receiver dislike each other, but agree on attitudes toward an object, the receiver will experience imbalance. Carl dislikes Sonja but both like Jazz. He will experience tension.

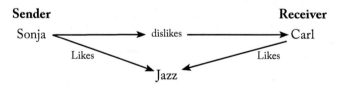

    Sonja offers Carl a ticket to an all day Jazz festival right beside her seat. Carl will experience the tension of wanting to hear the concert, but to be with other people—perhaps his hair needs washing instead?

3. The final way imbalance occurs is if the sender and receiver dislike each other and both dislike the object. Michael dislikes Amber and both dislike Jazz.

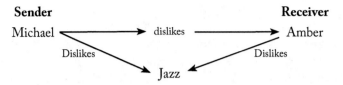

When Michael invites Amber to the Jazz festival, Amber wonders why because she knows he doesn't like either her or Jazz, so why would she ask—tension is created in the relationship.

Psychological imbalance creates an inner need to change. Persuasion is most effective when it influences an individual at the point of imbalance. If Sonja reads extensively on topics Carl likes to think about and spends extra time making herself physically attractive, she may begin to create a balance in Carl at the Jazz festival—he may begin to like both her and Jazz.

A balanced state occurs if all the relationships are positive or if two are negative and one is positive. All others are imbalanced. As mentioned previously, the significance of the imbalance will be directly related to the importance and relevance of the subject coupled with the degree of imbalance. For example: if tension is created in the area of funding public schools so that an imbalance is formed but an individual does not really care and has no children in the school system, then the likelihood of persuasive communication greatly impacting that person will be very small. Public persuasive rhetoric may motivate the individual to vote in a particular direction, but that position will have a greater likelihood of changing in the future than one derived through an issue that has deep personal beliefs and relevance such as if a child is entering the school or the resulting taxes means personal sacrifice.

Cognitive Dissonance

Leon Fesinger observed that the balanced perspective of persuasion helped people understand the quantitative relationships, but it did not deal with the qualitative differences. The continuum between like, being infatuated, and unconditional love is vast.

Congnitives are the thoughts, attitudes, beliefs, and values an individual holds to be true. Dissonance is a lack of agreement between our cognitives and actions or emotions. Consonance is the agreement between the thoughts and the actions or emotions. Individuals have a strong need for consonance, so they change when dissonance occurs. People tend to avoid the experience of dissonance and will actively avoid situations and information that increases dissonance.

Joe strongly believed his parents loved him, so when he overcharged his visa account, Joe asked his parents for extra money to pay the balance down to a manageable level. They declined stating the most loving thing would be to let him learn to manage his money on his own. Joe was exceptionally angry because his cognitive outlook said that those who have money and love a person in need should give or lend to that individual. The belief that his parents loved him and their actions of not loaning money to him were inconsistent in Joe's mind. Since his parents would not forward any money, Joe concluded they must not love him. In this instance he chose the belief that the one with money should give to the one in need as more powerful than the belief that his parents loved him, because of the dissonance.

Tension reduction is both quantitative and qualitative. The entire relationship may change along with the degree of significance of the beliefs and dissonance. People who dislike each other can fall madly in love—creating consonance out of dissonance.

Why do we expect our spouse to love us tomorrow? Why do we expect the professor to be in class? Why do we expect the car to run? Consistency. Humans seek a homeostatic balance, and when life is out of balance, the opportunity for persuasion is ripe.

Hypothesis #1: An individual's behavior may cause persuasion. Inconsistency between actions and beliefs brings about self-persuasion. The intrapersonal justification process brings about a change because of incompatible cognitions or actions.

Hypothesis #2: Humans tend to avoid the increase of dissonance. Persuaders need to be aware of the choice of persuasive channels as well as the message itself. Rhetorical sensitivity is the art of adapting to the audience. When a person holds position Y and X about similar beliefs a degree of dissonance may occur within their minds, often subconsciously.

Belief A

Y

Belief B

X

Positive   Degree of Dissonance   Negative

Two basic ways of reducing dissonance are to 1) change the proportions of consonant and dissonant elements (add new positive cognitions or delete negative thoughts) and 2) altering the importance level of the issue itself or the positive or negative elements involved (Simon, Greenberg, & Brehm, 1995).

The further apart two beliefs are, the greater the dissonance and the harder the reconciliation. The movie *Fiddler on the Roof* is an epic struggle between creating harmony between beliefs, values, attitudes, and actions that are in dissonance. Tevye was a poor Jewish milkman with five unmarried daughters living in the village Anatevka in Czarist Russia. The traditions of the community are broken step by step through the romantic relationships of his daughters within the greater dissonance of the community living in poverty yet hated because they supposedly are a major cause of economic injustice.

First, the oldest daughter falls in love with a tailor who asks Tevye directly for his daughter's hand rather than going through the matchmaker. The second daughter falls in love with a student who has liberal communist leanings and is soon confined in a Siberian labor camp. The final straw is reached when his third daughter marries a Russian. At this point Tevye cannot verbally give his blessing, but nonverbally comes to accept his son-in-law. Keeping the balance between the extremes of dissonance within both social and religious beliefs took Teveye into constant prayer for the reconciliation of values, customs, beliefs, actions, and love for his family. At the same time his place in society as a respected opinion leader among an impoverished, persecuted minority is uprooted and destroyed as the community is disbanded. Amidst this conflict he remains both human and faithful to his beliefs and traditions enabling a homeostasis of a different kind to sustain him for the conflicts ahead through the elimination of dissonance through prioritizing his daughters over customs by valuing virtue over legalism.

Information Processing or Perception Theories

The industry of the present and future is information. Having the correct information at the appropriate time is often the difference between profit and loss. While China, India, and other countries take over the manufacturing industrial complex the West is building an information-based economy. Creating new information, managing that information, and being able to access the best information at critical times is becoming a major factor in our world's economy.

Social Judgment Theory

Based on maxims or principles, social judgment theory connects a diverse variety of observations into a systematic understanding of persuasive public communication.

Principle #1

Beliefs, attitudes, and values are of different intentions or weights. The degree to which an individual adheres to a religion or political view is usually more significant and vital than the degree of adherence to which brand of gas is put in the car. In our postmodern culture, a philosophical deconstructionist position is lessening the value of simple consistency.

Principle #2

Communicators have categories of judgment in intrapersonal evaluation of persuasive communication. As the world has geographic latitudes, people have latitudes of acceptance and rejection ranging on a continuum from positive to negative. This measurement of attitudes enables a more sensitive discrimination between persuasion techniques.

  A. Raising student tuition (RST) is absolutely essential for the college to survive.

  B. RST is almost certain to be essential to the college's survival.

  C. RST will most probably assist the college.

  D. RST may assist the college.

  E. RST may or may not assist the college.

  F. RST may harm the college.

  G. Probably RST will harm the college.

  H. RST is almost certain to significantly harm the college.

  I. RST will almost certainly close the college.

Which position is adhered to by an individual will determine what the most preferred attitude is likely to be. Most people would be able to accept those attitudes immediately adjacent to their position as viable alternatives while rejecting those that are farther away. Understanding the continuum of attitudes becomes vital for a public advocate to ascertain in the best communicative strategies to use in an attempt to move the audience closer to the speaker's desired position or at least to be able to think about the position with greater respect.

Most people in an audience will not be swayed from their preferred position about abortion through one public communication. They may, however, increase the latitude of their tolerance, which may in time change the desired position. Many people in the example of college tuition increase may be persuaded through significant public argument in one debate, speech, or article. Public opinion about the Vietnam war and the war in Iraq can be changed over years of negative reporting by the mass media coupled with years of miscommunication by the government. The social judgment of the audience slowly changes along latitudes of attitudes.

Attribution Theory

Attribution theory is an attempt to describe how people explain elements of their world and experience. These attributions fall into two categories, internal and external. An external explanation assigns causality or motivation to forces that are outside of the agent of action. When Adam ate the forbidden fruit in the Garden of Eden, he blamed it on Eve, and she blamed it on the snake. Ever since people have held responsible outside situations, forces, or people responsible for their own actions both in their own thinking and in communication with others. The second kind of attribution is internal, from within the individual himself or herself. Motivation to action developed from inner resources make people directly responsible for their own behavior.

When Gail failed a midterm, she blamed the impossible to understand text, the boring lectures, the professor's oblique questions, her roommate for staying up till three, and the wasp up by the light during the test for distracting her: all these are *external attributions*. Here, the test is called the *entity*. The text, lecture, roommate, and wasp are *covariants* taken together she uses as reasons to explain the failure to herself and possibly others (especially her parents who are paying for the education). The process of taking the test is considered the *modality* for the failure. Taking it after a late night is the *time* frame. Gail works backwards from the failure of the test to inferences about the causes overlooking other influences that covary (like watching TV instead of studying and not completing the reading).

She studies hard earning an A on the final and credits it to her intelligence and hard work: *internal attribution*. Gail now celebrates her victory overcoming the previous causes or discounts the earlier causes. Where she assigns causality often will determine the future behavior of whether she studies or not. Honesty demands that she take another look at her own motivations and perhaps even check out possible covariant influences with a classmate (like the study group she joined after the midterm).

A marauding band of young men in LA smash windows, loot, and burn a store. Jessie Jackson blames the behavior on poverty, powerlessness, and racism: external attribution. The police prosecutor claims the behavior was the personal choice of the individuals: internal attribution. The judge and jury must decide the motivation that causes the behavior (freedom of speech or lawlessness). Where causality is assigned can determine both their degree of guilt and the resulting sentence.

The attribution of cause or motivation subjectively infers attitudes, abilities, intentions, and dispositions about individuals in the persuasion process. Honestly assessing probability, causes, and possible motivations facilitates accurate explanations of persuasive attempts and outcomes. This self-perception can also infer attitude changes based on actions ("I earned an *A*; therefore, I am becoming a good student," or "I am eating all of this spinach; therefore, I must really like it").

"Sally and I saw Joe at a pro-life rally downtown; he must really be becoming conservative since he is against abortion." The attributions that Joe has a pro-life belief structure, that the schemata is labeled *conservative*, and that he is against abortion are all inferred ascriptions from the behavior of being at a pro-life rally. Alternate causality such as he is doing research for a paper, he is with his girlfriend who is pro-life, or that he is attempting to gain a well-rounded perspective do not occur to those in the conversation.

One significant persuasive strategy derived from attribution theory is when an individual can influence the attributions another makes. Projecting probable causes for an audience can greatly influence their current attitudes and actions that last into the future. A second rhetorical strategy is that public communicators should provide several probable explanations for individuals to interpret observable phenomena and events in their world. A third aspect is to realize that the audience will likely judge a given public communication as to the degree of believability and probability of the rhetor's advocated position and explanation.

Cognitive Response Theories

As early as 1949, Hovland, Lusnsdane, and Sheffield found that persuasion is "best" when the persuadee actively thinks about the persuasive message. Petty and Cacioppo (1981, p. 93) observe that their formulations of persuasion owes much to the important work by Hovland and his associates, who identified a large number of important factors and interesting effects in persuasion. Recent theoretical advances in persuasion studies have emphasized a cognitive approach to attitude change in persuasive communication. The actual thinking that a person does during the persuasive process is considered significant in attitude and belief change. The basic focus of past cognitive theories has illuminated cognitive states resulting from persuasion attempts (Morley, 1987). Information processing theory has demonstrated that the cognitive response of an individual may be as important to the persuasion of that person as the message received from an external source (Pargament & DeRosa, 1985). Cognitive response theory purports that persuasion of a subject by an external message happens through issue-relevant thoughts generated by the persuasive communication. The receiver of a persuasive message is recognized as an active participator, not merely a passive receptor. Cognitive theory takes a step beyond information processing by predicting that the most effective communication will enhance significant issue-relevant thinking and, therefore, persuasion.

While not ignoring the persuader, cognitive response theory focuses on the internal schemata of the audience rather than external aspects of persuasive communication. More responsibility is also placed on individuals for their own actions, beliefs, and attitudes than on the rhetorical situation or the persuader. The intentional or unintentional selection of previously incorporated experiences, values, beliefs, and attitudes through schematic processes may be the most significant part of the persuasive process.

Heuristic Model

With the first full cognitive-response model, Chaiken supports the idea that high involvement leads auditors to use message-based cognitions to mediate persuasion (1980; Axsom, Yates, & Chaiken, 1987). Those in low involvement situations will use heuristic processing in which simple decision making methods or principles mediate persuasion. Pallak, Murroni, and Koch (1983) found this model to adequately explain variations in audience evaluations of various advertisements. As the name heuristic indicates, this model is a guide for thinking about and developing persuasive messages.

Persuasion most integrated within an individual audience member's mind creates a persistent attitude through the systematic processing mode. Here the listener mentally processes information received in persuasive communication by fully thinking through the implications and arguments. The heuristic model is based upon axioms that can be measured through social scientific methods to evaluate their relative impact on persuasive rhetoric.

The first of the heuristic principles is the credibility or ethos of the speaker. When the source of the persuasive message is strong, low-involvement listeners are more likely to believe the message. Some students will believe a message simply because a professor says it in a lecture. Some people will believe a message simply because a political leader from their party says it is true. Likewise some will reject anything the President says simply because he said it and he has low ethos in their eyes.

A second axiom is based on the degree the receiver is attracted to the sender of the message. When involvement in the issue is low, the degree to which the audience likes the initiator will influence the persuasive impact of the message. For example; if an audience member has experienced some near disaster in a kayak, then she will be more likely to believe a speaker's story of disaster on a category five rapids, while a person with no experience may be so far removed that the whole issue seems surreal. Woodworkers are more likely to tune into a carpentry program on TV, while golfers will be more likely to watch the PGA championship. Involvement in the activity is a key determinate in the audience's selection of the communication medium.

A third maxim is the consensus of those around the receiver. If a large number of individuals are positively accepting the message, then a low involvement individual will often positively respond to the message (Chaiken, 1987). When I was a pastor of an African-American church, I quickly realized how the interactive listening drew more hesitant members of the congregation into the key points of the worship and sermon. Those who do not believe or are doubtful would find themselves nodding in assent and finally respond in a positive manner. At Billy Graham crusades simply having the counselors come forward gives impetus for those who are contemplating conversion to join in the crowd who are going forward.

Like the Elaboration Likelihood Model (ELM), the Heuristic Model purports that persuasion can be achieved through two general avenues that change according to the amount of careful thinking involved by the auditors of a persuasive message. Unlike the ELM, the Heuristic Model suggests that these two processes of thinking are interactive or additive so that messages and effects may intertwine (Chaiken & Maheswaran, 1994). This flexibility is an important part of heuristic thinking.

Elaboration Likelihood Model

Petty and Cacioppo developed the Elaboration Likelihood Model (ELM) over a number of years. In the late seventies they published a number of articles individually and jointly that began to point toward an approach to persuasion based on the thought processes of a recipient of a persuasive message. They purport that persuasion changes as a function of the likelihood that receivers will engage in positive issue-relevant thinking.

According to the ELM, formation of attitudes is most effectively accomplished through fully and carefully thinking through each argument of an issue. This consideration is then internalized into the personal schema that results in a changed or strengthened attitude. When a persuader creates a situation in which the persuadees are likely to elaborate well-conceived arguments, then the elaboration likelihood is high and that advocate is expected to succeed. The likelihood of a person elaborating on a given idea is related in a specific manner to the person's motivation and ability to elaborate that particular argument. This central route to attitude change is the focus of the model.

The ELM has seven basic postulates (Berger, 1990; Petty & Cacioppo, 1986) that are advanced as essential premises in the process of persuasion. These postulates are presuppositions to a train of reasoning or hypothetical links in the theoretical chain of the ELM, thus they are essential parts of the whole as opposed to the maxims or axioms that can be more or less true independently of each other.

The first postulate is that people are motivated to hold correct attitudes. Festinger (1950) was the first to expound this idea in detail in his theory of social comparison processes. Each person subjectively evaluates the opinions of his or her own attitudes through perceived social norms and mores.

The ELM also postulates that although people want to hold correct attitudes, the amount and nature of issue relevant elaboration in which they are willing or able to engage in evaluating a message vary with individual and situational factors. The extent of issue-relevant cognitive response by a person who receives a persuasive message may occur along a continuum that extends from no thought about the information to complete elaboration of every argument with total integration into the person's attitude schema.

The third postulate asserts that variables can affect the amount and direction of attitude change by (a) serving as persuasive arguments, (b) serving as peripheral cues, and/or (c) affecting the extent or direction of issue and argument elaboration. "Persuasive arguments are viewed as bits of information contained in communication that are relevant to a person's subjective determination of the true merits of an advocated position" (Petty & Cacioppo, 1986, p. 16). The kind of information, presentation of that information, or the many other variables, which the subject may consider to be essential to the central merits of the issue, will vary from situation to situation and individual to individual. Peripheral cues are those stimuli that influence the attitude or issue without conscious thinking. Message elaboration, the third manner in which variables may influence persuasion, affects the extent and/or direction of issue relevant thinking. A practical difficulty arises within this postulate in that the advocate cannot determine which of the ways any particular variable will affect any individual in a given situation. Only the *likelihood* of elaboration may be predicted.

The fourth postulate of the ELM is that variables affecting motivation and ability to process a message in a relatively objective manner can do so by either enhancing or reducing argument scrutiny. People will attempt to come to a "correct" understanding of an issue (see postulate #1) in an objective manner when they have a high ability and high motivation to elaborate. Conversely, objective argument scrutiny diminishes when the individual has a lessened motivation or ability to process information. In practice most people will not have a perfectly objective schemata about any given issue, but will be relatively objective or relatively biased

The ELM also postulates that variables affecting message processing in a relatively biased manner can produce either a positive (favorable) or negative (unfavorable) motivational and/or ability bias to the issue-relevant thoughts attempted. When strong beliefs or attitudes already have become ingrained into the schematic processing of an individual concerning an issue, there is a high likelihood that one side will be supported more than another within the person's elaboration about that issue.

A sixth postulate affirms that as motivation and/or ability to process arguments is decreased, peripheral cues become relatively more important determinates of persuasion. For the best central route, persuasive processes require both high motivation and high ability. In all cases central and peripheral routes of persuasion are inversely related (this is in direct contradiction of the heuristic model). When the central route decreases, the importance of the peripheral route will increase. Likewise, as the peripheral route becomes operative in the process, elaboration will decrease in importance.

The seventh and last postulate of the ELM is that attitude changes that result mostly from processing issue-relevant arguments (central route)

will show greater temporal persistence, greater prediction of behavior, and greater resistance to counterpersuasion than attitude changes that result mostly from peripheral cues. The central route to persuasion will cause the subject to access the issue schema, rehearse relevant memories, strengthen interrelationships between ideas and levels, and thus render the schema more accessible, enduring, and resistant to change (McGuire, 1981; Petty & Cacioppo, 1986).

This model is inherently practical in that if a rhetor can create a message that moves the audience to elaborate in the central route in a positive direction, then the communication will have a favorable impact. The ELM, therefore, provides a framework to discover and use methods and qualities of rhetorical discourse for good.

Invitational Rhetoric

Invitational rhetoric intends to offer an alternative to persuasive rhetoric. Gearheart (1979) believes that "any intent to persuade is an act of violence" and thus persuasive rhetoric is indicted as criminal. Traditional rhetorical perspectives are viewed as masculine oriented with power appropriated to conquer others through the use of violent intention, method, style and content. Those who teach rhetoric "have been training a competent breed of weapons specialists who are skilled in emotional maneuvers, experts in intellectual logistics," and capable of creating a war of words where paternalistic propaganda overbears others for the good of the speaker (Gearheart, 1979). Foss and Griffin (1995) continue this frontal assault on rhetorical persuasion: "Embedded in efforts to change others is a desire for control and domination" where the self-worth of the auditor "is measured by the power exerted over others, and a devaluation of the life worlds of others." The critique of rhetorical persuasion contends that, masculine, hierarchical, judgmental and adversarial qualities are valued by traditional rhetoricians in a violent use of power in order to conquer others through coercive argumentation thereby gaining self-worth and more power. Along with this, Foss and Griffin (1995) maintain that the masculine understanding of an audience is that others are naïve, less expert and inferior "if their views differ from the rhetor's own" as though they are an "opponent" in a struggle to "impose" a specific perspective on each other.

The reformation idea of "invitation" was the focal point of Christian rhetorical persuasion; the theological constructs of equality (Galatians 3:28), human value (Psalm 139), and free will (Ephesians 1:3-7, I Timothy 2:4) were developed by Luther and Calvin. Along with these, the "priesthood of the believer" (I Peter 2:5-9), "human responsibility" (Matthew 28:18-20), "election" and "identification" (Romans 8:28-39), coupled with "faith" and "grace" (Ephesians 2:8-10), and the "voice of God" (Isaiah 55) all of which are important to the Christian idea of invitation within a theology of persuasive homiletic proclamation. Invitation is assumed to come in the conclusion of an informative, exegetical message.

Rather than taking a more holistic perspective, Foss and Griffin redefine the three selected constructs into a postmodern, humanistic philosophy calling them "feminist principles." This incomplete feminist perspective of invitation created in the *straw man* logical fallacy is far less than the rich heritage of theology and rhetoric.

The debate among clergy during the last five centuries does not envision a dichotomy between invitation (female) and imposition (male), as is the feminist perspective, but rather as a continuum from a persuasive "call" on one side to "invitation" in the middle, and "proclamation" of evidence on the other side. This conceptual basis for the purpose of persuasive communication allows the audience to make their own judgment at both ends of the ethical range. The question is not whether to give the audience a choice, that choice is assumed, but how directed should the decision or application be along the continuum between a "call for action" and a simple "proclamation of information."

A classical perspective of persuasion also makes a distinction between coercion, manipulation, and persuasion. Coercion and manipulation use power as the primary motivation, while persuasion attempts to motivate the auditor to change from within.

Traditional Rhetorical Perspective

Not persuasion	Persuasion
Coercion, manipulation	call to action, invitation, proclamation

In Christian philosophical rhetoric, decisions are made by a rhetor along a continuum of persuasion that avoids coercion and manipulation.

No distinct line between right and wrong may exist. For example, coercion of a two-year-old not to touch a hot stove is seen as ethically good. However, coercion of a twenty-year-old to vote in a specific manner is ethically evil.

In the realm of rhetorical persuasion manipulation and coercion are often ethically wrong because of the use of power by the communicator to get what is best of the speaker and not what is best for the audience. The debate as inherited from reformation thought is from a middle course of action (directing a specific change) to a proclamation (without a persuasive appeal). The radical feminist perspective creates a dichotomy between coercive manipulation, which they label as "traditional masculine rhetoric," and proclamation, which they label as "invitational rhetoric." Eliminating the middle ground where the majority of persuasive messages occur does not seem useful in persuasive argumentation.

Feminist Invitational Perspective

Traditional Rhetoric(s)	Feminist Rhetoric(s)
Male dominated	Female inspired
Traditionally static	New dynamic rhetoric
Power motivated violence	Relationally motivated
Imposition of will	Invitation to believe
Ethically wrong	Ethically right

Feminists see a dichotomy between kinds of rhetoric with discrete categories, according to Foss. Persuasion is violence while invitation is good influence. Different rhetorics may apply to divergent situations.

Critique of Feminist Invitation

Providing the listener with a choice based on love so that they are free moral agents is the difference between persuasion and manipulation not between male and female rhetoric. The logical fallacy these authors use by distorting traditional rhetorical persuasion through the use of violence, war, and power creates a false dichotomy and a "straw man" enemy, thus providing an illegitimate foundation for a feminist critique of persuasion. The mischaracterization of traditional rhetoric is so drastic Fulkerson (1996) indicates they "draw unnecessarily strong conclusions" while Bruner (1996) calls it "fictional." The classical "masculine" ideal of "speaking the truth in love" (Paul, Ephesians 4:15) is the opposite of this feminist characterization.

From the time Plato wrote *Georgias*, men have fought against those who use rhetoric to manipulate truth and coerce people for their own good. This feminist perspective of invitational rhetoric is asking people to move to Plato's "neuter" form of rhetoric from the *Phaedrus*. Plato sees three ways language can be used: 1) it can move us toward what is good—the noble lover. 2) it can move us toward what is wrong—the evil lover. Or 3) it can attempt to not influence the audience at all—the "neuter" lover (Weaver, 1985). The non-lover attempts to avoid responsibility assuming that by saying nothing persuasive, then the other person is free to make up her own mind. For Plato, and most others in the tradition of rhetoric, the position presented as feminist invitational rhetoric is devoid of love. As Weaver describes it, Plato in the Phaedrus "is asking whether we ought to prefer a neuter form of speech to the kind which is ever getting us aroused over things and provoking an expense of spirit" (1985, p. 5). Weaver moves on to critique what was then called "semantically purified" in style and form.

> *By this we mean the kind of speech approaching pure notation in the respect that it communicates abstract intelligence with impulsion . . . . But this neuter language will be an unqualified medium of transmission of meaning from mind to mind, and by virtue of its mind can remain in an unprejudiced relationship to the world and also to other minds.* (p. 7)

While championing the neuter speech, this feminist perspective attempts to force the "masculine" rhetoric into the second kind of love, that of the evil lover who exploits the audience. For this kind of speaker,

> *Love is defined as the kind of desire which overcomes rational opinion and moves toward the enjoyment of personal or bodily beauty. The lover wishes to make the object of his passion as pleasing to himself as possible; but to those possessed by this frenzy, only that which is subject to their will is pleasant.* (p. 10)

For Plato, neuter language, what is here called invitation, exploits rather than being an answer for exploitation. The response is found in the rhetorical tradition itself, the truth spoken in love (Paul, Eph. 4:15).

The "patriarchal" ideal as expressed by the Greek founders and current adherents conceptualize traditional rhetoric and persuasion as: a good man speaking well (Quintilian), developing the citizen orator (Cicero), enabling virtuous character and discovery of all arguments (Aristotle), with truthful content spoken in the character of love (Plato). Yes, some of these same male rhetors use war and violence as *metaphors* of argumentation, but not, as Foss and Griffin claim, a reality of violence (such as Cicero's metaphor or Aristotle's verbal defense [not offense] while Gearheart says it "is" actual violence). *The answer to neuter and exploitative rhetoric is noble, loving rhetoric that passionately moves the soul to become a better person.*

213

Far from the violence perspective of radical feminism, human change through persuasion from a character of love is both good and necessary. All traditional rhetoricians call for a choice to be given to the audience denouncing manipulation and propaganda. In the process of raising a child, if persuasion is eliminated, then physical violence is the primary method left for training. In the process of democratic government, if persuasion is eliminated, then totalitarianism is the major method left for civilization. In the process of business if persuasion were eliminated, then monopolies or government control would dominate the marketplace. In the process of social intercourse, if persuasion were eliminated, then anarchy would result. In the process of education, if a teacher does not attempt to influence or persuade students, education cannot take place. As the best *alternative to* violence, rhetorical persuasion widens ethical, kind and gentle manners of working within human realms while also allowing for appropriate assertiveness.

This traditional perspective of persuasive rhetoric based on truth and love does not remotely resemble the feminist re-interpretation of coercive power and imposition through authoritative manipulation as perceived by Gearhart (1979) and Foss and Griffin (1995). The "patriarchal" persuasion of traditional rhetoric is designed specifically to counter the cruel mistreatment of the persuasive process, yet radical feminist critique defines traditional rhetoric as the exploitation it was designed to overcome. Denying that some individuals do use words violently, that some do coerce, cheat, manipulate and lie would be unrealistic; however, these exploitations of rhetoric are not the teachings of traditional rhetoricians nor of men in general, they are the *misuse and abuse* of the good practice of persuasive rhetoric by both men and women.

The feminist dispute against persuasion uses two lines of argument: 1) persuasion is immoral as an attempt to dominate another through power and 2) cognitively females are biologically programmed and acculturated to think and interact differently than males, which gives them a disadvantage in argumentative discourse (Fulkerson, 1996). The moral issue is addressed in the development of a comprehensive ethical perspective and practice involving mutual respect and reciprocity. Isocrates' idea of service coupled with Plato's foundation of love provides the rhetorical counter argument. If persuasion in and of itself is unethical violence, then Foss and Griffin would be doing an immoral act by writing and publishing their paper because it is an argumentative essay designed to persuade the reader. The gender equity issue may be valid in some rhetorical situations and should be considered in all situations. In applying this logic to all persuasion, the argument is

self-contradictory (Foss and Griffin use liner hierarchical thinking expressing powerful ideas to say that women do not think in liner hierarchical
manners using power).

Underlying these arguments is the assumption that dividing all issues
by gender is vital to understanding. If both genders worked on the philosophy of rhetoric, the perspective could be broadened and include humans,
not just male or female. Foss and Foss (1983) indicate wholeness, process,
interconnectedness, approximation. and cooperation are the hallmarks of
feminist methodology distinguishing it from a masculine perspective. Why
not use these methods in describing "masculine" rhetoric instead of attempting to create enemies? If these were distinctives, then cooperatively
incorporating them into the mainstream of rhetorical thought instead of
alienating and recreating would be the appropriate argument for these female rhetors, yet they approach the "invitational" rhetoric through powerful persuasion instead of using their expressed ideals.

Place the postmodern invitational rhetoric back in the historical argument on the extent of persuasive appeal. No conclusive answer has arisen
from centuries of debate in the reformation tradition on the question:
"Should a persuasive appeal be given, inviting the audience to change or
make a decision, during or following a public speech?" Strategies of discussion, silence, narration, parable, poetry, music, meditation, and prayer have
all been implemented following public speeches in religious situations to
enable audiences to choose their own change based on the evidence provided rather than have the speaker direct the change. Many rhetors continue
to completely leave out any appeal in proclamation of their message; others
use the "invitation" where appeals are given for audience members to make
changes, but the specific change is left to the listener, and finally, some advocates prefer a "call" where a direct appeal for specific change is attempted
during persuasive rhetoric. Taking a small part of a theological-rhetorical
debate and placing it in the midst of postmodern secular humanism will
widen the discussion of important considerations beyond the confines of
the church allowing a debate of definitions of invitation and the ethical
appropriateness of stimulating change in others. This opportunity of envisioning a revised rhetoric within a new philosophical base is healthy but
would be far better placed in the continuum of persuasive rhetoric rather
than the dichotomy of extreme feminism.

The invitational rhetoric of Foss and Griffin calls attention to several significant aspects for the consideration of rhetorical persuasion in the
secular world. Directing a greater amount of attention to the open, interactive process of mutual respect and reciprocity is worthy for all rhetorical

situations. The concept of personal involvement through offering personal narratives adds to what Aristotle calls the ethos of the speaker and the relationship aspects of the content and situation, similar to the African style of relational speaking. Re-sourcement through dialogue gains the personal involvement of the audience and may be significant in developing issue-relevant intrapersonal elaboration, similar to dialogue preaching. Creating environments where individuals experience safety, value, and freedom allows relationships to develop in unique ways; pointing to the significance of this enriching environment in rhetorical situations should encourage positive interactions. If persuasion really is taught as violence, then their call for a step away from rhetorical persuasion is warranted; however, if their analysis is inaccurate and traditional rhetoric is not taught as they propose, then they could be seen as a moderating influence for the few who use power as a foundation for coercion and manipulation but Gearheart, Foss and Griffin, although they have a significant voice in postmodern circles, have little to say about classical public rhetoric.

Mass Media

Along side of public speaking and writing in traditional ways is the whole complex of modern mass media. Here is a very cursory overview of some of the major communicative theories that specifically address thinking about the messages of mass communication.

Lasswell

Lasswell's model is probably the best known of the mass media communication approaches. He says that the audience desires information. Journalists should provide correct, objective information that can be verified by other sources. He provides a series of questions to consider: Who? Says what? When? Where? In what channel? To whom? With what impact? As a continuing example, let's consider how the different models of mass communication would affect the audience's response to the idea of war. Lasswell's audience would ask: "Tell me the truth, what happened? What is happening?"

Magic Bullet

The Magic Bullet model believes people need information. Mass media reach people who are isolated in some manner. The messages of the media reach the audience at their point of isolation and will meet their need in a direct, immediate, uniform, and powerful way. The media serves society by meeting the needs of people. The ideal audience would respond to a message of war with, "Tell me more, help me understand, let's join together."

Hypodermic

In the Hypodermic model the audience is inoculated with a media message so that they believe the content and feel congruent emotions. This way of thinking stems from a perspective that commutation has a direct influence of communication on individuals. People change in the specific area of the message that should be factual, specific, and objective in nature. The audience would respond, "War is at hand! We are on the right side! We want war!"

Multistage

The Multistage model of mass media expects the audience to believe the opinion leaders, and the media augment those messages. This way of thinking is process oriented and considers communication to be both informative and entertaining and that both are persuasive. Influence of messages are first in thinking, then in values, and finally in behavior. The audience would respond, "This means war. People are saying we are at war."

Selective Process

In the Selective Process way of thinking, mass communicators anticipate the audience to interpret the message from their own experiences. Audiences select both the messages they listen to and their own beliefs and processes; the media simply provides opportunities to be aware of multiple messages along with corresponding information or content. People will be influenced only in the area where their attitudes already direct them to change. The audience would respond, "War, what war? or This is the moral equivalent of war."

Gratification

Similar to the Selective Process model is that of Gratification. People will chose those messages they want and reject what they do not desire to consume. They are entertained more than informed. Deep inner needs drive expectations so people become loyal to some media while neglecting most. Excitement and prurient interest are primary with change happening through deepening needs and gratification of those desires.

Social Learning

The Social Learning model believes people imitate media because they believe the real world is like the mediated world. The media simply reflects reality; therefore, the audience should respond to the mediated message. The mass media is part of social evolution that leads to different actions; thus, their primary task is to communicate specific behavioral possibilities. The audience would respond, "Let's go get 'em! Let's join!"

Priming

The Priming model of mass communication views the media as storytellers. Scripts of thought influence people because they picture life. When we face similar situations or information we will demonstrate a change to be like the story. Until then the message lies dormant in our life experience. The audience would respond, "Give me a gun. I'll pull the trigger."

Cultivation

The Cultivation model of mass communication assumes that the audience will adapt their worldview to what they see and hear through the mass media. Communication comes from the heart and influences the entire person: thoughts, emotions, attitudes, beliefs, and actions in a slow process of change. The audience would respond, "War is in our streets. It's a scary world out there! Our government should intervene."

Agenda Setting

The Agenda Setting model says the audience will make up their own minds, but they will think about the issues brought up by the mass media. The press determines the issues while people choose their own positions, so media influence is limited to the area of deliberation and critical thinking. The audience would respond with thinking and conversation, "What do you think about the war? I'm not so sure . . . ."

Catharsis

The Catharsis model considers mass communication from the perspective of vicarious experience so the audience joins in the process through the story. Communication is an existential reality where consumption of the messages becomes part of our life experience. The audience would respond, "What an awful fight." Or "I wish I had that dirty monger in my sights."

Hegemonic

The Hegemonic model indicates the audience knows the press is a vain attempt to confuse the masses in such a way as to keep the powerful in power. Communication primarily addresses money and power hoping the audience will become subservient to those who communicate by doing their bidding and keeping themselves in check. The audience would respond, "We are overcoming the evil enemy" or "Down with the war, overthrow the government! Our country is evil!"

Empathy

None of these approaches are adequate to explain the experience of the message of *The Passion of the Christ*. In that film Catharsis comes the closest, but it is not enough. Mass media messages are not consumed, but people enter into the story—it becomes part of our reality through vicarious experience. Feeling similar feelings about thinking similar thoughts through communication is the foundation of excellent communication. Like Plato's analysis of music in the *Republic*, mass media messages bypass the rational and enter into the heart of a person. Going straight to another's heart with a message intensifies when the communicators have a shared or similar past experience. It is also strengthened when approached from a shared worldview. It increases impact when a character in the story shares with us similar desires, passions, dreams, or goals. We enter into another's story, not just watch from the outside. This may be rare in mass media, but extremely powerful when it happens.

This proposal could explain the reaction of some people watching pornography or violence and then acting on it (if they respond as strongly to those items as I do to *The Passion*). This theoretical construct could also explain part of the behavior of extreme fans at sporting events. This could help explain the addiction of soap operas and sit coms. It could also begin to address the attraction of certain videogames and how they could have a benign impact on most people but move others to act in antisocial ways.

My addition to mass communication theory is that empathy can explain some reactions to media messages better than other theories. Some theories like Lasswell's can provide a great guide for construction of good media messages. Others give insight into the audience's reception of the communicative message and impact under normal situations.

Christian Responses to Mass Media

Bill Strom (2003) gives possible Christian responses to mass communication: 1) Reject media messages as well as the technology itself. This is the position of separatists. Some will reject specific kinds of electronic media such as movies or internet while accepting television and radio. 2) Reject the content of the media messages while accepting the technology. This is the position of the avoiders. They will either attempt to make separate channels with Christian messages or will be extremely careful about what is communicated. 3) Accepting the message along with the technology. Few Christians will accept all content messages but with varying degrees of freedom in consuming all kinds of communication. 4) Reform the message and use the technology. This is the position of most evangelical believers. Jesus said we are to be in the world but not of the world. Balancing that idea with skill is not easy. Attempting to further messages that conform to Romans 12:1-2, Philippians 2:5, and 4:8 while countering and avoiding messages that represent other kinds of thinking is not an easy task.

Avoiding the negative effects of media messages: secular values, temptation, objectification of people, and creation of power as the basis for relationships is not an easy task while consuming mass media messages. Even more difficult is the attempt to bring into the media culture specifically Christian messages or Christian ways of thinking. Overt attempts like *The Passion of the Christ* and more covert attempts like *The Lord of the Rings* can meet with great success. We need more Christians who are willing to take up the challenge to reform and redeem the mass media culture.

Conclusion

This simple overview of selected theory should be considered alongside of the historical review from chapters four through six and does not substitute for a complete survey of current communicative theories. What it does provide is a foundation upon which messages may be constructed and articulated in an influential manner. A number of mass media models were covered to broaden the understanding of media messages.

Chapter 9

Argumentative Forms and Methods

I speak the rhetoric of truth and reason.
Acts 25:26

THE GENERAL population of the United States thinks DDT caused the death of birds and destruction of environmental ecosystems. Banning it or as the US did, prohibiting foreign aid from going to any country that uses the pesticide, is effectively leading to the death of two million people a year from malaria. Persuasive, persistent, communication changed the beliefs of people in the face of strong contrary scientific evidence. Yet today congress holds to the restrictions and a majority of the population believes we are good to ban the substance. What brings about strong, persistent public perception—that is wrong? How can we be fooled in spite of the evidence? Logic and evidence that provides strong message quality and reflects truth is not always the argument that wins the day.

Persuasive communication must be placed by logical syntax and semantics into sentences that form ideas and thoughts presenting points of view. At other times stories or cartoons drive home the points. Even nonverbal means of persuasive communication such as a photograph of a soldier carrying a child hurt in a war have implied messages called enthymemes where the audience fills in the propositions and stasis implications. Public opinion is swayed through rhetorical discourse that involves argument, but not exclusively.

Dialectic, the Heart of Argument

A Socratic dialectic is to question an issue in order to derive an exact definition involving the Truth of an idea or thing. In Platonic dialogues dialectical conversation searches for exactitude in the definition and then categorizes the issue into specific species. Socrates sought to determine the essence of a thing or idea, what it always is, and then what it is not.

Reasoning about probabilities comes in the form of dialectic in Plato's perspective. Based on premises that are "generally accepted," dialectic builds arguments that persuade an audience. This is opposed to scientific demonstration based on observation and syllogistic logic. For Aristotle, dialectic enables intellectual training in argument, develops the ability to critically think through both sides of an issue, and enables a determination of truth all of which are useful in persuading an audience.

Dialectic is an art of communication based on a proposition or hypothesis and attempts to understand fully an issue from multiple perspectives. When we considered the ontological and moral perspectives of anthropology, we looked briefly into the views of Rousseau, Sartre, Hobbes, and a classical understanding. This was the beginning of dialectic; to complete it we would have to fully debate the issues.

This kind of philosophical conversation is best when more than one perspective is represented in the dialogue. Considering what Plato would have said, then considering what Aristotle would have said, then Paul, then Augustine . . . gives multiple points of view enabling a larger and more diverse dialectic. I have enjoyed greatly several post-doctoral conversations in ethics, philosophy, hermeneutics, homiletics, and rhetoric where a group of people with doctorates gathers to discuss issues. These keep me sharper intellectually than most conventions, research projects, or simple discussions. Rhetoric can be iron sharpening iron.

The heart of dialectic is asking great questions. Strangely, these are usually more difficult than the answers. Coming to agreement on what is the proper question for abortion—When does life begin? Whose rights are primary—mother's or child's? Is the right to life more important than the right to privacy? What is the essence of personhood? Agreeing on the right question to ask is actually more difficult than deriving a scientific, political, or personal policy.

Coming to agreement on definitions is also a very difficult process. For example, can you define *futile care* as in the case of delaying eminent death? Should futile care as practiced in our hospitals be categorized as euthanasia or allowing someone to die with dignity? Are food and water rights or privileges, medicine or essentials, in the struggle for life? Is removing a feeding tube and water, and not allowing food or water to be taken orally, a function of the individual, family, courts, legislature, or medical community? In a democratic republic we enter into many debates about what should be done. Listening to each other, taking each other into account, learning from each other are essential parts of co-existence. Dialectic is the key to this kind of public communication.

Logical Statements

Persuasive communication is rarely as exacting as putting together full syllogistic or formal statements in their entirety. However, Aristotle's enthymematic rhetorical reasoning understands that people often communicate by providing part of a syllogism and allow the audience to fill in the other elements, even if they are unaware they are doing so. In persuasive writing and speaking we often use part of the following reasoning patterns trusting the logical abilities of others for their persuasive impact. An enthymeme is an argument that leaves the audience to complete the premises.

Categorical Statements

Placing ideas in groups of similar elements allows comparison-contrast logic which enables our understanding. Calling the social issue of "gay marriage" a "civil right" places it among other "rights" giving it a particular perspective. Categorizing the issue as a "sin" places it among a different set of perspectives. Categorizing the issue as a "civil wrong" gives an entirely different impression. Categorizing it as a "drain on society" will give other implications. The essence of categorizing the issues of a proposition enables the listener to understand the issue in light of other similar issues because classifying according to categories enables understanding through comparison and distribution.

The category we place the argument in will often determine the range of questions available to ask and the kinds of evidence to be supplied. In the example of gay marriage, one of the issues brought up is that of health insurance. Culturally we have a difficult time arguing that since homosexual activity is so unhealthy it takes 20 years off the lifespan, should heterosexual people bear the burden of those extra costs? Because the category is "rights" and not "economics" or "healthcare."

Because much of real life is not as black and white in the details of categories, wise communicators often soften the impact with words like *usually, most,* or *probably.* If Bill is a member of a gang, a stereotypical minor premise, which arises in many of your audience member's minds, is that he breaks the law, skips school, or takes drugs can be a real danger for a communicator because the word gang connotes those things to many people.

Categorizing someone who commits suicide by blowing others up as a *freedom fighter* or *insurgent* places him or her in a different category than *terrorist* or *criminal.* Auxiliary categorization of the perpetrator as a Muslim terrorist, or Irish terrorist, limits the category even further by race or religion. Labeling a pro-life protester as a terrorist through blocking clinic access, places that speech issue on the same level as the criminal act of blowing up a clinic. The categories we use in public communication need to be carefully considered as the speaker forms the message for correct association.

Universal Statements

A universal proposition places the issue as always the same, in every situation. Formal logic attempts to deal with absolutes and universals as much as possible. Persuasive communication deals more often with latitudes of acceptance and rejection along lines of probability. Aristotle correctly noted that rhetoricians necessarily deal with degrees of probability. In a court of law the burden may be beyond reasonable doubt, while in a persuasive editorial for the newspaper you do not have three months of testimony to establish the position.

Universal statements can be diagramed as:

> All A are B (affirmative)
> All whales swim.
> When A (whales) is species of aquatic mammals.
> All females think.
> When A (females) is members of the human race.

> No A are B (negative)
> No whales climb Mt. Everest.
> When A is species of aquatic mammals.
> No females think.
> When A is species of moss.

Speeches and even books are usually presented in a manner such as to present an air-tight case for absolute universal truth. This book is a Liberal Arts approach to rhetoric and does not pretend to be the absolute universal truth about the subject. We touch on philosophy, ethics, theology, history, theory, psychology, and many other fields as we consider their relationship and influence on public communication. Rhetoric may be the queen of the Liberal Arts, but she is not a dictator of universals.

Does this mean no universal propositions can be made? Of course not. The evidence warrants many such propositions. The public communicator must be careful in using them. Not all Christians are Bible-thumpers, and not all Bible-thumpers are Christians. Not all students are capable, and not all capable people are students. Not all teachers are wise. Not all ministers have faith. Strictly speaking the earth is not round, only generally speaking. The sun does not rise; it only seems to as the world turns. Be careful how you state your argument. Does this mean you can never refer to a sunrise? Of course you can, even though strictly speaking it is not absolute truth, just a metaphorical way of referring to the phenomena we experience each morning. Learn to generalize without placing the argument in absolute universal terms.

"All space shuttle flights are deadly" is an overgeneralization stated as a universal proposition. The opposite is also not true, "All space shuttle flights are perfectly safe." While we know that many have been successful, two have ended in tragedy. A good public communicator will recognize the danger of universal statements in either direction and give an appropriate statement somewhere in the middle of the road with both danger and safety in balance.

One of the difficulties of knowing absolute truth is the difficulty of placing the application in absolute universal ways. All Christians must reproduce spiritually through evangelization. All Christians must believe that Jesus is coming again in bodily form. We all must not smoke, drink, dance, go to movies. . . . Be careful of placing a burden on others that we ourselves struggle to bear. The Pharisees got caught up in that external universal righteousness, and Jesus condemned them for it.

Particular Statements

The heart of most public communication is the individual example or particular. What is true in this instance, which axioms or principles apply to this idea, issue, data, or event are particulars. Much can be written on whether or not it is ethical to allow people to carry concealed weapons to public events such as a football game while still maintaining the constitutional right to the universal axiom to "keep and bear arms."

Particular statements can be diagramed as:

> Some A are B (affirmative)
> Some people are prejudiced.
> Some auto crashes are caused by distracted drivers talking on cell phones.

> Some A are not B (negative)
> Some prejudice is not bad or evil, but good.
> Some advertisements are not true.

These particular arguments allow for the flexibility for allowing people to make statements in a manner that reflects reality instead of pre-determined universal categories. Simply because some prejudice is evil, such as hating someone simply because he is of another race, does not mean that all prejudice is evil; some is good such as I love, value, provide for . . . my children more than I do for others. Being a father, that kind of prejudicial treatment of my own children is good, right, and just. Simply because some advertisements mislead, does not mean that all advertisements mislead the public; therefore, use care in developing true particular categories.

The universal ethical proposition that humans ought not to pollute water may be difficult to define, and virtually impossible to come to a working agreement with all interested parties. However we can write and speak publicly about whether to drink bottled water, restrict development, limit fertilization, or regulate industrial waste in a specific area. Oregon has found it next to impossible to reconcile: the needs of the farmers, protect the wild fish, provide for recreational use, and meet indigenous people's desires in the Klamath River Basin. Yet each party deserves to voice particular arguments in the dialectic leading to public policy whether it is for more irrigation, less pollution, decreased temperature, or grater volume of water. Competing rights and authorities have to communicate in dialectic in order for even a semblance of a fair and balanced agreement to be reached. Our job as rhetoricians is to give voice to these competing people, ideas, ideals, rights, and needs as particular statements aligning with the universal claims. We should be able to argue multiple sides of any issue.

Hypothetical Statements

Claims that are not true but can support an argument through allegory, metaphor, generalizations, or other means are called hypothetical. They often are used in "what if" scenarios. Many millions of dollars are spent annually in the Pentagon and at Langley attempting to decipher the possibilities present in our world. What are likely courses of action by enemies and terrorists? What if our cellular communications are cut off? What if radar fails? What if we are attacked with biological weapons? These scenarios are forecast in a manner that when similar events happen we will have possible courses of real actions to take. The hypothetical leads to better real action in that we have plans. Many families have escape plans if their house catches on fire. Most of us attempt to have available funds in case of a personal emergency. The whole idea of insurance is based on the probability of risk in a given situation to mitigate the financial loss if something unforeseen happens.

Hypothetical questions, statements, stories, and scenarios help people think of options and prepare for the future. Just like the very real hope that Jesus will come again leads people to be better individuals and do better things, hypothetical dreams lead people to start businesses, enter relationships, and persevere through college. Using these kinds of arguments in public communication can strengthen your appeal and influence the attitudes and actions of the audience.

Disjunctive Statements

Much practical reasoning follows a disjunctive form, setting something against two (or more) alternatives in the major premise, denying one of them in the minor premise, and affirming the other one through the conclusion.

Major premise:	Either A or B
Minor premise:	Not B
Conclusion:	Therefore A

A debate in Portland, Oregon, concerning purchasing PGE from Enron to supply the city's own electricity disjunctive reasoning in the local newspaper looks something like this:

> Either taxpayers will spend 2 billion on a public utility or the citizens will pay 4 or 5 billion over the next 3 years in rates to a private company.
>
> Paying twice as much or more to a private company is not wise.
>
> Therefore, the city should purchase a public utility.

This argument was countered.

> After paying 2 billion for an electric utility, the city will either have to raise rates or the service will decline because they have not considered the operating costs carefully.
>
> Raising rates and loosing service are both unacceptable.
>
> Therefore, the city should not purchase the public utility.

Disjunctive reasoning works only if the actual category is included in the major premise with all viable alternatives. Other information or options can easily change the reasoning process or the conclusion:

> A private company is already providing electricity to the city; in a capitalistic economy, socialism should not substitute for private ownership. Allowing for competition among providers will give the best rates to the citizens. We should not purchase the company but allow other private companies to enter the market.

Now add another alternative from a legal perspective:

> If the city purchases the utility, then they will have to pay workers salaries that are based on city and state law with "prevailing wage" and retirement clauses. The workers would both have an increase in wages and increase in retirement. Therefore, the operating costs would significantly increase. We should not purchase the company.

The debate can take on another principle:

> Enron unethically managed their company nationally; local control is better than unethical national control. We should purchase the company.

The disjunctive argument from the city leaders did not cover all alternatives so that the people were unconvinced, and finally Enron pulled out from the talks—no sale was made.

Another example of a failed disjunctive argument is: capital punishment is either murder or justice. This is a false dichotomy. Could capital punishment be cruel and unusual punishment? Could it be mistaken? Could it be vengeance? Could it be a deterrent of similar crimes? Disjunctive reasoning also needs to have each possibility to be separate and distinct. Several alternatives involving capital punishment may apply to the same case so that disjunctive reasoning cannot lead to a clear logical conclusion for that particular instance.

A simple disjunctive syllogism that does work could be: The girl in the corner is either a new student or she is visiting the class. She is not a student at the university. Therefore, she must be visiting the class. Sometimes just the minor premise and conclusion are given in public argument: The girl in the corner is not a student at the university; therefore, she is a visitor. Another statement of the minor premise and conclusion could be: That man is homeless; therefore, he needs help. The major premise of that argument would be: All homeless men need help. The ethical principle implied is: You and I (or the government, relief agencies, the church . . .) have a responsibility to provide that help.

A dilemma is a disjunctive argument that gives limited undesirable alternatives and asks for a forced choice. Usually the best choice is not one that is offered.

The spotted owl controversy in Oregon is one such argument. Either we stop logging old growth timber, or the spotted owl will become extinct. Based on the false assumption that spotted owls only live in old growth timber, this dilemma led to numerous court decisions and finally federal political policy. These pesky owls live not only in second growth timber; but also in charred landscapes after fires. Spotted owls nest in trees along major highways; and one pair nested in the broken corner of a neon hotel sign in the middle of a town. The inaccurate disjunctive reasoning still results in federal timber policy limiting logging.

Generalizations

Statements that assume what is true for part of a category or class is true for most other members of the same class are generalizations. The logic moves from some examples to reasoning about others of the same class. A stereotype is where the assumption is made that all individuals of a class are alike. To say, "All white trash are lazy rednecks" provides a population (those who are white trash), a quality (lazy), and a category (redneck). This is a generalization that is not helpful and will probably harm relationships.

To say, "Sally is white trash; therefore, she is a lazy redneck" is a stereotype that is probably false and definitely counterproductive.

Generalizations are similar to universal statements but they are usually less absolute in nature and easier to defend because the burden of proof is not as great. Careful thinking should enter into the general proposition and often warrants or qualifiers are used. Camping at Beachside State Park is fun (generalization) if you get a site away from highway 101 (warrant) and it doesn't rain (qualifier).

When all members of an ethnic heritage are measured by one or two experiences, then the process of generalization is misused. When a random sample of a group of people is used to observe specific behavior, then the generalization is more likely to be stable. The danger in persuasive communication is to make the assumption about an individual based on group characteristics or to make assumptions of groups based on too small of a sample.

Generalizations are necessary in public communication. The argument "taxation without representation" is a generalization that became the fulcrum of the American Revolution. Yet many states in our union allow the executive or judicial branches to increase fees and special taxes without legislative action. Generally speaking we are represented well in the tax structure, but not 100% or universally. Home prices are lower in Idaho than in California is a generalization that does not mean all homes for sale in Idaho are cheaper than all homes in California. However, without the ability to generalize, public communication would become extremely tedious and cumbersome.

Can you imagine trying to talk about stocks without being able to generalize to the market and indexes? Listing all of the businesses and attempting to discern directions would become impossible quickly. Comparing individual companies to other individual companies would take weeks of calculations instead of comparing an individual company to the market trend. Generalization is an economic necessity in our business choices.

Stasis of an Issue

Exploration into the depths of a subject leads to fascinating discovery with a wide range of implications. Beginning with a probative question the rhetor develops a thesis to answer and expand the subject. From the thesis, development of the essay or speech goes into a formative state where evidence (examples, testimony, facts, statistics . . .) is uncovered and major points (claims, propositions, principles . . .) are developed. The point of decision usually hangs on the *definition, fact,* or *quality* of an issue. Make certain that you engage the idea/issue at the point of greatest stasis.

Stasis is the issue upon which understanding and opinion hinge. Remember from our discussion of Cicero and Quintilian where he develops these ideas in detail. The example comes from a murder trial where Cicero successfully defended Milo who killed Claudius.

First, Did Milo kill Claudius? (fact) yes, fact admitted.

Second, Did Milo murder Claudius? (definition) murder is premeditated killing, Claudius lay in wait and attacked Milo in an attempt to kill him with malice and aforethought. Therefore, Milo killing Claudius is an action of self-defense not murder. The public communication therefore focuses on a clash in definitions.

Third, Was the killing of Claudius good or bad? (quality) it was good because Claudius was a person of evil temper and a bad citizen who often fought with others. The republic is better off with him dead.

The propositions of persuasive communication generally take the form of fact, value, quasi-policy, or policy. The propositions should focus their weight on the point of stasis—where the audience will make their decision on the matter.

Was the world created or did it happen by chance? The scientific facts vary widely with no conclusive answer. The definition of creation by divine rhetoric from nothing, by divine movement upon matter, or by divine work upon developing beings can be debated. The definition of chance and survival of the fittest must also be considered. The quality of life, ethical implications, and meaning of life that result from the two possibilities also should be part of the debate. Fully addressing the question should involve facts, definitions, and qualities. What we are to do about the answer is a policy (teach both in public schools).

Kinds of Propositions

Persuasive communication is often formed from propositional sentences. Most of them fall into four categories. To say that the electoral-college system is outmoded and should not be used in electing presidents is a *quasi-policy* proposition giving a direction for action. To say that Bush received fewer popular votes than Gore is a *factual* proposition that has truth-value. To say that the courts unfairly gave Bush the election is a *value* proposition affirming the degree of justness of judicial decisions. To say that the Electoral-college system should be replaced with a simple majority vote is a *policy* proposition supporting a definite strategic plan for action. All of the issues and arguments focus on the presidential election, but the reasoning and evidence would be different for each argument.

Propositions of Fact

Issues and questions of fact are primarily concerning events, relationships, states of being, or properties. They are not concerned with what "should" be (policy) or what is good or bad (value). Propositions of fact, according to Aristotle, focus on what was (past fact), what is (present fact), or what will be (future fact). They state what has been, is, or will be true or false.

Although absolute certainty is difficult, if not impossible to achieve in many instances; questions of fact must, therefore, involve what is verifiable, observably true, and beyond a reasonable doubt. Although philosophers may debate the ability of people to know anything in an absolute sense, we may be reasonably assured that Paris, France, is not the capital of Mississippi. We may be reasonably assured that the human body is primarily made of water. Factual argument can be based on the practical certainty of probability. Aristotle believed that the best persuasive communication about facts achieves a high level of *probability* with no demand for absolute certainty.

Past facts are those elements that are part of history—that existed in time and space—what was true or false. These can be events, statistics, objects, people . . . that have "objective being" in history. The majority of disputes are about events. A public opinion poll is a mathematical representation of what a statistically significant number of people think, believe, or perceive at a given point in time.

This becomes even more important in spiritual realms and events. Did Jesus die on a cross and rise to life? Did Moses bring the Israelites from Egypt; did he write the Pentateuch? Was Isaac offered by Abraham (Judeo-Christian tradition), or was it Ishmael (Islamic heritage)? Debates over the facts with religious implications are myriad. The arguments over these simple questions have often led to war.

Present facts are different facets of the current world that can be understood. Questions such as what is the current interest rate are easily confirmable facts. Much more difficult are propositions and questions about how the economy is doing. Hard science cannot come to a definitive description of whether the "greenhouse effect" or global warming exists. Objectivity in understanding our world is difficult at best and often impossible. But that does not relieve us from the responsibility of determining what is true and what is false.

Future facts are those that can be projected as impending. What will be true, in action, events, people, relationships, and being? When you observe certain romantic behavior between a young woman and a young man, you may predict the future fact of engagement and marriage. Observing different behavior between a young married couple may lead to a future fact of divorce. If this comes true, then it is true today; if it does not, then it is false today.

Different kinds of evidence support different kinds of factual propositions. Public opinion polls may be good evidence in a political campaign, but they have little relevance on the future fact of an individual couple getting married. Overall, propositions about the future take more discernment and better judgment on the part of those who make the arguments. Making propositional statements about the past is usually a matter of aligning statements with what happened in time and space. The question "Will the stock market stabilize, continue to rise, or fall?" is a harder question than did the stock market fall yesterday or the question "Is the stock market falling today?" Will unemployment rise or fall? People who can predict facts about significant issues based on reasoned judgments will always be in demand. Even though these facts have not yet happened, they are focused on what is true or false based on communicative probability.

The burden of proof in a fact debate is truth. Not absolute truth, but is it more true than false—probability. The degree of probability ranges from a majority (51%) to beyond a reasonable doubt. In spite of the intense philosophical debate, and in spite of the way many think about values and truth, in public communication truth means correspondence with reality.

Perception and fact are often different. During the past century Democratic presidents have gotten the United States into more wars than Republican presidents; however, public opinion may be the opposite of the fact—many people think the Republicans are more likely to lead the nation into war. People do not always believe or remember the truth which makes perception the foundation for persuasion. During WWII more than 70% of the soldiers who fought were drafted while in Vietnam more than 70% of the soldiers were volunteers, yet public perception differs from the reality of verifiable, past fact. Factual persuasive communication should attempt not just to prove the case, but to change the perception as well.

Emotion and fact also are different. People can and do have strong feelings which are counter to the facts. Issues and questions of ethnicity, race, freedom of choice, right to life, religion, sexual orientation and a host of others are all argued publicly with distortions and inaccuracies. These areas based on facts become propositions of value because the significance, worth, desirability, meaning, and implications are the essence of the argument. Factual debates cannot ignore pathos-emotional appeals without loosing ground. People may choose warm appealing probability over cold hard facts, so when we make out a case for an issue, taking the emotional impacts into consideration is essential.

Propositions of Value

When putting forward a statement of value with the intent of influencing others, the persuasive communication will usually include facts, but the fulcrum of the proposition is one of significance or moral import. The dialectic will lead to a discovery of whether the issue is good or bad, desirable or undesirable rather than true or false. Usually propositions of value have greater emotional and spiritual implications than those of simple fact.

The worth, merit, or importance of an issue is to some degree probable or relative. Sometimes, such as in the value of gold, property, or jewelry, an assigned or assessed worth is determined by objective appraisal because the standard of money is used as the value mechanism for an assessment of worth. Rarely is this the case for social issues, political subjects, religious belief, or a host of other kinds of concerns.

In most value debates the net worth is beyond price as measured by love, devotion, goodness, peace . . . . At the same time, emotions, qualities, and ideas cannot be reduced to a numerical appraisal or an outlay of wealth. Words like *beneficial, desirable, excellent, harmful, unfortunate, privileged, useful, advantageous, damaging, troublesome*, and a host of others form the positive or negative evaluation in value propositions.

Other value questions compare or contrast two aspects, ideas, approaches, or objects. Plato thought an oligarchy was a better form of government than a democracy. Most citizens of the United States believe a democratic republic is better than a totalitarian form of government. Some propositions of value would place one object—Toyota Pickup, against another object—Ford Pickup. The debate would entail specific evidence supporting the assertions so that the argument would not deteriorate into emotional assertions. Endless conversations, newspaper stories and magazine articles are written about which sports team is better.

An interesting form of persuasive communication involves competing values. Will the benefits of selective logging outweigh the costs to the forest environment? Or a more complicated issue: How should we weigh the public's right to know, the freedom of the press, the fairness of a trial, and the privacy of individuals in allowing cameras into courtrooms?

Usually a value argument would include the criteria necessary to weigh the issue according to the proposed value. The burden of proof for a proposition of value is that the value is the most relevant to the situation and that the criteria for weighing the value are upheld.

Some arguments contain both factual and value elements that change over time and lead to quasi-policy directions and ultimately to policy decisions. Was Iraq a terrorist threat to US national security, and upon removing that threat what is the responsibility of the US government? The facts of weapons of mass destruction, terrorist ties, and ill will toward the United States will be disputed for years to come. The values of security, freedom for all, democratically based governments, peace in the Middle East, and capitalist-based economies are part of the equation. The quasi-policies of what directions are desirable in securing the country, involving other nations, and establishing an infrastructure only begin the vast array of possibilities. These lead to the policy decisions of hunting down terrorists with force, giving contracts to large corporations who can build infrastructure quickly, and getting as many small interactions with other nations as possible. Often we communicate using only one kind of proposition; however, *complete arguments often involve all four major kinds of propositional statements, frequently on multiple levels.*

Quasi-Policy Propositions

Advantageous directions for action are chosen from among a variety of options long before specific action is contemplated. These are called quasi-policy propositions. Before you decide which movie to watch, you must select between watching a movie, going for a walk, reading a book, or a host of other alternatives. Usually a quasi-policy will place some kind of value judgment upon a specific policy. A claim that asserts, "Education reform is detrimental to student learning" would be a quasi-policy. A policy would be to debate the specific merits of the educational reform package "No Child Left Behind" as a course of actions.

The quasi-policy proposition point of decision usually hinges on a value concerning a bearing for action, not the action itself, or the value itself. In public debate value conflict about the impending action almost always is a precursor to the establishment of specific policies. Particular emphasis is usually placed on the motive of the actors giving a large place to why the policy direction should be sought. Using National Guard on the boarder is a policy decision that follows the quasi-policy of whether or not we should secure our boarders from illegal immigrants.

Quasi-policy communication does not have the burden of demon-strating necessary resources for completion of the action. But the quasi-policy usually address whether this is the best course of action among alternatives. Something of whether the policy will provide a level of solvency should be considered, but the major focus of the proposition is in the value of the direction for action.

The major difference between a quasi-policy and a policy is that a quasi-policy does not require the proposal of a plan of action, but endorses a value that may result in a specific policy of action. The senate vote in support of President Bush before the invasion of Iraq was one of quasi-policy that the administration used as a vote of confidence for a specific policy of military action. Years later both sides seem confused as to what the vote meant because the specific policy of invasion was founded on the vote for a direction of action against terrorism. In our form of government this is the appropriate way for action to take place (the executive branch is responsible for policy), but the communication should have been clearer.

Policy Propositions

A proposition of policy persuades an audience to follow or not follow a specific course of action. Policy is taken because of a problem in the status quo and the action will address or resolve the problem (solvency). Pro and con arguments are given to determine the costs and resources. New laws, programs, rules or expenditures are frequent legislative debates of policy. Although policy will usually entail discussions of fact and value, the primary point of stasis will be the course of action.

The first burden of a policymaker is to demonstrate the necessity of the proposition through expression of a significant problem. A prima-fascia case will demonstrate that taking no action will result in harms that are greater than the costs of taking action. Problems are usually assessed through an analysis of harms, costs, and benefits.

A plan to implement the policy is a burden of the person proposing the proposition. The United States entered the wars in Vietnam, Korea, and Iraq without a clear strategy to cover all contingencies. When unforeseen events took place, the policies or policymakers were not flexible enough to adapt to the situations.

The burden of covering the costs is a vital part of policy proposition. Where will human, financial, and material resources come from to bring about the change? Often supplying the needs results in unintended adverse consequences. President Johnson's great society experiment was to cost no more than three million dollars in any given year. But welfare has ended up costing the nation trillions. A good idea perhaps, but the cost is great. Besides the cost in dollars, the attempt to make women less reliant upon abusive men has in turn made millions of vulnerable women dependent upon the government instead.

Often policymakers must consider what others will do as a result of the proposal. While President Bush and the Republican led house and senate attempt to deal with a recession through tax cuts; several states, such as Oregon significantly raised taxes. This counter plan negates the positive impacts of the primary policy resulting in stagnating economy and loss of jobs for that part of the union. Interestingly enough, coming out of the recession those states that raised taxes generally speaking had a more difficult time than those who did not.

Another significant aspect of policy propositions is how long solving the problem will take. With the example of welfare from above, the check for rent and food can relieve an immediate problem while recovering from the negative consequences of people discovering they can have more money if they quit working than if they hold a job will take significantly longer.

Policy communication should also consider who has the responsibility and authority in the issue. Choosing the correct person, organization, or agency is essential to understanding an issue. Our creation of the Department of Homeland Security was an attempt to streamline the "who" of policy because by congressional law the FBI and CIA were not able to do the whole job.

Wrap-up

Factual, value, quasi-policy, and policy propositions form the way we approach social, political, and religious issues. The Bible is full of these kinds of claims that make cases for faith in God, the truth of ethics, and historicity of events. The Bible has many quasi-policies that pastors turn into specific policies in their application. We need to be careful in how conclusions are presented that we do not extend too far the message of scripture.

These propositions usually contain premises—a claim in an argument that provides a reason(s) for accepting the conclusion. Dependent premises need other claims to support them, while independent premises can stand alone in support for their conclusion. Rarely can one statement convince an audience, so most argument is formed of propositions with dependent premises but most effective argument is formed of examples or stories.

Chapter 10

Reasoning and Critical Thinking: The Process Forming Persuasive Communication

Come let us reason together
Says the Lord
Isaiah 1:18 NKJV

I N A criminal trial a verdict that evaluates and establishes the truth of a crime and perpetrator beyond a reasonable doubt is a question of fact. Whether the trial is fair is a question of value. What kinds of sentences are available are questions of quasi-policy, usually addressed by the judge. The application of the sentence is a separate proceeding evaluating the question of policy as it is applied to the individual. Each of these kinds of arguments needs to have careful reasoning and critical thinking before the message is sent.

Consider Multiple Viewpoints

Recently I had numerous difficulties with my neck, hands, and arm. One physician indicated that I had no physical problem, a dispute of fact, where he thought I suffered psychosomatic symptoms from stress. Not satisfied, I went to a second physician who wanted to do immediate exploratory surgery without a physical examination, quasi-policy without evidence. I never made a return visit to him. A third physician indicated a problem but concluded it was minor and should be treated with traction and therapy, a proposition of policy which I followed for six months without relief. A fourth physician, after exhaustive tests diagnosed a major problem with immediate radical surgery needed, a policy proposition based on a quasi-policy, in turn based on factual evidence. Because I valued the process of gathering evidence, could envision the problem on both MRI and CAT scans, understood the explanation of the harms, calculated the percentages of solvency risk, I believed the most reasonable course of action was radical surgery. This debate, which lasted more than a year, ended in a successful recovery, and I again have use of my neck, hands, and arms. Critical thinking about public communication begins with consideration of multiple perspectives. We regularly consider a second opinion with major surgery, but do you go out of the way to think from the different perspectives of the audience, Christian thinkers, non-Christian thinkers, and the general public?

This is dialectical reasoning-arguing from different worldviews, belief systems, and opinions. A rhetor does not have to consider every opinion available in the marketplace of ideas before wading into the raging waters of controversy; however, thinking through from multiple views that have been accepted by groups of people who have considered the issue carefully, is important. Dialectical thinking leads to consideration of more parts of the issue than any single view can. Sensitivity to others is usually an outgrowth of dialectic. Argument strength also results from thinking in multiple ways. Another benefit is that the style and wording will usually change in positive ways. Perhaps the most important result of carefully looking at the array of available positions on any given issue is that the advocate develops a position that can speak to others in a persuasive manner.

How often do we do all the homework necessary for a complete case before we attempt persuasion? Often we base opinions upon inadequate diagnosis, too few facts, not considering conflicting opinions, or simply because it is the way I *feel* about the issue. This chapter is a call for serious consideration and accountability for the messages Christian communicators put into the public arena. Rhetorical communication should be grounded in premises derived from dialectical reasoning and critical thinking.

Stating the Issue

The point or essence of what is put forth is the issue. When multiple perspectives can be taken, defining the issue often becomes the center of the dispute. The issue is *inherent* as a natural part of the dialectic derived from the definitions of the terms of argument. They form the evidence in such a manner as to directly prove or disprove the propositions. The issue of gay marriage can be approached as a civil right, as a poor attempt to redefine a social institution, as a sin against the holy God, as a bad idea for community change, or as a personal freedom; but the center of the issue remains homosexual and lesbian people joining together in matrimony.

Aristotle, in his book *Topics*, understood that considering the issue with dialectical reasoning about propositions could be approached with what he called *predictables* and *categories*. The predictables are: definition, property, genus, and accident. The categories are: essence, quantity, quality, relation, place, time, position, state, activity, and passivity. Although many centuries have passed, most of these forms of persuasive communication still hold sway in the center of issues. Any subject can be approached through one of these topics. If you are giving a speech, simply choose appropriate predictables and categories about the issue, support it with evidence, and you can produce the content of the speech.

Each day cultural battles are fought in our newspapers, magazines, books, airwaves, and classrooms over family values, sexual orientation, civil rights, and innumerable other issues. Each one is articulated in statements and propositions. Those that are supported by evidence become arguments; assertions are those propositions that stand-alone. The issues appear and reappear in different arguments. Critically thinking through the communication process is a necessary part of public rhetoric.

Testing Arguments

Assessing the aptitude of an argument prior to using it, or understanding the probable strength of another's persuasive communication is called *testing*. The following questions may assist in evaluating the claims made in persuasive argument:

What is the essence of the issue? At the heart of understanding any subject is an understanding of what we are talking about. A clear definition that we can either agree over as author and audience or an understanding that we can debate is necessary in order to continue dialogue. If the reader or listener is thinking about something else when a rhetor communicates a word, then the dance of meaning will be one of misunderstanding instead of an exchange of ideas or a persuasive attempt to change.

Is this the right issue? Closely related to the clear definition of the topic is a consideration of whether or not we are speaking of the correct ideas. Speakers and authors often have topics they feel comfortable with and view as important for audiences, and they bend other ideas to fit what they are most knowledgeable about.

Does the argument focus on what is most important about the issue? If the war in Iraq is part of the larger issue of terrorism then it might be important as part of the security of the Western world; however, if it is about protecting a source of oil, then we have a different motivation and the arguments will be very different.

Are the facts true, do they correspond to reality? All evidence should be considered and tested but at this stage double-checking the facts is important. In our data-driven environment be careful about simply googling a topic and accepting the top ten responses. Look at a data base where editors check the content. Consider the veracity of the cite and author, not simply accept the electronic information as correct.

Can I accept the premises? Evaluate the truth-content of the message to determine its worthiness of belief. Truth is often called *material logic*—conforming statements to reality. The propositions, premises, and conclusions should represent what exists in time and space.

Do both the premises and evidence support the conclusion? Evaluate the validity and strength of the propositions. They should join the argument with the conclusion. Are other possible versions or opinions supportable by the same information? Before you espouse a conclusion, know the legitimate alternatives.

What are the problems, harms, and benefits with possible unintended consequences? One of the primary difficulties with both politics and religion is that the leaders seldom are able to envision the results of their actions in real life. Consider that if the terrorist insurgents of the Middle East would stop their behavior for two years, the Western powers would pull out of their territories. How about the unintended result of the media publicizing the terrorist events? The fact is, they propagate them—suicide bombers do not claim and hold ground but only seek to communicate power, and the press gives them that power—without publicity terrorism would virtually stop.

What is the other side? Conflicting and contradicting propositions should be considered carefully to evaluate the scope and direction of every argument. This is the dialectical process that is essential to both the strengthening of argument and the persuasive communication of the position.

Mystery

How far away are the stars? Reason allows a finite number to be placed on the distance, measured in light years, for the distance in miles is incomprehensible. How many grains of sand are there on the beach? Reason suggests a finite number, but it is too great to count. How does a daffodil grow? Biology suggests processes, but life is irreproducible in the laboratory. Who can explain the intense emotional attraction between a husband and wife? Psychology can tap into smells, physical forms, and communication patterns, but these all fall short of a reasonable explanation for the phenomena of unconditional love. Even Solomon found "the way of a man with a maid" inscrutabile.

Mystery limits reason in many aspects of life. The ordered world crumbles into illogical forms, functions, and processes that baffle an ordered understanding. Logic cannot predict human behavior with certainty, such as, will a daughter return from a date before curfew. Cause and effect, punishment and reward, historical instances, national averages, not even syllogistic deduction nor inductive process can predict with certainty the outcome of an everyday event such as a date. Why does the rhythm of the seasons affect an individual with hope in the spring and melancholy in the fall? Biology is not adequate to fully explain the phenomenon. Why does a storm at sea give wonder and freedom tempered with fear? Meteorology is not adequate to fully explain the observable fact. Why does a robin bring a smile and a pause while we yell at a crow to chase it away?

Mysteries abound in life. Rhetorical persuasion recognizes the ambiguities and mysteries of life and, therefore, deals with *probability* or *likelihood* more often than with certainty. Communicating the essence of being human is usually not an absolute phenomenon, but a reasonable process, and is seasoned with mystery and beauty.

Critical thinking and reasoning are necessary as a process to understand the evidence and propositions of persuasive rhetoric. Stephen Lucas tells the story of Hack Wilson, a baseball star for the Brooklyn Dodgers in the 1930s.

> Wilson was a great player, but he had a fondness for the "good life." His drinking exploits were legendary. He was known to spend the entire night on the town, stagger into the team's hotel at the break of dawn, grab a couple of hours sleep, and get to the ballpark just in time for the afternoon game.

> This greatly distressed Max Carey, Wilson's manager. At the next team meeting, Carey spent time explaining the evils of drink. To prove his point, he stood beside a table on which he had placed two gasses and a plat of live angleworms. One glass was filled with water, the other with gin—Wilson's favorite beverage. With a flourish Carey dropped a worm into the glass of water. It wriggled hap-

pily. Next Carey plunged the same worm into the gin. It promptly stiffened and expired.

A murmur ran through the room, and some players were obviously impressed. But not Wilson. He didn't even seem interested. Carey waited a little, hoping for some delayed reaction from his wayward slugger. When none came, he prodded, "Do you follow my reasoning, Wilson?"

"Sure Skipper," answered Wilson, "It proves that if you drink gin, you'll never get worms!" (p. 437-438)

Evidence is only persuasive if the audience understands and follows the communicator's reasoning. The analogy above had alternative interpretations that could be used to support a counter claim. This chapter calls for the rhetor to make certain that the reasoning is sound before the attempt is made at public communication. Then, the content of the message should enable the audience to follow that reasoning by adopting it as their own method of thinking about the subject. Critical thinking is the process of developing clear, logical messages that are compelling to audiences.

Tests of Reasoning

The logic of argument demands critical thinking in the analyzing process. Both in listening to other's arguments and developing one's own, testing propositions will enable persuasion to be based on the best reasons. Getting in the habit of thinking through my own positions and statements enables me to hear, understand, and evaluate others' messages as well.

The first general test of a proposition is truth, accurately representing the facts through words and nonverbal communication. Plato's insistence on truth still stands millennia after he reconciled himself with the content of rhetoric in *The Phaedrus*. Truth is subject to human perception. A statement such as "the sea is calm today" means something far different to a professional fisherman than a seasick landlubber. Reality may be objective, but communication is often to people who rely on only perception.

The content of messages holds truth in tension with probability. Just a few lines ago, I wrote that public communication usually deals with uncertain claims, and now I am espousing truth as its most important aspect. All public rhetoric should seek truth and be based on truth. Great rhetoric communicates that truth with precision and clarity so that people know and understand the message and implications.

Closely following truth comes the test of good evidence. Is the argument supported by reasons the audience would consider to be persuasive? Without support, a proposition becomes an opinion, assumption, or premise rather than an argument. "Good" could be defined as important, interesting, and convincing (Vancil, 1993). If an argument is unsupportable, then it fails the test of good reasons.

Consider these conflicting arguments:

➤ The United States and Britain came under significant criticism after invading Iraq because the reasons they gave prior to the assault proved unfounded.

➤ The weapons of mass destruction that Iraq had were transported to Syria just prior to the invasion of Iraq (or were loaded on their two ships that have never been located).

➤ The evidence of weapons of mass destruction was faulty so that even if good comes from the war the irresponsibility of acting on poor evidence will haunt the victors.

➤ The real reason we attacked Iraq is control of the oil, our way of life and business interests come first.

➤ Having a stable country in the Middle East, is still of vital interest to the West.

➤ Therefore a new primary reason, freedom and democracy to the Iraqi people, takes precedence in the argument now.

These conflicting arguments float in the public arena through newspapers, talk shows, newscasts, books, and speeches. Supporting and countering the war is difficult and good reasons for one perspective will sound hollow to others.

A third examination for argument comes with evidence being relevant to the claim. The good reasons must support the truth of the proposition. This is where reasoning takes the forefront in persuasive rhetoric by establishing a relationship between the evidence and the propositions of communication that the audience can follow and accept.

➤ The terrorism perpetrated by Islamic extremists is about power and culture with little or nothing to do with US foreign policy.

➤ The polarization of American politics has more to do with the radical left and right being unwilling to move to the center than it does with Republican policy.

> Government health care has more to do with socialism vs.
> capitalism than the needs of the people.

Often the point of stasis and the presumption will center on the worldview of the audience. The speaker will then be challenged to demonstrate the relevancy of the argument rather than to simply bend to what will move the audience.

A fourth test for argument is the virtue of love. Truth should be tempered with the character, actions, motivations, passions, and value of unconditional love. Logic balanced in virtue is necessary for persuasive impact. Politics around the world is more centered on power than on love. Business around the world is more centered on money than on love. Classical rhetoricians will speak and write from a heart of love. Our views should be tempered in the furnace of passion (Plato) and offered in self-giving service (Paul).

Strong and Sufficient Argument

To be persuasive, we can reach beyond certainty to probability and argue with necessary and sufficient reasons that compose a "prima fascia" case. A set of arguments where the audience would be convinced *on the face* or surface, if no oppositional argumentation is present. The advocate of a position has the burden of providing enough argument to persuade the audience of the probability or likelihood of her position.

Arguments are built upon two basic kinds of foundations, evidence and reasoning. Evidence can be thought of as data discovered through observation and research. Reasoning is the logical process of developing or inferring new ideas, usually from already accepted premises or evidence. We will deal with reasoning in the next three chapters and evidence will be covered in chapter 14.

Persuasive communication is formed of *sound* argument. When a proposition is both valid and true, it is considered to be of sound reasoning. A series of logical steps that follows correct *form* leads to a valid conclusion. The study of formal logic analyzes how well an argument is put together to determine its validity. When the content of an argument accurately represents what exists in time and space, it is *materially* true.

Usually one sound argument is not enough to make a full case; therefore, sufficient logic and evidence should be given to persuade an audience. Evidence and reasoning can be carried on far longer than appropriate. In a recent speech where I thought the audience would need many examples, I used 12 specific instances from around the world where people were brutalizing others. While discussing the subject afterward with audience members, I discovered they were so overwhelmed with the examples that I lost much of the intended impact of the argument. Four specific examples would have been enough and the details could have been less graphic—then the impact would have been greater. This is part of the art of rhetoric, knowing the audience's likely response to the subject and using the appropriate means to arouse the response and passions.

Sufficiency, therefore, has both a logical and rhetorical dimension. Logically, is there enough support to establish the claim as believable so that we will accept the proposition? Then, rhetorically the argument has to be convincing to the audience. An argument can be good enough for some listeners while not enough for others. In the judicial system, the arguments of the prosecution may be sufficient to convince some members of a jury while others remain doubtful as to the guilt of the defendant.

Logical Reasoning

I am in the process of building a cabin near the beach. We designed a floor plan and then drew up a blueprint so that I understood all of the individual pieces of the house, where and when they fit into the whole, the relationships between the materials and the ultimate goal. If I neglected to place the water and electricity into the area before forming the foundation then I would have much extra work later in the building process. Likewise, the electric wires and plumbing go into the walls before drywall encloses them. Structural plans and overall perspectives enabling construction, maintenance and repair of a cabin, likewise, considering the logic of argument facilitates the construction and presentation of ideas as well as the prevention of counterpersuasion in argumentation.

Logical reasoning enables a well-constructed argument. Fallacies undermine the essence of that building. When you present the argument to others in order to influence them, illogical content will significantly decrease the likelihood of the argument impacting the audience in a positive manner. Often it will tend to push others to accept an opposing argument.

Inductive Logic

Reasoning from the particulars to general ideas is called inductive reasoning. Michael walked into class the first day of the quarter, right on time, but the professor was not in the room and neither were any other students. Considering the evidence before him (those who should have been present were not), Michael reasoned from the lack of evidence (students and professor) that the class had been canceled.

This logical induction brought Michael to a conclusion that could have different possibilities. Alternate causalities such as everyone else could be late, the schedule he referenced could have been wrong, the class could have been moved to another room, an event could be happening that took everyone away from the room, or any number of other causes could result in the present data of an empty room. Induction, therefore, is an exercise in probability where Michael choose the most plausible cause into his belief structure as an explanation of the observable particulars.

Inductive reasoning is similar to the process of addition in arithmetic. $1 + 2 + 3 + 4 = 10$ is a simple problem that most first grade students could solve. However, when considering communication or natural phenomena, the results are not quite as straightforward. Visiting Lima, Peru, and seeing person after person rush through the airport would not necessarily mean that everyone in the airport, everyone in Lima, nor everyone in Peru was in a hurry. Even though all of the observed phenomena pointed in that direction, the conclusions are unwarranted based on the inductive evidence. Inductive thinking "leaps" to draw generalized inferences from specific instances. The person is leaping from observable knowledge over the chasm of the unknown to a conclusion. Jumping to conclusions based on too few examples that are not randomly chosen can lead to inaccurate argumentation.

Unless all members of the observational class are observed, the conclusion is tentative. Propositional statements drawn from observations and research need to have qualifiers and softeners. When dealing with probability, the communicator cannot speak in absolute terms, but instead conveys claims as approximations, likelihoods, trends, and directions rather than certainties. Inductive conclusions should be considered to be temporary, tentative, and open to modification. Mature individuals, using sound inductive logic, are willing to be led in whatever direction the facts pilot us.

Also, unless all members of the observational class are observed in all situations, the conclusion is tentative. The behavior of people, animals, plants, even weather, liquids, and a host of items in the physical world cannot be predicted with simple behavioral linear logic. People have chaotic elements within us like emotions, values, and beliefs so that inductive logic has limitations when addressing human impacts.

Making good inductive arguments is an art. Some of the principles that can make that art have a greater impact on the audience are: Generalizations from induction need to have accurate quantifiers; so conclusions are not exaggerated. Typical instances should be selected for arguments that account for as many facts as possible. Think of alternative causes or opposing hypotheses before you use a given example. Avoid extreme simplicity or complexity for most audiences. Attempt to control for your own biases through considering the implications of the messages you send the evidence you use to support those claims.

> Specific instance: We go on vacation and the weather is rainy and cold but clears up the day we go home.
>
> Specific instance: My neighbors go on vacation and the weather is rainy and cold but clears up the day she goes home.
>
> Specific instance: My sister goes on vacation and the weather is rainy and cold but clears up the day they go home.
>
> Conclusion: When people go on vacation the weather will remain rainy and cold until the day to go home.

This reasoning from specific instances enables a conclusion that may not be accurate because no causal effect exists between vacation plans and the weather. A better logical induction could be it is better to take a vacation in August than in March when going to the Oregon coast.

Although limited in predictive value for individuals, inductive logic is excellent in determining trends or generalizations within populations. Planning an outdoor wedding in March on the Oregon coast is probably not the best idea without an alternative plan. The bride will be more likely to be happy with an August wedding on the sand.

Another example of inductive reasoning is measuring leave-taking communicative behavior at airports giving significant insight into how people communicate when parting for a significant amount of time. Measuring whether stress in increased or decreased and the kinds of nonverbal communicative behavior with separation being further removed in time and space from the airplane due to security changes would create an interesting study. Such observations provide insight into communication and relationships that deductive logic cannot provide.

Inductive logic is best at descriptive observations giving understanding of situations, populations, cultures, and people. Observing how my boss responds to certain situations can help me avoid those that are upsetting and to augment those that are pleasing to him, thus increasing the likelihood of a raise. Observing how parents respond to certain situations enable children to behave in appropriate ways which escalate the likelihood of pleasing their parents. This is inductive reasoning at work in our lives. Our challenge is to capture this natural logic and use it to further our message in public rhetoric.

Considering the specific instances where individuals are willing to commit suicide in order to kill others leads to the conclusion that the world has an increasing problem with terrorism. What was rare a few years ago is now a more common experience creating a foreboding anxiety among the people of the world. If it could happen in Israel, Iraq, Russia, Spain, Lebanon, and New York, it could happen to me—therefore terrorism is a significant issue.

Deductive Logic

Deductive logic is also an important part of persuasive communication. People naturally deduce individuations from general propositions. When an author writes a propositional statement such as the one Frederick Douglass' (1867) wrote about reconstruction:

> *Whether the tremendous war so heroically fought and so victoriously ended shall pass into history a miserable failure, barren of permanent results—a scandalous and shocking waste of blood and treasure—a strife for empire, as Earl Russell characterized it, of no value to liberty or civilization—an attempt to re-establish a Union by force, which must be the merest mockery of a Union—an effort to bring under Federal authority States into which no loyal man from the North may safely enter, and to bring men into the national councils who deliberate with daggers and vote with revolvers, and who do not even conceal their deadly hate of the country that conquered them; or whether, on the other hand, we shall, as the rightful reward of victory over treason, have a solid nation, entirely delivered from all contradictions and social antagonisms, based upon loyalty, liberty, and equality, must be determined one way or the other by the present session of Congress.*

This is one long sentence that gives voice to numerous socio-political ideas: nature of the civil war, heroism of the soldiers, failure of the congress, unity

250

of the nation, division of the people, patriotism of the victors, hatred of the conquered, physical union reestablished, spiritual union further divided and a host of other ideas with their accompanying emotions. The call for a heroic statesmanship that surpasses battlefield valor echoes down through the decades in a manner we can deductively apply to Middle Eastern politics of our day. These ideas are deduced from the statement and can persuasively be used in communication.

Another example of deductive reasoning is simpler: Reading out loud is easy. Oral interpretation is a freshman level course about reading out loud. Therefore oral interpretation will be an easy class. That kind of reasoning can lead a student to be very disappointed with the course when he discovers how challenging the curriculum can be.

The Apostle John uses deductive logic in the Gospel of John 1:1. He says, "In the beginning was the Word, and the Word was with God and the Word was God." Here the conclusion is derived from a general claim in an attempt to determine certainty. He backs up the deductive logic with an inductive claim in 1:14 that the Word dwelt among us. He furthers the inductive logical analysis in I John 1:1: "That which was from the beginning, which we have heard, which we have seen, which we have looked upon and our hands have handled of the Word of life." The Christology of John is based on both inductive and deductive logic, but is primarily revealed truth from a higher authority.

Syllogism

One of the classical forms of deductive reasoning is the syllogism moving the audience from the general to the specific in a symmetrical manner. Aristotle introduced us to this method of logical thinking:

> Major premise: All men are mortal.
> Minor premise: Socrates is a man.
> Conclusion: Therefore, Socrates is mortal.

Moving the audience to accept the conclusion is a matter of getting them to accept the premises. The conclusion is a logical necessity if the premises are true and if the form it followed making the argument is valid.

Syllogisms are only useful if the premises are true and the form is logically sound. Here is a syllogism that was used a few years ago in the media: No gravesites should be robbed. The wreck of the Titanic is a gravesite. Therefore, the wreck of the titanic should not be robbed. This kind of logic failed to sway most of the public in several ways: first the definition of *rob*, second the definition of *gravesite*, and third the declaration of the Titanic as a gravesite. The Apostle Paul uses a Sorites syllogism (one that links multiple premises together) in Romans 5:3-5:

> *We also rejoice in our sufferings because we know that suffering produces perseverance; perseverance character, and character hope, and hope does not disappoint us because God has poured out his love into our hearts by the Holy Spirit.*

Jesus uses a disjunctive syllogism in his logic about the place of an individual in relationship to God and the world as cited by Matthew in 6:24: *No one can serve two masters. Either he will hate the one and love the other, or he will be devoted to the one and despise the other. You cannot serve both God and money.*

The author of Hebrews may have used a hypothetical syllogism in 6:4-6: *It is impossible for those who have once been enlightened . . . if they fall away, to be brought back to repentance, because, to their loss they are crucifying the Son of God all over again and subjecting him to public disgrace.* These examples demonstrate that the revealed word of God contains sound logic in many forms. Although complex, the syllogism is a foundational part of human thinking.

Cause and Effect

Establishing a relationship between a phenomenon and action is causal reasoning. I forgot to turn in a paper, I didn't take the midterm exam, and I did very poorly on the final; therefore, I will fail the course—is causal reasoning based on the mathematical principles of learning assessment. The reason these were late is that I was out drinking instead of paying attention to my coursework never occurs to me, so the full cause-effect relationship does not sink into my consciousness. Most human behavior has multiple, complex causes.

One of Aristotle's *topoi* or topics, cause and effect is a way of organizing ideas that a reader or listener can easily understand because people organize their own thinking about subjects using these methods. Actions have causes that people will look for. Even in a court of law, we look for motivations that brought about or cause a crime.

A woman purchases a cup of hot coffee at McDonalds, tries to drink it while driving and talking on her cell phone, and spills it in her lap. The coffee scalds her so she sues the restaurant for the burns—not taking responsibility for her own actions. The cause of the burns is more her fault for driving, talking on the phone, and trying to drink at the same time. On the other hand, a elderly man enters McDonalds and slips on a patch of ice at the doorway falling and hitting his head. The restaurant is properly responsible to have a clear doorway if they are open after a snowstorm. Others sue McDonalds because they are overweight and eat regularly at the restaurant—not taking responsibility for the kind of food they consume or the amount. The cause and effect relationship also has elements of personal and corporate responsibility.

Reasoning that seeks to establish the relationship between causes and their effects is a significant part of persuasive rhetoric. Did America's need for oil cause the gulf war, or did France and Germany's need for oil cause them to counter the efforts of the US? The motivation to favor a specific course of action is the cause, and the same cause may be on both sides of an issue or action. In this instance, the cause is far beyond the simplistic exchange of blood (whether Iraqi blood under Hussein to keep oil coming, or soldier's blood in war for control of production) for oil.

Classification

Argument by classification divides what is being discussed into different groups of similar elements. Defining terms of argument in a manner that enhances understanding through close proximity with other issues is a significant part of persuasive communication.

Vague terms are those which lack specificity in a definitive meaning. The listeners can freely interpret vague terms to mean what they desire them to mean. Politicians are fond of using vague terms, having a "war on poverty" or "war on terrorism" is more popular than a "war on Iraq."

Equivocal terms have precise meanings, but they can be defined in multiple ways leaving the audience to interpret the specific meaning of the communication. Being a "fast" woman could be quickness physically, socially, or even sexually—the audience is left to make the decision as to the meaning.

Technical jargon has specialized meaning for words as used by different people. Mathematics, medicine, oceanography and even communication; virtually all areas of specialization find using words in a special way enables quick understanding that is not possible without jargon. Even nonverbal communication can be part of jargon, in electronically mediated journalism hand signals are used that indicate time signals, camera angles, and other specific actions that others outside of the occupation do not understand. Calling a person involved in a rhetorical communication a *rhetor* is new to some readers of this book, but is common to those who get a degree in rhetoric.

Where an item is classified can make the difference in understanding. The place of women in the church is hotly debated in many circles. Scott Bartchy makes a theological argument through the logic of categorization by labeling Galatians 3:28 as normative ("there is neither male nor female; for you are all one in Christ Jesus") along with passages such as Acts 2:17-18 with the Holy Spirit falling on both men and women, I Corinthians 7:4-5 with wife and husband having equal rights in marriage and I Corinthians 11:11-12 with men and women codependent. Opposing these "normative" passages are "descriptive" ones such as Acts 21:8-9 with Philip's daughters as prophetesses, Philippians 4:2-3 where Euodia and Synthyche are partners in the gospel, I Corinthians 11:4-5 with women who are praying or prophesying in the church to have their heads covered, Romans 16:1-2 with Phoebe a deacon, 3-4 Prisca and Aquilia partners, 7 Andronica an outstanding apostle. Then Bartchy labels other passages as problems such as I Corinthians 14:34-35 dealing with difficulties in worship and I Timothy 2:11-15 dealing with false doctrine. His categorization of these passages as normative, descriptive, and problems leads to an acceptance of women in all areas of ministry in the church. The logical analysis produces a hermeneutical pattern that many people find compelling while others find it difficult to swallow his categories.

Analogy

Reasoning sometimes includes analogical comparisons. When thinking from an analogy, the persuader likens two items that are similar in a number of aspects to also be similar in the additional characteristic. The classification of these items as similar enables understanding that goes deeper into the essence of the thing being studied. For example, Jesus' story of the weeds in Matthew 13 is an analogy with parts of the story representing or corresponding to various spiritual realities.

When the audience accepts the similarity between the cases, then what is true for the first case is true for the second. If the cases are dissimilar, then analogical logic fails to correspond between the two. Legal and policy arguments are often made from analogy. Universal health care is considered based on comparing the United States with other countries. Gun control, euthanasia, genetic research, these ideas where ethics meet public policy are argued on the basis of similarities to other cultures.

Case studies are exercises in analogical reasoning. An in-depth description and analysis is given of one instance and that is applied to similar cases. Business and journalism ethics often follow this path of reasoning. Much of US legal posturing is not based on a strict hermeneutic of the law, but rather on case study analogies. The Bible uses this kind of reasoning in suggesting that prior to the rapture the culture will be similar to that of Noah's time. Other places Paul derives doctrine from narratives because of the application of analogy.

Critical Thinking

We began this chapter speaking of the way people think. Drawing the strands together here at the end, we again come back to the idea of critical thinking: a thoughtful process of focused, organized deliberation concerning the logical relationships between ideas, events, people, and objects is necessary for rhetoric. Being able to systematize ideas into clear compelling linear logic enables audiences to follow your line of thinking concerning a subject. Both written and spoken communication demand a careful logic supported by evidence. The message must correspond to reality and thus be true. When an idea is "murky" in the mind, it will be muddy to the audience and will lose any persuasive impacts. Therefore, we need to consider our messages from a perspective of critical thinking.

Degree of Relevance and Cogency

Critical thinking, logical forms, and reasoning can be judged by the degree of relevance and cogency. The message should be significant or important to the audience containing or pertaining to the weight of values they already hold. If the audience cannot grasp why they should listen or read, then they will not process the material but will tune out the message. Likewise, if the argument is not applicable to real life but only an impenetrable esoteric statement, persuasion will not occur. Ideas have consequences and audiences instinctively reject those arguments that are not relevant to life.

The listeners need clarity and coherence to grasp logical arguments. Those that are not understandable with a timely significance are rejected. Simplicity of logic that makes transitions clear so the audience is drawn along creates an atmosphere of acceptance. Plain argument is usually accepted over complex obtuse reasoning. Thus the degree of relevance and cogency often determines the acceptance or rejection of the logical pattern chosen for communication.

Appropriate Depth and Breadth

People need to know enough to make appropriate decisions. In our age of sound bit images and mindless celebrity posturing, public rhetoric has a distinct need to develop in-depth information. Like a teen who asks to go to a movie, leaving out some of the people who will be there, the rating of the picture, and what will happen afterwards, our society is becoming lazy in thinking about important issues. Political and religious leaders often leave out the costs and the ripple effects that a policy or decision will bring about in the lives of the audience. Churches vote in programs that take more volunteer hours and cost more money than they envisioned when they made the choice. Legislatures enact a program to meet a current need that becomes much larger as soon as the solution is implemented. Much of "easy believeism" in Christianity can be traced to simply leaving out essential information for an individual who converts to Christ. Critical thinking calls for the communicator to give enough information both in depth and breadth for the audience to make an appropriate decision.

Catch phrases and sound bites may be enough to begin the emotional change of attitude, but for full persuasive impact so that the change is persistent, we need a complete message. What information do you need to make a decision at the point of stasis? What will the audience's point of stasis be and what information do you need to get them to that point, and then what do they need to know in order to make an informed decision? The answers to these questions will lead to researching the appropriate content. When evaluating others' messages in the public arena, a good critical thinker will ask similar questions: What is the point of stasis? What information do I need to make the decision?

Understanding Bias

All communication contains bias either in choosing priorities or creating prejudice. The extreme anti-republican bias of Dan Rather led to his demise on network news. When considering the needs of people around the world, I am biased to meet the needs of my own family before tending to others. Proper discrimination will enable a rhetor to discern where our own biases are and we can work to balance and mitigate the effects of that predisposition.

Elimination of bias is not possible; however, understanding and justice can reach an equilibrium where communication is truthful, fair, loving, objective, and balanced. Pastors will generally have an appropriate bias for ministering to the flock God has called them to serve. If they do not, then most would question the call. However, if that is not balanced with service to the community and individuals in need, then the Great Commission will not be fulfilled. In other words we need an appropriate balance in an occupation of service. Similarly, a local newspaper should deal more with news items from the community than those of the world in general. However, if national and international issues and information are left out entirely, readers will increasingly use other sources of news, and they will spend less and less time with the local paper. Bias needs a balance.

Conclusion

Rhetorical persuasion should be clear, accurate, precise, logical, relevant, cogent, of appropriate depth and breadth, and fair. This takes work in thinking through the issue, precisely defining what is at stake, understanding the point of decision, and providing all of the information necessary in a truthful, objective manner. Awareness of these responsibilities and holding ourselves accountable to them will enable our communication to affect others in a persuasive manner.

Chapter 11

Fallacies of Reasoning

He who walks in wisdom is kept safe
Proverbs 28:26 NIV

COMMUNICATED ARGUMENT ought to be logical in order for it to be persuasive; unfortunately this is not always the case. Illogical statements may occasionally draw some people in for a short time, but they will in the long term harm the rhetor, the audience, and the impact of the message. Errors in reasoning are called fallacies or said to be fallacious in quality. More than a hundred different kinds of fallacies have been identified, but here we will only consider a few of the most prevalent.

Whether writing or speaking to a public audience, careful deliberation should be given to avoid illogical reasoning in arguments. Some of the people may be fooled some of the time, but more will be alienated from your point of view if they detect a logical problem. In the long run, when people believe they have been intentionally or fraudulently deceived, they will respond in a very strong negative manner to further messages from the same source or about the same issue. Those who believed they were lied to about Vietnam or Iraq often become violently opposed to anything else the government is trying to do, even if it is unrelated to the specific argument simply because they feel deceived. This makes public argument in a democratic society difficult and yet very rewarding when done well.

Writing and speaking in a manner that builds credibility in public is best a search for truth through communication expressed through the virtue of love. Truth also needs to be considered in a logical manner so the conclusions are valid. Avoiding common pitfalls in logic is important to the lasting impact of the message. Another point in learning fallacies occurs when you can point out logical inconsistencies and errors in the opposition's positions, then the audience will be much more likely to accept your position on a given issue. A final reason for learning to identify fallacies is one of the best ways to remove bad argument from the debate—whether you simply drop your wrong thought or point out someone else's. Any way it goes, you are better off critiquing your own messages for logical errors than waiting and having someone in the audience notice, point it out to you, and then having to adjust your argument to rectify the deficit in your reasoning.

Two thousand years of contemplation of rhetoric, logic, and philosophy have done little to build on Aristotle's treatment in *Sophistical Refutations*. His original purpose was to uncover correct reasoning about why many of the sophists were wrong in their thinking and conclusions. The following chapter unabashedly borrows heavily from Aristotle's work.

Against the person

Argumentum ad hominem

Arguments that attack the speaker instead of the content of the propositions are called *ad hominem* attacks (Latin for "against the man"). Instead of communicating about the substance of real issues, the argument begins to focus on the people involved and their character. In the political realm we call this *mudslinging*, the art of dredging up past events and spinning them in a manner that gives the audience a bad image of an opponent. Character assassination leads to the downfall of many political figures. This fallacy attempts to directly tarnish the ethos: the audience's perception of the character, moral fiber, intelligence, goodwill, and leadership of an individual.

Argument against the person could be exemplified as:

> Joe says the economy is healthy. Joe is a bad person; therefore, the economy is in trouble.

> Fahad believes in Islam. Fahad is a good person; therefore, Islam must be true.

When Kenneth Star was investigating President Clinton, the president used systematic attacks on the prosecutor instead of answering the charges. This strategy was illogical, but it worked to refocus the hungry press and the American people away from the truth or falsity of the charges. Even though he had a strong case, Star lost the battle because he could not counter the attacks on himself. Vietnam Veterans attacked John Kerry's character while the press attacked George Bush's character in a series of ad hominem attacks in the political campaign of 2004.

This tactic also works in the courtroom. OJ Simpson's trial became focused on the police and the investigators instead of the murder. Michael Jackson's trial became a referendum on the accuser and his mother rather than on whether or not a crime was committed. These ad hominem attacks seem to work in both the legal realm and in the court of public opinion.

Not all attacks on character or integrity are fallacious. Sometimes people do things that are unethical and need to be called into account for what they have done. Martha Stewart's insider trading, Los Angeles police brutality, Enron's accounting, Exxon's shipping, and the list could go on and on because people are not perfect. In many cases a rhetor may raise the issue and remain logical—as long as the ethical lapse is the issue, or the substance of the message is addressed along with the character dimension.

Sadly, this kind of negative persuasion often works. Our political system is replete with *ad hominem* messages that attack people; whether the information is true or not, it is slanted or "spun" in such a manner that it impinges on the character of the person. With the ability of political parties and special interests groups to insulate a candidate from these kinds of messages, rarely does the sender receive consequences for these fallacies. Muckrakers simply leave, with other's character trampled in the dust, never looking back to consider the damages.

For those whose character has been misrepresented, to regain the trust and reputation can be nearly impossible. Recovering from an oblique attack is difficult. If someone can overcome mischaracterization, it usually happens through the audience's trust and through living a life of integrity over time. Often these persuasive appeals have just enough believability that many will accept the accusation in spite of the fallacious nature of the message. Be careful not to impugn an innocent person's character for the sake of a story or speech. Even when attacked, do not use the same strategy to get back at the attacker, instead point out the fallacy, and most of the audience will understand and the attack will backfire. Too often in our culture are journalists and politicians slinging mud that is only partly true, or has no factual basis. Getting caught up in passing on the gossip, believing the mudslinging, or passively sitting by and allowing others to suffer the words are all less than Christian.

From Ignorance

Argumentum ad ignorantiam

When someone reasons *a priori* or "in advance" of the facts, the argument becomes a deduction from assumed principles or ideas instead of from communicated evidence. Often this kind of reasoning becomes an *aprioristic* fallacy. Sound argument inducing principles and propositions based on relevant specific evidence is turned on its head. This kind of *invincible ignorance* often prohibits those who are convinced from even considering contradictory evidence. Arguments about life on Mars based on flimsy geological evidence of the possibility of water having been on the planet at an indeterminate past are fallacious. At this point people simply do not know; therefore, to conclude otherwise is a logical fallacy.

Argument from ignorance could be exemplified as:

Global warming is unproved; therefore, it is false.

Evolution cannot be disproved; therefore, it is true.

Some people have an *a priori* theology such as Dispensationalism or Armenianism by which they interpret the Bible, instead of allowing the Bible to speak for itself and the Holy Spirit to guide. Others may be so immersed in pre-millennial, pre-tribulational eschatological doctrine that they cannot hear a passage or person that may counter their position. Be careful not to take your assumptions as truth, but to always consider carefully the evidence.

A second type of appeal to ignorance is when something is not known and is, therefore, false or true. Some claim that intergalactic travel exists because life may exist in other solar systems with beings more technologically advanced than we are. This kind of reasoning from ignorance leads to illogical conclusions without fact.

My daughter and I could sit around the table and discuss nuclear power plants with a very small amount of information. Any assertions or claims we would make would be based on a lack of significant information for neither of us have an in-depth knowledge of the subject. We could share some values and judgments but very little factual information or other forms of evidence would enter into the discussion. That kind of persuasion is ripe for counter-argument based on solid argument with factual evidence. Ignorance is not a good foundation for persuasion.

Appeal to Pity

Argumentum ad Misericordiam

Love is an appropriate, secure foundation for persuasive communication, but when sympathetic emotional elements are used to manipulate a positive outcome the appeal has gone awry. The logical fallacy of pity occurs when the natural or supernatural charity of people is used as a means to accomplish the goals of the rhetor. Kant's Categorical Imperative places this kind of use outside the realm of ethical communication. My having love for the audience and others is a good healthy thing, but when I coerce your love into accepting or rejecting a position, then I am logically and ethically wrong.

The fallacy of pity can be exemplified in several ways:

Sally deserves pity because she is a widow (or lost her son); therefore, we cannot question her political opinion.

Joe had an accident and is physically impaired; therefore, his opinion on ethics is true.

Hell is a fearful condition and; therefore, should be avoided at all costs. Accept Christ or burn.

I hate Americans (Africans, Jews . . .); therefore, I am justified in killing them.

Sally will be broken hearted if Bill does not marry her; therefore, they should get married.

This does not eliminate the use of pity in persuasive appeals completely but as the grounds for decision making. Pictures of starving children are used ethically to entice people to give in support of those less fortunate. When a significant portion of that money goes to salaries, advertisements, and overhead, then the appeal is based on, rather than call forth the emotion. After 9/11, tsunamis, famines, earthquakes, and hurricanes, people are becoming calloused to the need for giving to alleviate the suffering caused by disasters. Therefore, a greater percentage of gifts are being used for fundraising and advertising with the consequence that the number of appeals to pity is increasing.

Another difficulty ensues when pity is the only reason supporting the appeal. If all evidence is against the message except the emotional element, then it is also wrong. Monroe's Motivated Sequence is a good example of how to use pity to enable the audience to feel a need while still providing evidence for the propositional argument that follows through to the appeal.

When fear is added, the fallacy can become a means of audience control. Informing people of hell will arouse emotions, but when that fear is the only form of persuasion used then it is often unethical evangelism bordering on coercion. Using fear of global warming as a socio-political tactic, many people are being manipulated to make decisions they would not make if the facts were used instead of fear. Lasting change will need to be based on more than repetition and fear.

Pathos, the Greek word for emotion also covers negative passions such as hatred and anger. When a message is given in hatred, then it will usually have logical errors. Some Muslims are so filled with hatred toward the Jews and the West that they are willing to become a bomb as long as they can kill others with their death. This kind of pathetic appeal leads to far worse abuses and logical errors than those of compassion, pity, and fear. Some people are so filled with hatred toward President Bush they will counter everything he stands for, even if it is right, simply because he holds to that opinion. This kind of thinking is illogical at best.

Everybody Else is Doing It

Argumentum ad populum Argument popularity
Argumentum ad numerum Argument from how many

Virtually all teenagers use this argument at one time or another. Everyone is getting a tattoo. Everyone is getting body piercing. Everyone is wearing mini-skirts. Everyone is going to the dance. Well, at least all the cool people are. Literally none of the time is the argument accurate—but it feels like it. This got-to-keep-up-with-the-Jones competitive or communal drive is part of many lives. The bandwagon is tempting, but assuming that something is popular and is, therefore, good, is a fallacy.

Argument from others could be exemplified as:

Many others are having extramarital sex; therefore, I ought to be free to have sex with whomever I want.

Many others believe media violence does not increase personal or social violence; therefore, I do not have to limit my DVD viewing or gaming.

The when in Rome do as the Romans do syndrome is an illogical argument. Although on rare occasions it may work, ad populum is an appeal that more often backfires on the rhetor. The fact more doctors prescribe, that movie stars use, or that more people purchase a product, does not make it better. More and more often our political system is considering public opinion as the primary factor in determining domestic and foreign policy. In a democratic republic opinion should be taken into account, but it does not mean that the idea is right or wrong. Advertisements may draw people in based on popularity, but thinking people do not yield to that kind of appeal. In speeches and writing, bandwagon arguments rarely work. Most teenagers find this kind of argument hardly ever succeeds with parents—yet they still use it time and again in hopes of getting to go somewhere or wear something. Justifying a proposition or action based on the common practice of others may be a democratic idea, but it does not logically persuade.

An interesting ethical twist on this fallacy is the country music and advertising slogan, "What is done in Mexico (Vegas . . .) stays in Mexico." Do things here that you want to do, but would not do at home. You can get away with anything because no one will speak of it. That kind of thinking will create more problems than it will solve.

In a democratic republic the bandwagon becomes a difficult proposition. Simply because a majority of people believe states should have the right to determine the behavior of their citizens, does not make it right to own slaves, pollute the environment, or sterilize mentally handicapped individuals. Simply because a panel of judges makes a decision to allow a practice; such as abortion or gay marriage, does not make the procedure either ethical or just. Simply because the president leads the country to war; and a majority of the people support him, does not make the war just. Public opinion is not always right; therefore, it may be important information to consider, but should not be the deciding factor in an issue. Although we govern through a majority opinion, that position is not always right, and it can change very quickly to a different stance on a given issue.

Appeal to Authority

Argumentum ad verecundiam
Ipse dixit he says so

Although authoritative testimony is a good form of evidence, when it is misleading, it becomes a fallacy. Many Christians appeal to the Bible, even when it is silent on an issue. Many humanists appeal to science, even when it is silent on an issue. Many politicians appeal to the constitution, even when it does not address a policy. Because these are our authorities, we want them to support what we believe, whether it is justified by the evidence or not.

Argument from authority could be exemplified as:

> Joe, who is an incredible actor, says to take brand X aspirin, so I will take brand X aspirin.

> Dr. B, my communication professor, says the earth is not round; therefore, the earth is not round.

> Dr. C, my Old Testament professor, believes in dispensationalism; therefore, it is true.

Many authorities are significantly biased. Going to Planned Parenthood, the American Civil Liberties Union, and the National Organization of Women for information on abortion will provide you unbalanced evidence from one socio-political perspective. To make a good decision you would have to go to people from an opposite perspective as well, such as Focus on the Family, the American Center for Law and Justice, Excellence in Broadcasting, or the Moral Majority. Getting balanced information, or at least information from both sides, will lead to logical understanding.

Another significant issue occurs when a non-authority is used for the persuasive appeal. Advertisers will choose actors who play doctors on TV programs to endorse their products. This empty content is misleading at best, but it draws in those who view the program with favor. Individuals who are authorities in a different area sometimes crossover to argue issues they do not understand. If you were to argue physics based on my testimony, you would be using an appeal to false authority, because I am not an expert on physics. If you were to argue rhetoric based on my testimony, you would be using a proper source.

Some people will believe anything if it is linked to a specific authority. Simply mentioning a Bible passage before making a claim, even if the issue at hand has nothing to do with the meaning of that text, will convince some people the statement is correct. In a sermon, if an appeal to the Bible is not used, many fundamentalist listeners will not believe the message no matter what other evidence is used. In a similar fallacy, others will doubt anything simply because of the source of authority, whether it is the Bible, the Book of Mormon, the ACLU, or Planned Parenthood. The message is wrong, because of the authority behind the information or claim.

Another logical fallacy about authority is when one cannot be questioned. Christopher Reeve calling for increased stem cell research could not be addressed simply because he was a famous actor prior to having an accident. Some of the widows from the 9/11 tragedy speak out against the administration, and they cannot be questioned because of their status. Cindy Sheehan lost her son in Iraq, and she cannot be questioned about her politics because of that loss. These people are effective advocates, but their message should be able to be supported by logic and evidence and not simply rest on the untouchable nature of their opinion.

False Cause

Non causa pro causa

A boat capsizes when going over the bar in rough weather; what is the cause of the accident? The answer may not be immediately evident. Some will blame the Captain for attempting an inadvisable action. Others will blame the wind and waves for creating the dangerous situation. Others will blame the boat manufacturer for making a non-seaworthy hull. Still others will call it an act of God and blame him for the victims' misfortune. Even others will be resigned to fate because the accident was predetermined from eternity past. What is the real cause? That is hard to determine, but if harm results, lawyers will probably create reams of arguments to persuade judge and jury of their hired perspective.

The Fallacy of false cause could be exemplified as:

> Jill did not study for her midterm philosophy exam and got a high A; I studied all night and failed; therefore, I will not study for the final.

> America went to war and the stock market rose; therefore, war is good for the economy.

> Our tomato plants withered when the temperature reached 100; therefore, you should avoid planting tomatoes in hot climates.

Most often a false cause is a post hoc, ergo propter hoc, Latin for "after this, therefore because of this." Simply because an event follows another, does not mean that either event causes the other; they could be coincidental or caused by a different event. Basketball players have certain warm-up routines before shooting a foul shot. Shaq is still searching for the right routine that will enable him to make foul shots. Most sports have participants who gage their performance through this kind of fallacy. If the president makes a specific economic policy and the stock market plummets, many journalists will use this fallacy in their front-page news. Yet the reason for the drop in the market is probably unrelated to the President's action, but as soon as it is in print others will believe it.

A second causal fallacy is assuming only one cause when most events have multiple factors as causes. Too often we look for simple causes when reality is complex and multifaceted. Authority and responsibility are shared in most situations rather than falling on one factor alone. Many people believe Muslim terrorists are motivated by US foreign policy decisions when the truth is far more complex and US policy is most probably a secondary consideration—exporting our decadent culture through mass media, support for Israel, and business practices are all unquestionably parts of the issue.

Irrelevant Conclusion

Ignoratio elenchi
Non sequitur

A catch all type of fallacy that is used in numerous situations, this kind of illogical communication is one of the most commonly used logical errors. Usually beginning with a true premise or factual evidence, the rhetor proceeds to draw a conclusion that is false or not demonstrable from the evidence.

Irrelevant conclusions can be exemplified as:

> The United States led the free world against Iraq and freed Kuwait, thereby demonstrating the superiority of democracy over dictatorship.

> Families need time together in order to develop healthy relationships. Parents who work outside of the home take time away from their families; therefore, mothers should not work outside of the home.

The premises might provide insight into a situation, but the conclusion distracts from the issue or uses incorrect evidence to support the issue. In the examples given above, the winning of a war says more about military resources and power than about the political system. To conclude that mothers alone should not work outside of the home based solely on parents spending time away from home is fallacious because it ignores the father, whether or not the kids are at home, and the use of time when at home. Although possibly true, the conclusion is irrelevant to the evidence and original premise.

Many pastors approach a scripture passage and develop a message from their own hearts rather than the message of the text. Pretending a message is from God when it is really the worldview of the pastor is a logical fallacy.

Appeal to Power

Argumentum ad baculum

When someone in a position of power uses threats or hegemonic coercion to direct people, an illusion of persuasion exists. When Iraqi kidnappers coerced a "confession" from a victim, the illogical result is that many believe the message.

Insertion of power into argument can be exemplified as:

> If you do not agree with me, you will get an F in the course. I believe Aristotle is the greatest philosopher of all time; therefore, Aristotle is the greatest philosopher.

Similar to a misuse of an appeal to authority, the appeal to power is more overtly illogical. Might does not make right. When disagreement is feared because of the social, physical, or spiritual power of the persuader, then the rhetor needs to be very careful in development of the message. The emotion of fear that results from the possible use of retaliatory power becomes the reason for compliance rather than pertinence of information or validity of argument. All of us are in positions of power to some audiences; therefore, we should be aware of that power and be conscious of how that works subtly within the persuasive context of a communication.

Many pastors fall into this fallacy in preaching. Not relying on the persuasion of the Holy Spirit the sermon is filled with words like, must, should, absolute, and required. Insertion of power into religious persuasion will weaken the argument and chase many people away.

Begging the Question

Petitio quaesiti
Petitio principii "request for the premise"

Avoiding answering the question, usually by answering a different but semi-related question is a common political version of this fallacy. Like attacking a person instead of the issue, begging the question avoids addressing the issue at hand. Another form of begging the question crops up when the proposition is used to prove itself or it assumes the issue the argument aims to prove. Begging the question can also be not addressing a major issue but focusing on minor ones instead. Arguments for evolution and creation often fall into this fallacy.

Begging the question could be exemplified as follows:

> Some palentologists prove the age of rocks by the fossils they contain being of a certain era in history while the geologists prove the age of the rocks through the kind of fossils in the same strata.

> Getting an "A" in a class implies the student knows the material and has skill in using it correctly. Suppose Jose is going to get an A in psychology; therefore, we ought to get him to explain the material to us.

Politicians become very adept at giving answers to questions that are not asked in a manner that sounds very good to a general audience. The sound bite statements are worked out ahead of time, and then when a question arises that is remotely similar, they simply give the prepared answer. When asked about the increasing federal budget deficit, making a statement about tax refunds is begging the question. When asked about weapons of mass destruction in Iraq, focusing on human rights is begging the question. When asked about sex in the oval office, arguing about the definition of "is" begs the question. At best it fudges by distracting the audience to a new focus; at worst it misleads the audience about the essence of the issue.

Political press conferences, campaign debates, and public interviews are becoming a dance of getting the message out that the speaker desires while avoiding any uncomfortable revelations. Actually answering a question is becoming rare while the participants awkwardly reposition and frame their chosen message. Little real communion takes place in such encounters.

Equivocation

Giving one definition in one place and changing it in another, or not giving enough relevant information is called equivocation. This fallacy is one of lexicon or meaning rather than of form. It takes advantage of ambiguity because the same word can mean two or more different things.

Take for instance this syllogism:

Hot dogs are better than nothing.
Nothing is better than steak.
Therefore, hot dogs are better than steak.

By changing the definition of "nothing" from the major premise (no food) to the definition used for "nothing" in the minor premise (all other food), this syllogism becomes an equivocation. The message is, therefore, illogical.

The fallacy of equivocation can be exemplified as:

"If we don't hang together, we will hang separately," Ben Franklin.

All banks are beside rivers. Therefore, the financial institution where I deposit my money is beside a river.

All wars are immoral. Therefore, the war on poverty is immoral.

The average family in the United States has 2.5 children. Bill and Sue are an average family; therefore, they must have 2.5 children.

Laura, wanting to go to see a movie, asks her parents if she can go with Shannon leaving out the plan to have Gabino and Nate meet them there. If her parents knew the whole plan, they would say no, so Laura equivocates by leaving out the relevant information that would be counter productive to her goal of seeing the movie with her friends. Theologians call this a lie of omission—a sin of communication. Logicians recognize this as another form of equivocation by leaving out necessary information.

Equivocation fallaciously misleads the audience in an intentional manner by evading the truth, or at least part of the truth. Hedging by giving partially true information, evading by omitting some of the important information, or lying by changing definitions are all examples of fallacious reasoning sometimes called equivocation. Political parties often adapt the vocabulary of their opponents and change the definition to refocus the argument. "Family values" supported by the Democrats are vastly different from the family values promoted by the Republicans. Yet Bill Clinton was able to take the words of the issue from President George Bush during a presidential campaign through equivocation. Because of the popularity of the phrase "family values," it was a worthwhile redefinition. The debate continues more than a decade later with both sides talking past each other because they mean different things by the same words.

By deceptively advertising one item, the retailers hope to get the customer to purchase something else that will bring the store more money when they sell it. Or a merchandizer will order only a limited number of a product at a fantastic price, but when the customer in need of that product arrives, none are left, so he must buy a similar product at a much higher price—or go away empty handed.

Composition

When an argument is formulated in such a manner that we believe that what is true of one part, is necessarily true of the whole. This fallacy is usually developed from a hasty generalization where we move from the specific to the general in inductive processes or use an associational logic to link an individual aspect to a whole category.

This fallacy can be exemplified in the following arguments:

> One rich white man driving a Mercedes does not mean all rich white men drive them or that no poor people have a Mercedes.

> One democrat wanting to raise taxes does not mean all democrats do.

> Neither are all students at a specific school more intelligent than those at another school.

> Nor do all lawyers cheat.

Often fallacies of composition happen because we do not see another factor that links the issue. Simply because two states institute medical marijuana laws allowing people with specific diseases to use the drug, and then illegal use increased, does not mean that the same pattern will hold true for the other 48 states.

The impact of fallacious reasoning may be fearful. Was the "weapons of mass destruction" argument for Iraq based on a hasty generalization? Do the munitions of degraded chemical warfare demonstrate a justification for war? Even though the concept that Iraq had weapons of mass destruction was universally accepted, the evidence to date does not support the conclusion that the Iraqi army had sophisticated capabilities of killing many people at once through biological or nuclear means. What are unquestionably found are cruel attempts at manipulating and killing many people.

Division

The opposite of the fallacy of composition is believing what is true of the whole is necessarily true of the individual parts without justification or evidence. A second version of the fallacy of division is to assume that what is true of a collective is true of the individual constituents. Moving from the general to the particular in an illogical manner comes from illogical deductive reasoning.

The fallacy of division can be exemplified with:

> Table salt (sodium chloride), can be ingested by humans safely; therefore, the constituent elements sodium and chloride can be safely eaten.

> African-Americans get paid less than European-Americans; therefore, Michael Jordan gets paid less than Bill Smith.

Understanding that the county government is replete with bureaucratic red tape does not mean the clerk's office is necessarily the same. Knowing that insurance companies are out to make a profit does not mean they will deny a specific claim. That handguns are generally manufactured and purchased for self-defense does not mean that every person who purchases one does so for that reason. Because most students on probation did not study hard does not mean that any particular student who is on probation is not trying. We can observe that most freshmen are less mature than most seniors, but we cannot give the particularization that the freshman Sam is less mature than the senior Gretchen. Division is an active part of many unreasonable arguments.

Straw Man

Claims that misrepresents an opponent's actual position and substitutes a distorted or exaggerated claim and thus misleads the audience, and then arguing against that made-up stance is a fallacy. Instead of listening, understanding, and using the arguments of the opposition, focusing the facts on a false target that is easier to refute is a tactic used by lazy public rhetoricians. One of the reasons political debates are so important to a campaign is that the opposing voices must confront each other in person rather than a characterization of their arguments. Focusing on a bogus claim that is weaker than the opposition's true ideas makes an argument appear to be stronger, but is really a form of counterfeiting or deception.

The straw man fallacy can be exemplified by:

> The Democrats just want to raise taxes and spend more public money not solve real problems.

> President Bush is offering amnesty to illegal aliens to solve the boarder problem.

Pro-life advocates demonize pro-choice advocates by overstating their position. Pro-choice advocates return the favor with neither side able to understand, characterize, or effectively be heard by the other. Until they can listen to each other effectively without pre-conceived labeling, no community solution will be reached. Raising an issue such as "When does life begin?" even though the opposition does not address the issue is not a straw man fallacy because it strikes at the heart of the debate. Focusing the debate on the medical training, cleanliness of facilities, or prayer outside clinics does detract from the main issue of abortion and right to life.

In a similar manner, liberal Christians speak of unintelligent fundamentalists who cannot think for themselves, while the conservatives speak of wishy washy liberals who cannot take seriously the sovereignty of God nor the authority of the Bible. Both sides are arguing against a false conception of the other. Until a full listening occurs where both sides stop arguing against a false conception of the other, no good writing or speaking will take place to heal the splits. Denomination after denomination and church after church have discovered the hard way the serious conflicts that can occur through this logical error.

Red Herring

In an attempt to keep fox hunters out of their crops, farmers in England would hang herring along their fields so that the hounds would loose the scent of the fox. A red herring is an attempt to throw the audience off track through stating an attractive but irrelevant issue. The opposition or audience is diverted into arguing a different concept that has little relevance to the original subject and thus avoids persuasive argument.

Red Herrings can be exemplified with:

> Lethal injection may be determined to be cruel and unusual but the cost of all the trials necessary to put the criminal on the gurney is definitely a crime.

Most students have attempted to get a professor to talk about something other than the curriculum plan. This is a game played in many classrooms in an attempt to shift the attention of the teacher away from the intended subject. In arguing about increasing the height of Shasta Dam of Northern California several radio talk shows gave a reason for not doing it as "Those whacko environmentalists who oppose anything that makes sense for people." This has nothing to do with whether or not billions of gallons of water should be stored at that place for human consumption. This kind of smokescreen would only be persuasive for people who are strongly against the environmental movement while alienating those who are part of the movement and confusing the issue for those looking for solid evidence and reasoning about the issue.

Sidetracking can be an art of avoiding an issue by shifting the attention away from the question at hand. Many people who argue death penalty justice believe that some convicted criminals may actually be innocent and then executed. Therefore, the death penalty should not be used. To advocates for the death penalty, this is a separate issue—where unjust verdicts are given, so occasionally the waters may be muddied through red herrings.

False Dilemma

Socrates in Plato's dialogue Euthyphro asks "Is what is pious loved by the gods because it is pious, or it is pious because it is loved by them?" The good has only two choices—something greater than the gods or something arbitrarily chosen by the gods. Other options exist such as the Judaic and Christian idea that good is based on God's nature or the Eastern idea that it is a path and not an ultimate good. We have a dilemma attempting to force an issue because of false categorization of answers. This is precisely why so many people are frustrated in taking personality tests because they require multiple false dilemmas in order to place us in a forced choice situation determining preferences.

The fallacy of false dilemma can be exemplified with:

> We must cut defense spending this year or the deficit
> will bankrupt the country.

> America: love it or leave it.

Either you are a Republican or a Democrat. What about all the independents, reformers, and Green Party advocates? What about those who choose to not be involved? Politically we often place ourselves into a false dichotomy (Christians certainly wouldn't do the same thing with denominations and churches).

Time

Argumentum ad novarrum – newness
Argumentum ad verecundiam – authority in the sense of tradition

The fallacy of the newness of an argument is ad novarrum while over reliance on the tried and true nature is the fallacy of ad verecundum. Neither the good old days nor the current fads have inevitable truth. Simply because something is typed on a word processor instead of written with a pencil and paper does not mean the text is a better quality.

The time fallacies can be exemplified as:

> The new morality of accepting people with promiscuous and alternative sexual lifestyles is better than the barbaric old ethic of monogamous heterosexual marriage.

> My grandfather served in the army in World War I, my father served in the army in World War II, I served in the army in Vietnam, now it is your turn to serve in the Middle East.

The Jewish character Tevye in Fiddler on the Roof cites as reason for many things in life—tradition. All that is necessary to continue a practice is that is the way it has always been done. Yet his passionate love for his family, his wisdom, his pride, and his faith help him overcome this fallacious reason to give him the ability to face extreme oppression in turn-of-the-century Czarist Russia.

Novelty is also a part of this fallacy. The "new and improved" glue for flooring I purchased recently was more expensive, harder to use, and less efficient than the previous glue. In America we practically worship the young and the new. We are obsessed with the newest video game, the newest fashions, the newest electronics, the newest ideas, fads, and political whims. Just because a startup company goes public in the stock market does not mean it will be a success.

Argument by Repetition

Argumentum ad nauseam - Argument to the point of nausea
Argumentum ad infinitum - Argument into infinity
Argumentum verbosium - Proof by verbosity

Franklin Roosevelt said, "Repetition does not transform a lie into a truth." On the other side of the Atlantic, Joseph Goebells is reputed to have said, "Tell a lie that is big enough, and repeat it often enough, and the whole world will believe it." Yet decades later we are still wrestling with claims that counter the evidence repeated over and over so that people believe them. Another kind of repetition fallacy is to argue the same thing over and over until the opposition no longer challenges the issue.

Saying President Bush lied over and over has most of the world believing the claim, yet no-one can point to a specific lie that has evidence to support the assertion. Michael Moore claiming that the U.S. government gave $245 million to the Taliban government in Afghanistan is a distortion because that aid consisted of food and food security programs administered through the U.N. and other non-governmental agencies to relieve famine. Numerous other lies from Moore are accepted as truth so that international film festivals give him honors for the documentary movies that are so inaccurate Time magazine made up a new category called politainment or political entertainment rather than documentary.

The fallacy of repetition can be exemplified with:

> Where there's smoke there's fire.

> Some teams of lawyers attempt to win suits by overwhelming the opposition in a storm of paperwork—verbosity.

In an age when the associated press is quoted around the world as journalistic gospel, any argument that makes the wire becomes spoken of and written over and over without critical appraisal of the veracity of the information. Public relations firms make their living off of "talking points" that provide quotable short phrases for media to use in their articles. Whoever gets the first perspective in the public sphere is likely to win the battle for public opinion.

Conclusion

These pseudoreasons should be avoided in public communication because in the long run they alienate more people than they persuade. Although sending a teacher on a rabbit trail may be fun during a class period, when it comes to the final exam, the students pay the price for the distraction. Without proper debate over an issue, we the people will bear the burden in a lack of knowledge and bad decisions. When reason gives way to misdirection, misunderstanding, weakness, or mistakes whether intentional or unintentional, persuasive rhetoric becomes an exercise in absurdity rather than influential impact.

This brief review of fallacious argument is not an exhaustive list of the possible ways people will subvert sound reasoning or distort truth. Some illogical rhetoric is an innocent mistake made through a lack of background work in constructing sound reasoning. Other illogical communication is intentional attempts to manipulate the audience and win an argument.

Even though some people will be persuaded in a given situation through fallacious reasoning, they will do so with less confidence, shorter duration, and be more open to counterpersuasion than if solid reasoning and evidence are used. This is especially true if the fallacy is tied to emotions such as fear, guilt, pity, or pride. Eventually the public will uncover the fraudulent or sloppy thinking and reject the rhetor's message usually with a greater zeal than they accepted it at the start. When people think they have been duped, they respond with extreme skepticism to the next message from the same source.

Chapter 12

Evidence

So I turned my mind to understand,
To investigate and to search out wisdom
And the scheme of things
Ecclesiastes 7:25 NIV

SUPPORTING THE propositions of arguments is the backbone of rhetorical persuasion. Rhetors should be able to effectively use a wide variety of forms of evidence adapting them to particular subjects and audiences. Without specific and generalizable evidence, the claims of rhetorical addresses are mere assertions. Being able to recognize and evaluate evidence in other's argument will empower the rhetor's ability to understand and criticize the discourse in a meaningful way. Resourceful skill in researching, observing, and discovering evidence for your own argument and effectively using it, will enhance your ability to persuade others.

Evidence can be anything that furnishes proof for or against a proposition. Defined in this manner, evidence is an audience-particular element of discourse. What may be accepted as proof for one audience may increase the skepticism of another group of people. The fact that we are experiencing more recorded earthquakes and volcanoes for one audience may support the proposition that increased technology allows us to become more aware of the world upon which we live. The same fact for another audience may be evidence that the Bible's prediction of an increase in earthquakes is a sign of "the end of the age," thus indicating that the world as we know it will soon end. This same fact for another audience may be an indication of the tectonic movement of the earth's crust. For others it may be an indication that Southern California, Afghanistan, Japan or wherever it occurs, has sinned and is being judged by God. Evidence functions within persuasive writing and address as audience centered content that supports the major propositions of a communication.

Specific data, particulars, or instances logically substantiating claims are called evidence. This support transforms a claim into a persuasive argument instead of a simple, unsubstantiated opinion. Evidentiary reasons build the logical stability, demonstrability, and persuasibility of a claim as opposed to personal rationalization of opinion.

One of the mistakes rhetoricians make is to use a single kind of evidence to support a speech. If too many statistics are used, some members of the audience may not be able to compute the meaning. If only examples are cited, some of the audience may think of examples that do not fit the mold. Using multiple forms of evidence with each claim is usually better than relying on any one particular class alone.

> Claim: In a democratic republic every vote counts.
>
> Example: Bush/Gore presidential race.
>
> Statistics: Few people vote, often less than 50%, so those who do have a greater voice.
>
> Fact: Bush won the Electoral College vote and is therefore president, even though Gore won the popular vote.
>
> Fact: The Supreme Court of the United States held the Supreme Court of Florida to Florida's own election laws and federal laws thus determining the Electoral College vote of Florida.
>
> Fact: Painfully slow recounts show that for those ballots that can be counted, Bush won the election in Florida.
>
> Testimony: "Once I began to vote, I became more aware and involved in the political processes that make a real difference in our community."
>
> Appeal: So your vote counts, please vote.

A combination of evidence like this will make a claim stronger than if only one kind was used. They have an "additive" effect where the support multiplies the dynamism and impact of the claim making it more rhetorically persuasive.

Some claims may lend themselves to different kinds of evidence. A value claim may need explanation, examples, analogies, and testimony while a factual claim may need data, particulars, statistics, and specific instances. Virtually any of the kinds of evidence can support any claim, but a claim of fact supported only by analogy would be weak and probably not persuasive to a counterattitudinal audience. The mix of evidence used in substantiating a claim is part of the art of persuasion. No persuasive communication can exhaust all of the available information or all of the forms of evidence in support or countering a claim.

The amount of evidence depends on the audience, speaker, subject, and occasion. The twin rules of necessity and sufficiency apply to how much information is needed to be persuasive. The speaker or writer's first obligation is to discover what evidence is essential as necessary to make her point. Then the speaker should evaluate the extent or sufficiency of the evidence needed to convince the audience of the validity of her argument. Giving fourteen forms of statistics may be confusing and detract from persuasion while two specific statistics might be necessary for a favorable reception of the message.

Kinds of Evidence

For centuries the list of forms of evidence has swelled and abated with different thinkers and theorists. Aristotle noted 28 different types of evidence in *The Rhetoric*. Others have added to and subtracted from the list. Here we will not exhaustively consider all forms of evidence, but consider some of the most common kinds of substantiation used in persuasive argument. Just because something does not appear in the list here does not mean that it will be ineffectual in persuasion. Also note that simple nonverbal additions to evidence such as visual representation of processes, charts, graphs, objects, or correlations can greatly enhance your ability to persuade either in writing or through speaking.

Explanation

Argument By Amplification

Argument by explanation implies that understanding the meaning of a proposition will build the persuasive power of the statement. Explanation is the elaboration of the physical attributes, description of the context (historical, social, spiritual, geographical . . .), or annotation of the constructs in a manner that clarifies the important parts for audience perception of the subject.

Expositional evidence can be used persuasively through *ethos, pathos,* and/or *logos.* A "liberal" audience may think a "conservative" speaker is intellectually inferior. By using adroit explanation of a current event, the audience's perception of the speaker's intelligence could be enhanced. Officiates at weddings often desire to increase the impact of the service on the participants. Explanation of the ritualistic symbolism being used can add to the *pathetic* appeal of the service possibly influencing the future of the people involved, making divorce less likely. An archeologist can use descriptive explanation of the customs of a culture to increase an audience's cognitive understanding of artifacts discovered in a dig. Explanatory evidence often increases appropriate persuasive appeals (*ethos, pathos,* and *logos*) through audience knowledge, awareness, and comprehension.

Explanations should be tested for their lucidity, fairness and applicability.

1. What is the argument claim?

2. Does the explanation clarify and lead to understanding?

3. Is the explanation generalizable?

4. Are the terms adequately defined and differentiated?

5. Is the argument plausible?

6. Is the argument true?

7. Does it take into account counter possibilities and interpretations?

Be sure to think through the strength and truth of the explanation before using it in a formal communication situation.

Specific Instance

Argument by Example

A real or hypothetical event in which the proposition actually happens is an example of a specific instance. Sometimes examples are considered to be brief reports while specific instances are longer with more details. Examples serve to illustrate the specific argument by illumining or enlightening the idea. Usually an example is representative of a group or type of similar phenomena. Sometimes an example is given as an illustrative ideal or pattern to be imitated or not to be followed in applying an argument to real life. The activities of an individual lamb may be taken as representative of an entire flock of sheep. The history of a typical stock may be typical of the index.

Taking an individual incident as representative of other events and using it as support for a claim is an inductive use of an example. When an advocate uses an example as evidence to support a claim, an assumption is being made that an aspect of the example is true of the rest of the instances in the group.

When President Bush makes the claim that terrorists ought to be eliminated from causing active harm to others and follows it up with a war on terrorism, the world carefully considers his claim. The vast majority of people from around the world agree, and in turn support the United States in the following military endeavors in Afghanistan. But when President Bush puts pressure on Israel to negotiate with the Palestine Liberation Organization, then many in the world wonder why Yassar Arafat should not be considered a terrorist. Dozens of examples of terror activities can be traced directly to the highest levels of the PLO. Bush cites their willingness to negotiate and sign treaties as evidence that Arafat is not a "terrorist." Examples are used on both sides of the debate as evidence to support whether or not the definition of "terrorist" should apply to the PLO in general and Arafat in particular. Another example is putting the "terrorist label on Saddam Hussein and Iraq by President Bush, and the nations dwindle from supporting the war on terrorism. Following these events Arafat dies and the Hamas party is elected in Palestine and now most of the Western world is putting pressure on the government of Palestine to denounce terrorism. Israel's Likud party is attempting to negotiate, but the efforts are falling short. Hesbolah, Hamas, and others shelling Israeli cities; and Israel returning with overwhelming military force. The UN condemning Israel and not the Arab terrorists is adding to the strain in the situation. By the time this book enters your hands the situation concerning terrorism and the specific examples will change. Many examples are, therefore, time sensitive.

Examples can be tested to ensure their soundness in the argument. Analyzing our own evidence should be done prior to publicly presenting the claims; these same tests can be used to critically evaluate other's arguments.

1. Does the example(s) cited actually *support* the whole claim? Or even part of the claim?

2. Is the *number* of examples sufficient to support the generalization offered in the claim?

3. Are the instances cited *typical* of all cases covered by the claim? Do they represent other cases in the classification well?

4. Do any negative examples exist to *contradict* those given?

5. Is the example *accurately portrayed* in the observation and reporting by the rhetor?

6. Is the example of *recent* origin, or has time blurred the audience's ability to relate to the illustrative quality?

7. Are *factors other than the claim* more important in understanding the example?

8. What is the historical situation? Context similarity?

These questions can lead to choosing stronger examples or using the cited examples to support only that part of the claim it really does elaborate.

When speaking of God's care in what really matters in life, Jesus used examples of the birds not worrying about food, people worrying about life, and flowers not worrying about clothing (Matthew 6:26-30). The conclusion of having faith rather than worrying is a natural form of induction from example. Examples are also support for deductive logic. In Galatians 3:2 Paul uses an example in the form of a question to move the reader to accept a premise deductively. The proposition is: "You are wrong in leaving the faith to go back under the law," and is supported by the example of when they received the Holy Spirit it happened through faith, not obedience to the law. Examples are forms of evidence and reasoning that can be used either inductively or deductively.

Accurate Depictions of Reality

Argument by Facts

Factual evidence describes or reports what exists in reality—events, objects, places, persons, and phenomena. These can be verified to be either true or false. Direct factual evidence is that which the participants in the persuasive situation can observe. Indirect factual evidence can be uncovered from authorities and others who have directly observed the phenomena. Explanations or evaluations usually are needed to function as warrants or logical links for facts to support propositions. Both indirect and direct facts describe or report what exists in time and space—objects, persons, phenomena, or events. They should correspond to the reality of the audience or inform them in a believable manner.

The vast majority of factual evidence used in persuasive communication comes from the observations of others. Therefore, the source of the material should be carefully noted. In I John 1:1 the Apostle John cites specific empirical data as evidence: which we have seen, which we have looked upon, and our hands have handled.

Usually auditors interpret facts in presenting them to audiences. The observable reality that George W. Bush was elected president by the Electoral College process even though Al Gore received more popular votes could be stated as an opinion:

> America is *lucky* George Bush was elected president even though Al Gore received more popular votes.

Often facts will be spoken with value-laden words meant to shape the listener's perspective. Dan Rather will label Republican politicians as *conservative* or religious individuals as *fundamentalist* yet rarely states the opposite such as *liberal* Democrats or *left wing* radicals. The language chosen for those he disagrees with demonstrates a bias in reporting. This bias became so strong he either fabricated or at least refused factual evidence when reporting about President Bush's military service. Even though the narrow-mindedness or openness of a person's perspective has nothing to do with which part of the spectrum she is from (right or left, conservative or liberal). The adjectives placed in front of the fact communicate value-laden opinion rather than objective reality. When the audience assumes the speaker's opinion is fact, misunderstanding is perpetrated creating an illusion of knowledge rather than a solid base for persuasive claims.

Some of the tests for factual evidence are:

1. Is the fact true (corresponding to reality in time and space)?

2. Is the fact subjective (developed by human thought)?

3. Is the information plausible (believable)?

4. Is the information relevant to the claim?

5. Is the information recent enough to be related to the present situation?

6. Does the fact have a reliable source with appropriate credentials to observe the phenomena?

7. Does observation of the fact involve assumptions?

8. Can others independently verify the information presented?

9. Is the information generalizable to the entire claim, or does it support only part of the proposition?

10. Are interpretations of the fact lucid?

11. Are implications of the fact ethical?

12. What counter facts are present?

Factual evidence should be questioned whether in a news broadcast or presidential speech. We should clearly understand the best information before attempting to persuade an audience.

Testimony

Argument by Authority

The verbal or nonverbal communication of someone who supports a specific proposition is called testimony. Statements by others are usually expert, where someone who has the qualifications to related knowledge makes a statement. Testimony can also be "lay" where someone with simple experience in the area covered by the argument makes a statement. Usually expert opinion is stated in the form of opinions that interpret or evaluate facts.

When testimony provides a foundation of logical organization of experience and fact for an audience along with ways to judge claims, it fulfills the best function of testimonial evidence. When testimony is simple opinion, it is not persuasive in a way that will provide lasting strong change in the audience.

The audience provisionally accepts opinions when the source is credible. If an expert is believed to be capable of observing and offering testimony, then the judgments by that individual are more likely to be accepted. Alternatively, if an expert expresses an opinion that the audience already believes, then the person giving the testimony will have a more positive ethos.

Why are the experts that the mainstream press relies on so slow to understand the finding of weapons of mass destruction? World Net Daily reported in 2004 that evidence was being found. Now in 2006 that evidence is verified—yet the press is reluctant to publish the facts of what is being uncovered. People have accepted the conventional wisdom and knowledge that no weapons existed, so we only listen to those who say what we already believe. Counterevidence and expert opinion that violates what is believed have very little impact on public opinion.

For many audiences the persuader becomes an implied expert through the act of communicating a message. The ethical responsibilities of significant research, understanding the issues, and accurately representing factual data increase with the acceptance of the audience.

A number of tests exist for evaluating the testimony of both expert and lay testimony.

1. Does the person have relevant training, background, or personal experience (is the authority credible)?

2. Is the testimony relevant to the claim?

3. Is the source trustworthy?

4. What is the motivation of the individual who is testifying?

5. Is the source of the testimony biased in a significant manner so the opinion is not objective?

6. Is a reliable base of factual evidence for the opinion available?

7. Are contradictory opinions available of equally qualified individuals?

8. Is the testimony of direct or indirect evidence?

9. If the testimony is from a published source, is the publisher credible?

10. Is the testimony substantive content or does it critique?

Understanding the people involved and their perspectives will enable good use of testimony. The internet is an increasingly tempting source of simple quotations that purport support for propositions, yet they often come from unreliable or immature sources.

Lay testimony is imputing authority to someone who has specific experience in the issue rather than occupational or educational qualifications. This kind of evidence has a different list of tests.

1. What is the experience that gives him the right to speak to the issue?

2. What is the duration of the experience?

3. Does the person have other similar experiences?

4. What gives the person the ability to judge or critique?

5. What is the likelihood or plausibility of the experience?

6. Is the person impartial to the issue at stake?

These kinds of questions will enable the audience to evaluate the objectivity and believability of the lay testimony.

Analogy

Argument by Comparison

An analogy compares or contrasts elements of two different subjects. The purpose of an analogy is to make a new idea more picturesque and accessible to the listener. Analogies are logical inferences that if two things are similar in one aspect, they are also similar in others, or that two items are dissimilar in one aspect so they are also different in other ways. The similarities between American style football and rugby could be stressed, such as the kind of ball, things done with the ball, and movement within the rules. Soccer also has many things in common with football; then we could compare the similarities with baseball and still find logical parallels. All of these have more in common than football and chess, and yet even that association could be useful for analogies about strategy, problem solving, and character development.

The similarities between football and stock trading on Wall Street are a stretch, but the contrasts could be quite interesting (spectators, players, activity, purpose . . .). When an analogy is used to contrast traits, it is called *figurative* because it combines subjects from different realms of experience or quality. Many times figurative analogies make indigestible ideas digestible to an audience. Often the complexity of an issue or situation can become clear and simple through analogous reasoning.

In order for an analogy to be compelling, the audience has to interpret it as significantly parallel to induce the conclusion that what is true of one instance is also true of the other. The rhetor's assertion that two different things that are similar in several ways are also similar in the specific point being argued must be adopted by the audience for an analogy to work.

Tests for analogous argument:

1. Are the cases really comparable in their essential characteristics?

2. What is the extent of the contrast (non-analogous part)?

3. Does this comparison or contrast logically lead to the new manner of identification between the two?

4. Are the cases based on verifiable description?

5. Are collaborative forms of evidence available?

6. What is the logical link between the cases?

7. Will the audience easily grasp the meaning so the claim is illuminated, or will the analogy need further explanation?

8. Is the analogy impartial?

Analogies effectively add color and emotion to argument, yet care should be used not to place too much emphasis on the logical elements of parallelism.

Narration

Argument through Story

Stories are one of the most powerful, yet often overlooked, forms of evidence. While falling well short of Fisher who explains all of life through narrative, story can accomplish far more in argument than what first meets the eye. In one sense, narration is an extended example or illustration, but in another sense, narratives are far more complete because of the extra dimensions they bring to the table. Stories engage audiences in life situations and support the propositions of persuasive argument by adding positive ethos to the speaker, generating positive pathos for the subject, providing identification with the characters, and applying the logos of the claim.

Narratives begin with people. The characters of a story should be realistic and believable. Listeners will identify with the actors in the story envisioning themselves in different roles.

Details such as dialogue between characters, colors, textures, and smells allow the story to come alive to the audience. Search for the most meaningful images that draw emotions into the content of the message. Engage the imagination so the mind pictures the scene and action adds visualization to persuasion. Lengthy descriptions can slow a story; use active details to embroider the action and carrying the audience to the enthymematic conclusion.

The action follows a plot line with development, complication, climax, and resolution of the sequence. Accounting the incidents and events of individuals working through to a climax involves the imagination and logical progression toward a claim in an inductive manner. The action of characters primarily differentiates a story from an example.

Narratives are powerful because the audience discovers truth in them. The thesis of the message becomes their personal creation of meaning from the story involving a high degree of personalization and relevance with added emotion and commitment to the ideas. Stories also generate the ability to understanding future events that are similar in a way that creates meaning and gives the audience a way of responding to the future situation. The difficulty is that the audience may come to a different conclusion from that of the advocate.

Some tests of a narrative:

1. Does the story lead the audience closer to adopting the claim of the argument?

2. Does the action and characterization represent reality in a manner the audience can identify with?

3. Will the audience be able to adopt proper application in real life situations on the basis of this narrative?

4. Is the originality of the expressions drawing the senses into the subject?

5. Will the emotional response to the story augment the proper pathos of the claim?

6. Does the narrative lead to ethical action?

7. Does the story have coherence and fidelity?

Narratives involve the audience in the action of a speech so the participants discover the message. Often the story is remembered long after the other parts of the speech are forgotten.

Humor

Argument by fun

Fraught with peril, humor remains a significant part of persuasive appeals and as evidence to support cases. Humor often arouses inappropriate emotions, degrades people and diverts logical argument in a compelling dismissive degradation of people who are worthy of respect. Ridicule can be a fallacy that should be carefully avoided.

Billy Graham often began sermons with humor as a form of identifying with the audience. The laughter helps eliminate other concerns and put everyone on the same page, ready to hear the real message. Ronald Regan had a dry sense of humor that was woven into the heart of some of his speeches. Whatever the place of the joke, allusion, or tease, it can disarm opponents and further the humanity of the speaker or writer.

1. Is the humor appropriate to the issue?

2. Does the humor attack the person or the idea?

3. Does the humor include ridicule?

4. Does the humor harm anyone (especially the opposition)?

5. Is the punch-line justifiable?

6. Does the humor lead to understanding and clarity?

Most humor falls into logical fallacies and should be taken with skepticism. Often advocates will resort to humor when other forms of evidence are not available or significant counterevidence is available. When well done, the use of humor can be one of the most powerful forms of rhetorical evidence. People who cannot quickly grasp the physics of a nuclear bomb can immediately grasp humor about it.

Numeric Argumentation

Argument through Statistics

Expressing the nature of a phenomena in quantitative form can be strong support for a claim. Expressed in percentages, ratios, graphs and tables, statistical information that is readily accessible by the audience moves people to understand the relationship of a claim to other assertions. Ross Perot's presidential campaign used statistical graphs to help the voters' understand the implications of his positions in such a strong manner that he received more third party votes than any other candidate since the Bull Moose election in the early 1900's.

Because statistics are easy to manipulate, they are often mistrusted by audiences. Many of the statistical representations of claims will be gathered from sources the speaker has no control over. Therefore, great care should be used in determining the reliability of the numbers, citing the sources when using them, and usually using other evidence along with the numbers.

A significant portion of the audience grasps the importance of numbers when they are expressed in a graphic word picture. When talking about trillion dollar debts of the federal government, compare the number of dollars in a wallet, how high to reach $1,000 (height and thousand are easy to grasp) and then how high to reach a million, billion, and finally a trillion. Or, the speaker could relate how much to spend each second in order to spend a trillion in a year? Yes, it takes more work than copying the source, but the audience impact is worthwhile.

Tests for statistical evidence:

1. Was the evidence compiled by a disinterested source? Planned Parenthood, National Rifle Association, People for the American Way, the American Civil Liberties Union all produce their own statistical evidence which is usually suspect by counterattitudinal audience members.

2. What was the wording of the question that produced the statistic? Walking down the sidewalk at the University of Oregon, I was asked among questions about friendships, "Have you ever been attracted to someone of the same gender?" Nothing in the question suggested sexual attraction, yet the pollsters concluded, based on that question, more than 10% of the student body had homosexual tendencies. Nowhere in the poll did it even ask if I were a student, yet the conclusion was that anyone walking through campus was a student, and attraction was automatically interpreted as sexual orientation.

3. Another major question to ask is the size and randomness of the sample. Simply taking a sample from a phone book is not adequate because many people do not have listed numbers, others use only cell phones and a few choose to have no phones at all, so a random sample of a community derived from a phone book is not an adequate source for the population of a community.

4. Statistical measures change rapidly, so was the study done recently enough to be relevant to the claim?

5. Where alternative causalities considered?

6. Are the figures open to a different interpretation?

7. Are supporting evidences available?

Be careful when quoting statistics as evidence in a persuasive speech to use them ethically. Also, citing too many will confuse an audience more than illuminate the claim. In our information age, statistics are often necessary to convince an audience. Statistical evidence demonstrates a serious consideration of the issue and often how others perceive the implications. Being able to objectively demonstrate the substance through numbers will move some of the audience most of the time.

Evaluating Evidence

The major tests of evidence are truth, relevancy, recency, credibility, accessibility, sufficiency, and ethics. These are integrated into many of the questions from the earlier sections, but they should be considered in the use of any evidence. Audiences should not believe argument simply because it is written or spoken, but because it is true, convincing, and significant.

Truth

The primary characteristic of evidence is truth. Does the information correspond to reality—what exists in time and space. If the evidence does not speak the truth, then it should be rejected. For items without a specific truth value like critique, explanation, and narration, the degree of accuracy should be taken into account. Truth can also be considered from the advocate's motivation; if the purpose is to deceive the audience, then the evidence should be considered with skepticism. The veracity of an advocate will often be judged on the basis of his honesty and integrity in dealing with truth. Sincerity of belief is not enough to convince most; it takes building a case with sound reason and truthful support to substantiate the propositions.

Relevant

Evidence should have a direct bearing on the subject at hand. A pertinent connection allows the audience to draw focused conclusions that will be resistant to change when counter information is provided. Germane evidence also is more capable of moving the audience to adapt applications to real-life situations in their own life, making personal action based on the persuasive message more likely.

Recent

Although some forms of evidence such as analogies or literary allusions maintain their potency over time, most evidence looses persuasive value the further the audience is from the source. Examples from the mid 18th century are unlikely to significantly move a 21st century audience. Currency is most critical in the use of statistics and public opinion forms of evidence. Citing a public opinion poll about President Clinton's approval rating from more than a decade ago holds no persuasive power in determining the popularity of a current president. Even public opinion polls from early in a term have little to do with what happens a year later because of the changeable nature of opinion. Other evidence has little to do with passing time. Gravity, light, and the pyramids of Egypt contain facts that do not change with time.

Credible

Speakers should always consider whether the audience is capable of believing evidence. Believability is most important for unfamiliar audiences and cross-cultural situations. Remember, all evidence is audience centered, not what will it take for the speaker to believe the proposition, but what information will enable the audience to accept the persuasive message. Credibility is closely related to the diction, style, and ethos of the rhetor. The way something is framed will often determine the believability of the evidence.

Accessible

Is the argument supported by evidence that is available to anyone, or is it private? "Secret government documents" have been used as evidence to prove that aliens landed in the desert, that Lee Harvey Oswald acted with the CIA and FBI to assassinate President Kennedy and that Elvis is still alive. Since the source is not accessible by those in debate, the evidence must be accepted on the veracity of the arguer alone and should, therefore, be treated with skepticism.

In this age of the internet, much information, true and untrue, good and evil, accurate and inaccurate is available in seconds by the push of a button. Public communicators need to access that database of public information and be willing to have their evidence considered openly by a skeptical world.

Sufficient

The amount of evidence provided should be sufficient for the purpose of the communication. For most arguments, clear, compelling, and convincing evidence is enough to persuade an audience. If the guilt of an individual is in question with the possibility of execution, then the standard of evidence is much higher. Occasionally one piece of evidence is so compelling that it will persuade; however, more often multiple forms put together into a full case will be necessary for moving an audience.

Ethics

Good argument leads to ethical actions with the appropriate kind and intensity of emotion. The impact of argument should result in an exercise of love and justice. One of the primary ways to consider the authenticity and significance of an argument is to analyze where it leads. Although the ends do not justify the means, often, the ends do give significant information about public communication. If a policy leads to evil action, then its consequences should be considered prior to putting it into practice. Possible unintended impacts and consequences should also be researched before action is urged. The quality of significance compels argument when it leads in a good direction.

Another Way of Considering What to Use

Michael and Suzanne Osborn (2003) give the following guidelines for making wise choices to select supporting material for a speech:

1. If an idea is *controversial*, rely primarily on facts, statistics, factual examples or expert testimony from sources the audience will respect and accept.

2. If your ideas or concepts are *abstract*, use examples and narratives to bring them to life. Use comparisons, contrasts, or analogies so that your listeners grasp your ideas and develop appropriate feelings about them.

3. If an idea is highly *technical*, supplement facts and statistics with expert testimony. Use definitions, explanations, and descriptions to aid understanding. Use examples, comparisons, contrasts and analogies to help listeners integrate information.

4. If you need to *arouse emotions*, use lay and prestige testimony, examples or narratives. Excite listeners by using contrast and analogy.

5. If you need to *defuse emotions*, emphasize facts and statistics and expert testimony. Keep the focus on definitions and explanations.

6. If your topic is *distant* from the lives of listeners, draw it closer to them through information, examples, and narratives, activated by descriptions, comparisons, and analogies.

Conclusion

Although the need for particular types of supporting material may vary with different topics and audiences, a good rule of thumb is to support each main point with the most important and relevant facts and statistics available. To clarify each point, use testimony, and provide sufficient definitions, explanations, and descriptions. Additionally, support each main point with at least one interesting example or narrative. To make your presentation more dramatic or memorable, emphasize examples and narratives, brought to life through striking comparisons, contrasts, and analogies.

In writing, evidence will be even more important with readers paying careful attention to the manner and kind of substantiation. Those who read or listen will dismiss claims and opinion that are not supported by significant evidence; or else they will have to look for grounds to confirm or deny the argument. A good public communicator will provide sufficient, strong evidence in support of claims made when speaking or writing.

Part IV

Practicing Public Communication

Doing the work of communicating involves putting the message into relationship with information, then choosing the best and most beautiful words, and finally presenting them to an audience is the practice of public rhetoric. Putting the foundations and theory into form still requires style and delivery to applied with vitality and dynamism. This comes through communication in an appropriate style and charisma with eloquence. Traveling two thousand miles to Hawaii just to sit in a car and watch the sun set without the feel of sand between the toes or the froth of waves bubbling against your ankles would be unfulfilling. Great ideas will not have great impact unless they are framed in an appropriate style and presented with magnetism.

Organization of the content into a form that the audience can experience and understand enables them to follow through the thinking process increasing the likelihood of a positive impact.

Style is the choosing of words, phrases, and approaches in eloquent aesthetics that impact the heart and mind. How we say what we say is often as important as what we say.

Delivery is the presentation to the audience of the message in a manner they can receive for maximum impact.

Chapter 13

Organization

Make plain to everyone the administration
Of this mystery,
Which for ages was kept hidden in God.
Ephesians 3:9 NIV

WHETHER BEGINNING with a question, a reaction to someone else's thoughts, or an inspiration, persuasive communication starts through forming a topic into an argument. Opinions tend to grow in random ways unless they are carefully pruned, cultivated, watered, and fertilized. Selection, propositional formation, and organization are the method used to nurture an idea into persuasive rhetoric. Aristotle called the process invention and organization: the discovery, development, and logical arrangement of an idea into a persuasive unit.

Topic Selection

The first part of organization of ideas is to select a topic that is appropriate for the audience, communicator, and occasion. Sometimes a speaker is given a topic, such as a request to submit a proposal for a board, a sales presentation, or a special occasion. Sometimes a limitation on source or evidence is given such as speaking to a worship service or in a classroom. Other times the occasion to speak is given without limits on the subject such as at a graduation or civic club. Narrowing the topic into a subject that can be adequately covered in the allotted time can be difficult. A boss assigns some persuasive written work, while other times we can write whatever we want. Also, limiting the topic to what can be covered in a given time frame is important. No one can adequately cover geologic history in a ten-minute speech, but giving some specifics about an individual rock can be enlightening. No one can adequately cover the subject of rhetoric in a ten-page paper, but considering how to select a topic can be covered.

Narrowing the speech or essay involves a balance between the needs of the audience, the appropriateness and purpose of the occasion, and the knowledge and your ability as the rhetor. Sometimes the topic is narrowed through understanding the limitations of expertise and research that the author can accomplish in the allotted time. A professional photographer speaking on the use of light in portraits would use far different information than an amateur who has rarely looked through a SLR lens. Sometimes the topic is narrowed through the limitations of space allotted to the writing or time to the speech. A three-page essay has different demands than a fifteen-page treatise. Sometimes the topic is narrowed through the specific audience. For example, a speech on NASA's Mars exploration would look very different in a third grade classroom compared to a speech on the same topic in a Senate subcommittee.

Purpose of the Rhetoric

The specific purpose of the paper or speech develops through the narrowing of the topic as balanced with the audience. Most people find it helpful to write out the purpose in one sentence before beginning research on the topic. A general topic such as "space exploration" typed into Google will yield about 15,600,000 hits. No one has the time to analyze all of the information available. Concentrating your general topic through creating a specific purpose will save you a substantial amount of research time by focusing the search on specific information. Consider the specific purpose statement: "I will attempt to persuade the senators in the subcommittee that future space exploration on Mars is a worthy goal for the United States." The essay would be focused on a specific goal that saves significant time and effort. A Google search gives one cite at nasa.gov for research saving much time. If the purpose were a general statement such as: "To persuade the senators about space exploration" the persuasive effort would probably fail. The effort would be too diffuse with an insurmountable amount of evidence required. A speech on homosexual marriage could have the following purpose: "I will attempt to persuade the college class that sexual orientation should not be part of the constitution." Given a different perspective: "I will attempt to persuade the reader that marriage between a man and a woman ought to be part of our nation's constitution." These specific purpose statements allow you to spend more of your preparation time discovering evidence that will support your idea rather than wandering through the volumes of information available on the general subject.

Sometimes purpose statements are written as infinitive phrases rather than full sentences: "To persuade the geography teacher to consider geologic evidence that the Grand Canyon was not carved over millions of years, but accomplished in a single catastrophic action." The subject "I" is implied and the mechanism of a paper written for a class is also implied. The audience and specific purpose is evident. Students who begin writing "in order to get an A" will have a more difficult time completing the persuasive rhetoric.

Most purpose statements begin with the subject of you, the communicator, and include your target audience. These two ideas will enable you to discard much information that would not be persuasive. The purpose plan should form the goal of the effort; what you would like to accomplish.

The purpose should be accomplishable. When speaking to a group of women who are members of "NOW," the purpose should not be: "I will persuade these women that all abortion should be outlawed immediately." Given their socio-political perspective, radical transformation will not happen in one short speech or even an entire book. A much smaller step may be possible: "To persuade the audience a pre-born baby is not simply a part of her mother's body, but is a new life," may be possible for an individual but not the whole audience. More likely would be a goal to: "Lead the audience to respect those who disagree with them" or "To convince members of the audience to respect the viability of other arguments." This smaller step gives the persuasive communication the rhetorical characteristic of *plausibility* to the audience. Often the purpose statement is not stated in the speech or paper, but only used by the author.

Aristotle limited the purposes of public speeches to: to persuade (to convince), to activate (to do), to teach (to inform), and to inspire (to entertain). These should be the major purposes realizing that a good speech should have some elements of all four, the best speeches will only attempt to accomplish one of the goals.

Thesis Sentence

A rhetorical approach to public communication calls for congruency between the content of the message, the audience, the speaker, and the occasion. Seen most clearly in the style and delivery of the thesis sentence, the ideas should grasp and hold the mind and heart of the rhetor and audience. Sometimes in journalism or in public speeches this will become the center of a *nut graph* or a paragraph that fleshes out the entire role of a thesis.

Transforming ideas into one sentence takes time, imagination, and effort. The central idea of the communication, whether written or spoken persuasion, should be reduced to one sentence. Sometimes this is called the central idea or the proposition. Formed into a concise statement, the thesis sentence expresses the message you desire to communicate. As a clearly stated proposition, the thesis is not a question or a fact.

The thesis sentence should avoid figurative language. Metaphors, similes, tropes, and figures give beauty and depth to language, but they are also rhetorical structures that give ambiguity, indefiniteness, and indirectness when the message should be clear and certain. The thesis sentence may answer a question, but it should not be the question itself. Rhetorical questions allow the audience to develop their own answers through thought patterns that are not directed by the author or speaker.

The thesis sentence should be one complete idea. Do not try to accomplish too much in a persuasive communication. People who already agree with you may believe you did well, but those on the fringes with whom you want to have a greater influence will be driven away. The idea should be manageable for the audience and the length of the speech. A comprehensive understanding of Jewish theology based on the book of Deuteronomy is not possible in one hour or one magazine article. Considering the implications of one of the Ten Commandments may be accomplished during that time. Persuading the audience to obey one would be well worth the effort.

Thesis statements should be significant to the author or speaker and the audience. If the writer does not think the topic is important, then the effort will be wasted, and the reader will probably not be engaged in the thinking. Because the major proposition gives direction to the speech, it needs to strike to the essence of an issue that impacts the audience.

Often the thesis will be formed later in the preparation time and be refined over time. When this is done, the issue or theme should be narrow enough to limit the amount of time spent in research. The thesis should also fulfill the promise of the purpose statement. As a summary of the idea you want to communicate, this is the most important part of a paper or speech. The thesis needs to be supportable by evidence and illustrations.

The interrelationship of the topic, purpose, and thesis should create a communication of high rhetorical quality. Characteristics of novelty, relevancy, plausibility, and audience appropriateness should enable the effort to be affective.

Topic: Alternative Energy Sources

Speaker: Informed Consumer

Audience: Local electric board

Occasion: Regular board meeting

Purpose: I will attempt to persuade the board to experiment in wind generating capacities for local electric consumption.

Thesis: Given our geographic location and the stability of the wind in the west hills, generating electricity through windmills could be a significant way to meet our growing need.

Evidence should include specific information concerning the technology of windmills, the likelihood of sufficient winds to generate adequate supply, funding, availability, adverse consequences, and community support. You should also consider the cost of generating a kilowatt-hour of electricity from wind power compared with the cost per kilowatt hour of hydroelectric power.

The topic, speaker, audience, occasion, purpose, evidence, and thesis all work together to form a united whole for the rhetoric. The topic is appropriate to the audience who has jurisdictional power over the decision and the message is specific enough to be considered. Unless the speaker has overwhelming evidence, a decision is highly unlikely in the near future, but the discussion can begin and advocates won on the board. Most likely this would have to be part of a campaign in which written articles would be printed in the paper, inserts in the electric bills, interviews for radio and television news and talk shows could be given, along with other speeches in civic groups. Accomplishing the goal will take convincing the board and enabling them to move the whole community.

Topic: Sexual Harassment

Audience: Students at a local Liberal Arts College

Occasion: Martin Luther King Jr. day celebration

Purpose: Following the speech the audience members will respond to sexual harassment appropriately instead of accepting it.

Thesis: In whatever form it takes, humor, manipulation, intimidation, attempt at compliance, or advantage; sexual harassment is wrong and must be stopped.

Evidence: include specific examples from similar colleges and local stories that students can relate to immediately.

The thesis needs to be memorable. If an audience member were at home reading your persuasive communication, could she look up after finishing and remember the thesis and general argument? The thesis statement encapsulates the message in a manner that presents the heart of the issue in a cogent manner.

Topic: Charitable Giving to the United Way

Audience: Employees at a local car dealership

Occasion: Memo prior to the Quarterly Staff Meeting

Purpose: I would like to motivate all of last years participants to sign up again with equal or greater contributions plus seven of the twenty-four who did not give last year.

Thesis: The United Way provides a flexible way to support charitable services in our community, across the United States, and around the world.

Evidence: include local examples of where the money has been spent in the past and where it is likely to go in the future.

Here the persuasive communication must be succinct, positive, and convincing at the same time. You may have an opportunity to verbally encourage participation at the meeting, but the primary impetus to charitable contributions needs to come from the pen.

Thesis sentences may come at the beginning, in the middle, at the end, or at all three places. Sometimes they are short and simple. Other times they are more complex. Well written statements are always worth the effort.

Organizational Principles

Communication is arranged along patterns of thinking which articulate relationships between elements of the content. A fishing trip may be arranged along the geography of a river. A furniture store may be arranged according to the rooms of a house. A clothing store may be arranged by the gender of the intended wearer and further by the size, income, occasion, or taste of the audience. Human endeavors are arranged according to patterns. These organizational principles usually flow from the goals of the communicator.

If the goal is to sell furniture, a store arranging the showroom by size may have the dining room tables next to beds and couches as large items, while putting the matching chairs next to ottomans and nightstands. Consumers would have a difficult time visualizing how they match and a decrease in sales would probably result. Also, impulse buying of the china cabinet would probably suffer greatly. Appropriate organization is necessary in accomplishing the purpose of virtually any human activity. Written and spoken communication is no different.

Persuasive rhetorical argument is more likely to be accepted when it is arranged in a coherent manner. Enhancing the audience's ability to understand and accept a given communication will enable them to agree with the speaker of persuasive communication.

A labor union organizes workers into a community of people who are focused on similar goals and issues. Instead of dealing with the people one at a time, the organization has to deal with all at once. The evidence of a persuasive speech is usually stronger and given with greater import when arranged in conjunction with other evidence. The speaker gives a fuller account and thus increases the likelihood of acceptance through a strong use of persuasive communication.

Patterns of Arrangement

A logical formation of information into a persuasive written document takes place through consistent patterns. An attention-gaining introduction forms the start of a paper or speech, creating exigence, the desire of the audience to read on or listen to what comes next. Then the body of the paper or speech fills the majority of the space. Finally the conclusion wraps up the speech.

Introductions

"It was a dark, story night . . . " Snoopy's quintessential opening line to a novel never written. Grasping a reader's attention with a title and cover gives you the opportunity to have a first sentence. The majority of people will reject the reading simply on the basis of the cover. Little do students realize how difficult the teacher's task is when confronting a pile of ten page persuasive essays carefully crafted by college students. Like a fisherman searching for the right fly to entice a trout to bite, you need to carefully select the words that will hook the audience to your presentation.

Introductions primarily provide a motivation or *exigence* for the reader or audience to continue to participate in the communication situation. Usually an introduction funnels the attention of the audience into the direction the rhetor desires their thinking to go. Most of the time an introduction will initiate or kick off the topic of the speech or paper. Often introductions give a synopsis of the communication content.

Methods of beginning a paper or speech are varied. Here are a few of them. Starting out with a reference to the audience and establishing a relationship between them, you, and the topic is a good way to begin. Another way is to create a word picture, metaphor, or analogy where the reader or listener can graphically picture action related to the issue. A story or narrative will usually serve as a good foundation for persuasive communication. Sometimes startling listeners with a statement that engages their thoughts in a novel manner will be an effective introduction. Humor often works when the writing is clean and appropriate. Apt quotations will often enable the speaker to enter with candor and authority. Sometimes a question will open the dialogue in an effective manner. Description of a local or world event that links the people to the topic can be very valuable in starting a persuasive communication. Using a poem or literary citation can begin a persuasive effort with a feeling of academic or artistic encounter.

Public communication is not simply about gaining and maintaining interest. Creating *exigence* is not enough. We have to have something significant to say in a manner that piques the interest in the subject matter. However, content that does not engage the mind and heart will not persuade or move the audience into action.

Organizing the Body

Arranging the body of the rhetorical communication to communicate in a logical manner is essential for effective communication. Sequencing the ideas so that the audience can hear or see the logical progression enables a full understanding of the content. The best pattern for a given speech is determined by the interaction of the speech topic, the audience, the occasion, the purpose, and the speaker. Often thought of as the strategy of public communication, organizing the ideas into a whole takes time and practice. Choosing the best pattern for the author or speaker to address any particular idea to a particular audience is one of the aspects that make communication an art.

Sometimes a series of messages are presented in the same order, such as a syndicated political column in a newspaper or a series of magazine articles on the war in Iraq. Other times a series can follow multiple formats such as approaching the topic of marriage in eight sermons may tell narratives, be propositional, give advice, chronologically consider or any number of organizational approaches. Some are more apt to persuade a given audience than others. Therefore, an intentional approach will enable you to accomplish more with the same time and effort.

Topical

The vast majority of papers and speeches are arranged around a topic. Feature articles in newspapers and magazines are usually topically arranged. After developing your thesis, purpose, and analyzing your audience, begin researching the topic. From the vast amount of information three to five key points or subtopics usually arise that will supply the progression of the body of the speech or story. Intuitive logic concerning the most important aspects of the topic enable the rhetor to cull out what is less vital for that which naturally demands more attention. The entire speech focuses on the evidence that supports the *subtopical* ideas (major points).

Inverted Pyramid

A basic journalism model of public communication is the inverted pyramid. This is a specialized form of the topical approach. Beginning with a thesis sentence in a nut graph that grabs the reader's attention, the article expands to include all the relevant information going from most important to least important or from general to particular. The farther into the article the reader goes, the more detail is given. Often the general facts and significance is highlighted early, and then a chronological pattern follows culminating with relevant fine points.

Spatial

Using geographical space as an organizational tool will enable the audience to follow the speech from east to west, top to bottom, front to back, left to right . . . any given route. Describing the wounds of a victim going from head to foot or inside to outside, is a spatial organization. The designs of a building may go from foundation to roof, or from exterior to interior. Articles and speeches about specific environmental issues may be covered partially or wholly from a spatial organization pattern.

Chronological

Construction processes, cookbooks, event stories, and many speeches follow time through a sequence of stages forming a way of chronological thinking. Narrating a series of events, phases, or steps enables the audience to follow the process through the essential parts. How to plan and build a deck, make fresh salsa, or write a Ph.D. dissertation are all chronologically oriented processes that must take into account time. Some items like a travel log, scientific exploration, or documentary may be both chronological and spatial with the time-space continuum the major organizational pattern.

Problem/Solution

Many written articles, especially for magazines and newspapers take on a problem/solution form of reasoning. Whether the problem is a major social issue like homelessness, poverty, the economy, transportation, or a personal issue like health, home, or fashion, people are faced with problems and decision-making. Much of public communication is dedicated to solving those problems. From the trivial, like should the hometown basketball team draft a center or power forward, to the significant, like should the US sanction gay marriage, problems arise that must be addressed in public dialectic. The speech has two main points or movements, one dealing with the problem, the other with the solution. The solution should cover as much of the problem as possible, especially as it deals with the audience.

Eugene Lowery couples the problem-solution method with the psychological theory of reducing dissonance into an organization of sermons: 1) upset the equilibrium of the audience, 2) analyze their problem, 3) consider the discrepancies in their lives, 4) provide a solution, and 5) help them anticipate the consequences.

Cause/Effect

Many effects can be seen such as rising water temperature, unknown diseases, and stock market volatility. The public is interested in the causes. One of the significant responsibilities of public communicators is to explain what is happening in the world and society in a manner that the audience can understand the implications of who is doing what. The two sections of the speech, article, or book can be separate: cause then effect or effect then cause. They can also be entwined: part of effect, part of cause, another part of effect, and another part of the cause. The author should always be clear as to what is being addressed in each part of the communication.

For example, we could begin with a description of an airplane crash while fighting a fire. Transition the reader into a history of the individual plane. Transition again into a statement of the larger effects of aging out-of-date airplanes that were not designed to fight fires, but are being used that way. This would give depth to the current story of an individual airplane crash with plausible cause and effect relationships. The same story could be written from a human perspective on the pilot and crew detailing their situation, what happened prior to the crash, the crash itself, and the results.

Narrative

Choosing to address an issue through a story enables the audience to understand the content in a unique and dramatic channel. The characters, setting, and plot unite to move the audience toward accepting the issue. The narrative form will magnify the human elements and decrease the logical import. Novels and short stories fall into this category as well as biography, eulogy, and most current events. Narrative is the universal human language and art form; everyone in every society loves a good story. From a sage recounting a history in the glow of the campfire to the President of the US giving a State of the Union speech, narrative interacts with the audience in such a manner that people are drawn into the topic.

Question/Answer

Not you as the speaker asking the audience questions for them to answer, nor having the audience ask questions for you to answer, but think through what questions they would have about the topic and then research and answer them yourself. Each major point becomes a question that builds to the conclusion. From the sale of a new line of tractors to the implications of foreign policy, people are naturally skeptical and have numerous questions. Sometimes a wise public communicator approaches a topic by thinking of the questions, categorizing them, and then answering them one by one. Often news conferences begin with a statement designed to answer most of the questions and then take live questions. Public Relations people usually create documents that answer questions about their organization. Universities and others who recruit people may have a frequently asked questions segment of their presentation, website, or printed material. Samuel Procter outlines this form as: 1) introduction, 2) transition, 3) relevant question, and 4) synthetic answer.

Cicero's Debate Formula

Understanding the diverse desires of a communicator, different audiences, topics, and occasions; this is one of the most dynamic and flexible methods of organization because each part has different functions and objectives allowing a wide range of topics and purposes. The pattern has six parts: exordium, narration, partition, confirmation, refutation, and peroration (sometimes digression is added as a seventh).

Exordium: As an introduction the exordium (1) brings the essence of the topic to the forefront of the mind of the listener. Cicero goes beyond this to say the rhetor should (2) gain the goodwill of the audience. They should become favorably disposed to listen to your case in a manner that identifies the audience with the subject. The exordium should also (3) begin to wrap the audience in the proper emotion with the appropriate degree of intensity. This will engage the mind and heart in the topic so that the audience can think and feel along side the author as the speech or story progresses.

Narration: A brief story of the thesis enables the audience to comprehend the whole in such a manner that the rhetor can then fill in the full evidence. This part of the communication provides a complete but not comprehensive look at the author's line of thinking about the topic. As a brief, clear, plausible look at the content, the narration will give a framework of understanding. The narration is the second part of the opening statement or introduction in which the story is placed into the arena.

Partition: Make the essence of your argument clear concerning the story—what are you going to say about the thesis? Usually summarizing the stasis of the issue (where the reader/listener will make his decision about the topic), the partition ends the introduction with the focal point of the communication. Sometimes the partition is simply a question or list of issues.

Confirmation: This is where the rhetor proves what needs to be proved. Point by point walk through the case giving specific evidence that supports your perspective. In journalistic writing most public communicators begin with the strongest point and progress to the weakest. Public speakers often have the strongest first, then weaker ones ending with a reiteration of the strongest point. This process obscures the weaker points by providing them in the middle.

Refutation: Providing an answer to the opposition, weakening their story, and giving counter evidence will usually enable the audience to comprehend and accept your perspective over alternatives. By diminishing the opposition we gain those who are already predisposed to counter them, we make the audience skeptical concerning what they have to say, and provide good reasons to accept our perspective.

Peroration: As the conclusion to the communication, the peroration summarizes the stasis, thesis, refreshes the memory of the evidence, and calls for appropriate action—all in a manner that heightens appropriate emotion with proper intensity. Recognizing the importance of the conclusion, Quintilian in his *Institutio Oratoria* said, "It is in the peroration, if anywhere, that we must let loose the whole torrent of our eloquence."

Digression: Cicero recognizes that occasionally something that is not part of the argument needs to be dealt with in a manner that will allow the audience to understand the issues or emotion more fully. Although usually placed after the refutation, a digression may occur wherever appropriate.

Monroe's Motivated Sequence

Drawing the audience through five stages emotionally, logically, and socially calls for specified action that will solve a problem or meet a need. This organizational pattern draws heavily on a psychology of the audience—needing to understand them and what happens as they hear or read different parts of a persuasive presentation.

Attention: the successful public writer or speaker arouses audience attention through creating exigence with novelty, activity, contrast, intensity, and relevance. Getting the audience involved in the topic, people, and problems that your communication addresses takes knowledge of people as well as the content.

Need: when necessary, the speaker must demonstrate a need so clearly and graphically that the audience feels the urgency of the problem or need. This step takes description that gives hope that the need can be alleviated, the question answered, or the problem solved, but focuses on the presentation of the need in a way that neither overstates nor understates the situation. In a country where no public schools exist, ignorance blossoms into poverty and rage. This step brings knowledge and emotion into the communication.

Satisfaction: the answer to the need is presented so that the consequences are mitigated in a manner that satisfies the heavy costs of not solving the problem. The satisfaction needs to be relevant and plausible with an explanation as to how it works—the realization of hope. How can AIDS be contained, not spread to any others? This step brings understanding and wisdom of a means for a workable solution.

Visualization gives faith to the people in a manner that they can picture the problem being solved. What would the world be like when this is no longer an issue? The positive results may not solve the entire problem; my giving cannot stop a famine, but it can save one family—so picture that. This step gives a vision for the future.

Action: calling the audience to do—to put your answer to work raises the probability that the need will be satisfied. Passing the hat or getting commitments to give, challenging the audience to do, or giving a personal dedication that others can follow are all ways to activate the audience. The final step provides a means and challenge for personal involvement.

Monroe's motivated sequence can be used in advertisements, sales pitches, speeches, articles calling for volunteers, or a host of other kinds of public communications. A popular Bible study outline uses this idea: 1) hook—introduction, 2) look—consider the human situation, 3) book—what does the Bible say about it, and 4) took—application and conclusion.

Conclusions

Drawing the speech or article to a close is an art. Billy Graham begins the conclusion before the introduction. He says something like, "We will invite you to come forward and receive Christ." He warns them of his persuasive intent before he even begins the message. Many salespeople deny they are attempting to sell a product until they get to the end. Recently I had a young man attempt to sell me an alarm system for a home. He introduced himself as an installer, yet after describing the system, he had a very tough sales approach. When I refused to purchase the system from him, he wanted to call my wife, who was at work. The organization and pressure was so great even if I were to purchase the system from his company, I would ask for a different sales person.

Conclusions come in many types including:

➤ Personal stories

➤ Emotional appeals

➤ Humor

➤ Summarizing the speech

➤ Quotations

➤ Dramatic illustrations

➤ Word picture—metaphor or simile

➤ Re-connect with the introduction

➤ Real life examples

➤ Appeal to application or action

➤ Visualize what will happen if we do not act

Ending well will draw the message to a close and be the only chance the rhetor has of completing the mission of persuading the audience. One of the primary mistakes made by public speakers is to leave the conclusion for the moment.

Many opinion pieces forget to draw implications concerning their message. If you consider the facts in this manner, what will the impact be on other perspectives? Actions? On the people involved? Conclude in a manner that makes clear the message and what inherent change should happen as a result.

Transitions

Leading the audience from one idea to another, from one event to another, from one point to another in a way that enables them to understand your logical connections is a necessary part of public communication whether in a speech or a written article. Tying the introduction to the body, the body to the conclusion, and holding the body together are signposts or movements that readers and listeners find necessary to join the parts of an argument into a logical whole.

Many times transitions are sentences or paragraphs that warrant the information in a logical manner. Sometimes they are internal summaries that lead the audience through the logic from the thesis to the present part of the speech—these are especially used prior to the conclusion. They set a direction for people to think along side of you.

Michael and Susan Osborn (2003) have a useful division of transitions:

To Indicate	Use
Time changes	Until, now, previously, later, following, before, At present, eventually, meanwhile, earlier . . .
Additions	in addition, moreover, furthermore, besides . . .
Comparison	as compared with, both are, likewise, similarly, of equal importance, another type, like, just as . . .
Cause-Effect	therefore, consequently, thus, so, as a result, since, because of, due to, for this reason . . .
Numerical order	first . . . , to begin with, initially, next, finally . . .
Spatial	to the North . . . , alongside, left, above, in front of, behind, next to, below, in the distance . . .
Explanation	to illustrate, for example, for instance, case in point, in other words, to simplify, to clarify . . .
Importance	most importantly, least, above all, keep in mind, listen carefully, take note of, indeed, remember . . .
Ending	in conclusion, finally, in short, to summarize . . .

Wrap up

The organization of ideas and information into a persuasive public communication is an art that develops through use. Like a painter mixing a palate for a landscape, carefully consider the principles that lead to an artistic artifact whether it is a speech, an article, or a story. The judgment of the rhetor in determining how to present the case will be one of the significant elements in whether or not the audience will be persuaded.

Introductions that create exigence, thesis statements that grasp the essence of the issue, logical progressing bodies, with apt conclusions will make written and spoken rhetoric effective. Without significant effort put into the organization, many readers will simply put down the article, listeners will tune out the speaker, and the rhetor will not have a persuasive impact.

Chapter 14

Style: Adding Eloquence to Personality

The Lips of the righteous
Know what is fitting
Proverbs 10:32 NIV

MEANING COMES through the individual's use of words to communicate specific ideas. Persuasive style is the art of managing the impact of language on the audience in a manner that reflects the personality of the advocate and the level of eloquence appropriate for the audience, subject, and situation. When people talk of "mere rhetoric," they are denigrating the use of style and consider it to be a substitute for substance of content. Style is not superficial, but goes directly to the ability of words to communicate a message in a manner that impacts the auditor. The ornamentation of substance-less ideas in an effort to impress with empty decoration is not rhetoric, but a cruel imitation of truth spoken in love. As in most art, rhetorical style adds the appropriate emotion at the proper intensity to the substance of the message making the impact accomplish the goal.

Spinning and framing are ways of communicating an event, or a person, or an object, or a place from a particular perspective. Political "spin doctors" come up with creative ways of understanding significant events in a positive or negative manner. The human brain thinks in images and icons. Speech that frames or spins graphic, relevant, and active images will be more likely to produce the kind of positive elaboration that leads to persuading the audience to change.

Grasping a hold of an audience's emotions and leading them through a series of *pathetic* responses paralleling the cognitive elements is largely a

316

matter of speech style. The way a speaker chooses to express the content of a message largely determines the extent of persuasion as well as the integration of the advocacy into the soul of the audience.

Centuries ago Augustine noted the low, middle, and grand styles of rhetoric not only applied to the kinds of speeches (informative, deliberative, and forensic), but also to the kinds of audiences. Some people are more apt to respond positively to some forms of style while others favor a different style. Cultural rhetorical styles can vary widely so that what is most appropriate for one audience may become counter-productive for a different audience. Understanding the audience is as important as discernment of your own personality when choosing a style of communication.

Also, the topic of the communication may indicate suitable and unsuitable rhetorical styles. Shakespearian dialect possibly will make a humorous approach to asking for a date, but would probably receive more negative responses than positive ones. Using flippant remarks while considering presidential candidates in a political convention would also be out of place. Sacred subjects, formal meetings and tucking a child into bed all call for a difference. Hermongenes in On Style lists seven virtues of rhetorical style: clarity, grandeur, beauty, rapidity, character, sincerity, and force. These will combine to form the most appropriate style for the audience when the rhetor asks questions of each virtue for the audience (What will make the message clear [grand, beautiful, quick . . .] to this particular audience?).

Art

Written and spoken rhetoric is an art that can be beautiful when speaking the truth in an attitude of love or dark and menacing when distortion turns phrases. Plato in the *Phaedrus* came to terms with the artistic nature of language recognizing that it must be taught and practiced in the public arena. Rhetoric is a science because it has principles that can be discovered and applied; it is also a humanity because it is formed by humans made in the image of God, and it is an art because we have degrees of competency and beauty in writing and speaking.

We all recognize the art of great literature in the works of Shakespeare and Tolstoy. We all recognize the art of public speaking in the speeches of Martin Luther King, Jr., President Regan, and Billy Graham. Moving from recognition of powerful examples of public communication that moves audiences, we need to practice the techniques of the art in a manner that produces desired results. The art of rhetoric is not so much creating a great

317

communication product, whether written or spoken, as it is constructing a great communicator.

Integrating eloquence into the personality may be a daunting task, but can also be an exploratory adventure. A speaker's style is first seen in the verbs chosen, then in tropes and figures, also in picturesque nouns, and finally in syntax and semantics. The process of developing an eloquent style gives a window into the soul of the advocate. "Which words are chosen?" "Why?" and "For what effect?" are questions whose answers lay deep in the heart and motivations and are thus the essence of style.

Practice is necessary for artists to perfect their art. Nothing is as important as writing and speaking in the development of an eloquent rhetor. I suggest that public rhetors develop poetic habits. Technical writers should speak their message out loud. Prose should still have snap and vigor, while speeches need to keep the audience more than awake—sitting on the edge of their seats wanting to know what comes next. Storytellers, whether in a novel or from a stage; need to be able to engage the audience in a plot and envision themselves in the characters. Artistic use of language comes through reading, writing, and speaking. So keep doing all three no matter what your specialty will become. As Solomon eloquently noted (Proverbs 25:11), a word aptly for fitly spoken is "like apples of gold in settings of silver" more beautiful than fine jewelry.

Diction

The choice of words is vital to the persuasive impact of rhetoric. We postmodern people avoid the word *diction* as though it denotes an indistinct exactness of grammar beyond the capability of any but the most fastidious and crotchety old professors wearing wire glasses with pop-bottle thick lenses, probably half bald if male or wearing a two-century old cotton dress if female, with nothing to do but pour over sentence construction all day.

Diction is perhaps the most important part of rhetorical style. J.R.R. Tolkien in *The Two Towers* has Gimli the dwarf explain to Legolas the elf the art of cultivating beauty in the caves of Helm's Deep:

> 'No, you do not understand,' said Gimli. 'No dwarf could be unmoved by such loveliness. None of Durin's race would mine these caves for stones or ore, not if diamonds and gold could be got there. Do you cut down the blossoming trees in springtime for firewood? We would tend these glades of flowering stone, not quarry them. With cautious skill, tap by tap—a small chip of rock and no more, perhaps, in a whole anxious day—so we would work.'

That is the way with the art of rhetoric; perhaps a whole anxious day to discover a verb or grow a noun. Word choice can mean the difference between a reader continuing to read, or turning on a videogame. Word choice can mean the difference between the audience daydreaming or elaborating during the speech. A careful turn of a phrase or word creates great literature as opposed to fire fodder.

Is the adult female a lady, a woman, or a chick? Is the individual in the wheelchair disabled, crippled, immobilized, enabled, differently-abled, or handicapped? Is the man on the corner a vagrant, a tramp, a hobo, a beggar, an itinerant individual, or a homeless person? Is the dark skinned citizen of Chicago a black, Negro, African-American, or colored person? The denotations may all refer to the same thing but the connotations are very different. If "the man took a knife from his belt," the audience will have a different emotion than if "the bearded pirate drew a dagger," as opposed to "the thug pulled out a switchblade and casually flipped it open with an evil smirk." If you ran from him into "the forested hinterland," the audience would have a different emotion than if you "escaped into the trackless jungle," or "took flight under the canopy of the virgin rainforest." The denotation may be the same, but the connotation is vastly different. The art of choosing the right words and phrases will greatly impact the conveyed meaning and emotion. Style does directly impact the content and impact of the message.

Diction is especially important when using figurative language. Choosing the right words to express the content can make the difference between affective eloquence and ineffective drivel. Yards of unnecessary lace make a gaudy dress. Caked makeup with layers of cheap costume jewelry turn the beauty of a woman into haughty vanity. Even so, too much rhetorical flair and finery will twist solid content into unrecognizable rubbish. Even solid content will become distorted and discarded refuse when lace overtakes function. The art of diction is to find the balance that will entice the reader or listener, awaken the proper emotion, and drive home the content with clarity and muscle—eloquence.

Framing

Choosing how to say what you are going to say is called framing. Speaking or writing with words that the audience understands, knows (or can find out with a minimum of effort), and fit together into a comprehensive whole enables the author to direct the reader's interpretation.

For example, the U.S. government framing those taken on the battlefield in Afghanistan as *enemy combatants* instead of *foreign criminals* or *prisoner's of war* enables the United States to "legally" hold them indefinitely without trial. The individual will have to judge whether that is good (keeping terrorists out of the war and gaining intelligence) or bad (holding people without due process and violating inalienable human rights). The words chosen to describe these individuals make the difference between the prisoners having international rights as a prisoner of war, having legal rights of a citizen under our constitution, and the government having military rights as the country who took possession of enemy personnel on a battlefield. Framing in this instance has specific legal and international implications. The Supreme Court decided the words *enemy combatant* were not as applicable as *prisoner of war* so the legal process changes from a military tribunal to a trial—a dispute over how to frame and categorize people.

Another example of framing is that of *weapons of mass destruction* as justification for attacking Iraq. President Bush used this as *a* major reason, but not the only reason for Iraq being a threat. Yet the press largely tells the story as though it is the *only* reason, and since few of these weapons have been found, none of which were a direct military threat to the territory or people of the U.S., we are in Iraq as *conquerors* and *occupiers* who have no right—and therefore ought to pull out as soon as possible. As long as the press frame the argument in this way, they have a strong position and are winning public support. However, if they argued against the President's entire position instead of this weakness, the story would be significantly less convincing. If we used the word *liberator* instead of *occupier* for our troops, the perception of the audience would be different. If we used the word *terrorist* instead of *insurgent* for the continued enemy, the perception of the audience would be different. If planting roadside bombs were *crimes against humanity,* instead of *resistance* the perception of the audience would be different. In other words, this is a war of public relations, and the U.S. is loosing that battle in the press, both here at home and abroad. What most of the press does not realize is that they (the press) are the major weapon of the terrorists. If the atrocities and crimes went unreported, they would stop because the goals can only be accomplished through media. Likewise, if the media through their framing universally condemned the attacks, then the terrorists would loose most of their power. Similarly, the Palestinian attacks on Israel are terrorist crimes, not meant to gain or maintain the territory in dispute, they are instead public relations attacks. Israel responding by taking more territory is a great military tactic but they loose in the court of public opinion because the world's press frames the conflict in favor of the Arab terrorists.

A parent who frames an argument, "You must be home by 10 pm," in terms of power, "because I said so," is likely to gain compliance only through threat of punishment. The same issue framed as safety or school tomorrow is more likely to have a willing teenager be persuaded rather than manipulated into obedience.

Arguments need to be framed in ways in which the audience can both understand the message and feel the emotional vibration within the communication. Often careful planning is necessary to think through the issue, the audience, the occasion, and who you are as a speaker before choosing a frame for the word pictures you are painting.

Through extensive historical research, David McCullough wrote a history of the American Revolutionary War entitled *1776*. The story is told through correspondence and journals written at the time that frame the war in a realistic manner. George Washington had to learn to be a General and to lead a different kind of soldier than the British ideal. King George III needed to learn to be "royal" in a political and a cultural sense. England's General Howe knew patience and courage, but needed to learn innovation and respect. The chief characters are developed through what they lacked, then learned, as a rebellion became violent and determined. The frame is different from that of other histories, heroes who had to learn to become heroic. The frame is believable and fresh in a graphic re-telling of a well-worn story with new details from dusty, faded correspondence.

Grammar

Should language be spoken and written as it is used to transfer meaning between people (functional linguistics), or do we have a universally accepted norm for proper form of language use (structural linguistics), or is grammar embedded into our brains and thinking (psycholinguistics)? Of these three schools of thought, which is most appropriate for public communication?

The best use of grammar is to communicate a message clearly and eloquently to the intended audience. Therefore, I am a functional linguist who places emphasis on discourse analysis and understanding. At the same time, I recognize that grammatical errors or irregularities often detract from the audience's acceptance of your message. In persuasive public communication this means following the best universally accepted grammatical constructions for the audience. Different standards do apply. Usually the audience will demand greater exactness from writing than from speaking. The more educated in language an audience is the greater an impact grammatical errors will have on the acceptance or rejection of your message.

In public writing, most mediums have a *style sheet* that gives specific guidelines for punctuation, word choice, and other details. The readers are then able to comprehend, find sources, and interpret the message in a manner similar to other writing with the same publication or publisher. I catch many errors in my student's work while I make the same errors unseen in writing this book so that an editor has to catch the grammatical mistakes. Having a good friend or spouse who can give an objective outside opinion to your public communication, before you put it in print or speak it from a podium, is of immeasurable help.

Vividness

Active, transitive verbs pump the lifeblood of persuasive communication into the audience with vividness and verve. They drive the listener forward along with the speaker into new parts of the message. Especially when sprinkled with details, verbs will enliven communicative power: "The boy had come to the train station to meet the girl" or "Breathless from his sprint to beat the train, Casy leapt onto the platform, heart pounding, eyes searching for Sheryl's long hair and blue coat." Which style leaves the audience wanting to discover what happens next?

The verbal action of *leapt* and *searching* are more powerful than *had come* and *meet*. The proper names of Casy and Sheryl replace the generic boy and girl. The sprint to the door in competition with a locomotive gives an emotional edge that *train station* cannot muster. *Heart pounding, eyes searching,* and *long hair and blue coat* all give a more romantic feel to the sentence that *he looked for her* does not have. The details such as naming the characters instead of generalized pronouns and describing instead of telling are also significant in adding vibrancy.

Descriptive nouns provide picturesque details that generic nouns or pronouns could never appropriate. "Moss filled the bark's crevasses converting the gnarled oak into a scrubby, bearded appellation awaiting Shannon as she jogged closer" will create a different meaning and different emotions than "the oak tree stood by the jogger's path." Nouns that grab the reader or listener almost always create a more intense meaning or emotion than adding adjectives and adverbs.

Adverbs and adjectives color the message in ways that intensify or soften the emotional import of the message. These familiar, concrete words enable understanding of more abstract concepts. *Unbridled* freedom gives a very different idea than *simple* freedom. The *moving* car and the *speeding* car may be doing the same thing, but in a report of an auto accident they can make a great deal of difference to the mindset of an insurance adjuster. *Walking* quickly or slowly is better than just *walking*; however, walking doggedly will create an even better impact. Today's temperature is not simply hot, we have a *searing* 117 degree day or *frying* (yes, we could literally fry eggs without a stove on my deck this afternoon). *Hot* simply does not do justice to nature's unfunneled oven, we call it Redding, California, in June.

Recently I watched a weather report from South Florida on one channel. The reporter was standing in a downpour with bits of shingles and debris flying through the air. She said something like, "Hurricane force winds are blowing across Florida." I turned the channel where another reporter was in the same situation. He said something like, "About 10 minutes ago this palm tree blew over. Look, there goes a piece of someone's roof. Just down the street you can see the sparks as power-lines whip along the ground in the hurricane-force wind." One person simply reporting the facts with detachment, another giving specific details that pictured the scene with objective descriptive vividness: which one would you watch?

Word pictures generate images with vivid clarity in the minds of the reader or listener. Creating in the mind a sense experience so that the audience can feel the texture of the grass under bare feet, smell the fresh cut flowers, or hear the moist silence of the forest is an artful use of words. Making someone angry about the squalid conditions of an orphanage may be the first step to getting help for them—so choose your words carefully to match the message. Painting the scene in the reader's head, telling the story visually, or graphically speaking will make the message come alive through words.

The movie *Jurassic Park* is filled with special effects that live on the screen, yet the novel by Michael Crichton does a much better job through the imagination.

> *The late twentieth century has witnessed a scientific gold rush of astonishing proportions: the headlong and furious haste to commercialize genetic engineering. This enterprise has proceeded so rapidly—with so little outside commentary—that its dimensions and implications are hardly understood at all.*

With those words he introduces a social critique of our cultural use and acceptance of science in the form of a story. Through characterization, plot, and dialogue, Crichton artfully produces a damming criticism of the use of scientific power demonstrating some of the ethical limits enlivened through the use of narrative. The same message could be propositionally stated: "Scientists through the scientific method are incapable of governing the power discovered through its use." This message is watered down in the movie where sense experience takes president over the truth of the proposition. Painting the picture graphically through an entire novel enables us to live the message and thus comprehend it in multiple layers and then question our worldview and values. The art of verbal style makes the message powerful to the audience.

Rhetor

At the center of style is the rhetor. Only a few people with specific thinking patterns could call the dark-skinned citizen of Chicago a Negro or colored in today's culture. Diction says much about level of education, social experience, and empathetic thinking. Use of grammar, ability to spell, and artistic use of words all speak of who is saying what is being said. The amount of work spent in discovering appropriate words and setting them in descriptive phrases indicates much about the originator of those words.

People have more style than sermons, speeches, articles, or books. Their style will come through in writing and speaking. This book has much in common with my first book, *Oral Interpretation of the Bible*. However, some significant differences occur in the message and language. That book was a compilation of my class notes; this book was written from scratch. That book was written in a month; this book is taking several years. The style is very different. Declaring multiple authors wrote the Pentateuch, or Isaiah, based on a stylistic analysis is weak evidence at best, but it should be carefully considered.

Oral and written style are also different. Oral focuses on the ear while written communication is based on the eye. A speech can usually use greater spontaneity and directness while a written public communication will be more formal and distant. Audiences will hold a speaker to a lesser degree of exactness than the words of a writer that are published. For example, students will hold me to a greater degree of accountability for these words than they will for the notes they write from a class session.

Tropes and Figures

The aesthetic beauty of language use increases with the artful use of tropes and figures. When integrated into the content, they become a significant part of the message enabling graphic visualization of the communicated substance. Using tropes and figures gives the advocate a greater level of influence on the audience's emotional responses to the message and thus adds to the impact. These stylistic elements assist the communicator in developing a specific emotional response. "Turning" that passionate development within the audience from the metaphorical idea onto the message content elements leads the audience to positive elaboration.

These imaginative uses of language enliven ideas and make them accessible to the audience. Yes, they can be overdone. Understanding of a clear message is more important than the bells and whistles or flowery frills of linguistic gymnastics. Mixing may be good for cookie dough, but not for metaphors. Use sufficient rhetorical plans to plummet the point as perfectly as possible, but pass up profoundly ponderous phrases.

Rhetorical Figures

Alliteration: the repetition of a consonant or related consonants, usually at the beginning of words but occasionally in the middle or ends of words. Like assonance and onomatopoeia, alliteration is a scheme that exploits the sounds of words creating an almost poetic aesthetic to a persuasive communication.

> *I would suggest to you that as foot soldiers in the fight for world food security, we must take the lead in preventing [starvation] from happening.* Thomas J. Donohue, *World Hunger*

> *Our next step will be to scrap the current, fatally flawed internal revenue code and replace it with a fairer, simpler, flatter system.* Jack Kemp, *The American Dream*

> *Civility is significant and essential because it cements civilization. Courtesy, common sense and civility promotes meaningful relationships, communication and cooperation.* Roberto D. Garton, *Public Discourse.*

Anaphora: the repetition of a word or phrase at the beginning of successive clauses. Exceptionally effective use can be made of this technique when ascending or descending a ladder of abstraction or specificity.

> *Revolution is bloody, revolution is hostile, revolution knows no compromise, revolution overturns and destroys everything that gets in its way.* Malcolm X, *The Black Revolution.*

[Oedipus] represents for us all the ways in which we can unwittingly be the architects of our own misfortune, all the ways in which we refuse to see the truth, all the ways in which we unconsciously fulfill our destinies even as we struggle to avoid them. Richard Monette, *Lunatics, Lovers, and People of Business.*

Women are also dying from diseases that should have been prevented or treated; they are watching their children succumb to malnutrition caused by poverty and economic deprivation; they are being denied the right to go to school by their own fathers and brothers; they are being forced into prostitution, and they are being barred from the ballot box and the bank lending office. Hillary Rodham Clinton, *Women's Rights are Human Rights*

Limited understanding means limited appropriating, limited release from our burden, limited joy. Myron S. Augsburger, *The Cross is Timeless*

Standing with God and the crushed and bleeding slave on this occasion, I will, in the name of humanity, which is outraged, in the name of liberty, which is fettered, in the name of the Constitution and the Bible, which are disregarded and trampled upon, dare to call in question and to denounce, with all the emphasis I can command, everything that serves to perpetuate slavery—the great sin and shame of America! Frederick Douglass, *The Hypocrisy of American Slavery.*

And this is the way of prudence certainly because to hope for more than the possible is to court despair. To hope for more than the possible is to risk becoming the ones who wait, helpless and irrelevant in their white robes, for a deliverance that never comes. To hope for more than the possible is a kind of madness. Frederick Buechner, *The Hungering Dark.*

Antimetabole: the repetition of words in reverse grammatical order. Contrasting the ideas can turn an accepted phrase to a new direction.

Ask not what your country can do for you; ask what you can do for your country. John F. Kennedy, *1961 Inaugural Address*

The important thing is that you must play a role, for while not everything that is faced can be changed, nothing can be changed until it is faced. Myron H. Wahls, *The Moral Decay of America.*

Assonance: the repetition of vowels in stressed position. The repetition tends to give phrases grater impact with accenting the expression as a whole.

326

> *The great Mississippi, the majestic, the magnificent Mississippi, rolling its mile-wide tide along, shining in the sun* . . . Mark Twain, *Old Times on the Mississippi.*

> *Now there is instantaneous freezing and microwave heating and printed electrical circuitry and computerized economics and open-heart surgery. Who needs God anymore!?* John Killinger, *There is Still God.*

Asyndeton: the omission of a conjunction where it would ordinarily occur.

> *[Confidence] thrives only on honesty, on honor, on the sacredness of obligations, on faithful protection, on unselfish performance; without them it cannot live.* Franklin D. Roosevelt, *1933 Inaugural Address.*

Climax: the arrangement of words, phrases, or clauses in order of ascending importance.

> *Let's face it. Let's talk sense to the American people. Let's tell them that there are no gains without pains.* Adlai Stevenson, *1952 Democratic Nomination Acceptance Speech.*

> *This day started at the end of World War I to commemorate the armistice which was signed on the eleventh hour of the eleventh day of the eleventh month on 1918.* Carroll Letellier, *Tribute to Veterans.*

> *After decades of assault upon what made America great, upon supposedly obsolete values, what have we reaped, what have we created, what do we have? What we have, in the opinion of millions of Americans, is crime, drugs, illegitimacy, abortion, the abdication of duty, and the abandonment of children.* Robert Dole, *The Best Days are Yet to Come.*

Climax is particularly effective when combined with anadiplosis or epanastrophe, repeating the last word of one phrase or sentence at the beginning of the next.

> *They call for you: The general who became a slave; the slave who became a gladiator; the gladiator who defied an Emperor. Striking story.* Brian Fairbanks, David Franzoni, John Logan and William Nicholson, *Gladiator.*

> *Knowing that tribulation worketh patience; and patience, experience, and experience, hope; and hope maketh not ashamed because the love of God is shed abroad in our hearts by the Holy Spirit.* Apostle Paul, *Romans 5:3-5 KJV*

Ellipsis: the omission of a word or group of words. Allowing the audience to supply the missing ingredients can be effective because they discover the meaning for themselves. Aristotle considered this a kind of enthymeme.

> *We in America today are nearer to the final triumph over poverty than ever before in the history of any land.* Herbert Hoover, 1928 Stump Speech.

> The full form is "nearer than anyone has been ever been before."

Ellipsis is also common in the idiom—for example:

> *if [it is] possible; for [a] long [time].*

Epanalepsis: the repetition of a word or phrase at the beginning and end of a single clause.

> *You bleed when the white man says bleed; you bite when the white man says bite; and you bark when the white man says bark.* Malcolm X, *A Message to the Fleeting Hearts.*

> *I'm gonna sing when the Spirit says sing, I'm gonna shout when the Spirit says shout, I'm gonna pray when the Spirit says pray, and obey the Spirit of the Lord . . .* African-American Spiritual

Epanastrophe or anadiplosis: the repetition of a word or phrase at the end of one clause and the beginning of the next.

> *If we fail in this defense it will not be for lack of money. It will be on account of money. Money has been the most serious handicap that we have met.* Clarence Darrow, Leopold and Loeb murder trial.

> *The central government didn't tell [the farmer] what to plant and he got to keep what he produced. All powerfully motivating forces, forces which ultimately increase the food supply.* Richard McGuire, *Property Rights and the Food Supply.*

Epistrophe: the repetition of a word or phrase at the end of successive clauses.

> *If slavery is not wrong, nothing is wrong.* Abraham Lincoln, *1864 Defense of Allowing Blacks to Serve in the Army.*

> *What we are learning around the world is that, if women are healthy and educated, their families will flourish. If women are free from violence, their families will flourish. If women have a chance to work and*

earn as full and equal partners in society, their families will flourish. Hilliary Rodham Clinton, *Women's Rights are Human Rights*

As the impact is international, the response must be international. So, together, we must design a new international financial system for a new financial age. Tony Blair, *A New International Financial System.*

Hyperbaton: a variation of the standard positions of words. Common forms of hyperbaton are as follows:

Anastrophe: a departure from or inversion of the natural word order.

In our image of the Negro breathes the past we deny, not dead but living yet and powerful, the beast in our jungle of statistics . . . James Baldwin, *Many Thousands Gone*

While ever a state of feeling such as this shall universally or even very generally prevail throughout the nation, vain will be every effort, and fruitless every attempt, to subvert our national freedom. Lincoln, *Address before the Young Men's Lyceum of Springfield, Illinois*

Take that fact I have spoken of, that appalling fact that, even now, it is harder to live than it was in that dark and rude age five centuries ago—how do you explain it? Henry George, *The Crime of Poverty.*

Parenthesis: an abrupt and sometimes permanent syntactic break.

When I came out of prison--for someone interfered and paid the tax--I did not perceive that great changes had taken place . . . Henry David Thoreau, *Civil Disobedience.*

The next five or six weeks were too complex, aggravating and frustrating for me to express with any real degree of truth but, in a nut-shell, the red-tape, the heart-breaking hurdles to be crossed and the details of such a venture made me a nervous wreck (this on top of trying to cope with my first year of House Mastering made me impossible to live with for many I'm sure). Albania, Macedonia, and Montenegro were out of the question as transportation to these areas was booked solid . . . Clayton W. Johnston, *The World is Our Village.*

Onomatopoeia: the use of words whose sound suggest the meaning.

It got wild on the airways. There was a great manic competition going on, shrieks, giggles, falsettos, heaving buffoonery, laughing gargles, high school beat talk, shouts, gasps, sighs, yuks, loony laughs, nonsense rhymes, puns, crazy accents . . . Tom Wolfe

Whatever sense anybody might have had of its being a holy time and a holy place was swallowed up by the sheer spectacle of it—the countless voices and candles, and the marble faces of saints and apostles, and the hiss and shuffle of feet on the acres of mosaic. Frederick Buechner, *The Hungering Dark.*

Parallelism: the symmetrical arrangement of related words, phrases, or clauses:

We need the storm, the whirlwind, and the earthquake. The feeling of the nation must be quickened; the conscience of the nation must be rousted; the propriety of the nation must be startled; the hypocrisy of the nation must be exposed; and its crimes against God and man must be proclaimed and denounced. Frederick Douglass, *The Hypocrisy of American Slavery.*

There is no height to which I have risen that is high enough to allow me to forget [my family], to allow me to forget where I came from, where I stand, and how I stand, with my feet on the ground, just as a man, at the mercy of God. Robert Dole, *The Best Days are Yet to Come.*

This nation stands before the world as perhaps the last expression of the possibility of man devising a social order where justice is the supreme ruler and law but its instrument; where freedom is the dominant creed and order but its principle; where equity is the common practice and fraternity the common human condition. Myron H. Wahls, *The Moral Decay of America.*

Opposing ideas may also be juxtaposed in parallel form.

They are not moral: they are only conventional. They are not virtuous: they are only cowardly. They are not even vicious: they are only 'frail.' They are not artistic: they are only lascivious. They are not prosperous: they are only rich. They are not loyal, they are only servile; not dutiful, only sheepish; not public spirited, only patriotic . . . George Bernard Shaw, *Man and Superman.*

In Christ there is love, not hostility; forgiveness, not revenge; peace, not violence; submission, not resistance; service, not dominance. Myron S. Augsburger, *The Cross is Timeless.*

Chiasmus: the inversion of syntactic elements in successive clauses.

Englishmen, Sir, are . . . too apt to be sullen when they are silent; and, when they are sullen, to hang themselves. Benjamin Franklin, *The Grand Leap of the Whale.*

Homoeoteleuton: the use of identical or similar sounding suffixes on the final words of phrases or clauses:

> *We cannot dedicate, we cannot consecrate, we cannot hallow this ground . . .* Abraham Lincoln, *Gettysburg Address.*

> *It is not only aptitude but attitude that will determine your altitude. If you can conceive it and believe it, you can achieve it.* Myron H. Wahls, *The Moral Decay of America.*

Polysyndeton: the use of more conjunctions than grammatically necessary.

> *The past, at least, is secure. There is Boston and Concord and Lexington and Bunker Hill; and there they will remain.* Daniel Webster, 1830 Second Reply to Hayne.

> *They fished all night and caught nothing. It sounds like a page out of the life of every pastor I know. The let down periods. When the dust has settled, and the reception is over, and the search committee has gone back to their jobs, and it's just you and her and the dog and two homesick kids and boxes and strangeness and four hundred miles from any friend you have.* Roger Lovette, *Night Fishing.*

> *Manufacturers of watches, of farm implements, of Linotypes and cash registers and automobiles, and sewing machines and lawn mowers and locomotives, are now making fuses and bomb packing crates and telescope mounts and shells and pistols and tanks.* Franklin D. Roosevelt, *The Arsenal of Democracy.*

TROPES

Erotema: the rhetorical question, a question that answers itself.

> *But what else can one do when he is alone in a narrow jail cell, other than write long letters, think long thoughts, and pray long prayers?* Martin Luther King, *Letter From Birmingham Jail.*

Euphemism: the substitution of a mild, vague, or polite term for one that is more exact but considered unacceptable in the circumstances. Euphemisms are closely related to irony, litotes, and periphrasis.

> *Yet there is in the land a certain restlessness, a questioning.* Lyndon B. Johnson, *1968 State of the Union Address.*

I hardly think I ought to engage in any hostilities with a woman, especially a woman usually thought of as the friend of all men rather than the enemy of any one. Cicero, *In Defense of Caelius.*

Hyperbole: an obvious overstatement, an exaggeration, usually for emphasis.

O God, I could be bounded in a nutshell, and count myself a king of infinite space, were it not that I have bad dreams. William Shakespeare, *Hamlet.*

I cannot forecast to you the action of Russia. It is a riddle wrapped in a mystery inside an enigma. Sir Winston Churchill, 1939 Radio Broadcast.

All the armies of Europe, Asia and Africa combined, with all the treasure of the earth (our own excepted) in their military chest, with a Bonaparte for a commander, could not by force take a drink from the Ohio or make a track on the Blue Ridge in a trial of a thousand years. Abraham Lincoln, *Address Before the Young Men's Lyceum.*

But I forbear, and come reluctantly to the transactions of that dismal night when in such quick succession we felt the extremes of grief, astonishment and rage; when heaven in anger, for a dreadful moment, suffered hell to take the reins; when Satan with his chosen band opened the sluices of New England's blood, and sacrilegiously polluted our land with the dead bodies of her guiltless sons! John Hancock, *Boston Massacre Oration.*

Irony: the use of words to convey the opposite of their literal meaning.

Brutus is an honorable man . . . so are they all, all honorable men. William Shakespeare, *Julius Caesar.*

Those words seem clear to me, but as we all know, the Constitution can't be read accurately by ordinary folks. It requires expert lawyers to discover what these simple words really mean. Richard McGuire, *Private Property and the Food Supply.*

Paralepsis is a form of irony in which a statement is made and at the same time described as not worth mentioning or too obvious to mention.

I am convinced that [these witnesses] are the most reputable characters, first of all, being on such intimate terms with so fine a lady, and then, volunteering for this mission to be stowed away in the public baths. . . . Observe their valor, their self-denying energies: "They hid in the bath-

house." That's the sort of witness we like to have in court. Cicero, *In Defense of Caelius.*

Litotes: understatement; usually the expression of an affirmative by negation of its opposite. This emphasizes the magnitude of a statement through understating coupled with negation.

> *Three of my friends were killed in the last three weeks in Chicago. That certainly isn't conducive to peace of mind.* Al Capone, After his arrest in Philadelphia.

> *I am a Jew from Tarsus in Cilicia, a citizen of no ordinary city.* Apostle Paul, *Acts* 21:39.

Metaphor: an implicit comparison of literally unlike things. It attempts to establish a relationship between two items.

> *The moral fiber of the American people is beset by rot and decay.* Barry Goldwater, 1964 televised Stump Speech.

> *The hydrogen bomb is history's exclamation point. It ends an age-long sentence of manifest violence.* Marshall McLuhan, *The Medium is the Message*

> *A total military victory is not in sight or around the corner.* Robert F. Kennedy, *Pentagon Papers.*

> *An iron curtain has descended across the Continent.* Sir Winston Churchill, *1946 Iron Curtain.*

> *Our legal systems, our political systems, our educational systems, our economic systems: those are the constructs that enable us to function as a community, rather than as an anarchic rabble of isolated individuals. They are the traffic lights of being, if you will.* Richard Monette, *Lunatics, Lovers, and People of Business.*

> *The challenge before us today is to face with courage, unity and resolve all attacks on free societies and free institutions, to face, in particular, terrorism, which is a dagger at the back of all free societies.* George Bush. *Defending Freedom.*

> *When [Man Thinking] can read God directly, the hour is too precious to be wasted in other men's transcripts of their readings. But when the intervals of darkness come, as come they must—when the sun is hid, and the stars withdraw their shining—we repair to the lamps which were kindled by their ray, to guide our steps to the East again, when the dawn is.* Ralph Waldo Emerson, *The American Scholar.*

Metonymy: the use of a suggestive word for what is actually meant. Similar to a euphemism.

> *I urge the Congress to stop the trade in mail-order murder by adopting a proper gun control law.* Lyndon B. Johnson, *1968 State of the Union Address.*

> *How can the so-called Negroes who call themselves enlightened leaders expect the poor black sheep to be integrated into a society of bloodthirsty white wolves, white wolves who have already been sucking on our blood for over four hundred years here in America?* Malcolm X, *The Black Revolution.*

Oxymoron: a combination of contradictory words or of words incongruous in context.

> *living death*
> *friendly enemies*
> *sweet sorrow* William Shakespeare.

> *His honour rooted in dishonour stood,*
> *And faith unfaithful kept him falsely true.*
> Alfred Lord Tennyson, *Richard III.*

Paradox: a statement that is apparently self-contradictory (an amplified form of oxymoron). Paradoxes seem to oppose common sense yet have a measure of truth.

> *War is Peace, Freedom is Slavery, Ignorance is Strength.* George Orwell, *1984*

> *The primary purpose of our arms is peace, not war.* John F. Kennedy, *1961 Inaugural Address.*

> *If we have to resort to force, it will not be just a war about oil. It will not be a war about hostages. It will not be a war about democracy. It will be a war about peace—not just peace in our time, but peace for our children and grandchildren for generations to come.* Richard M. Nixon, *A War about Peace*

> *Would [Caelius], if he wanted to avoid work and were enmeshed in the toils of pleasure, daily do battle here in public?* Cicero, *In Defense of Caelius.*

> *What is the current explanation of the hard times? Overproduction! There are so many clothes that men must go ragged, so much coal that in the bitter winters people have to shiver, such over-filled granaries*

that people actually die by starvation! Henry George, *The Crime of Poverty.*

Periphrasis: circumlocution; the phrasing of an idea in a roundabout and usually abstract way. A thought may be extended by means of repetition or qualification strictly unnecessary to the sense.

> *And I report to you that I believe with abiding conviction . . . they and those for whom they speak and all of us are going to suffer very serious consequences.* Lyndon B. Johnson, *1968 State of the Union Address.*

Antonomasia: another form of periphrasis, involves the use of an epithet or descriptive phrase instead of a proper name or the substitution of a proper name to suggest a related quality.

> *To our sister republics south of our border . . .* John F. Kennedy, *1961 Inaugural Address*
>
> *Informed sources reject reports that. . . .* New York Times
>
> *I share the view of the Founding Fathers who thought it was a good idea if the king's reach stopped at the front door.* Richard McGuire, *Property Rights and the Food Supply*
>
> *What an affront to the King of the universe, to maintain that the happiness of a monster, sunk in debauchery and spreading desolation and murder among men, of a Caligula, a Nero, or a Charles, is more precious in his sight than that of millions of his suppliant creatures, who do justice, love mercy, and walk humbly with their God!* Samuel Adams, *American Independence.*

Personification: the representation of a thing, quality or idea, as a person.

> *Father Time; Mother Nature; Uncle Sam; Uncle Tom; Jim Crow; John Doe.*
>
> *This Constitution is said to have beautiful features; but when I come to examine these features, sir, they appear to me horribly frightful. Among other deformities, it has an awful squinting; it squints towards monarchy.* Patrick Henry, *Shall Liberty or Empire be Sought?*
>
> *The army and the navy are the sword and shield, which this nation must carry if she is to do her duty among nations of the earth.* Theodore Roosevelt, *The Strenuous Life.*
>
> *And though the murderers may escape, the just resentment of an enraged people; though drowsy justice, intoxicated by the poisonous draught pre-*

335

pared for her cup, still nods upon her rotten seat, yet be assured such complicated crimes will meet their due rewards. John Hancock, *Boston Massacre Oration.*

Pun: a play on words based on a similarity of sound or root and a disparity in meaning or grammatical function. Common forms of the pun are as follows:

Antanaclasis: the exploitation of different senses of the same word.

The business of America is business. Calvin Coolidge, 1925 *Speech to the ASNE Convention.*

Somewhere I read that the greatness of America is the right to protest for right. Martin Luther King, Jr., *I See the Promised Land.*

The 'haves' have not and the 'have nots' have not at all. Repeated studies have shown a direct correlation between the lack of basic human needs being met and the escalation of crime. Myron H. Whals, *The Moral Decay of America.*

Polyptoton: the use of different grammatical forms of the same word or words of similar derivation.

A victor's terms imposed upon the vanquished. Woodrow Wilson, *Peace Without Victory.*

His griefs grieve on no universal bones. William Faulkner, 1950 Nobel Banquet Speech.

His eyes rolling back in his head, he snatches up quill, brush or chisel, and leaps to his task. We get a close-up, showing an expression of agonized ecstasy—or ecstatic agony—then fade to black. Richard Monette, *Lunatics, Lovers, and People of Business.*

Simile: an explicit comparison of literally unlike things.

Good prose is like a windowpane. George Orwell, *Why I Write.*

Friends have asked me what it was like to visit the camp and, like Santa Claus, be the bearer of all sorts of goodies for the children there. Clayton W. Johnston, *The World is Our Village.*

Religious people use God's Law as a yardstick against which to measure others. Jesus wants us to use God's Law as a mirror in which to examine ourselves. Bruce Hedman, *Casting the First Stone.*

Synecdoche: the substitution of a part for the whole, singular for plural, species for genus . . . and vice versa.

> *Standing here on the shore of the Atlantic and contemplating certain of its biggest literary billows* . . . Mark Twain, 1877 At the Whittier Dinner, Boston.

> *The white man discovered the Cross by way of the Bible, but the black man discovered the Bible by way of the Cross.* James Baldwin

> *"Nearly sixteen million hands will aid you in pulling the load upward, or they will pull against you the load downward.* Booker T. Washington, *Speech at the Cotton States Exposition.*

Conclusion

These are a few of the tropes and figures used in rhetorical communication. One mistake is to reduce rhetoric to simply using these in communication to form artistic eloquence. The Eloqution movement of the 1800's and early 1900's devoted all of rhetorical understanding to these elements of style and how they were delivered. Tropes and figures should be used to enhance the truth of the content and intensify the impact of the attitude of love in which the message is given. Ornamentation for ornamentation sake is never good, but to more adequately relate to, address, or impact an audience or to call forth the proper emotion to the proper degree, then using these will enable the rhetor to speak more eloquently.

Coupled with an expressive vocabulary, these tropes and figures will become even more influential. Many in the press will speak of right-wing Republicans, but do not use the metaphorical adjective left-wing for Democrats, or speak of fundamentalist Christians, but not use a similar adjective for members of NOW, Greenpeace, or NAMBLA. This bias for the left is demonstrated through the semantics and syntax of style when providing information.

This means that style is often significantly related to truth. Exerting persuasive influence over others through the use of rhetorical tropes and figures will impact the way they think about the content of the message. Carefully consider the impact your words will have, how they could be misconstrued, and how they align thinking to the message prior to speaking or writing.

Chapter 15

Delivering Public Rhetoric Persuasively

We know that you speak and teach what is right,
and that you do not show partiality
but teach the way of God
in accordance with the truth.
Luke 20:21 NIV

A FEW WEEKS after I was hired as a youth pastor in a church of about 800 members, the pastor went on vacation, and I was to preach in the Sunday morning worship service. With a layman in charge, the music was over, the offering taken, special music and the choir sang all in about twelve minutes. I had 48 minutes to fill with a 25-minute sermon. My mind raced with things to add as I approached the pulpit. The first sentence was right off my notes, "We are the elect of God." As I said the last word of the first sentence a woman in the second row from the front screamed, threw her hands up in the air, and went into an epileptic seizure.

What should I do: Having prepared the content, having considered the audience in relationship to God and the text, and in the midst of adapting to the occasion. The unexpected enters into public communication, and the principles of delivery need to take over. Delivery is the fifth of Aristotle's canons of rhetoric and is concerned with how something is communicated to augment the content or what is communicated. The Greek word for delivery is *huperkrisis;* Aristotle uses the same word for dramatic acting and oral interpretation of poetry. Delivery is the doing or action of communicating.

338

Content Based Delivery

The first and most important principle of delivery is to add to the substance of the message. Anything that subtracts from what you are trying to say or write should be avoided. Thou shalt not detract from the message.

A student from Los Angeles who believed God was calling him to minister to small, rural churches dressed in wild colors, had multiple body piercings, and talked with an in-your-face attitude. When I asked if he was willing to give up his attitude, his slang, his dress, and his jewelry he was shocked by the idea. These things were part of "who he was" and had nothing to do with preaching God's Word to people. He graduated from college and could not get a job in a church, he went to seminary and tried again after he had his masters, and he was still not called to a church. He tried selling cars, working for a printing company, and finally landed a job delivering mail. Focusing on being who he was physically was more important to him than conforming to the image of God and allowing God to speak through his nonverbal communication. He was more important than the message. People refused to listen because they knew character was more important than tattoos or piercings and they did not want someone with his attitude and nonverbal communication representing them in the community as their pastor.

In a freshman public speaking class I was teaching at the University of Oregon, one young man brought in a large, dirty, mossy rock and placed it on the table. His speech had nothing to do with rocks and at the end he picked it up and carried it back to his seat. When asked about it, he said he wanted to give people a place to focus their attention instead of on him. If they were wondering about what a rock had to do with his speech, they would be distracted from watching him—bad idea. We were so focused on the rock that we did not hear his message.

If the PowerPoint presentation, if the movie clips, or if the setting is so novel, so unusual, so engrossing that the audience pays more attention to the electronic delivery than the message, then it is a bad delivery. The first principle of delivery is to always put the message first. Just like using too many rhetorical tropes and figures may detract from clarity and make them counterproductive, delivery can also become distracting.

Natural

The second overarching principle of delivery is to be natural when speaking and writing persuasive rhetoric. Thou shalt not be artificial. Do not become someone who you are not, in order to give the message. Some of our culture will think the young man who gave up God's call on his life, so that he could remain "himself" in outward dress and adornment, did a noble thing. Most will understand that what is inside is what really counts so that if God calls you to go somewhere, you have to make some adjustments in outward things. The flip side of that same issue is hypocrisy, pretending to be someone you are not. You can fool some people as a public communicator—but you will not fool all of the audience.

Another aspect of being natural is speaking conversationally, using the appropriate style for the people and occasion. Usually prior to giving a public speech, I will talk to members of the audience and then in the presentation use their words to present my idea. Doing so matches my vocabulary style with their conversation and makes a natural delivery. When writing for a newspaper or magazine I look at the words the editors use in editorials before I write the article.

A third aspect of naturalness concerns the body. Stiffness, except in rare formal situations, come from being uncomfortable in front of the audience. Relax. Move some.

A final part of being natural in delivery is vocalics. Learn to control the voice so that it is not strained but conversational in tone and quality. Be careful of affected pitch or volume as well.

In written rhetoric naturalness comes to me when I can read something over a cup of coffee on my deck. Does the story flow from the pen as a good friend would tell it to me amidst the birds and trees? Yes, I know that some writing and speaking is designed for other purposes, however, we need to master natural delivery before we can affectively alter it to something else.

Interest

How you say what you say should add interest to the message. Thou shalt not be boring. Delivery should aid the audience in knowing what is most important through nonverbal emphasis that adds weight to the words. Rhetorical strive to create exigence—the audience sitting on the edge of their seats eager to hear the next word, tuning out all distractions.

Some delivery practices distract audiences. When my Dad taught, he would twirl his reading glasses when he wasn't reading from his notes. College students would inevitably mimic him, yet he never broke the habit. Some speakers wipe their nose with their hands, twist their hair, pace, or any number of things that decrease interest in the material and place emphasis on the delivery.

Modern journalism and nonfiction authors have adapted a good strategy of placing sidebars, text boxes, and related columns in order to add to the interest, cover necessary information, and apply the text. This is a way to emphasize the written text where an oral presentation would become louder or softer.

Flexibility

This chapter opened with an illustration from my life with a question-what would you do if someone had a seizure while you are speaking? I called for a doctor and asked the ushers to come up and help him. Then, I asked a couple deacons to come up front and over to one side, so the audience could focus on them, and God, not the woman, and we prayed for her. When she was safe, they carried her from the sanctuary, we sang a hymn and then went back to the sermon. Can you think on your feet to appropriately address a situation?

Another time I was speaking to about 500 high school students at a camp. The person at the soundboard simply could not get the mike right. It would squeak, then go dead, then gave high pitch squeal, then a loud hum. . . nothing would work. He kept adjusting the sound as I spoke and I realized the message was not going to come across. I turned off the microphone, stepped out in front of the platform, and raised my voice. The effect for most of the audience was that the volume decreased, so they sat forward in their chairs to hear the message. Are you flexible enough to deal with a faulty microphone?

While I was speaking in a college chapel one time, a mouse ran in among the students. Girls squealed, people raised their legs, and in general the mouse stole the attention of the entire student body. I asked everyone to raise their feet, but that was a failure because the mouse still had their attention. The mouse went too close to a farm boy, a good stomp and it was history, but afterwards people remembered the mouse—not the message. I never did regain the full attention of the student body, some laughing, some grossed out, all distracted. Are you flexible enough to realize that some failure in delivering the message will be beyond your control?

Flexibility is also needed in written communication. The ability to deliver the same message in a short newspaper editorial, in a feature article for a magazine, and in a scholarly publication takes serious consideration of the appropriate way to approach each audience with voice, style, and vocabulary. Delivery will make the difference in whether or not they are of publishable quality.

Another aspect of flexibility in written rhetoric delivery is that of scoop. Journalists are becoming so lazy that the first person to publish on an issue gets to set the approach everyone else uses. We need a greater variety of interpretations of events and vigorous debate within the media concerning the viability of specific interpretations. Rigorous evaluation of the tone and words used in reporting will change the impression of readers.

Delivery of Written Rhetoric

Written public rhetoric has most of the delivery decisions taken away from the author. When writing for a newspaper, you may argue for which page a particular article will appear, whether it is above or below the fold, and perhaps something about the surrounding advertisements. However, the font type and size, paper quality, and ink contrast are not negotiable. In magazines or journals authors have few choices; the publisher largely makes them. Books leave a little more up to the author with photographs, a wider range of paper, cover design, font, and size all of which are nonverbal parts of the delivery of the message.

For authors, choosing which magazine, which newspaper, or which book publisher is therefore a larger consideration than it may appear because it is usually the extent of the control the author has over delivery. Look carefully through the writer's guidelines, samples from the publisher, and internet cites before you submit your work for publication. Sometimes you want to contain complete control of the content—like when Billy Graham allowed an interview to be published in *Playboy*. In order to reach the people who read such magazines, he interviewed with them, but only allowed them to publish what he said with strict guidelines on what appeared alongside his words.

Delivery of Oral Rhetoric

The strongest message quality and the best preparation are not communicative unless the audience is able to hear and comprehend the message.

Engaging the audience is necessary. When this becomes the primary consideration the communication is no longer rhetoric but *technical* in the sense that technique and style are foremost. When this is overemphasized through the greater impact delivery can have over solid content then *sophistic* communication is the driving paradigm. In *philosophical rhetoric* from a Christian perspective is used, the truth of the message is primary, love for the audience from a person of virtue is secondary, process and method are then considered and delivery is de-emphasized, but not eliminated, from the rhetorical task.

Vocalics and Vocal Properties

Variety is the spice of vocalic communication. Yet a rhythmic pausing and phrasing based on the ideas will create an interesting delivery. These need to be held in balance. A sing-song rhythm will make many sick to their stomach, while a monotone drone will put them to sleep.

A speaker should think in phrases and sentences rather than in individual words. The ideas communicated come through the syntax more than the semantics, so the phrases should hang together in the delivery in a manner that emphasizes what is most important about the thought.

The real key to vocalic rhetoric is to have all of the elements fit into a whole that is congruent with the message and the speaker. Speaking is not simply the vocalization of a written text; it is a different kind of message with a different kind of relationship established with the audience. All of the elements should align in order for maximum impact.

Pronunciation: having the correct sound.

Each area of the world has an "accent" that distinguishes those who grew up there from speakers from other areas. Some accents are more distinct than others. Most of us could differentiate between native English speakers from Mississippi, New Jersey, London, and Seattle. However, the difference between a speaker from Seattle, Washington and Portland, Oregon, would be more difficult. This is a good, healthy aspect of diversity that should be enjoyed and celebrated. One accent is not right with another wrong.

Pronunciation is the first thing people notice about speaking any language. Audiences will not pick up on a poor vocabulary or simple grammar nearly as fast as they will immediately become aware of whether or not you use the correct sounds. Many in the audience will simply not understand the message because they are spending so much effort attempting to hear the correct words.

While in a rhetoric class for my Ph.D. at the University of Oregon, one of my professors gave a lecture on hermeneutics but the entire time he mispronounced the word as "her-me-net-ics." Even worse, he spent a lengthy time attempting to establish his expertise in the area. Uninformed audience members may have been suitably awed. My impression, however, of his expertise dropped considerably for the entire course because he was pretending to be an authority on a subject he could not even pronounce correctly. Even though I tried to give him the benefit of the doubt cognitively, emotionally he never regained the status he had in my heart—simply because of a mispronounced word.

A teacher I had in high school escaped from Communist China and made her way to the US. Her pronunciation was so bad that we had to work at listening, and even then she had to write down much of what she taught. One of her idiosyncrasies was to add an "er" to the end of everyone's name, to her I was Daner. As she taught literature, we learned of characters such as Kneehighmier (Nehemiah), Hisesskyer (Hezekiah), Ohteller (Othello), and Brutusser (Brutus). Her ethos was not harmed by her pronunciation because we knew her as one who hungered so much for the stories, that she read her family's hidden treasures in a concealed basement room with a candlelight lantern, and then she escaped on a boat taking only a deep passion for literature and the clothes on her back from her homeland. Decades later I can still hear her voice as it added to the mystery of those stories. Sadly, by the end of her first year, she had worked so hard at learning to speak English she could correctly pronounce almost anything, except our names, they still had an "er" on the end. Pronunciation is the key to perceived competence. Talk to people who know your subject before you speak in public so that you can adapt the pronunciation of difficult and jargon words. Enough electronic resources exist that you can probably find an internet cite with a video stream that will give you the cue you need to correctly decipher the sounds of any unknown words.

Enunciation: having the correct emphasis.

Enunciation provides the emotional cues for the audience as well as the relative importance of an individual word to the whole communication. Placing the correct emphasis on the right syllable as well as stressing or destressing words and phrases connects the audience to the emotional level of competency of language use. As a noun, *enunciation* indicates speaking in such a way that the audience clearly understands the words along with their relative importance in the syntax: making known words by the voice. As a verb, *enunciation* is the action of utterance or the vocalization of the sound with the correct stress.

As the audience listens to enunciated words, they will make a connotative connection with the speaker leading to understanding the appropriate emotions of the rhetorical event. When I clearly enunciate my daughter's name, Charity, with staccato rhythm, getting higher in pitch, increased projection and with greater stress on each syllable, she knows she is in trouble or that something is dreadfully wrong. Adding her middle name and continuing the pattern of getting higher and louder with stress on the last syllable will further indicate to her the emotional state of the communication sequence.

Articulation: having clear sound.

Pronunciation is having the correct sound. Enunciation is having the correct emphasis on the syllable, word, or phrase. Articulation is the degree of distinctness or clarity of the sound of syllables, words, and phrases. The extent of articulative clarity is directly related to the audience being able to differentiate precise words from other words and, therefore, pinpoint meaning.

In music an articulation is a relationship of notes to each other such as: ties, slurs, staccatos, accents . . . giving the musician a cue as to the degree of distinctness an individual note should have in relationship to other notes in the score. In speech, articulation is the distinctness of an individual sound, syllable, or word in relationship to other words in the phrase or discourse. Consonants are differentiated by where they are physically shaped: labial (lip), coronal (front of tongue), dorsal (middle/back of tongue), radical (tongue base with epiglottis), and laryngeal (the larynx).

Training the mouth to work together with the stress is one of the more difficult aspects of language acquisition. Like music finds meaning in the phrases with the correct sound, correct stress, and relational clarity spoken, rhetoric uses the correct sound, correct stress, and relational clarity to create meaning. Together these enable the eloquent artist to create intelligibility and enhance impact.

Resonance: having full sound.

The quality, tone, or texture of the voice is largely determined by the resonance. Each human voice has a distinctive character and degree of richness as determined by the physical resonance of the voice. The air cavities of the mouth, sinuses, and nose intensify vocal tones through vibrations in the process of speaking. We call that intensification, or lack thereof, *resonance*. Vibrations of the voice can echo in the soul of the audience creating a relationship of meaning and emotion that goes beyond simple understanding of the words.

Sometimes known as the timbre or quality of the voice, resonance give color to the tone. The Germans call it the *ring* of the voice. As such, resonance can add feeling such a being *blue* or *golden*. Providing a spiritual connection with the message, the resonance creates more than a vibration of sound waves in a chamber, but a deep inner relationship of people and content.

Volume

The degree of loudness is the volume of a speaker. Closely related is the ability to project the voice to a specific target. With their dependence upon electronic amplification, modern speakers have largely abandoned the aptitudes and skills related to variation in sound. We even record music, radio, and television programs to have a largely monotone volume so that they can be heard in cars and over other noises. I think of these as the ability to fill a room with my voice and the ability to hit a target with my voice. This encourages me to exercise my vocalics more than many speakers do.

The movie *Sister Act* has the new nun lead a convent choir and tells them to sing over the clamor of a restaurant full of people who are eating, talking, and dropping silverware—to project the voice with appropriate volume. Jesus could speak to 5,000 people on a mountainside. The Roman coliseum seated 50,000 people who could all hear one speaker. George Whitefield and John Wesley spoke to crowds over 20,000 in open fields. Most speakers today want a microphone if they are speaking to 100 in a closed room.

Rate

The speed of speaking is more than the rapidity of words. Rate includes how quickly the individual words are spoken and the frequency of pauses between phrases and words. This is one of the first areas affected by nervousness. Many beginning speakers talk so rapidly, the words are difficult to differentiate no matter how well they are articulated and enunciated. Some speakers talk faster the closer they get to the end of the speech. Others talk fast at the beginning and partway through relax and begin to speak normally. All of these ways of misusing rate distract the audience from the message. Some speakers seem to be afraid to pause in a discourse. Audiences need time to absorb what a speaker says; they cannot go back and re-listen to a passage the way a reader can re-read if he misses something.

Slow down, speak as though you are in a natural conversation, and pause often. I do this through speaking phrase-by-phrase rather than word-by-word. Thinking through the units of meaning and stressing them enables me to pace the communication in a way the audience can enter the rhythm of the content.

Pitch

Where a sound falls on a musical scale is called pitch. If you want to sound scared, a high piercing pitch will avail the purpose. If you want to sound bored, a low slow pitch will be better. The change of pitch in a speaker produces what is called inflection. The highest possible sound to the lowest sound capable of being made by an individual speaker is called the range. Training can usually increase the range and inflection significantly.

While resonance provides a deep spiritual connection and meaning, pitch gives a more overt emotional depiction to the message. Enunciation provides the kind of emotion and nuances of meaning; intensity of emotion and distinct changes of meaning are achieved through pitch. Infliction also relates to a speaker's personality in that patterns of pitch are connected to certain situations, words, and phrases.

Facial Expression

Eyes are the window to your soul; let the people see you seeing them. The visual cues of your facial expressions will provide the audience with important information about how to interpret your message.

When the face is congruent with vocalics and they match the content of the speech, the audience is more likely to believe what you have to say. A speaker who does not look the audience in the eye will usually be considered to be either incompetent, shy, or worse, trying to lie to them. Staring at the audience the entire time without breaking eye contact may bring about the impression of a "used car salesman" or "slick Willie" kind of presentation. A confident speaker will create a relationship with the audience through eye contact and maintain that contact with boldness.

Emotions can also be important parts of facial expression. Fear can be wide-eyed, leaned back, and mouth open. Surprise raises the eyebrows, opens eyes and mouth, and smiles. Normal expressions for the emotions will enhance the audience's ability to feel those same things. The speaker should exhibit one degree of intensity more than what we want the audience to feel. If you want them to get angry, do not express rage, just be a little angrier than you want them to feel. Incorporate smiles, head nods, and openness into your speaking, and the audience will respond appropriately.

Body Movement

How you "carry" yourself says much about who you are as a person and your attitude about the subject and people in the rhetorical situation. A straighter posture, open arms, along with a smile sends a subconscious message that you are competent, at ease with who you are, alert, and ready to communicate. Slouching, sluggish movements, crossed arms, and a furrowed brow will communicate something very different. Comfortable erectness with arms uncrossed is the basic speech posture.

During the speech if at all possible you should move some. Even if it is only to step back and turn your torso to one side, hold it there, and then to the other, you will engage those on the sides of the audience through movement. I usually prefer to walk around some during a long speech, walking to a position on the stage, stopping to make a point, and then walking back. Especially in long speeches the movement tends to engage the audience in the subject more than simply standing still. Constant movement with pacing is worse than not moving at all, you should be comfortable enough to pause in movement, just like you should be comfortable enough to pause in talking.

Gestures are closely linked to body movement and should be coordinated with vocalics and facial expression to augment the argument. Some speakers have trouble knowing what to do with their hands. Sometimes hold them in front of you and make small movements. Sometimes hold them behind you in a kind of parade rest position. Sometimes get them out from your body in larger movements that emphasize the points you are making. In other words, no one thing is right; the best thing you can do with your hands is to use them in different ways at different parts of the speech. Watch yourself and others in interpersonal conversations and take note of how we use our hands, then, do similar things when speaking in public. Make sure you use some larger movements because the audience is larger.

The best gestures are timed to emphasize the content of the speech. If you are using a visual aid, point out what you are talking about. You can also use gestures to mimic real life, especially in how to or informative speeches. Good public speakers get into a rhythm of speaking where the gestures match the phrases and emotions.

Personal Appearance

Combed hair, being clean, dressed one degree above the average of the audience . . . being careful your personal appearance will enhance your credibility and thus add to the impact of your speech. Generally speaking, your clothing should stand out from the background. If you are speaking in front of a curtain or wall, you should wear a contrasting color to set you apart from the background. Generally speaking you should wear nicer clothing than most of the audience, avoid speaking to a group of farmers in a tux, come in clean denim and an ironed shirt.

As mentioned earlier, if you are a professional communicator like a pastor, teacher, or politician you will want to adapt your personal appearance to your primary audience. That may include not wearing too much jewelry, putting the tie-dyed shirt in the bottom of the drawer with the miniskirt that has a hole in the side. Do this not because you are pretending to be someone you are not, but because your message and the impact you have on others is more important than the outward display. Hanging up the cowboy hat may not be easy, but professionals have to make decisions on what sacrifices should be made in order to be the most effective at any job. Public communication is simply more overt than some other positions.

Visual Aids

Intentionally augmenting the speech through appropriate physical supports will strengthen the intended results of the event. Visual aids can be objects or artifacts such as a goldfish, a basket, or electric drill. I've used sledge hammers, an ancient stone adz, antique books, musical instruments, and even a garbage can as props in speeches. People are intrigued both by ordinary things and unusual things. Visual aids also include verbal augments presented electronically, or on a chalkboard, on charts, or on overheads.

Here are some principles that should guide the use of visual aids in speeches:

1. The visual aid should emphasize the content of the message.

2. The visual aid should be appropriate to the context, audience, and situation.

3. The visual aid should simplify and explain material, not complicate the issue.

4. The visual aid should not detract from the speech.

5. Choose a visual aid that tells the "story" of the speech.

6. Be certain the visual aid is accurate and ethical.

They serve many purposes. Complex statistics can be visualized in a graph easier than explained in prose. Sometimes a photograph will enable the audience to visualize people or situations. Often a visual aid can demonstrate relationships between ideas in a fashion that is difficult without the visual element. Many visual aids will enable the speaker to cover more territory in less time with less repetition.

Stage Presence: Congruency and Charisma

When some people walk into a room and onto a stage, by their very presence the situation is changed and the audience takes note. The magnetism, grace, and relational captivation some people have as a public figure or performer is called charisma. When the audience perceives a sincere desire for their good from a person who confidently engages them in a speech, they will respond. Arrogance is the opposite of confident stage presence. Some people have a charisma of thought, others of the voice, others a grace of body; all of them have a sincere congruency of who they are coming through what they are doing on the stage.

What are the components of the almost indescribable gift of stage presence? It's not beauty, but attractiveness helps. It's not ability, but that may help. It's not simply intelligence, but it may be impossible without some level of intelligence. It's definitely not credentials, but most people with charisma attain some.

1. Confidence in some aspect of the message and themselves, especially when it leads to being unflappable under pressure.

2. Sincere love for the audience and desire for interpersonal interaction, not simply performance.

3. Being prepared for the rhetorical situation, accurately speaking the truth, having done the research and knows, not just giving someone else's speech.

4. A significant level of competence that can be observed by the audience, but is not overstated.

5. A willingness to being transparently real, to share a little of who you really are with the audience, having a fresh innocence.

6. Most people with charisma enjoy doing what they are doing; it is more than an assignment or a job, but a passion to communicate.

7. A stage presence can often be seen when something goes wrong and the person can laugh at himself and the situation, even if it is embarrassing.

8. In public speaking it also means creating exigence and quitting while the audience still wants to hear more.

These are some of the qualities individuals can build into their own speaking and being—you can develop a stage presence that captivates an audience simply by being.

Empathy

The end of rhetorical persuasion should be an experience of empathy. Feeling similar emotions about similar thoughts within similar circumstances is what empathy is about. Public speakers who develop the ability to project themselves emotionally and intellectually into the subject matter, the situation, and the audience will create a spiritual-psychological relational bond that enables significant communication to persuasively impact the audience.

Most thinkers about public rhetoric ignore this aspect of the discipline. Others, like Kenneth Burke, touch on it through the concept of identification. Others simply call it a relationship and leave it alone. I believe the mystery of the spiritual bond of communion established in the sharing of understanding can go well beyond the easily identifiable assessments of social scientific research or the qualitative methodology of the humanities.

Empathy is the mystery of spiritual unity of heart and mind when a speaker's being touches the listener's being. On certain occasions this inscrutable event changes those who participate so they become different through the rhetorical event. This happens when a social event becomes fellowship, when diversity becomes unity, when individuals become partners, and when God enters the human sphere. The unfathomable richness of an empathetic encounter through communication leaves us hungering for more. The empathetic relationship of love enabled, deepened and established through public communication fulfills the ethical function of rhetoric and adds to the meaning of life.

Bibliography

Adams, S. (1989). American independence. In J. Andrews & D. Zarefsky (Eds.), *American voices: Significant Speeches in American History, 1640-1945* (pp. 66-77). New York: Longman.

Augsburger, M. S. (1994). The cross is timeless. In R. A. Bodey (Ed.), *If I had only one sermon to preach* (pp.13-21). Grand Rapids: Baker Books.

Blair, T. (1998, October 15). A new international finance system. *Vital speeches of the day, LXV.* No.1, 2-4.

Barnet, S., & Bedau, H. (1999). *Current issues and enduring questions: A guide to critical thinking and argument with readings.* Boston: Bedford/St. Martin's.

Baltimore, C., & Meyer, R. J. (1969). A study of storage, child behavioral traits, and mother's knowledge of toxicology in 52 poisoned families and 52 comparison families. *Pediatrics, 44,* 816-820.

Berger, D. (2003). *Oral interpretation of the Bible.* Eugene, OR: Wipf and Stock Publishers.

Bettinghouse, E., & Cody, M. (1994). *Persuasive communication* (5th ed.) (pp. 185-188). New York: Harcourt Brace.

Bizzell, P. & Herzberg B. (1990). *The rhetorical tradition: Readings from classical times to the present.* Boston: Bedford.

Blair, T. (1997). Welfare reform: Giving people the will to win. *Vital speeches of the day. LXIII,* No. 18, 549-552.

Boethius, A. M. S. *An overview of the structure of rhetoric,* (J. M. Miller Trans.) (1973) pp. 425-430. In P. Bizzell and B. Herzberg (1990) *The rhetorical tradition: Readings from classical times to the present.* Boston: Bedford Books.. (Original work published in 524?).

Boethius, A. M. S. *The consolation of philosophy,* Trans. W. V. Cooper (1902) in Golden, J. L., G. F. Berquist and W. E. Coleman, (1997) *The rhetoric of western thought,* 6th ed., Dubuque, Iowa: Kendall Hunt Publishing Company. (Original work published in 525?)

Bragg, B. W. (1973). *A good idea but are they too much bother: An analysis of the relationship between attidtdes toward seat belts and reported use.* Ottawa: Department of Transport, Road and Motor Vehicle Traffic Safety Branch.

Buechner, F. (1978). The hungering dark. In J. W. Cox (Ed.), *The Twentieth Century Pulpit,* (pp. 20-29). Nashville: Abgindon.

Burke, K. (1969). *A rhetoric of motives.* Berkley: University of California Press.

Bush, G. (May 15, 1986). Defending freedom. *Vital speeches of the day. LII,* 450-454.

Campbell, G. (1835). *Philosophy of rhetoric* (new edition) Boston: J. H. Wilkins & Co., Hilliard, Gray, & Co., and Gould, Lincoln, & Kendall.

L. P. Pojman, (1998). *Classics of philosophy*. New York: Oxford University Press.

Caputo, J. D. & J. Derrida (1997). *Deconstruction in a nutshell: A conversation with Jacques Derrida*. New York: Fordham University Press.

Chaiken, S. (1980). Heuristic versus systematic information processing and the use of source versus message cues in persuasion, *Journal of personality and social psychology, 39*, 752-766.

Chomsky, N. (1965). *Aspects of the theory of syntax*. [Massachusetts]: Massachusetts Institute of Technology.

Cialdini, R. B., Levy, A., Herman, P., Kozlowski, L., & Petty, R. E. (1976). Elastic shifts of opinion: Determinants of direction and durability. *Journal of Personality and Social Psychology, 34*, 663-673.

Cicero. (1967). *In defense of Caelius*, In *nine orations and the dream of scipio*, P. Bovie (Trans.) (pp. 229-270). New York: Mentor Books.

Clark, G. H. (1984). Knowledge. In Elwell, W. A. (Ed.). *Evangelical dictionary of theology*. Grand Rapids, Michigan: Baker Book House.

Cleaver, E. (1971). Meditation on the assassination of Martin Luther King Jr. In D. J. O'Neill (Ed.). *Speeches by black Americans*, (pp. 229-233). Encino, California: Dickenson Publishing.

Clinton, H. R. (October 1, 1995). Women's rights are human rights. *Vital speeches of the day. LXI*, No. 24, 738-740.

Corbett, E. P. J. (1971). *Classical rhetoric for the modern student*, (2nd ed.). New York: Oxford University Press.

Crosswhite, J. (1996). *The rhetoric of reason*. Madison: The University of Wisconsin Press.

de Man, P. (1990). *Blindness and insight: Essays in the rhetoric of contemporary criticism*. Minneapolis: University of Minnesota Press.

deTurck, M., (2002). Persuasive effects of product warning labels. In J. P. Dillard & M. Pfau (Eds). *The persuasion handbook: Developments in theory and practice*. (pp. 345-367). Thousand Oaks, CA: Sage Publications.

Derrida, J. (1976). *Of Grammatology*. G. C. Spivak (Trans.). Baltimore: Johns Hopkins University Press.

Derrida, J. (1981). Semiology and grammatology. In *Positions* A. Bass (Trans.). Chicago: The University of Chicago Press.

Dole, R. (September 1, 1996). The best days are yet to come. *Vital speeches of the day, LXII*, No. 22, 674-679.

Donohue, T. J. (1999). World hunger. *Vital speeches of the day. LXIV*, No. 18, 567-571.

Douglass, F. (2000). *The hypocrisy of American slavery. modern history sourcebook*. Retrieved March 31, 2000. http://www.fordham.edu/halsall/mod/douglass-hypo.html.

Du Bois, W.E.B. (1971). Address to the national Negro convention. In D. J. O'Neill (Ed.). *Speeches by black Americans* (pp. 88-101). Encino, California: Dickenson Publishing.

Emerson, R. W. (1989). The American scholar. In J. Andrews and D. Zarefsky_(Eds.). *American voices: Significant speeches in American history, 1640-1945*. (pp. 154-167). New York: Longman,

Erickson, M. J. (2001). *Truth or consequences*. Downer's Grove, IL: InterVarsity Press.

Festinger, L., & Mccoby, N. (1964). On resistance to persuasive communication. *Journal of abnormal and social psychology, 68*, 359-366.

Fishbein, M. & Ajzen, I. (1975). *Belief, attitude, intention, and behavior: An introduction to theory and research*. Reading, MA: Addison-Wesley.

Fisher, W. R. (1987). *Human communication as narration: Toward a philosophy of reason, value, and action.* Columbia: University of South Carolina Press.

Foss, S. K., Foss, K. A., & Griffin, C. L. (1999). *Feminist rhetorical theories.* Thousand Oaks, CA: Sage.

Foss, S. K., & Foss, K. A. (1994). *Inviting transformation: Presentational speaking for a changing world.* Prospect Heights, IL: Waveland Press.

Foss, S. K., & Griffin, C. L. (1995). *Beyond persuasion: A proposal for an invitational rhetoric.* Communication monographs. 62:1; 2-18.

Foss, S. K., Foss, K. A., & Trapp, R. (1985). *Contemporary perspectives on rhetoric.* Prospect Heights, IL: Waveland Press.

Foucault, M. (1990). *The history of sexuality,* New York: Random House.

Garton, R. D. (1999). Public discourse. *Vital speeches of the day. LXIV,* No. 18, 564-567.

Gearheart, S. (1979). *The womanization of rhetoric.* Women's studies international quarterly, 2:195-201.

George, H. (1989). The crime of poverty. In J. Andrews & D. Zarefsky (Eds.). *American voices: Significant speeches in American history, 1640-1945.* (pp. 313-330). New York: Longman.

Gibbs, T. J. (1993). Memorable munificence. In J. W. Cox (Ed.). *Best sermons 6,* (pp. 68-75). San Francisco: HarperCollins.

Givon, T. (1979). *On understanding grammar.* New York: Academic Press.

Grice, H. P. (1975). Logic and conversation in P. Cole & J. L. Morgan (Eds.). *Syntax and semantics: Speech acts.* (Vol. 3) (pp. 41-58). New York: Academic Press.

Griffin, E. (2005). *A first look at communication theory* (6ᵗʰ Ed.). Boston: Mc Graw Hill.

Groothuis, D. (2000). *Truth decay: Defending Christianity against the challenges of postmodernism.* Downer's Grove, IL: InterVarsity Press.

Hancock, J. (1989). The Boston massacre oration. In J. Andrews & D. Zarefsky (Ed.). *American voices: Significant speeches in American history, 1640-1945.* (pp. 40-48). New York: Longman.

Hauerwas, S. (1981). *A community of character: Towards a constructive Christian ethic.* South Bend, IN: University of Notre Dame Press.

Hedman, B. (1993). Casting the first stone. In J. W. Cox (Ed.). *Best sermons 6,* (pp. 85-89). San Francisco: HarperCollins.

Herrick, J. A. (1997). *The history and theory of rhetoric: An introduction.* Scottsdale, Arizona: Gorsuch Scarisbrick, Publishers.

Johnston, C. W. (1999). The world is our village. *Vital speeches of the day. LXIV,* No. 18. 576-581.

Kemp, J. (September 1, 1996). The American dream. *Vital speeches of the day. LXII,* No.22, 679-681.

Kennedy, G. A. (1980). *Classical rhetoric and its Christian and secular tradition from ancient to modern times.* Chapel Hill: University of North Carolina Press.

Killinger, J. (1978). There is still God. In J. W. Cox (Ed.). *The twentieth century pulpit* (pp.108-114). Nashville: Abgindon.

King, M. L. (2000). *I see the promised land.* Retrieved March 31, 2000. http://members.aol.com/clove01/promland.htm.

Letellier, (1999). Tribute to veterans. *Vital speeches of the day. LXIV,* No. 16 pp. 435-439.

LaPiere, R. (1934). Attitudes versus actions. *Social forces.* 13, 230-237.

Lincoln, A. (2000). *Address before the young men's lyceum of Springfield, Illinois.* Retrieved March 31, 2000. http://douglass.speech.nwu.edu/linc_a69.htm.

Lovette, R. (1993). Night fishing. In J. W. Cox. (Ed.). *Best sermons 6.* San Francisco: HarperCollins.

Lucaites, J. L., Condit, C. M. & Caudill, S (1999). *Contemporary rhetorical theory: A reader.* New York: Guilford.

Lucas, S. E. (2004). *The art of public speaking* (8th ed.). Boston: Mc Graw Hill.

Marwell, G. & Schmitt, D. (1967). Dimensions of compliance-gaining strategies: A dimensional analysis. In *Sociometry* 30, 350-364.

Malcolm X, (2000). *The black revolution.* Retrieved March 31, 2000. http://sac.uky.edu/ ~jfmcdo00/bookshelf/blackrev.html.

Manley, D. (2002). *Wisdom: The principle thing.* Enumclaw, WA: WinePress Publishing.

Maslow, A. H. (1970). *Motivation and personality,* (2nd ed.). New York: Harper and Row.

McDaniel, J. M. (1998). Rhetoric reconsidered: Preaching as persuasion, *Sewanee Theological Review.* 41:3, 241-257.

McGuire, R. (August 15, 1995). Property Rights and the Food Supply. *Vital Speeches of the Day. LXI,* No. 21, 657-660.

McGuire, W. J. (1964). Inducing resistance to persuasion: Some contemporary approaches. In L. Berkowitz (Ed.) *Advances in experimental social psychology, 1,* pp. 191-229. New York: Academic.

Monette, R. (April 15, 1998). Lunatics, lovers, and people of business. *Vital speeches of the day. LXIV,* No.13, 411-416.

Nixon, R. M. (April 1, 1990). A war about peace. *Vital speeches of the day. LVII,* No. 12.

Osborn, M., & Osborn, S. (2003) *Public speaking.* Boston: Houghton Mifflin.

Packard, V. (1957). *The hidden persuaders.* New York: David McKay Company inc.

Reid, R F. (2000). Forward: A long and proud tradition, *Arugmentation and advocacy,* River Falls; Summer 2000 37:1 p. 1-11.

Perelman, C. & L. Olbrechts-Tyteca (1969). *The New Rhetoric.* (New Ed.). Notre Dame, IN: University of Notre Dame Press.

Perelman, C. (1982). *The Realm of Rhetoric.* Notre Dame, IN: University of Notre Dame Press.

Perloff, R. (1993). *The dynamics of persuasion.* Hillsdale, NJ: Lawrence Erbaum Associates.

Perloff, R. M. & Brock, T. C. (1980). And thinking makes it so: Cognitive responses to persuasion. In M. Roloff & G. Miller (Eds.) *Persuasion: New directions in theory and research* (pp. 67-100). Beverly Hills: Sage.

Petty, R. E., & Cacioppo, J. T. (1981). *Attitudes and persuasion: Classic and contemporary approaches.* Dubuque, IA: William C. Brown Co. Publishers.

Petty, R. E. & Cacioppo, J. T. (1986). *Communication and persuasion: Central and peripheral routes to attitude change.* New York: Springer-Verlag Inc.

Resner, A. (1999). *Preacher and cross: Person and message in theology and rhetoric.* Grand Rapids: Eerdmans.

Richards, I.A. & C. K. Ogden (1923) *The meaning of meaning.* London: Oxford University Press.

Richards, I. A. (1936). *The philosophy of rhetoric.* New York: Oxford University Press.

Ross, R. S. (1994). *Understanding persuasion* (4th ed.). Englewood Cliffs, New Jersey: Prentice Hall.

Powell, A.C. (1971). Can there any good things come out of Nazareth? In *Speeches by black Americans,* D. J. O'Neill (Ed.). (pp. 193-199). Encino, California: Dickenson Publishing,.

Rhodes, C. B. (1993). How, then, shall we live? In J. W. Cox (Ed.). *Best sermons 6,* (pp. 76-84). San Francisco: HarperCollins.

Rokeach, M. (1968). *Beliefs, attitudes, and values: A theory of organization and change.* San Francisco: Jossey-Bass.

Rosenstand N. (2005). *The moral of the story.* (5ᵗʰ ed.). Boston: McGraw Hill.

Roosevelt, Franklin D. *The arsenal of democracy.* Retreived March 30, 2000. http://www.tamu.edu/scom/pres/speeches/fdrarsenal.html.

Saussure, F. de. (1966). *Course in general linguistics.* C. Bally & A. Sechehaye (Eds.). W. Baskin (Trs). New York: McGraw-Hill Book Company.

Schultze, Q. J. (2000). *Communicating for life: Christian stewardship in community and media.* Grand Rapids: Baker Book House.

Schultze, Q. J. (2002). *Habits of the high-tech heart: Living virtuously in the information age.* Grand Rapids: Baker Book House.

Shavitt, S. & Nelson, M. R. (2002). The role of attitude functions in persuasion and social judgment. In J. P. Dillard & M. Pfau (Eds.). *The persuasion handbook: Developments in theory and practice,* (pp.137-153). Thousand Oaks, CA: Sage Publications.

Smith, Loren A. (August 1995). Lawyers, garden slugs and constitutional liberty, *Vital bpeeches of the day. LXI,* No. 20, 613-615.

Strom, B. (2003). *More than talk: Communication studies and the Christian faith,* (2ⁿᵈ ed.). Dubuque, Iowa: Kendall/Hunt Publishing Company.

Tyson, L (1999). *Critical theory today: A user-friendly guide.* New York: Garland Publishing Inc.

Van Dyk, W. (2002). *The word in reformed worship.* Retrieved April 10, 2002. http://www.pastornet.net.au/rtc/word.htm.

Vancil, D. (1993). *Rhetoric and Argumentation.* Boston: Allyn and Bacon.

Verplanken, B. (1989). Involvement and need for cognition as moderators of beliefs-attitude-intention consistency. *British journal of social psychology, 28,* 115-122.

Wahls, M. H. (1997). The moral decay of America. In C. M. Logue & J. DeHart (Eds.). *Representative American speeches 1996-1997.* New York: H.W. Wilson.

Washington, B. T. (1971). Speech at the cotton states exposition. In D. J. O'Neill (Ed.). *Speeches by black Americans.* (pp. 73-86). Encino, California: Dickenson Publishing.

West, R. & Turner, L. H. (2000). *Introducing communication theory.* Mountain View, CA; Mayfiled.

Whately, R. (1854). *Elements of rhetoric: Comprising an analysis of the laws of moral evidence and of persuasion, with rules for argumentative composition and elocution* (new edition) Boston and Cambridge: James Munroe and Company

Whately, R. (1864). *Miscellaneous remains: From the commonplace book* Miss E. J. Whately (Ed.). London: Longman, Green, Longman, Robrets, & Green.

Whedbee, K (May, 1998). "Authority, freedom and liberal judgment: The presumptions and presumptuousness of Whately, Mill and Tocqueville" *The quarterly journal of speech* vol 84 #2 [on line: proquest] p. 171-189.

Wheeless, L. R., Barraclough, R., & Stewart, R. (1983). Compliance-gaining and power in persuasion. In *Communication Yearbook 7.* (pp. 105-145). Beverly Hills, CA: Sage.

White, J., (1994). Protestant worship of the reformation Era. In R. E. Webber (Ed.). *Complete library of Christian worship: Volume 2, Twenty centuries of Christian worship.* Nashville, TN: Star Song Publishers.

Woodward, G.C. & Denton, R. E. (2000). *Persuasion & influence in American life.* Prospect Heights, IL: Waveland Press.

Yoshida, S. (Nov. 15, 1996). Japanese corporations react to new global economic pressures: American and Japanese competition and collaboration are progressing. In *Vital speeches of the day. LXIII*, No. 3, 92-96.

Young, W. M. (1971). Can the city survive? In D. J. O'Neill (Ed.). *Speeches by black Americans.* (pp. 177-191). Encino, California: Dickenson Publishing.